REPRINTS OF ECONOMIC CLASSICS

THE DISTRIBUTION OF WEALTH

THE

DISTRIBUTION OF WEALTH

A THEORY OF WAGES, INTEREST AND PROFITS

BY

JOHN BATES CLARK

PROFESSOR OF POLITICAL ECONOMY IN COLUMBIA UNIVERSITY
AUTHOR OF "THE PHILOSOPHY OF WEALTH"

REPRINTS OF ECONOMIC CLASSICS

Augustus M. Kelley, Bookseller
New York 1965

Library of Congress Catalogue Card Number
65 - 19641

PRINTED IN THE UNITED STATES OF AMERICA
by SENTRY PRESS, NEW YORK, N. Y. 10019

PREFACE

IT is the purpose of this work to show that the distribution of the income of society is controlled by a natural law, and that this law, if it worked without friction, would give to every agent of production the amount of wealth which that agent creates. However wages may be adjusted by bargains freely made between individual men, the rates of pay that result from such transactions tend, it is here claimed, to equal that part of the product of industry which is traceable to the labor itself; and however interest may be adjusted by similarly free bargaining, it naturally tends to equal the fractional product that is separately traceable to capital. At the point in the economic system where titles to property originate, — where labor and capital come into possession of the amounts that the state afterwards treats as their own, — the social procedure is true to the principle on which the right of property rests. So far as it is not obstructed, it assigns to every one what he has specifically produced.

In a series of articles and monographs, published at intervals since 1881, I have endeavored to formulate the parts of this theory relating severally to value, capital, wages, interest, rent and profits. These papers appeared in the *New Englander*, the *Quarterly Journal of Economics*, the *Yale Review*, the *Political Science Quarterly*, the *Annals of the Academy of Political and Social Science*, the *Revue d'Economie*

v

Politique, the *Dictionary of Political Economy*, and the series of monographs and studies published by the American Economic Association. These partial statements are now brought into an orderly arrangement and extensively supplemented.

The term *natural*, as used by classical economists in connection with standards of value, wages and interest, was unconsciously employed as an equivalent of the term *static;* and it is such natural or static standards that this volume undertakes to present. It aims to show to what rates the market prices of goods, the wages of labor and the interest on capital would conform, if the changes that are going on in the shape of the industrial world and in the character of its activities were to cease. It tries completely to isolate the static forces that act in distribution from the dynamic forces. Actual society is always dynamic, and the part of it that we are most concerned with is highly so. Change and progress are apparent everywhere, and industrial society is constantly assuming new forms and discharging new functions. Because of this continual evolution the standards of wages and of interest to-day are not what they will be ten years hence. There are, however, normal standards to-day. In the midst of all changes there are at work forces that fix rates to which, at any one moment, wages and interest tend to conform. However stormy may be the ocean, there is an ideal level surface projecting itself through the waves, and the actual surface of the turbulent water fluctuates about it. There are, likewise, static standards with which, in the most turbulent markets, actual values, wages and interest tend to coincide.

What would be the rate of wages, if labor and capital were to remain fixed in quantity, if improvements in the mode of production were to stop, if the consolidating of capital were to cease and if the wants of consumers were never to alter? The question assumes, of course, that industry shall go on, and that, notwithstanding a paralysis of the forces of progress, wealth shall continue to be created under the influence of a perfectly unobstructed competition. The values and the rates of wages and interest which, under such conditions, would prevail, are those to which, in spite of all disturbances that progress occasions, the rates in the actual market tend, at any one time, to conform. They are the theoretically "natural" rates which science has been seeking.

In presenting the laws by which such rates are fixed, this volume tries to perform a work that is constructive and not controversial. At a few points it will gain something, in the way of clearness, by calling attention to contrasting theories, but it will offer no systematic criticism of them. An adequate treatment of the various theories of distribution would require a book not less extensive than this one devoted wholly to controversy. The plan of making relatively few references to other writings may leave a reader in some uncertainty as to whether a particular part of the present work may have been borrowed from existing economic literature, and it seems therefore necessary to say that no part has been consciously borrowed in this way. At the dates when I first published the several parts in the series of articles above referred to, only one important point could, so far as I now know, have been thus obtained. One very important point might have been taken from the writings of the early economist, von Thünen; and if I had seen the passage in his works in which it is stated, before pub-

lishing certain articles which contained a similar
statement, those articles would not have failed to
refer to the work of this brilliant pioneer in economic theory. The omission is now remedied. In
an extended note I have pointed out the resemblances and the differences between von Thünen's
final-productivity theory of wages and interest and
my own. Up to a certain point the two theories
can be stated in identical terms; and yet the difference between them is in reality a radical one.

It was the claim advanced by Mr. Henry George,
that wages are fixed by the product which a man can
create by tilling rentless land, that first led me to
seek a method by which the product of labor everywhere may be disentangled from the product of
coöperating agents and separately identified; and
it was this quest which led to the attainment of the
law that is here presented, according to which the
wages of all labor tend, under perfectly free competition, to equal the product that is separately
attributable to the labor. The product of the "final
unit" of labor is the same as that of every unit,
separately considered; and if normal tendencies could
work in perfection, it would be true not only of each
unit, but of the working force as a whole, that its
product and its pay are identical.

There are resemblances and contrasts between the
theory that is here presented and those of the Austrian economists, Karl Menger and Friedrich von
Wieser; and one feature which distinguishes the
present system from the others is a recognition of
the difference between permanent capital, or an
abiding fund of productive wealth, and particular
capital-goods, or instruments of production, which
perish in the using. The relation that this theory
bears to the fascinating one recently published by

Ex-minister von Böhm-Bawerk can best be made
clear after a later volume on the dynamics of distribution shall have seen the light. If my present
plan had admitted it, I should have been glad to
cite and to discuss many specific contributions to
the literature of the theory of distribution, such as
those made by Professor Alfred Marshall, President
Francis A. Walker, President Arthur T. Hadley,
Professor Frank W. Taussig, Professor William
Smart, Mr. John A. Hobson, Dr. Charles W. Mac-
Farlane, Dr. Stuart Wood and Mr. Herbert M.
Thompson. To three men I am indebted for general stimulus and suggestion, the effects of which
must have appeared in any theoretical work that I
have done. They are my teacher, the late Professor
Karl Knies of Heidelberg, and my early associates in
economic work, Professor Franklin H. Giddings of
Columbia University and Professor Simon N. Patten
of the University of Pennsylvania.

For an understanding of the plan on which this
book is arranged, it is necessary to note that the
principle of final productivity — which, as the work
claims, is at the basis of the law of wages and interest — can be stated in a few words ; but that,
when it is so stated, the significance of the terms
used requires very extended defining. Interest, for
example, is said to depend on the productive power
of the final unit of social capital. What, however,
is such a final unit, and in what sense can it be
called social ? Is it highly composite, and is it
apportioned, by some nice adjustment, among all
the industries of society ? Does it consist in concrete things that can everywhere be distinguished ?
It is said, in the theory, that this increment of productive wealth, on the efficiency of which the rate of
interest depends, consists of a quantity of " perma-

nent capital." Concrete instruments, however, are
not permanent. They perish and require continual
replacing, and it is essential to know the true relation between the instruments which are thus perishing and the fund of wealth which is abiding. In
the apportioning of this fund among different industries, the market values of different products have
their influence; and it is necessary to ascertain the
relation between the laws of value and those of
distribution. Moreover, incomes that are determined by the final-productivity law may also be
translated into a form that makes it possible to
apply to them the principle of rent. The nature
of rent and its relation to wages and interest need
to be ascertained. Extended statements on many
other points are required, if the apparently simple
final-productivity formula for wages and interest is
to have definiteness of meaning and a character of
reality that will cause it to interpret the practical
facts of life.

Now, it would have been possible to make these
explanatory statements first, and to reserve the presentation of the law of final productivity till every
term that a statement of it would use should have
been fully defined and made to represent something
in actual business. It would have been possible to
discuss the nature of capital and of capital-goods,
value, group relations, rent, etc., before presenting
the main proposition, concerning the final-productivity law of wages and interest. There would have
been a logical justification of such an arrangement,
since the explanatory statements would have prepared the way for a brief concluding thesis, which
would have contained the essence of the theory.
The work would then have culminated in one all-
embracing statement. But the use of so much of

the book for preliminary definitions and discussions would have made a large demand on the reader's patience, and would have added to the difficulty of connecting the explanatory matter with the principal thesis. I have, therefore, preferred to state the main proposition early and the explanatory ones afterward. The variety of these latter statements is such that, unless the central truth — the final-productivity law — be kept in mind from the outset, it is not entirely easy to bring them into apparent unity. To make the logical connections more apparent, I have given to the table of contents the character of an outline of the series of leading ideas contained in the several chapters, without any attempt to make it an abstract of the entire contents of the chapters. Many paragraphs are not referred to in it, but the general argument of the book is, I hope, the better given by reason of these omissions.

The plan of advancing early the chief thesis of the work and causing the full meaning of it gradually to unfold itself requires that a subject such as rent or value be treated in more than one part of the book. If rent were to be discussed for its own sake, the treatment of this subject should, of course, be consecutive; but as the purpose of each reference to rent is to add something to the meaning of the thesis which states the final-productivity law of distribution, it is best to forego the attempt to finish the treatment of rent in one passage and, rather, to give the amplifications of the main thesis in a natural order.

The mathematical modes of statement that have been adopted in many parts of the book have been purposely made entirely simple and untechnical. Not even the notation that is in vogue in mathematics has been used.

In the final preparation of this volume I have
received assistance that I desire gratefully to ac-
knowledge from my colleague, Professor E. R. A.
Seligman; from Professor H. L. Moore, of Smith
College ; from Mr. A. S. Johnson, Fellow in Columbia University; and particularly from Mr. A. M.
Day, Instructor in Political Economy and Social
Science in the same University, who has read the
work repeatedly in the manuscript and has made
very many helpful suggestions, and, in connection
with the revising of the proofs, has rendered in-
valuable aid.

JOHN BATES CLARK.

TABLE OF CONTENTS

[Containing a condensed statement of the leading idea of each of the different chapters, but not a complete analysis of the entire contents of the chapters. For a summary of the contents of parts of chapters the reader is referred to the marginal analysis accompanying the text.]

CHAPTER I

Human welfare depends on incomes, which are fixed by contract, but are really controlled by natural law. Wages, interest and profits are the products of three different functions, and the theory of distribution traces these incomes to their sources. Whether a producer gets the amount that he creates is one question ; and whether the amount created is large or small is another. Ethical issues are connected with the incomes of different persons, but are settled by a study of the incomes connected with different functions ; since, if every function is paid according to its product, every person is also thus paid. Whether labor gets its product or not is a question of fact ; but if it does not, the laborer is robbed.

CHAPTER II

Since the traditional divisions of economics are not really distinct, it is necessary to rearrange economic theory. Production, as carried on by society as a whole, includes exchange and distribution. The fixing of market values, which is traditionally placed under exchange, determines the distribution of social income among producing groups, among sub-groups and, finally, among the factors of production within each sub-group. Market values tend, however, toward normal standards. These standards are the result of a force in distribution that equalizes

Three kinds of force are working together in social
economy. The study of these resolves economic science
into three natural divisions. There is a distinct set of
laws that are not dependent upon organization, but act in
all stages of social evolution. These laws are the subject
of the first natural division of economics. There is a
second set of laws that are dependent upon exchanges and
the organization of industry. These are the subject of
the second natural division of economic science. In a
broad sense, the science of distribution embraces the social
laws of economics ; for it treats of the relations of the
groups to each other and of the relations between classes
within the groups. Social production may be thought of
as static. Only in a static society can values, wages and
interest be " natural," in the traditional sense. Static
laws only fall within the second division. In an actual
society, however, there are dynamic forces at work, as
well as static. These forces and their effects are the subject of the third natural division of economics.
These divisions are distinct, though interdependent. A
theory of dynamic social economics presupposes the conclusions attained by a study of static social economics,
and this in turn presupposes the conclusions gained by
the study of universal economics. Consumption is studied
in the first of the three divisions. The static theory of
distribution is included within the second. The dynamics
of distribution belongs within the third.

CHAPTER IV

This work deals mainly with subjects that fall within the second natural division of economic science, but derives premises from the first division, and only enters the field of the third so far as is necessary for showing that static forces dominate dynamic societies. Isolated life reveals the essential attributes of wealth and the law of diminishing utility of successive increments of it, though the action of this principle in adjusting market values is confined to social life. An apportionment of labor among different occupations is necessary in primitive life; but such apportionment by means of groups, with the phenomena of prices that result from such organization, involves a social mode of living. So the principle of final productivity of labor and capital acts in isolated life, but causes the phenomena of wages and interest only in social life. The static theory of distribution, therefore, takes premises from the facts and laws of a universal economy.

CHAPTER V

While the laws of primitive economic life are everywhere active, organization of society has brought new forces into play. These forces are explained by the science of catallactics. Catallactics treats of the motive for exchanges, the gain from division of labor. Division of labor organizes society into groups and sub-groups. Catallactics shows that the incomes of groups, of sub-groups and of the factors within the sub-group are their own virtual products. Catallactics falls into two divisions, statics and dynamics. The dynamic study explains the changes in the functions and structure of society that result from the five generic changes which constitute progress. The static study explains the laws of industrial life, exclusive of the laws of industrial growth. All societies are dynamic; but, nevertheless, static law is everywhere operative, and must be explained before the laws of dynamics can be understood.

CHAPTER VI

Movements of labor from group to group show that society is dynamic ; but they are themselves the effort of society to put itself into the shape that static law, at the moment, calls for. The movements of labor and of capital tend to render each of these agents as productive in one group as it is in others. If dynamic influences should cease, competition would equalize the products of labor and of capital, and we should have a static state, with mobility without motion. Were dynamic influences to act intermittently, we should have a series of static shapes. Let the forces of change act continually, and we shall have a continually changing standard shape to which society will tend to conform. This is the actual condition of society. Static science must find the natural condition of society at any given time ; dynamic science must explain variation and progress. Ricardian economics made an unconscious and imperfect static study. If the Ricardians had recognized that their study was only partial, and had followed it with a separate study of dynamic forces, they would have given to their science a realistic character. Dynamic forces are not to be treated as merely disturbing elements. They are in accordance with nature ; and the science that shall explain them will interpret the phenomena of progress which historical economics records and measures. Dynamics is a deductive science which analyzes change qualitatively ; historical economics is a quantitative study of change.

CHAPTER VII

Competition is the force that makes prices "natural." Prices would conform to natural standards, if either the forces of growth were eliminated or the friction that keeps labor and capital from being perfectly mobile were removed. In the former case, permanent static standards would gradually be reached ; in the latter, prices would conform perfectly to perpetually changing standards. In a dynamic society there is a normal variation from static standards. In like manner, there is a theoretical standard

dynamic movements compel both labor and capital to change their concrete forms, and changes in the relative quantities of labor and capital do this. Wages and interest are fixed by the final productivity of these permanent agents. When to a given field labor is applied unit by unit, the product of the final unit measures the effective product of every one, since they are interchangeable. If the field is isolated, this final product is the standard toward which the wages of each unit tends. In the economic world *the wages of each unit of social labor tend to equal the product of the final unit.*

CHAPTER XII

To illustrate the law of final productivity of labor, we build up a working force unit by unit, leaving the amount of capital unchanged. These units of labor are composite, containing representatives of each occupation. With only one unit the capital will assume costly forms. When a second unit is added, the forms of the capital will be more simple. The total product will be increased by the presence of the second unit, and the increase is what is attributable to the labor alone. If units are supplied till all the labor of society is set working, the increase which is due to the last unit is its virtual product. Since any unit is final in an economic sense, the product of the last unit of labor is the product of any unit and is the standard toward which wages tend under the pressure of competition. A reversal of this imaginary process reveals the law of interest. The product of the last unit of capital is the virtual product of any unit and sets the standard of interest. In actual society capital tends to outgrow labor; and, therefore, we see it assuming more and more costly forms, which earn a continually diminishing fraction of their cost.

CHAPTER XIII

It has been customary to treat ground rent as a unique form of income. In a discussion of the laws of wages and interest, however, we must place land on the same footing as other capital goods. The differential formula is more accurately applied to the earnings of the fund of permanent capital and of the whole force of social labor. If on an isolated farm we introduce laborers one by one, each except the last creates a surplus. The sum of these sur-pluses is the rent of land, or the part of the general product that is attributable to the land. If, instead of an isolated farm, we take a fixed social capital, and supply labor unit by unit, the labor will be subject to a law of diminishing returns, each unit creating a surplus over the product of the last. The sum of these surpluses is the rent of the fund of social capital and equals total interest. If we reverse the process and supply capital by units to a fixed amount of labor, capital will be subject to a law of diminishing returns. The surpluses created by the earlier units are in this case the rent of social labor and equal total wages. In a static state the two rents make up the whole of the social income. From one point of view each is measured directly; from another it is measured residually.

CHAPTER XIV

The principle of rent applies to social capital, as this is apportioned, by a nice adjustment, among all the industrial groups and sub-groups; and it applies to labor in the same way. Group incomes, composed of wages and interest, are governed by a different application of the general principle that fixes wages and interest themselves. Group incomes depend on values; and these are fixed by the principle of final utility applied, not to commodities in their entirety, but to what may be called value elements in commodities. In this way the law applies to a series of increments of social consumers' wealth, as well as to increments that are used by an individual; and the final social increment of such wealth is a composite of innumerable value elements, but contains few entire articles. Increments of capital are to be distinguished in the same analytical way; and a final increment of social capital is a composite of many capital elements in instruments, but of few instruments in their entirety.

cal improvement of the productive equipment of society. It is the productive power of qualitative increments, thus added to the working outfit, that fixes interest. Competition eliminates the *entrepreneur* in whose hands such final increments do not earn normal interest. It is capital, as such, which is the subject of competition, though *entrepreneurs* may be said to compete for capital goods that are about to be. Each *entrepreneur* embodies the capital in such forms as are needed in his business. Generally the additional capital that an *entrepreneur* secures takes the form of improved quality of an existing plant. These qualitative improvements are the final increments of capital.

Capital grows mainly by qualitative increments infused into capital goods. A new increment of general capital is apportioned by a natural law among all the different industries, in each of which it takes, in the main, the form of improvements in the working equipment. Labor is apportioned in the same way, though the growth of it is mainly by quantitative increments. Capital, as we have seen, lives by a self-transmutation, by which it passes from one set of forms to another. There is an industrial group of which the function is the replenishing of the tissues of active capital. Any increase in social capital requires an enlargement of this group; and this in turn results in a general improvement of the capital goods that are in process of being used up and replenished.

CHAPTER XIX

The apportionment of labor and capital is normal, when each agent is everywhere uniformly productive. A movement of either agent from group to group affects the producing power of the other. The mechanism that replenishes the tissues of fixed capital also moves it from one group to another, whenever such a transfer is required. Labor is apportioned among the groups in a way that tends to secure uniform productivity. The movements of both labor and capital are governed by a general law, which both fixes values and determines the physical productivity of these two agents of production. If labor and capital are misadjusted, this law tends to restore the equilibrium. When the supply of one productive agent in a group becomes smaller, the power of a unit of this agent to produce goods becomes greater, and the value of the goods that are specifically attributable to this agent rises. In two ways, therefore, the power of this agent to produce value is increased. Under the same conditions the other agent loses power to create goods; but, as the goods that it still creates have an increased value, the true wealth-creating power of this agent may be nearly unchanged or it may, in some minor degree, become greater or smaller. These influences insure, in the end, a normal apportionment of the two agents. It is the *entrepreneur* who moves both labor and capital, and gets the advantage of any exceptional productivity of either of them. The apportionment of producing agents among the sub-groups within a general group is effected by the same influences that control the adjustments among the general groups themselves; but the need of maintaining a uniform flow of products in different stages of approach to completion makes a quick and accurate adjustment among the sub-groups imperative. The same law adjusts the relative proportions of fixed and circulating capital, and determines how much land shall enter into the equipment of each group.

CHAPTER XX

If consumers' wealth is advanced by one class of persons to another, it is by the highest sub-groups to the lower ones, and not by capitalists to laborers. Irregularities in production and consumption involve storing of goods, but this influence is not here to be considered. It is the rapidity of a uniform flow of ripened consumers' wealth that affects all incomes; and well-coördinated capital enables producers in the lower sub-groups to get without waiting ripened goods that, virtually but not

literally, they have produced. Capital goods seem to
compel some producers to wait for their rewards; but
capital relieves them from this necessity. Without pre-
existing and coördinated capital, effort and time are the
requisites of the production of ripened goods; but with
such capital the industry of every sub-group produces an
immediate and fully ripened return.

CHAPTER XXI

The theory of final productivity, when it is presented
in an imperfect form, leads to the inference that labor is
exploited by the action of a natural law. For the correction of this inference it is necessary to complete the theory
and to show to what cause the surpluses connected with
early increments are due. If the number of units of
labor that are employed with a fixed amount of capital
is increased, each of the earlier units must surrender a
part of the capital by which it has been aided. The diminution in its product that this entails shows the part that
is imputable to the surrendered capital. *At a given time* all
units are equally productive, and there is no exploitation
involved in giving to each what a final one produces. In
this way the product of labor on the zone of indifference
is a correct test of the productivity of all labor, provided
that labor and capital are properly apportioned throughout the group system.

CHAPTER XXII

In popular usage the term "rent" designates the earnings of concrete instruments, while "interest" designates
the earnings of a sum of "money" invested. This usage is
based on the distinction between capital and capital goods,
and is more correct than is the scientific practice of confining the term "rent" to the earnings of land. The
basis of the old distinction between land and capital was
that the quantity of land is fixed, while capital can be
increased, and that the earnings of land can be measured
differentially. In a static study neither distinction has

validity.   Total capital is fixed ; but the amount which may go to any group can be changed, if there is offered an inducement for changing it.   This is also true of land. The earnings of all artificial instruments, as well as the earnings of land, may be computed by the differential formula.   There is a margin of utilization of artificial instruments, just as there is a margin of cultivation of land, and these margins are fixed by the same law.   It is increasing productivity that extends the margins, and it is not the extending of the margins that raises rents.   All incomes, even wages, may be computed residually ; from another point of view, however, they are determined directly.   *All rents are true products, which can be traced to distinguishable agents.*

CHAPTER XXIII

It has been generally believed that "rent does not enter into price."   But the amount of any agent in a group affects the product of the group and thus affects price.   The rent of any concrete instrument is primarily its product, considered in kind ; and this must enter into the supply of goods, on the basis of which the value of such goods is determined.   What the classical economists have really shown is that the destination of rent makes no difference in price.   If this reasoning could really prove that the rent of land does not enter into price, the same reasoning would show that neither wages nor interest enter into price.   All real rents, including real wages, are quantities of actual goods placed on the market, where, of course, they affect supply and market value. It is not true that different parts of the supply are produced at different costs, leaving rent as a mere residuum, or a gratuity having no price-making power.   The same argument will prove that wages and interest are also residual amounts having no price-making power; and this is an absurdity.

A measure of wealth is needed that will not depend on
reciprocal comparisons of different kinds of goods, but
will measure all kinds in absolute sums. Effective utility
is an element common to all kinds of wealth, and it may
be measured in terms of social disutility. Pleasures of
many kinds may be measured in terms of the homogeneous sacrifice that is incurred by labor. The costliest
labor is that which is performed at the close of the working day, and this measures the utility of the least necessary
part of social consumers' wealth. The *effective* utility of
all goods produced at uniform cost in labor is equal ; and
the *effective* disutility of all equal periods of labor is equal,
however unlike the *absolute* disutility of the labor of
different hours may be. The individuals who make goods,
and incur the sacrifice that this involves, do not consume
them and get the offsetting benefit. The benefits that
these individuals get come from other goods ; and these
persons cannot bring the sacrifice incurred in producing
these goods and the gain from consuming them to an
equation. Society as a whole can do this ; and, moreover,
society can put a price in terms of collective sacrifice on
each kind of goods. Each article is worth the social
sacrifice that society incurs in *acquiring* it, and this is
measured at the terminal point of the social working day.
*The sacrifice that, at this point, society incurs in getting
different forms of consumers' wealth is the ultimate unit of
value.*

Static standards of value, wages and interest are "natural," in a sense ; but dynamic changes are natural in a
broader sense, and they disturb all static adjustments.
They can be understood, however, only by means of a
knowledge of static laws. Dynamic movements must be
studied first singly and then in concurrent action; and,
in view of the fact that at each instant a dynamic society
tends toward a single definite static adjustment, dynamic

forces account for variations from the static standards and for constant and progressive changes in the standards themselves. Different dynamic movements neutralize each other, so far as causing variations from static adjustments is concerned. Velocities of movement are dynamic subjects, and they are directly connected with the income distinguished as pure profits. Friction has a connection with this income, and also with the rate of dynamic movements. Certain permanent variations from static standards result from continuous dynamic changes. Some of these changes are mutually neutralizing, so far as movements of labor and capital in the group system are concerned, as illustrations show ; and the efficiency of static forces is in proportion to the activity and the *diversity* of dynamic ones. Certain steady movements of labor and capital are the resultant of all these dynamic forces — namely, a flow from the lower sub-groups to the upper ones and movements to and fro within each horizontal range of sub-groups. One mode of creating for study an imaginary static state is to stop all dynamic changes and then to wait long enough to permit the slowest of all the static adjustments to be made.

CHAPTER XXVI

Certain parts of a general static adjustment encounter special obstacles, and a quasi-static adjustment may be made by carrying to completion the remainder of the general process. A movement that, for the world as a whole, is a part of a static adjustment may be, within a particular part of the world, equivalent to a dynamic influence. Thus a static unification of methods of production in the world as a whole would be the cause of grand dynamics in Asia. The scope of an economic study may be locally limited. An economic centre of the world may be defined, and its relations to the outer zones may be treated as causing dynamic influences within the centre. A static state may, for purposes of study, be created within the centre itself ; and this would exclude migrations of labor and capital to or from the outer zones, but not the exchanging of products with those zones. Three different standards of wages are to be recognized in economic theory, and in practice these are never to be brought to an equality. Dynamic gains are forever accruing in the economic centre, and economic theory has to concern itself, primarily, with static rates of gain within that local area, and, secondly, with rates of change and amounts of variation caused within that area by dynamic influences. Ultimate standards, proximate ones and the relations between the two kinds of standards are to be studied. The full effects of economic friction must be taken into account. Changes in wages, interest and profits that are to take place in the future are to be accounted for by influences that can be defined in the present, and such studies compose the most difficult and the most fruitful ones that it is possible to make.

THE DISTRIBUTION OF WEALTH

THE DISTRIBUTION OF WEALTH

CHAPTER I

ISSUES THAT DEPEND ON DISTRIBUTION

For practical men, and hence for students, supreme importance attaches to one economic problem — that of the distribution of wealth among different claimants. Is there a natural law according to which the income of society is divided into wages, interest and profits? If so, what is that law? This is the problem which demands solution.[1]

A majority of men live chiefly by labor; and for these men the resultant of all the economic forces takes the practical form of wages. Arts have been mastered, labor has been divided and subdivided, and machinery has been set working; and as the result of it all, that which comes to wage-earners is the pay that employers give to them. The amount of this pay fixes the degree of comfort that these men themselves can enjoy, and the amount of culture, health and well-being that they can insure to their children. Moreover, the effects of high or low wages upon the welfare of the working class are cumulative, as generations succeed each other. The money that a man earns may be thought of as poten- *Men's welfare dependent on their shares of the social income.*

[1] By "wealth" is meant those sources of human welfare which are material, transferable and limited in quantity. See the first chapter of *The Philosophy of Wealth*, by the author of the present work.

1

The personal effects of increasing wages cumulative, as generations succeed each other.

Wages governed by a natural law, though adjusted by personal bargaining.

The gross income of society resolvable into wages, interest and profits.

tial well-being condensed into a material form; and if workers now get enough of it to put them on a high plane of comfort, their descendants will probably reach a higher plane. It is, then, the nature of the law of wages which determines whether the continuous life of working humanity shall have a rising or a falling trend.

Wages are usually paid by one person to another. The amount thus paid is adjusted by bargain, and may seem to depend on the comparative power and the adroitness of the parties to the contract; for commercial strategy is an important art, practised by both employers and workmen according to their several abilities. There is, however, a market rate of wages; and this is, in the main, controlled by ulterior and positive forces. The so-called "higgling of the market," in fact, affects the rate of pay for labor only in a local way and within narrow limits. The amount that workmen can generally, by any shrewdness or firmness, exact from employers is limited, as we shall show, by the productive power that resides in labor; and the forces that control the prevailing terms of wage contracts are those which determine the amount of that productive power. There is, in short, a deep acting natural law at work amid the confusing struggles of the labor market.

The function of this natural law is to separate the gross earnings of society into three generic shares that are unlike in kind. It causes the whole annual gains of society to distribute themselves into three great sums — general wages, general interest and aggregate profits.[1] These are, respectively, the earnings of labor, the earnings of capital and the gains

[1] The rent of land is to be regarded — for reasons that will appear later — as merged with interest. This, however, involves an extension of the traditional theory of rent, rather than a denial of it.

from a certain coördinating process that is performed by the employers of labor and users of capital. This purely coördinating work we shall call the *entrepreneur's* function, and the rewards for it we shall call profits. The function in itself includes no working and no owning of capital : it consists entirely in the establishing and maintaining of efficient relations between the agents of production.

We have said that the pay which, with all the bargaining strategy that they can use, workmen get from employers is limited by the productive power that resides in labor itself, and that a study of the wage law must search for the influences that fix this productive power. We may now advance the more general thesis — later to be proved — that, *where natural laws have their way, the share of income that attaches to any productive function is gauged by the actual product of it.* In other words, free competition tends to give to labor what labor creates, to capitalists what capital creates, and to *entrepreneurs* what the coördinating function creates. *These shares naturally equal the products created by three distinct functions.*

The entire study of distribution is, in this view, a study of *specific production.* It is an analysis of the wealth-creating operation, and a tracing to each of the three agencies that together bring wealth into existence of the part which it separately contributes to the joint result. To each agent a distinguishable share in production, and to each a corresponding reward — such is the natural law of distribution. *Distribution resolves a composite product into its component parts.* This thesis we have to prove ; and more hinges on the truth of it than any introductory words can state. The right of society to exist in its present form, and the probability that it will continue so to exist, are at stake. These facts lend to this problem of distribution its measureless importance.

The welfare of the laboring classes depends on whether they get much or little; but their attitude toward other classes — and, therefore, the stability of the social state — depends chiefly on the question, whether the amount that they get, be it large or small,

The disposal of the part created by labor a critical issue. is what they produce. If they create a small amount of wealth and get the whole of it, they may not seek to revolutionize society; but if it were to appear that they produce an ample amount and get only a part of it, many of them would become revolutionists, and all would have the right to do so. The indictment that hangs over society is that of " exploiting labor." " Workmen " it is said, "are regularly robbed of what they produce. This is done within the forms of law, and by the natural working of competition." If this charge were proved, every right-minded man should become a socialist; and his zeal in transforming the industrial system would then measure and express his sense of justice. If we are to test the charge, however, we must enter the realm of production. We must resolve the product of social industry into its component elements, in order to see whether the natural effect of competition is or is not to give to each producer the amount of wealth that he specifically brings into existence.

In case it shall prove to be true that products and shares do thus coincide, we need further to know whether each of these separate incomes grows absolutely larger or smaller. We must ascertain whether

The increase or diminution of this product important. evolution makes labor more productive, and therefore better paid, or less productive, and therefore worse paid. We need also to know whether it treats capital and the undertaking function, in these respects, well or ill. As evolution proceeds, do owners of capital and users of capital become better off or worse off? Having first tested the honesty of the social state, by determining whether it gives to every man his own, we have next to test its beneficence, by ascertaining whether that which is his own is becoming greater or smaller. The *right* of the present social system to exist at all depends on its honesty; but the *expediency* of letting it develop in its own way depends entirely on its beneficence. We therefore need first to know whether we have the right to let natural economic forces work as they are doing; and we need next to know whether, on grounds of utility, it is wise to let them work thus.

The whole income of the world is, of course, distributed among all the persons in the world; but the science of distribution does not directly determine what each person shall get. Personal sharing results from another kind of sharing: only the resolving of the total income of society into wages, interest and profits, as distinct kinds of income, falls directly and entirely within the field of economics. Each of these shares is unlike the others in kind, since it has a different origin. One comes from performing work, one from furnishing capital and one from coördinating these two agents. Nearly every man's income, furthermore, is more or less composite. Laborers own some capital, capitalists perform some labor, and *entrepreneurs* usually own capital and perform a kind of labor. To what extent a particular man's income is derived from one source or another, depends on a wider range of influences than our present study can include. We cannot inquire *how much* labor a capitalist naturally performs. What we wish to ascertain is solely what fixes the rate of wages, as such, and what fixes the rates of pure interest and of net profits, as such. When these rates are determined, a particular man's income depends on the amount and kind of work that he performs, the amount of capital

Personal distribution and functional distribution contrasted.

that he furnishes, and the extent and kind of co-ordinating that he does. That which is beyond his control, and fixed by a general and purely economic law, is the determination of the product that labor and capital, in themselves, can create and ultimately get.

We are, then, to seek only to discover the forces that fix the amounts of the three kinds of income. It is a striking fact, however, that, even though we thus restrict the inquiry, we do, if we are successful, settle the great personal issues that range men in hostile classes. By discovering the law that fixes the rates of wages, of interest and of pure profits, we decide whether the man, A, has a grievance against B. We have not, indeed, thus ascertained why one of them has only $500 a year, while the other has $50,000; but we have ascertained something about the two incomes that decides whether each of them rightfully belongs to the man who gets it. The two kinds of distribution, however, though thus closely related, must be kept distinct.

Personal distribution decides what is the income of particular men. It gives to A $500 a year, to B $50,000, to C $500,000, etc., regardless of the way in which any one income is obtained. What we call *functional distribution* decides how much is secured in a particular way. It makes the pay for a certain grade of labor $1.50 a day, regardless of who performs the labor. It makes the rate of interest five per cent, regardless of who gets it. The difference between these two kinds of distribution is marked and important, for the dividing lines that are drawn by one of them cut across those which are drawn by the other. Taking the income of a particular man, as a dividend, by a functional distribution you may separate it into wages, interest and profits; for this individual man may get something in each of these

Functional distribution a resolving of men's personal incomes into parts unlike in their origin.

ways. Taking all wages, as such, as a dividend, you may, by a personal distribution, separate this gross amount into the pay that goes to each one of a myriad of different men. Profits, in the abstract, be it noted, are not under a moral obligation to wages in the abstract; although the *entrepreneur*, who gets profits, may owe something to his workmen, who get the wages. Rights are always personal; and only a sentient being has claims, as only an intelligent being has duties. There is, then, no issue of right or wrong involved in the fact that wages, as such, fall from a dollar and a half a day to a dollar; but the taking of a half-dollar from the daily pay of each member of a force of men, and the adding of it to the gains of an employer, raises between the parties a critical issue of justice or injustice. The question is: Has the employer taken something that the laborer has produced? Exactly this issue is forever pending between industrial classes. Every day a definite amount is handed over by one class to another. Is this amount determined by a principle that humanity can approve and perpetuate? Does it treat men fairly? The issue is personal; but it is settled by a knowledge of purely functional distribution.

If each productive function is paid for according to the amount of its product, then each man gets what he himself produces. If he works, he gets what he creates by working; if he also provides capital, he gets what his capital produces; and if, further, he renders service by coördinating labor and capital, he gets the product that can be separately traced to that function. Only in one of these ways can a man produce anything. If he receives all that he brings into existence through any one of these three functions, he receives all that he creates at all. If wages,

Grievances depend on personal distribution,

but they are removed by a normal functional distribution.

interest and profits, in themselves considered, are fixed according to a sound principle, then the different classes of men who combine their forces in industry have no grievances against each other. If functions are paid according to their products, men are also. Hence, while rights are personal, the issue of rights that is involved in distribution is settled by a functional study.

We might, indeed, go into a further and purely ethical inquiry. We might raise the question, whether a rule that gives to each man his product is, in the highest sense, just. Certain socialists have, indeed, contended that such a rule cannot attain justice. Work according to ability and pay according to need, is a familiar formula, which expresses a certain ideal of equity in distribution. This rule would require the taking from some men of a part of their product, in order to bestow it on others who might be more necessitous. It would violate what is ordinarily regarded as a property right. The entire question whether this is just or not lies outside of our inquiry, for it is a matter of pure ethics. Before

Whether labor gets what it produces or not a question of fact, not of ethics. us, on the other hand, is a problem of economic fact. Does natural distribution identify men's products and their gains? Is that which we get and which the civil law enables us to keep really our own property by right of creation? Do our actual estates rest, from their very beginnings, on production?

When a workman leaves the mill, carrying his pay in his pocket, the civil law guarantees to him what he thus takes away; but before he leaves the mill he is the rightful owner of a part of the wealth that the day's industry has brought forth. Does the economic law which, in some way that he does not understand, determines what his pay shall be, make it to correspond with the amount of his portion of the day's

product, or does it force him to leave some of his
rightful share behind him? A plan of living that
should force men to leave in their employers' hands
anything that by right of creation is theirs, would be
an institutional robbery — a legally established viola- Institutional
tion of the principle on which property is supposed robbery.
to rest.

This is the problem that we have to solve. It is
an issue of pure fact. If the law on which property
is supposed to rest — the rule, " to each what he
creates" — actually works at the point where the
possession of property begins, in the payments that
are made in the mill, etc., for values there created,
it remains for practical men so to perfect the industrial system, after its kind, that exceptions to this
prevalent rule may be less frequent and less considerable. We can deal otherwise with robberies that are
not institutional; but it is evident that a society in
which property is made to rest on the claim of a
producer to what he creates must, as a general rule,
vindicate that right at the point where titles originate — that is, in the payments that are made for
labor. If it were to do otherwise, there would be at
the foundation of the social structure an explosive
element which sooner or later would destroy it. For
nothing, if not to protect property, does the state
exist. Hence a state which should force a workman
to leave behind him in the mill property that was his
by right of creation, would fail at a critical point.
A study of distribution settles this question, as to
whether the modern state is true to its principle.
Property is protected at the point of its origin, if
actual wages are the whole product of labor, if interest is the product of capital, and if profit is the
product of a coördinating act.

CHAPTER II

THE PLACE OF DISTRIBUTION WITHIN THE TRADI-
TIONAL DIVISIONS OF ECONOMICS

WE have undertaken to solve a test problem of
distribution — to ascertain whether the division of
the social income into wages, interest and profits is,
in principle, honest. We have seen that this compels us to enter the realm of production, in order to
find whether these incomes are earned. Is each of
them specifically created by the agent that gets it?
If it is, the entire science of distribution is nothing
more than a science of the process of specific production. In any case, the relation of the wealth-creating
process to the wealth-dividing process needs a most
searching examination.

The terms, Production, Distribution, Exchange
and Consumption, have been used to designate four
divisions of economic science. These, however, are
not distinct divisions; for one of them includes two
The social of the others. The production of wealth, as it is
process of
production carried on by an organized society, is a process that
includes ex- embraces within itself both exchange and distribu-
change and
distribution. tion. This fact makes it necessary completely to rearrange economic theory, for purposes of study, and
to divide it according to a new principle. The old
landmarks of the science will not entirely disappear,
for it will still be necessary to speak of production,
distribution, etc., as processes that are going on, and
that can be defined and understood. As divisions

10

of the science, however, they will vanish; for the
demarcations that have been made between them
correspond to nothing in actual life.   They are
forced distinctions, made for the sake of resolving
into smaller areas a field that is too large to be dealt
with as a whole.   As we throw them away, the economic field takes on an entirely new appearance,
and it will soon be seen that this is its true and
natural appearance.   This field will still, however,
have its divisions; and it is a striking fact that the
study which shows how hopelessly blended are exchange, distribution and production has also the
effect of revealing three divisions of economics that
are natural and clear.   We attain the true divisions,
in fact, by perceiving why we may not use the old
ones.

Production is the bringing of commodities into
existence; and in any social state except a primitive
one it is accomplished by a division of labor.   The
modern producer is a specialist, selling one article,
or a part of an article, and buying what he needs
with the proceeds.   Only society in its entirety is
an all-around creator of goods.   This is equivalent
to saying that social production is now accomplished
by means of exchanges.   The passing of goods from
man to man enables all society to make all goods;
and the two expressions, "division of labor," on the
one hand, and "exchange," on the other, merely
describe in different ways the organized process of
creating wealth, as contrasted with the method of
isolated and independent production.   Where a thing
stays in one man's hands until it is finished and in
use, production is not yet socialized.[1]   Society in its

[margin notes:] Production, distribution, exchange and consumption definable, though not distinct from each other.

"Exchange and "division of labor" both describe the organized process of creating wealth.

---

[1] An article is not finished, in the economic sense, till the retail
merchant has found the customer whose needs it satisfies.   The sale
of completed articles is thus the terminal act of social production.

entirety is the one producer of wealth. Exchange is, then, the socializing element in production. It is a characteristic part of the comprehensive process.

The essen-
tial relation
of man to
nature un-
changed by
social or-
ganization.
The relation of man to Nature in the productive operation remains unchanged, however much society may be organized. The earth still gives matter, and man transforms it. The making of a steel tool in a modern shop is, in this respect, akin to the fashioning of a stone hatchet by a prehistoric man. What is new in social production is the relation of man to man. Interdependence has supplanted independence: a great organization has taken the place of a mass of unconnected producers. Specializing and exchanging have made this difference.

Production by society as a whole, moreover, involves a fixing of values. If we part with our own products, something must decide how much we are to get in return for them. The ratios of exchange that a market establishes have, not unnaturally, been treated in that division of the science which is customarily entitled exchange. Is that, however, the proper place for them?

The fixing
of values
equivalent
to group
distribution.
There is a kind of distribution that does not fix the rates of wages and interest, but determines how much one industry, as a whole, including its laborers, its capitalists and its *entrepreneurs*, shall get, as compared with other industries. It determines whether one whole branch of business shall be more prosperous than another. This is an intermediate part of the general distributing operation, and it is accomplished by means of prices. When wheat, for example, is high in price, the farming industry is well paid, as compared with others; and when wheat is cheap, that industry is ill paid. If what we have in mind is the so-called " market price " of an article, — the immediate price of any given supply of an

article, — this kind of value governs what we may call group distribution. If steel, for example, sells at a high rate, a large income goes to the group that produces it. This income distributes itself somewhere in the group; but how much of it laborers get, and how much capitalists and employers get, is a question that we do not now raise. This is determined by an ultimate distribution taking place within the groups. Group distribution is a preliminary division of the social income, and it deals with branches of industry in their entirety. The terms of this primary division of the social income depend on the prices of different kinds of goods. Farmers want wheat to be dear, as miners want ore to be dear, etc. Prices, then, fix the incomes of these groups. *The prosperity of a group dependent on market prices.*

The great income of all society — that which is to be distributed — really consists of concrete articles, all for some use. Most of them are goods for consumption; and they serve to stock retailers' shops, while waiting for purchasers. In some way this promiscuous stock of consumers' goods gets divided into shares, of which every man, whether he be a laborer or a capitalist, gets a part. There is no way in which the fixing of the terms of this division can be begun and completed after the goods are finished and exposed for sale. If, before the stock of goods was ready to be taken by consumers, nothing had been done to decide how much each laborer and each capitalist might have, the distribution would have to be made according to some arbitrary rule and by some officer of the state. The terms of the division that is actually made, however, are fixed as the production of the goods goes on: the goods are really apportioned in the making. *Wages and interest fixed by an earlier adjustment.*

The creation of such a general stock of commodities for use is a great synthesis, which goes on in a systematic way.   One group of producers makes the article A, another group makes B, another C, etc. As A is sold, the sum that is paid for it is apportioned among the entire group that makes it; and as B is sold, the returns from this sale are divided, in the same way, among all who have helped to make this article.   The prices of completed articles thus fix the incomes of groups in their entirety.   These groups are, in an equally exact way, divided into sub-groups.   Thus it takes farmers, wool merchants, manufacturers, dyers, cloth merchants and tailors to make a coat.   Each of these classes constitutes a sub-group; and each gets a share of the returns of the general group — a share in every case dependent on prices.   If wool is dear, farmers thrive; and if the difference between the price of wool and the price of cloth is large, manufacturers thrive.   It is market values that fix the incomes of sub-groups, as well as those of groups.

Prices affect the incomes of groups in their entirety,

and also those of sub-groups.

Neither of these price-adjusting operations, however, directly fixes wages and interest.   This is the final and critical part of distribution.   It takes place within the sub-groups, and it constitutes the third and final division that has to be made.   The portions of income that fall to farmers, manufacturers, etc., as such, have to be further subdivided; for a share must be paid to every laborer and to every capitalist. This last division is not made, however, as the more general divisions are made, by a mere sale of finished goods: finer and more difficult adjustments are involved.   We need now to have clearly in mind the systematic way in which the division of the grand stock of usable goods proceeds, the manner in which it follows the stages of production and the part that the fixing of exchange values has in it.   This distribution goes on in three distinct stages.   There

are to be made a division, a subdivision and a final
subdivision of the social income. The first division
fixes the income of industrial groups; the second
fixes that of sub-groups, and the final division adjusts
wages and interest within each of the innumerable
sub-groups in the system. The shares of the groups
and those of the sub-groups depend entirely on the
prices of goods, and therefore the fixing of market
values results in the adjustment of the terms of
group distribution.

A'''	B'''	C'''
A''	B''	C''
A'	B'	C'
A	B	C

Thus, let A''' represent some one completed product,
say bread; and let A represent raw material, the
standing wheat of which it is made. A' may then
represent the wheat as threshed and conveyed to the
elevator of a milling company, A'' may represent it
as it is ground into flour, and A''' may represent it
baked into loaves. In like manner B, B', etc., represent another commodity — say, woollen clothing — in
its several stages of advancement, and the series of C's
represent still another commodity. All the A's constitute the product of one general group; and the
price of A''' fixes the size of its entire group income. The prices of B''' and C''' likewise fix the
general incomes of the two groups that make them.
Similarly, the difference between the price of A'' and
that of A''' fixes the income of the sub-group that
transforms the one article into the other. In this
case the difference is the gross income of the baking
industry. In the same way, the difference between
the price of A' and that of A'' determines the income
of the flouring industry, etc. *The income of each sub-
group in the whole series, then, depends directly on prices.*

Incomes of
groups and
sub-groups
determined
in the first
two stages.

A philosophy that goes behind such market prices, however, brings us to what are called "natural" or "normal" prices. These are the values, expressed in terms of money, to which, in the long run, market values tend to conform. These normal values are also, in another way, phenomena of distribution; for a certain force that operates within the sphere of group distribution establishes the normal standards to which market values tend to conform. We have just seen that market prices fix the incomes of the different groups, as such, and so control distribution in its early stages. We have now to see that a deeper force, and one that also acts in distribution, controls normal prices. Market prices are the cause of group distribution; normal prices are the effect of a certain phenomenon of distribution. The adjustment of natural or normal prices is a part of the distributive process. The movements that make prices "natural" are, in fact, efforts on the part of different men to get their natural shares of income.

Prices are at their natural level when labor and capital in one industry produce as much and get as much as they do in any other. Normal prices mean equalized wages and equalized interest. If the prices of wheat, wool, iron, lumber, etc., were such that no laborer and no capitalist could acquire an enlarged producing power by leaving the industry that creates one of these commodities, and betaking himself to one that makes another, the price of each of the commodities would be normal.

The familiar definition of natural price is: that which conforms to the cost of production. The economist has been in the habit of putting himself, in imagination, in the business man's position, and of considering the money that he pays out in producing an article as the cost and what he gets by selling the

article as the return.   The tendency of competition,
according to this conception, is to bring the price down
to the point at which the return equals the cost.   This
is, however, an individualistic and limited view of
the law of normal prices.   It presents that law as it
appears to a man who is performing his one particular part of the social operation of creating wealth.
The broad view, on the other hand, presents the law
as it appears to a student who has all society within
the range of his vision.   It is, indeed, true that the
normal price of each article is its cost.   The cause of
this, however, is not local in the industry: it is not
anything that takes place within the one group that
makes the commodity.   The influence that brings,
let us say, cotton cloth to a natural price is one that
works throughout the productive system.   A broadly
social tendency it is, in fact, that makes any one
price normal.   The traditional statement of the law
of normal price is not incorrect; but it is misleading,
because it is partial and inadequate.   It presents
things from an *entrepreneur's* point of view, instead
of from a social point of view.

It will be seen, when we make a fuller study of
this subject, that a condition in which all things sell
for the amount of money that they have cost —
including interest and wages of management, as elements of cost — is a state in which the gross gains of
the different industrial groups are brought to *pro rata*
equality, that is, to a condition in which the returns
of all groups yield the same amounts per unit of
capital and also the same amounts per unit of labor.
Cost prices, then, are those that give equalized
earnings.

It is comparative gains, and not the gains of any
one group, that test prices, and determine whether
they are normal.   Thus, the present price of wheat

is such as to afford a larger product per unit of
capital than is afforded in some other industries:
it is above the natural standard, and would be so
even if wages and interest were locally so high
that *entrepreneurs* got nothing above cost of production.   If the result of this should be to draw
men and capital from other occupations to the raising of this cereal, the operation would end by reducing to nothing the excess of gains that is now secured
in this occupation.   Prices would then be normal,
provided that no other causes had meanwhile acted
to disturb the equality of the earning power of labor
and capital in the group system.   It is because the
prices then realized would afford to the different
industrial groups equalized returns, that the prices
themselves are to be called normal.   The term really
signifies that group distribution is in a natural state.
Equal products everywhere per unit of labor and
equal products per unit of capital — this is the condition that affords natural prices of goods.   Incidentally, this condition gives what have been defined as
cost prices.

When, therefore, men have no further inducement
to move from one group to another, — that is, when
group distribution is natural, — prices are natural.
This requires that labor and capital shall be so apportioned among the various industries that there is
neither overproduction of one article nor underpro-
duction of another.   Society must, in short, so direct
its productive energies as to make different goods
in the right quantities.   The production of each
specific article must be normal in amount, in order
that the price of it may be normal.   The influence
that brings production to this natural state is the
effort of laborers and capitalists to seize any special
gain that may be offered to them, by moving to any

A natural
group distri-
bution the
condition of
a "natural
price" of
any article;

this depen-
dent on the
apportion-
ment of
producing
agents
among the
groups.

group in which the price of the product is high.
This is clearly an operation in group distribution.
Thus an influence that originates in distribution
brings about a state of social production in which
exchange values are normal. Where, then, within
the four traditional divisions of economic science
should the study of exchange value be located? The
phenomenon itself is directly connected with exchange; the proximate cause of it is a state of
production; the ultimate influence that controls it
is an action of the forces of distribution.

Value gov-
erned by
comparative
group pro-
duction, and
ultimately
controlled
by forces of
distribution.

It is clear that the study of market value falls
within the science of distribution. On the surface,
it is current market prices that control the distribution which takes place among different groups or
specific industries. These prices, however, are transient, and they fluctuate about certain more permanent standards. The tendency of group distribution
to become normal — that is, to bring wages and interest to an approximate equality in different industries
— draws prices toward the normal standard.

The theory
of value in-
cluded with-
in the theory
of distribu-
tion.

What, then, is left to be treated under the title,
exchange? Only the actual passing of goods from
hand to hand. This process results in ranging men
in distinct groups, each of which has its part to play
in the process of social production. Exchange fixes
the form of organization of industrial society. Back
of each finished article that the shops offer to us
there is ranged a series of specialized producers, each
of whom has taken his turn in putting a touch upon
it. Intricate, indeed, is the organization of society
for productive purposes ; but the principles that give
shape to it are simple. They are the subjects of the
theory of exchange, which is the theory of the organization of industrial society. When we examine
the system of groups of which society is composed,

Exchange
signifies the
organiza-
tion of
industry.

we shall perceive the full meaning of this statement. For the present, be it noted that exchanges divide and subdivide industry: they range its forces in groups and sub-groups, the functions of which are determined by natural law.

It is, further, clear that all this disposing of the agents of production — this putting of some labor and capital here, and other labor and capital there — is a phenomenon of social production, a part of the social productive organization. It is a certain marshalling of the productive forces, placing them where they will do the most good. Production, in fact, embraces every economic operation except consumption. Exchange is merely the typical feature of production, as carried on by groups. Under this head we shall describe the group system of industry. We have seen that an influence which acts in distribution fixes the sizes of the groups and the amount of goods that each shall create. In the way that we have just noted, it guards against the production of too much of one commodity and too little of another. This is also a part of the all-embracing process of social production.

There is another and an even more important kind of distribution that falls within production. The distribution which connects itself with values, and the study of which gives a science of value, is that which takes place between different industries in their entirety. Thus, a high price for wheat makes the raising of that cereal a well-paid occupation, and puts a large sum into the possession of the group of laborers, capitalists and *entrepreneurs* who jointly raise it. How much of this large return goes to laborers? How much goes to capitalists? How much remains in the hands of *entrepreneurs?* These, as we noted, are questions involving distribution of another kind.

Exchange a phenomenon of production.

Socialized production the all-inclusive process.

Within each industry there is this final division to be made. After the returns of each sub-group, taken as a whole, have been determined, this lump sum is to be apportioned among different claimants within it; and this is the final process in the distributing of the social income.

Final distribution a process within the sub-groups.

In the final division that takes place within the sub-groups — the division that separates the gross earnings of each of them into wages, interest and profits — a law of production rules. So far as natural laws are unperverted, labor tends to get, as its share, what it separately produces; and capital does the same. The laborer who has helped a farmer to raise wheat naturally gets the value of that part of the wheat crop which is separately due to his labor. This statement requires proof, and will receive it; but it must stand for the present, as a thesis to be established by a later study. What is now clear is that, if it should be established, the whole of distribution, as well as the whole of exchange, would be included within the organized process of producing wealth. Unravel the web of the social product, tracing each thread to its source, and you will have solved the problem of distribution. This is an analytical study. It traces backward, step by step, the synthesis by which, through the putting together of many different things, the great social dividend of usable goods is created. It first traces to each group its share in the creating of the grand total; then it traces the part of this that each sub-group has contributed; and finally it attributes to labor and capital their several shares in the creating of the sub-group product.

Wages, interest and profits determined by the specific products in each industry, of labor, capital and coördination.

The problem of distribution solved by tracing the social product to its sources.

We may, then, gather into the comprehensive science of production all the economic processes that go on in an organized or social way. There

is, then, it appears, no separating of the processes
that traditional theories have treated as distinct
divisions of the science. Here, for example, working in a shoe shop, is a man who gets two dollars
a day. Let us set before ourselves the problem of
accounting for the amount of his wages. He is a
part of a sub-group; and we have first to account
for the way in which society has thrown itself into
the systematic shape of groups and sub-groups, which
exchange products with each other. We discuss the
theory of exchange, in the narrow and accurate sense
of the term, when we account for this group arrangement which is brought about for the sake of
carrying on production in an organized way. In
treating exchange, therefore, we are entering on the
treatment of production. What the man gets is a
part of what his sub-group gets; and this is fixed
by the law of group distribution — the law of
market value. Market value, however, depends on
the relative quantities of the different articles that
are produced; and this is saying that it depends on
comparative group production. We are, then, still
within the more general science of production when
we thus try to trace to its causes the income of the
sub-group from which the shoemaker's wages are
taken. When we have discovered the influences
that act on the sub-group's income, we must see why
the shoemaker's share of that income is two dollars
a day. This will take us into a further study of
specific production. We shall have to find out, first,
whether the man's pay tends to equal what he separately produces; and, secondly, what fixes the
amount that he is able to produce. This is the study
of distribution in its final stage, but it is also a study of
production. We have, then, studied in part each
of the four traditional subjects except consumption,

in investigating the causes of the two dollar wage for the shoemaker's labor; and yet we have been, all the while, within the subject of social production. Consumption alone remains an individualistic process. We produce our food coöperatively, but we eat it each one for himself. Society makes our clothing, builds our houses, etc.; but when we get our clothes, we wear them without assistance; and we dwell under our roofs in the same independent way. Society, however, reacts on our natures, and changes and multiplies our wants. A desire to associate with others, while consumption is going on, may even give a kind of collectivity to the process by which some products are used. Thus, we enjoy dining together; and we listen to music and addresses in assemblies, getting a part of our pleasure from the presence of others; but there is no coöperation in the consumption of goods that resembles what takes place in the production of them. There is no obvious group system, and no coöperation of agents such as labor and capital. It is to the sensibilities of individuals that products address themselves; and therefore consumption is the individualistic part of social economy.

Consumption an individualistic process.

If we look, then, at the relations of man to man, we find that production and consumption are not on the same plane. One is a collective operation: it is nothing, if not organized. The other is an individualistic operation: it consists in the using by each man of what society, by its intricate system of production, has made for him. In an accurate sense, the one process is a part of social economy and the other is not.

Production and consumption not coördinate, so far as men's relations to each other are concerned;

If we look at the relations of man to nature, we find that production and consumption are entirely coördinate, — that one of them is the reversal of the other. Man acts on nature in the one case, and nature acts on man in the other. Cultivate the earth till it gives you food, and you have produced a kind of wealth by acting on nature; but the food restores your wasted tissues and your lost energy by acting on you. Man making wealth and wealth making man constitute the whole economic operation. Humanity takes the active and aggressive attitude in the former part of the process, and it takes the passive and recipient attitude in the latter part. In the simplest mode of living these two processes are the only ones that take place. A primitive man, living alone, would kill game and eat it; he would make clothing and wear it; he would build a hut and live in it: in short, he would act on nature and let nature react on him, and that would constitute the whole of his economy. He would have nothing to do with exchange and distribution. This, indeed, is all that an economic society does, if we consider it only as a unit. It produces its food, its clothing, its shelter and its myriad of articles of comfort and luxury; and then it uses them. It produces them in an organized way, indeed, and it uses them in an unorganized way. Incidental to the making of them are the trading and sharing processes that are termed exchange and distribution; but production and consumption still exhaust the whole economy: there is no phenomenon of wealth that lies outside of them.

These are the facts to be recognized in entering on the study of distribution. In carrying that study to completion we cannot get outside of the field of social production, and we cannot avoid including within our more limited field the subject of exchange. Value is the chief subject that has customarily been treated in the division of exchange; but the theory of value and that of group distribution are one and the same.

but coördinate, so far as the relations of man and Nature are concerned.

Production and consumption constitute the whole economic process.

Distribution as a part of social production, and as including exchange.

CHAPTER III

THE PLACE OF DISTRIBUTION WITHIN THE NATURAL DIVISIONS OF ECONOMICS

THERE is, we may now note, a mode of dividing the field of economics that will enable us to study distribution without forgetting its relations to exchanges and to production. In social economics there are three distinct kinds of force working together. If we study them separately, we shall resolve economic science into three divisions, the boundaries of which have been drawn by nature. Man modifies matter by production, and matter modifies man through consumption. These processes do not require any organization on the part of the men who impart and then receive impressions. All this could be accomplished by an isolated man, or by men living together for protection or for the mere pleasures of association, without any system of exchange of products. Let every one make his own goods and consume them, and an economic life of a certain kind is complete.

The relation of man to nature not dependent on social organization.

The distinctive feature of such a life is that it establishes direct relations between the individual man and nature. Every man subdues for himself a part of his material environment; and he gets the direct service that this bit of nature, when thus subdued, can render. Under these conditions, there are no disguises thrown over the relation that workers sustain to the earth. Obvious dependence

This relation undisguised in primitive life.

25

on nature, obvious independence of other men — such is the rule of every one's economic life. Out of materials furnished by the earth each producer creates his own income; and connected with this process there are no problems of distribution.

Yet, in this mode of living, which puts every man face to face with nature, there is room for the action of all of the more fundamental laws of economics. Here, for example, is a hunter in a primeval forest, converting the flesh of animals into food and their skins into clothing and shelter. He is creating something that can be defined as wealth. It has the essential marks that analysis detects in the wealth that crowds the shops of the modern city. The man uses capital, and includes in his equipment both the fixed and the circulating varieties of it. His consumption has its laws; and the chief of them is the one that calls for variety in the things consumed. He must not make and use too much of one kind of product and too little of another — he must guard against glutting some wants and letting others go unsatisfied, if the wealth that he creates is to do him much good.

The fundamental laws of economics here in operation.

There is, then, a distinct set of economic laws, the action of which is not dependent on organization. They are fundamental; and we now have to note that they are universal. They act in the economy of the most advanced state, as well as in that of the most primitive. Wealth has everywhere the same distinguishing marks. The producing and the consuming of it are always subject to the same general conditions. The first natural division of economic science should, therefore, present the universal laws of wealth: it should discuss the more general laws of production and all the laws of consumption.

Universal laws the subject of the first division of economic science.

A second series of phenomena is traceable to a

further set of forces which originate in relations between man and man.   They are made to work wher- A second set
ever persons begin to exchange products ; for this of laws
dependent
organizes society into groups or specific industries. on the exchanging of
Let some men produce food and others build huts, products.
exchanging products with each other, and things
happen that are not accounted for by the laws of
that general economy in which the direct relations
of man to nature are explained.   Exchanges involve
the determining of values ; and these, as we have
seen, fix the terms of group distribution.

The organization of society is further extended How eco-
when, within each group or specific industry, there nomic society is organ-
arise employers paying wages to the men who ized.
labor and interest to those who furnish capital.
Distribution, in a broad definition of that term,
results from such an organization of the wealth-
creating powers.   The division of economics that
treats of it will first deal with group distribution,
which depends on exchanges, and then deal with
that final distribution which takes place within each
sub-group, fixing the wages, the interest and the
profits that are there received.   Broadly conceived,
and made to include a description of the group
system and its exchanges of products, the science of
distribution embraces the social laws of economics.
Such a science begins with a description of the group
system of industry.   It accounts for the terms on
which the groups buy and sell from each other, and
shows on what the income of each group in its
entirety depends.   It further shows what becomes
of the income which in this way comes to a group
as a whole.   Laborers get some of it, capitalists get
some, and *entrepreneurs* get the remainder — if there
is one.   In short, the distinctively social relations Relations of
that are created when society as a whole becomes groups and
of classes

within them described by the term, distribution.

the producer, may be treated under the title, distribution. This term, however, cannot be used as the title of a scientific division, if this use of it carries with it the idea that what is treated under this title is not production and is not exchange. Distribution is a process which, in its completeness, includes exchange, but it falls within production. It is not expedient, therefore, to characterize the second natural division of economic science as the science of distribution; since the idea of distinctness from production and exchange attaches itself, in the public mind, to this term. It is best described as the division that treats of the social laws of economics, as distinct from the general laws. When we know what happens in consequence of the economic actions and reactions that are taking place between man and nature, we need further to know what takes place in consequence of relations between man and man.

Distribution partly treated in the second division of economic science.

This division occupied with social, as distinct from universal, phenomena of wealth.

It is conceivable that production might go on in an organized way without any change in the character of the operation. Men might conceivably produce to the end of time the same kinds of goods, and they might do it by the same processes. Their tools and materials might never change; and they might not alter, either for the better or for the worse, the amount of wealth that industry would yield. Social production can thus be thought of as static. In such a changeless mode of social industry, distribution, with all that it involves, would take place. Groups would exchange products, and each would be dependent on the value of its own goods for the amount of its collective income. The price of agricultural produce would determine the income of farmers, and the price of ore would fix that of miners. The gains of a group as a whole would be divided among the sub-groups composing it, and would then by a

Distribution in an unchanging state of industry.

further operation be parted into wages, interest and profits.

What are called "natural" standards of values and "natural" or normal rates of wages, interest and profits are, in reality, static rates. They are identical with those which would be realized, if a society were perfectly organized but were free from the disturbances that progress causes. Far more than classical economists were aware of is involved in a thorough-going study of what they called natural values.

"Natural" values, wages, interest and profits equivalent to static rates.

Reduce society to a stationary state, let industry go on with entire freedom, make labor and capital absolutely mobile — as free to move from employment to employment as they are supposed to be in the theoretical world that figures in Ricardo's studies — and you will have a regime of natural values. These are the values about which rates are forever fluctuating in the shops of commercial cities. You will also have a regime of natural wages and interest; and these are the standards about which the rates of pay for labor and capital are always hovering in actual mills, fields, mines, etc. In this connection, the terms, natural, normal and static are synonymous. That division of economic science which presents natural standards of values, wages and interest ought consciously to take the shape of a theory of Social Economic Statics. Such a theory would treat of distribution as it would go on if there were taking place none of those grand disturbances — changes in the modes of production, etc. — that are forever causing market quotations to vary from the natural standards that figure in classical economics.

These rates approached, though with variations, in actual markets.

A static state, however, is imaginary. All natural societies are dynamic; and those which we have principally to study are highly so. Heroically theoretical is the study that creates in imagination a

Societies always dynamic, but still dominated by static forces

static society. In the actual world unceasing
changes thrust labor and capital, from time to time,
out of one occupation and into another. In each
industry they change, again and again, the modes of
production and the kinds and the quantities of the
goods produced. Yet this does not invalidate the
conclusions of a static theory; for static laws are
nevertheless real laws. The forces that would work
in a world that should be held in a fixed shape and
made to act forever in a fixed manner still operate
in the changing world of reality. We can always see
them working in connection with other forces, but we
have to imagine them working alone. We study them
separately, in order that we may understand one part
of what goes on in dynamic society. To do this we
imagine a static society, thus making a heroic but
necessary application of the isolating method.

Static forces
to be distin-
guished
from dy-
namic ones.

Only by reason of its omissions, however, is the
imaginary and static state unlike the real and dynamic one. All the forces that would work in the
unchanging world are not only working in the changeful one, but are even the dominant forces in it. They
do not keep values exactly at the natural standards,
but they keep them fluctuating about those standards;
and they keep real wages and interest always comparatively near to the natural rates.

We have now described the boundaries of two of
the natural divisions of economic science. The first
treats of universal phenomena, and the second of
static social phenomena. Starting with those laws of
economics which act whether humanity is organized
or not, we next study the forces that depend on
organization but do not depend on progress. Finally,
it is necessary to study the forces of progress. To
influences that would act if society were in a stationary state, we must add those which act only as society

Forces of
progress the
subject of
the third di-
vision of
economics.

is thrown into a condition of movement and disturbance. This will give us a science of Social Economic Dynamics. It will bring the society that figures in our theory into a condition like that of the actual world. It will supply what a static theory openly and intentionally puts out of sight — namely, changes that alter the mode of production and act on the very structure of society itself. A study of these changes is the content of the third natural division of economic science.

Wants are changing, and the kinds of wealth that are produced must change with them. New mechanical processes are coming into use. Machines supplant hand labor, and efficient machines displace inferior ones. New motive powers are taken into service, and new raw materials are used. Population increases and migrates, taking with it some of the increase of its wealth. Large industries grow up and crowd small ones out of the field. The earth becomes crowded with life and wealth. None of these changes, however, serves to suppress the action of static forces; nor do all of them together do so. Not one jot nor one tittle shall fall from the law of natural values, or from that of natural rates of wages, interest and profits. A different set of forces is acting in connection with the static ones; and real values, wages, etc., are the resultant of the two kinds of force. In advancing to the study of dynamic phenomena, our theory completes itself; and the effect is to make it fully interpret the world of fact. A theoretical dynamic world is exactly like the actual world, if the theory that constructs it is a valid and complete one. It has the elements of disturbance and of friction to which men of business point, as influences that invalidate theoretical conclusions. If the study of it were carried to completion, it would

The nature of the changes that are taking place.

Dynamic forces act in connection with static forces. A dynamic theory, if complete, is realistic furnish what has heretofore been lacking — namely, a science of economic friction and disturbance.

So far as method is concerned, a theory of economic dynamics must use deduction, as did the theories of the Ricardian school.   It must base itself on the conclusions of economic statics, which, as we have seen, are uncompromisingly theoretical.   Yet realism is the striking trait of the dynamic theory.   It includes in its field of view just the elements that have been needed to make a deductive economic science fully interpret the world of fact.

In the markets of all parts of the world where competition rules the standards about which prices fluctuate are set by static forces, and the fluctuations are accounted for by dynamic ones.   Actual prices are now above the standards and now below them, as a pendulum is now on one side of an imaginary vertical line and now on the other.   This vertical line coincides with the position that the pendulum would hold, if it were under the influence of static forces only.   The oscillations are due to dynamic forces; and these can be measured, if we first know the nature of the static forces and the position to which, if they were acting alone, they would bring the pendulum.   The oscillations of prices about the natural standards can be accounted for only by a like method of study.   The same thing is true of natural wages and interest, and of the fluctuations about these standards that actual rates show.   Static forces set the standards, and dynamic forces produce the variations.

This, however, is not the largest effect of dynamic forces.   We shall not have learned the most important thing about them, when we have accounted for the deviations from natural rates that actual values, wages and interest show.   We shall see that dynamic forces create new conditions in which static forces

Standards of price set by static laws; oscillations about them accounted for by dynamic influences.

Changes in static standards them-work. In these new conditions natural values, etc., are not what they were in the former conditions. Thus, the price of cotton cloth that is entirely natural when this fabric is made by hand is far from natural when it is made by machinery. The normal price of cotton cloth fell in consequence of the inventions of Watt, Hargreave, Arkwright and Crompton. Before these men did their work, the price of the cloth was fluctuating about one natural standard; afterward it fluctuated about another. Similarly, the normal level of wages is rising and that of interest is falling, in consequence of far-reaching dynamic influences. At any one time there is one standard of value, wages and interest set by static forces, and at that time the temporary fluctuations of actual rates about these standards are due to dynamic causes. At a later time it will be found that the standards themselves have undergone a change; and these grander effects are the most important ones that are attributable to dynamic forces. A theory of disturbance and variation is, indeed, included in the science of economic dynamics; but the most important thing that is included in it is a theory of progress. The normal wealth of the world will be greater, and the natural level of wages will be far higher in the year 2000 than they are to-day, if the greater forces of economic dynamics continue to work.

We have now before us the boundaries of the three natural divisions of economic science. The first embraces the universal phenomena of wealth. If anything is true of the wealth-getting and the wealth-using process under every condition of social development, it is material for this division. The second includes social economic statics, and tells what further happens, in connection with wealth, if society is organized. and if no change takes place in

selves accounted for by dynamic laws

Universal phenomena, static social phenomena and dynamic social phenomena — the subjects of the three divisions of economic science.

its form of organization or in its mode of action. The third division includes social economic dynamics, and tells what still further happens, as regards the wealth and welfare of the community, by reason of the fact that society is changing in form and in modes of activity.

Relations of the new divisions to the old.

If we wish to note the relation that these three divisions bear to the four traditional ones, we shall see that the first division, treating of universal economic phenomena, includes fundamental concepts and facts that are naturally put into an introductory division or *Grundlegung*. Yet this division may be made to include all needful discussion of consumption, since this is an individualistic operation, of which the fundamental laws are the same in all social conditions. The second division discusses value, which has been commonly treated under exchange, and natural or static wages and interest, which have been commonly treated under distribution. The third division is devoted to the dynamics of production, which include changes in value and the whole of the dynamics of distribution. And, as changes in human wants constitute the dynamics of consumption, the effect of such changes enters as an element into the material with which this division deals. The three divisions here proposed are quite distinct from each other, though they are interdependent and consecutive. The second division takes among its data the facts and principles presented in the first; and the third begins by assuming all that is stated or assumed by the second. Of the four old divisions, three are hopelessly merged in each other; and none of the four accurately corresponds to either of the three divisions that we have called natural.[1]

Consumption offers material for the first division, and exchange and distribution material for the second.

The dynamics of distribution offers material for the third division.

These three divisions distinct. The four traditional divisions merged in each other, and nowhere coincident with the three here proposed.

[1] If the term "statics of distribution" had been used and had been very broadly defined, it might have been made to coincide in

It is already clear that the field for new investiga- Economic
tion offered by economic dynamics is an indefinitely the most
fruitful one. It would become still clearer that this field.
is the fact, if it were practicable here to describe, in
a more detailed way, the particular problems that
have to be solved in a theory of social economic
progress. They include every possibility of gain
that can come to humanity by economic change.
They are essentially new problems, because the prevailing mode of economic study has not heretofore
isolated them, brought them clearly into view and
afforded the data for solving them. Not without its
references to progress has been the theory that has
founded itself on the old and baffling plan of a four-
fold division of the whole science into production,
distribution, exchange and consumption ; but it has Successful
not been in a position to solve the problems that dependent
progress presents, for the reason that a knowledge on a knowl-
of static law is universally needed as a preliminary static law.
to a knowledge of dynamic law. As is the case in
mechanics, the forces of rest must be known before
those of movement can be understood.

its scope with the second of the three proposed divisions ; but this
would have involved attaching a broad meaning to the term, distribution, since it would thus have made it to cover the organization
of productive society into groups.

Dividing a field by two intersecting lines makes four divisions
instead of three. A treatment of every possib'e phase of economic

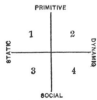

life would require us to study field 1 of the
accompanying diagram, or primitive economic statics, and then field 2, or primitive
economic dynamics. If after this we were
to enter the social territory, we should at
once be in field 4, that of social economic
dynamics, and should have passed by the
indispensable division of social economic
statics. As our entire purpose is to understand the laws of a
dynamic social industry, we attain our end by covering only fields
1, 3 and 4.

CHAPTER IV

THE BASIS OF DISTRIBUTION IN UNIVERSAL ECONOMIC LAWS

THIS work will first present the static laws of distribution — a subject that falls within the field that we have defined as belonging to the second of the three Scope of natural divisions of economic science. It will offer the present a pure theory of what may be called natural wages work: and interest. Statistical studies it will not make; and it will not discuss in detail the practical mechanism by which exchanges are effected. It will contain no treatment of money and banks, of taxation, or of political action that is taken for the purpose of influencing the terms of distribution.

The laws of distribution, as broadly defined and made to include those of exchange, are the distinctively social laws of economics, since they account for the organization of society into producing groups, and for the organization of each group into classes of laborers, capitalists and employers. They account also for the transactions of these groups and classes with each other. Static laws furnish the natural standards to which the incomes of economic groups and those of laborers and capitalists within them tend to conform. Dynamic laws, on the other hand, account, first, for the variations of actual incomes from these natural standards; and, secondly, for the slow and steady change that, as time progresses, is taking place in the standards themselves.

36

Natural wages to-day are not what they will be a
year hence. If society is evolving in a normal way,
the standards of pay in the future will steadily rise.
The actual rate of pay, as the evolution goes on, will
pursue the rising theoretical standard, but will lag
behind it in its upward movement. The rate at
which the standard of pay rises and the influences
that determine the extent to which the actual pay
of labor varies from it are typical subjects of a
dynamic theory of distribution; and so far as this
work discusses any of these subjects, it will enter
the domain of the third natural division of pure economics. A theory of distribution, static and dynamic, would constitute the greater part, though
not the whole, of the second and third divisions of
a complete economic theory. The field of social
economic dynamics, however, is the unexplored part
of the general economic field. If present plans shall
be realized, this work will in due time be followed by
another, which will deal with the distinctly dynamic
laws. In the present work the "natural" — or, more
accurately, the static — standards of wages, interest
and profits will be presented; and dynamic movements will be described only in the most brief and
general way, for the sake of making clear the fact
that static laws dominate the activities of a real and
dynamic society. Wages in the practical world, with
all its radical changes and with all the friction that
it offers to the action of pure law, actually hover
about the static standards; and their variations from
these are themselves subject to law. In particular, it
is necessary to know that the primitive law which
puts a man face to face with nature and makes him
dependent on what he personally can make her yield
to him is still, in essence, the law of the most complex
economy.

it falls mainly within the limits of social economic statics,

but will try to show that static laws dominate dynamic societies.

If we were to assume, at the outset, that all of the universal truths of economics are known, we should pass completely over the first division of a general economic theory and begin with the second. Principles that in reality apply to all industrial life are thrown into prominence in elementary treatises, although these consciously aim to explain the economy of organized societies. Such treatises have never divided the theory of economics in the manner here proposed, and have never presented the universal truths of that science in a division by themselves, in a way that marks the distinction between them and those facts and laws which depend on social organization. What they have done, however, in the way of presenting these truths, has made it possible to discuss the social laws of economics without rehearsing at the beginning many of the more general laws. We know what wealth is, what its varieties are, and what agencies act in the production of it. We have in mind definitions of labor and capital, and the usual distinction between fixed capital and that of the circulating kind. We are familiar with the so-called law of diminishing returns, by which land under tillage rewards labor and capital less and less bountifully, as more and more labor and capital are used on a given area. We know the essential laws of consumption. In short, we possess a body of truth which, although it has not been separated from truths of a distinctively social economy, makes it possible for us to study the social problems without an extended introduction to them.[1]

Acquaintance with most of the universal economic ideas assumed.

[1] The reader is referred to the English works of J. S. Mill, Henry Fawcett, Sidgwick and Marshall, to authoritative foreign treatises, and to such American works as those of F. A. Walker, Hadley and others, for able presentations of economic truths that are universal in their application, although these are not formally

Some general questions in economics, however, have not yet been treated in the way that furnishes the needed basis for the study of distributive problems. In these instances we shall be forced to make brief statements that would naturally fall in the introductory division of a general treatise on economics, if such a division were offered. On controverted points, moreover, we must take a definite position and assign grounds for doing so.

It happens that in an earlier work the author of the present volume has presented some of the universal laws of wealth in a form that makes them harmonize with the theory here to be presented and constitute, in so far, an introduction to it.[1] The treatment that these laws there received was, however, not complete. Moreover, the work was not prepared with a view to its serving as an adequate introduction to the present treatise. For such a purpose, what is especially needed is a sharply defined boundary line separating the field of universal economics from that of social economics. How much, then, is contained in the first of these fields?

We have said that the universal laws of economics depend on relations of mankind to nature, while the social laws, as included in a theory of distribution, depend on relations between man and man. This generalization will guide us in defining the scope of the preliminary division of the general theory. We have said that the essential laws of consumption and all those laws of production that act in the absence of exchanges are subjects for this introductory division of the general theory. What we need particularly to know is how much of what is separated from those which are limited in their application to a social economy.

[1] See *The Philosophy of Wealth.*

of distribu-
tion found
among the
universal
truths.

contained in such a division of the subject has to
be used in the second division. How far does a
statement of universal laws of economics go in the
direction of furnishing premises for a theory of value
and for a theory of wages and interest?

It will be recalled that in our analysis the fixing
of values is the same thing as the adjusting of the
terms of group distribution, while the fixing of wages
and interest is the making of the final division of

Value,
wages and
interest, as
adjusted in
the market,
social phe-
nomena.

incomes within the several sub-groups. Value, wages
and interest [1] are, therefore, the distinctive subjects
of the second of the proposed scientific divisions,
since they are essentially social phenomena. The first
division, on the contrary, must include nothing that
depends on exchanges: it must put out of sight the
organization of society and whatever that entails.
Under these limitations, does a theory of universal
economics offer any materials for a study of values,
wages and interest? We shall see.

Take away exchanges. In imagination sweep out
of existence the industrial institutions of modern
society. This is annihilating the most of what is
known as civilization: it leaves the individual man
face to face with nature, and under the necessity of
making a living by his efforts and her bounty. He
must make his own goods and use them. He must
begin with the rawest material and fashion goods
to completion. Under such circumstances it is a
short list of articles that a man can have. Rude
must they be, and awkward must be the process of
making them. By some tests the man who should
live without exchanges would be less civilized than
are bees, ants, beavers and other animals whose production is organized; yet he would still lead an eco-

---

[1] The reason for omitting to treat profits at this point will soon
appear. See p. 70, also p. 78 *et seq.*

nomic life. He would possess wealth, and some of it would be capital. His production and his consumption would be subject to laws. Since production acts on nature for no other purpose than that nature may react on the producer himself, the economy of every man resolves itself into a process by which he indirectly serves himself, using natural material as a means. This " means " is wealth. Through the medium of things, man serves man in any system of economy. In the primitive system the same man is server and the served, whereas in a social system one man serves another. Wealth is, nevertheless, always the means employed. The goods that an isolated man would make for himself are the concrete forms that his wealth would assume ; and the attributes that would distinguish them are the same that in a commercial city make the difference between what is wealth and what is not.

Production and consumption not limited to social life.

The economy of an isolated man.

In every stage of economic evolution wealth consists of useful material things ; but their utility is of the kind that we may call *specific*. Each part of the supply has some importance attaching to it. Such goods are unlike air or salt water, of which any specific cubic yard might be removed without doing harm. If the goods are of such a kind that by adding to the supply of them you make some one better off, and by taking away any of them you make him worse off, they are wealth. Outward material things that are appropriable and, in this specific way, useful, are economic goods. They are commodities, or concrete forms of wealth ; and this description applies as perfectly to the canoe of a savage and its load of fish as it does to an Atlantic steamship and its rich and varied cargo.

Specific utility the universal attribute of wealth.

If an article is useful to one man, it is usually so to another, and it is therefore in itself exchangeable.

It will, in fact, probably be exchanged, if a social economy is established. It has the qualities that would induce a person other than the owner to make some sacrifice in order to get it. In considering how much it is best to give for it, — say, in the form of labor or of the product of labor, — such a person would apply the principle with which all readers are now familiar, under the title, "final utility." As this term is usually defined, it means the degree of usefulness that the last of a series of similar articles possesses. Give to a man one unit of the article A, and then another and another, till he has ten of

The diminishing utility of successive increments of commodity a general principle. them. While each of the articles in the series may do him some good, the amount of the benefit will steadily diminish, as the number of the articles grows larger, and the tenth one will benefit him least of all. In order to add to his stock of A, the man will never sacrifice more than what is, in his view, a fair offset for the benefit that he will get from the tenth and last unit of it. In order that an article may be wealth at all, each unit of the supply of it must, as we have seen, be of some importance to its owner. The law that we have just cited marks the last unit of the supply as the least important unit. This is one of the universal laws of economics.

There is much to be said as to the completeness and the accuracy of this conception of the law of final utility, which modern theory puts at the basis of the theory of value. We shall see what an important change has to be made in it, if it is to be brought into conformity with facts. For the present, we may put it into the form of a hypothesis and use it provisionally. If men do in fact use a number of units of consumers' goods, all of a kind, and if the specific utility of these goods diminishes as they get more and more of them, then what they will give for any of them will be gauged by the specific utility of the last one. If these familiar premises of the modern theory of value correspond with the facts of life, the theory explains the prices of goods in a modern market: it is a true philosophy of a most important social phenomenon.

The action of this principle in social life.

The line that separates universal economics from social economics runs between the principle of final utility and the application of that principle in a theory of value. The primitive economy that we have imagined cannot test final utilities in a market, for it has no exchanges. Can it not, then, test them at all, and does it not find it necessary to do so? We may easily see that it does this, and that the purpose is exactly like that for which organized society makes the same test. The principle of final utility belongs in the first division of a theory of economics and has to be assumed in the second division.

The action of it in isolated life.

There is always a gain in diversifying the articles that men consume. This is a principle of human nature that affords a universal law of consumption. The industry of the savage state cannot carry the diversifying process far, because it cannot produce many kinds of goods. A man who should try to make many different kinds of articles entirely for himself would be a jack of all trades, and would be so poor in most of them that he would lose as a producer more than, through the diversity of the articles, he would gain as a consumer. Making a few things only, the savage can glut his desires for any one of them by an overproduction of it. The diminution in the utility of successive units of goods of one kind makes itself keenly felt, if he works too long in one occupation. If, then, he has so much meat on hand that more will be of little use to him, he

Diversifying one man's consumption everywhere gainful; diversifying his production everywhere wasteful.

may turn to hewing out canoes, fashioning bows and arrows, or building huts. Otherwise, he will do nothing; since the utility of a further unit of an overproduced kind of wealth will not be enough to keep him working.

The law of final utility fixes the point at which such a producer will stop creating one product and begin making another. A modern laborer, with money in his pocket, is supposed to consult the law of final utility in making purchases and to spend each dime where, in view of the supply of different things already on hand, it will do him the most good. The savage in our assumed case has, not dimes, but efforts to expend; and he directs the expenditure of them according to the same principle. When he has dulled the keenness of his desire for one thing, he makes another. While markets and prices are, therefore, modern phenomena, the study of which has no place in a division of the science devoted to universal truths, the law of final utility which directs the purchases that are made in a modern market also directs the production of the isolated man, and is a universal law of economics.

An isolated man's labor apportioned among his different occupations by the law of final utility.

Draw the line, then, between a theory of exchange economy, or catallactics, and a primitive economy that treats of actions and reactions between man and nature. On the one side of this line you will find markets, values and like phenomena; on the other side you will find those laws of consumption which govern values. In modern life these laws direct the social demand for different goods offered in the shops; but in primitive life they control the manner in which a man husbands his productive power and uses it where it will do him the most good. The law of final utility is common to both economies.

This a law of consumption and universally operative.

This is not all. The picture of an isolated man
turning his own labor from making one thing, of
which he now has a supply, to the making of a
thing that has a higher final utility, illustrates a
characteristic of modern life which is in danger of
being overlooked. Through the laws of value
society, in its entirety, is doing exactly this. It is
turning its collective energies from one direction
to another, according to the law of final utility.
Markets and values afford the mechanism for doing
this. Think of society as an isolated being, turning
its collective energy to the making of one thing till
it has enough of it and then making another, and
you have the fundamental fact. The science of an
exchange economy must tell us how this change is
made.

The labor of
the social
organism as
a whole
apportioned
among dif-
ferent em-
ployments
by the ac-
tion of this
law.

When we look solely at individuals in a modern
state and see how they deal with each other, we lose
sight of fundamental truths. The difficulty of seeing
a forest, by reason of the trees, is small in comparison
with the difficulty of getting a view of society, because
of individuals and their intricate dealings. We must,
therefore, take a broad view : we must not put ourselves in one man's place, and look at things solely
through his eyes. There is no doubt about one fact
— the fact that an oversupply of any one article in a
market means a social glut of a specific kind. In
such a case, the effective demand for this article in
society as a whole is more than met. Then it is that,
through the mechanism of a falling price, society is
warned to turn its energies to the making of something else ; and its whole procedure is nothing more
or less than doing what an isolated man would do,
if he found his want of one commodity becoming
satiated.

If, then, we individualize society — if we make

it to be in its entirety one isolated being, and if we give rein to that philosophy which treats a body of independent beings as one organism —we find it doing what a solitary man would do, under the influence of the law of diminishing utility. Putting a price on each article in a market is the act of the collective organism in estimating the importance to

Changes in price express the need of changing this apportionment of labor.

itself of each of its own products. Theoretically, it takes the whole of society to make any one article rise or fall in price. The movement of labor and capital from an industry the product of which has fallen in price to one the product of which has risen in price is also a social operation. It is the act of society in economizing its productive forces and turning them where they will do to itself the most good. The motives in this movement are individualistic, but

Prices are social phenomena, but the principle that determines them is universal.

the resultant is collective. Each man pursues his own interest; but, as the outcome of his activity, society acts as a solitary man would act under the influence of the law of diminishing utility. The law itself is universal, and the statement of it belongs in the first division of economic theory; but the description of the mechanism by which the law works in a society belongs in the second division.

The deepest economic problems have reference to wages and interest. These incomes are fixed by that final distributing operation which takes place within each of the industrial groups. Let an employer sell his product, pay for his raw material and use the money that he has left in paying wages and interest, and this final distribution is complete. Nothing of this kind, however, takes place in primi-

The dividing of an income into shares is a social operation;

tive life. Selling products and dividing the returns carry us to an advanced or social state. Where a man makes all his own goods, is there any trace of distribution in his economy? Of the separating of a collective income into shares there is certainly nothing; and yet the principle that in social economy governs the separation has as clear a field for its action under primitive conditions as it has under any other.

Market value, then, is a social phenomenon; but the principle of final utility, by which values are fixed, is universal in its scope. So, too, the division of the income of an industrial group into wages and interest is a social phenomenon; but the principle that governs that division — the principle, namely, of specific productivity — is as dominant in primitive life as it is anywhere. but the principle of final productivity, which is at the basis of such a distribution, is universal.

The specific productivity of labor fixes wages — this is the thesis that is to be supported in this volume. Ascertain how large a product is to be attributed to a single unit of labor that is employed in raising wheat, making shoes, smelting iron, spinning cotton, etc., and you have the standard to which the pay of all labor tends to conform. In like manner does the specific productivity of capital fix the rate of interest. Ascertain how large a product is due to the presence of the single unit of capital in each industry, and you have the standard to which all interest tends to adjust itself. The specific productivity of labor the basis of wages, and that of capital the basis of interest.

This principle of specific productivity acts in all stages of economic life. It reveals itself, however, in one way when a man lives in isolation, and in a very different way when he lives in a commercial state. When labor and capital everywhere coöperate, there is, if we are discerning enough to see it, everywhere a definite product that can be attributed to a single unit of each of them. One hour of labor that a savage bestows on the making of a canoe creates a certain amount of wealth, and so does a unit of labor that he gives to any other of his small list of occupations. This principle operative in all stages of economic life.

A man living in solitude and making all his own goods, by the aid of his equipment of working instruments, has to form some conception of the productivity of a unit of labor. He may have an hour which is available for fishing or for working on a canoe that will make future fishing more productive. An hour may be devoted to gathering fruits or to fashioning a spade, for working the soil and thus making food in the future more abundant. In making a decision between two such uses of his time and effort he measures, in his own rude way, the productivity of a unit of capital and that of a unit of labor. The canoe and the spade stand for capital; and the hour that is spent in perfecting such an equipment adds one unit to the man's small fund of it. The hour that is spent in fishing or in fruit gathering adds a unit to the day's labor. Which, on the whole, is the more productive? The answer depends on a law that is the basis of distribution in a modern society, but the law itself is universal.

As consumers' goods grow less and less useful, when a series of units of them are supplied, so producers' goods, or forms of capital, if they have to be used by one man, grow less and less productive. The last tool adds less to man's efficiency than do earlier tools. If capital be used in increasing quantity by a fixed working force, it is subject to a law of diminishing productivity. This law determines how much labor it is best to withdraw from the securing of what ministers directly to wants, for the sake of making an addition to the equipment of working instruments. The choice between casting a line from the shore to catch fish and working on the construction of a canoe, like the choice between climbing a tree for wild fruit and working on a spade for future gardening, is determined by exactly the same principle that is at work

How the final productivity of capital has to be tested in isolated life.

Diminishing returns from capital the check on the making of tools.

in fixing the point at which the labor force of a civilized state shall be taken out of the shops that make goods for consumption and put into those that make tools, machines, etc. The principle of the final productivity of labor and capital everywhere determines how much capital it pays to accumulate.[1]

What we have now to note is the fact that the diminishing productivity of labor, when it is used in connection with a fixed amount of capital, is a universal phenomenon. This fact shows itself in any economy, primitive or social. The statement of the general principle belongs in the first division of economic theory, while the application of it to a theory of natural wages in a social state belongs in

The law of diminishing returns of labor general.

The application of this law to a theory of wages a part of social economics.

[1] Here the greatest of care has to be used in the definition of terms. We have said that the *specific* productivity of labor fixes wages; and this means that pay conforms to the amount of product that is specifically imputable to any one unit of labor in a working force. This implies that the products of the different units are equal. In like manner, the *specific* productivity of capital fixes interest. The earnings of a dollar are what the dollar creates; and this implies that in any one fund of capital, as it is described in terms of money, the products of all the different dollars are the same. Yet the law of diminishing productivity seems to require that the products of different units of labor and of capital should be unlike and that final units should be the least productive. Here is, apparently, a startling contradiction; but it will soon disappear. If terms be defined with care, final productivity and specific productivity mean the same thing. Only when the terms are so used is it correct to say that wages are fixed by the final productivity of labor and interest by that of capital. Moreover, when the term final productivity is otherwise defined, it leads to a theory of the exploitation of labor. If units of labor that stand early in a series continue to create more wealth than they get, labor is robbed. The theory that makes society honest and the one that makes it to be a system of organized plundering of labor are distinguished by the two unlike definitions of the term, final productivity. We must soon make clear the nature of these opposite views that may be stated in the same terms. We must separate the concept of final productivity that is identical with specific productivity from the one that is unlike it. This, however, is the work of a later chapter.

the second division. It is this application that we have to make in the present volume.

The law of the diminishing returns of capital universal.

In like manner, in connection with capital, the line that divides the first division of economic theory from the second runs between the law of diminishing productivity and the application of it. Supply capital in successive units to a fixed force of laborers, and everywhere you get, as a result, smaller and smaller additions to your output. This is a universal law, which vitally affects the conduct of men, even in a primitive wilderness, in deciding how large an equipment of capital it pays to create. In such a state there are no wages or interest to be paid, and no market rates of any kind to be determined; but the principle of final productivity reveals itself with entire clearness in the simplest economy. It is when this

Social applications of this principle the basis of a theory of distribution.

principle acts in such a way as to determine how many laborers and how much capital there shall be in one of the industries of a civilized state that it produces a social effect. This action of the general law is a fitting subject for the theory of social economics; and here it becomes the basis of a theory of distribution.

Universal principles, then, and the social applications of them, are the two contrasted things. There are no markets in a wilderness; yet the law of final utility, which governs markets, is there in action. There are no wages and interest to be paid in the economy of solitary life; yet the law of the final productivity of labor and of capital is there, as everywhere, in action. These two principles are the ones that we take from the omitted first division of economic theory, as we enter on the second discussion, which deals with distribution. We tacitly assume all the familiar facts about the nature of wealth, and about the character of the economic process, as a subjugation of nature by man. For immediate use, moreover, we need a knowledge of three laws, of which the first is one that we may term the law of the varying efficiency of consumers' wealth, which is the basis of natural value; the second is the law of the varying efficiency of producers' wealth, which is the basis of natural interest; and the third is the law of the varying efficiency of labor, which is at the bottom of natural wages. These are among the universal truths of economic science.

The law of varying efficiency of consumers' wealth, of producers' wealth and of labor, as borrowed from universal economics, a premise of the theory of distribution.

CHAPTER V

ACTUAL DISTRIBUTION THE RESULT OF SOCIAL ORGANIZATION

Primitive
life worthy
of study, be-
cause the
essential
laws of it
are still
operative.

EXCHANGES add much to the economy of primitive life, but they subtract nothing from the essential laws of it. Man must still tame the forces of nature and transform materials into commodities. The general laws of the wealth-creating and the consuming process are the same in all economics; and it is this persistence in civilized conditions of the laws that govern primitive life which makes it worth while to study that life at all. It is in such simple conditions that these laws act alone; and it is here, therefore, that they can be separately examined. It is not because the life of a Crusoe is of much importance that it has been introduced into economic discussion: it is because the principles by which the economy of an isolated man are directed still guide the economy of a modern state.

Catallactics
the science
of what is
added to
primitive
life by or-
ganization
and ex-
changing.

There are, it is true, new forces now in action, in connection with the old ones; and it is absolutely necessary to make a separate study of these new forces. Catallactics, the term once suggested as a title for the whole of economic science, is an accurate name for that division of the science which treats of phenomena that are attributable to exchange only. It assumes, at the outset, the facts and principles that are common to all economics; and then proceeds to examine those which are peculiar to an exchange economy. The interchange of products disguises, but does not destroy, the dependence of the individual on nature. A laborer's income may seem to come to him as a payment from another man; but in essence it is still the response that nature makes to his own labor — it is his own virtual product.

Incomes apparently paid by employers really wrested from nature, as in primitive life.

A study of exchanges naturally notices at the outset the motive for resorting to them. This motive is the gain that is inherent in a division of labor. This principle, however, is only the reversal of one that we have referred to in connection with primitive life. We there saw that the diversification of employments by an isolated man involves a loss of productive power. Whoever thus does many things, does them slowly and ill, and he is sure to have few and poor appliances for aiding him in the processes. Since the diversification of a man's productive action is a loss, specialization is a gain. Moreover, the farther the specializing is carried, the greater become the celerity and the accuracy of the man's work.

The gain from division of labor due to the reversed action of the law of waste from diversifying one man's work.

This principle of loss from doing many kinds of labor, and of gain from doing a few kinds, is one that applies to all economic states; but what is not universal is the opportunity for specializing that an exchange economy offers. The organization of society into producing groups and sub-groups makes it possible for a man to produce only one kind of product, or, in the end, only one minute fraction of a product, while still satisfying his omnivorous wants.

Specialized production, with diversified consumption, possible in society.

Let us, then, withdraw from the persons who are making everything for themselves the single function of making shoes and assign it to a distinct class, who shall provide foot-wear for the community. This industry may not absorb their whole time and energy; but, so far as they are engaged in it, they constitute one industrial group. Assign, now, the making of clothing, the securing of meat, the raising of cereals, etc., each to its own separate group, and we have made the first and most general organiza-

tion of society for production. We have thus multi-plied many fold the product that can be created, and we have also made the income of each group depend on the exchange value of its product. The market prices of goods fix the incomes of groups in their entirety; and, as we have already indicated and shall hereafter state in greater detail, the movements of men from groups in which returns are low to those in which they are higher has the effect of drawing the price of each article toward a natural standard. We have seen that normal prices are those which afford equal gains to the labor and the capital in different groups. Wherever normal prices rule, they indicate such an arrangement of the groups that a day's labor in one produces as much,

and gets as much, as it does in another. When the adjustment is complete, the income of such a group, if it be reduced to value, is its own virtual product. The members of it may retain none of their own merchandise; but they get the "dollars," or units of wealth, that they produce. This is a thesis for the theory of catallactics to establish.

Now push the differentiating process further, and let the making of each completed article become the joint function of several sub-groups. Let some men raise cattle, others tan hides and others make shoes. Let the work of making clothing, food products, etc., also be subdivided. The gain that is inherent in spe-

cialization is increased. The income of each sub-group is now the value, not of a completed article, but of the one particular utility that it imparts to that arti-cle. It is a distinguishable something, indeed; but it is something that is merged and lost in an indivisible commodity. In *kind*, it is a quality imparted to the article ; in *value*, it is a fraction of the article. A thesis that the theory of exchange economy has to establish is that such particular utilities, or sub-products, have their prices, and when these are normal, each sub-group gets, as an income, the value that it creates.

Now carry the differentiating process to completion. Within each sub-group there is labor to be performed, and there is capital to be furnished. The sub-group that turns leather into shoes must have its factories full of machines and men to run them. We will let a distinct class of persons furnish the factory with machines and with the raw material. The theory of catallactics has to prove that the income of the one class that labors and that of the other which furnishes capital is, in each case, its virtual product. If the adjustments that take place within the sub-groups are perfectly normal, the classes of which the sub-groups are made, as well as the sub-groups in their entirety, get their several products. Catallactics has to study the structure of such a society as this, has to trace the divisions and sub-divisions that it makes in the producing operation, and has to see how the law that tends to identify the income of each agent with its virtual product acts in spite of the complications that disguise it. This is a comprehensive study, structural and functional, of the group system of production. Values, wages and interest are to be accounted for ; and the study that does this must analyze the entire producing operation.

Catallactics, as a whole, falls into two divisions, of which the first includes the statics and the second the dynamics of an exchange economy. Progress is mainly the result of the social relation. One function of economic society is that of growth. It is becoming larger and richer, and its structure is changing.

The income of each agent within a sub-group naturally its product.

As time passes, it uses more and better appliances for production. The individual members of it develop new wants, and the society uses its enlarging process to gratify them. The organism is perpetually gaining in efficiency, and this is promoting the individual members of it to higher planes of life. In the producing operation there is more and more intelligence used, for the forces of nature are better understood and there is a better coördination of all the participants. There is more bounty on the side of nature, since more forces are placed at man's disposal; and there is more efficiency in the industrial ranks themselves.

Five generic changes are going on, every one of which reacts on the structure of society, by changing the arrangements of that group system which it is the work of catallactics to study : —

1. Population is increasing.

2. Capital is increasing.

3. Methods of production are improving.

4. The forms of industrial establishments are changing: the less efficient shops, etc., are passing from the field, and the more efficient are surviving.

5. The wants of consumers are multiplying.

Every one of these changes acts on the structure of the producing organism, society, for it alters the relative sizes of the different industrial groups.

A'''	B'''	C'''
A''	B''	C''
A'	B'	C'
A	B	C

Let us recur to the illustrative table that was used in an earlier chapter. There is one sub-group engaged in getting out of the earth the material that, when finished, will be the article A''' and in passing it in the form, A, to another set of workers. These

Marginal notes:

Social progress develops men's wants and their powers.

Five generic changes in progress.

Each changes the sizes of the industrial groups.

impart to it the utility that changes it into A'. A third set of workers now puts its touch on it and carries it, by one point, nearer to completion.   It becomes A'', and in that shape goes to the last subgroup to be finished.   Here it becomes A''', a commodity ready for use, and seeks the individual who is in need of it. B is a second raw material; and in the hands of a series of sub-groups of workers it becomes B', B'' and B'''. In the last of these shapes it also is a finished commodity. C, the third raw material, goes through its transmutations in a similar way and ripens into C'''.

A may be the skins of live cattle on a western ranch; A' may be hides in a warehouse ready to be shipped to a tannery; A'' may be tanned leather and A''', shoes. B''' may be woollen garments that, by passing through kindred transmutations, have grown out of the fleece of sheep into this completed condition. C''' may be bread that has been made out of growing wheat and has passed through all the distinct stages in the entire process. All persons in the series that, in the end, makes A''' constitute a producing group; while those at either A, A', A'' or A''' constitute a sub-group. In like manner, all persons in the B''' series or in C''' series form a general group, which is composed of sub-groups.

The plan of social production illustrated by a simple table.

This represents the plan on which production goes on. With this illustration simplified to the last degree, not three products, but a countless number are in the retail shops, awaiting consumers. It is, moreover, not a uniform course of ripening, in which each has passed four stages, that has brought them into the finished state. A great variety of ripening processes is represented. Some articles go through many hands in the making, and some go through few. Some also contain many kinds of raw materials.

These complications will be examined in due time. At present it suffices to note the effect that changes of the five kinds above referred to have on the form of this society. Each one of them takes men out of some sub-groups and puts them into others. The mere act of exchanging products carries with it, not only the fact of a general social organization, but a certainty of change and progress in that organization. It is thus impossible that any one of these five changes which characterize a dynamic economy should take place without producing an effect on the social structure. As the simplest and most obvious result, the comparative sizes of the different groups must change, if any one of these dynamic movements is in progress.

Movements of labor and capital the sign of a dynamic economy. It is possible, therefore, to identify a dynamic social state as one in which there are labor and capital that are shifting their places in the economic system, and thus making some of the sub-groups larger and others smaller. Some labor and some capital may be actually deserting certain sub-groups and betaking themselves to others. Even if a sub-group is not actually losing equipment, it may be growing relatively smaller, by reason of new labor and capital that are adding themselves to other sub-groups.

Such quantitative changes in the groups are not the essence of a dynamic social state : more fundamental changes are taking place. Society changes its structure as a means of changing its producing function. It aims to produce goods in greater quantity and greater variety, and with more economy. It is mov-**Change in function the essence of it.** ing upward in the scale of power to create and power to enjoy. Functional change, indeed, is the essence of dynamics. We avail ourselves of the changes that take place in the sizes of sub-groups as the most available test of the presence of dynamic forces. If society begins to produce new kinds of

goods, or more goods, or if it begins to use new processes, etc., it is bound to reveal the fact by rearranging,
to some extent, its system of industrial groups and
sub-groups. A''', for example, may take more men,
and B''' fewer. A dynamic state may, therefore, be
described as one in which changes in the mode of
production are taking place and are acting on the
structure of industrial society.

In the sense in which we use the term, then, social
dynamics does not consist in mere activity, provided
that it is not of a kind which changes the social structure.
In a physical sense, all action is dynamic; and indus-   All industry
try is always action. A physically static industry is   dynamic in
                                                         the physical
obviously a contradiction in terms. On every farm,   sense.
men, tools, the chemical elements of the soil, and the
light and heat of the sun are acting. In every mill,
machines are going through their intricate movements
and materials are growing into useful shapes. All
this, however, resolves itself into an elementary kind
of dynamics: it is action on the part of the men,
tools and materials — the agents of production. But
if there is no change in the mode of the action, there is
none of that grander progressive movement by which
the structure of society is altered. If no labor and
no capital shifts its place from group to group in the
industrial system, there is none of that type of movement which, in a special and higher sense, we here term
dynamic. Till the ground forever with the same tools
and get the same kinds of crop, work in the same
mills with the same machines and materials—in short,
change nothing in the mode of creating wealth — and
you have a socially static industry. The producing
organism then keeps its form intact.

A world with none of the physical activities of industry would, of course, be a dead world; but a state
can be imagined in which the social organism should

keep its shape intact and in which life should continue.   Men might work and eat, they might be
born and die, in a world in which the forms of industrial organization should show no change. As generations should succeed each other, the men of each
would take up the trades of their fathers and trans-
mit them to their children.   As tools should be worn
out, they would be replaced by others exactly like

An industry them.   Changeless in its population, its wealth, its
without
change of   local abodes, its modes of production and the forms
mode imagi-   of its wealth, such a society would live, indeed, but
nable.
it would show no change in its organic form. Having
life, but not growth, it would be what we identify as
a static society.

This is an imaginary state, but it reveals facts of
real life.   There is, it is true, no society that is thus
static.   Even the Oriental world is merely less
changeful than the Western.   Countries can be found
where progress is very slow, but it is nowhere altogether absent; and contact with progressive countries
induces movement in the most unprogressive.   The
economy of the world,as a whole, is certain to be in-

The imagi-   creasingly dynamic. Why, then, do we wish to know
nary static
world re-   the laws of an imaginary static state?   Because the
veals certain
forces of   forces that act in such a state continue to act in a dy-
real life act-
ing alone.   namic one.   They are even the more powerful of the
two sets of forces that there operate.   We shall soon
see how the two kinds of force mingle in a modern
state ; and we shall see how unlike are their effects,
and how essential it is that we should examine them
separately.   The study of the unreal static state is a
heroic but indispensable use of the isolating method
of study, that is adopted in every science where complex phenomena are analyzed. We are, then, studying
the realities of the modern progressive state, when we
examine the characteristics of the imaginary static one.

We have specified five kinds of change that constitute a dynamic condition. All of them are in progress in a modern society, and all are acting on its structural form. As population increases, the new laborers apportion themselves in an irregular way among the different groups and sub-groups into which the producing society is divided, and some of the sub-groups increase more rapidly than others. As capital increases, there is the same irregularity in the apportionment of it; for some of the sub-groups get a disproportionate share of the new productive fund. A theory of economic dynamics should tell by what principle these apportionments are governed.

Mechanical inventions, in particular, are obvious disturbers of the group relations. Much labor saving in one part of the system is, so far as it goes, the cause of a natural drifting of labor to other parts. New kinds of goods call for new industrial groups to make them, and these are created by taking men and capital from old ones. Thus, every one of the general changes that we have specified, as keeping society in a dynamic state, declares its presence by acting on the social structure. Mere industry is the self-maintenance of society, while growth and change are further phenomena. It is as important to separate the two as it is in hydraulics to examine the properties of a particle of water in a tranquil pool, as distinct from the further properties that it acquires when it is projected into the pit in which a turbine wheel is turning. In dealing with the complex problems of an advancing economy, the key of success is the separate study of the static forces that constantly act within it.

Why static studies must precede dynamic ones.

CHAPTER VI

EFFECTS OF SOCIAL PROGRESS

THE changes that take place in a civilized society affect its entire collective life, and even the lives of its individual members. Every man in such a community acts and thinks differently, and comes in time to be a somewhat different being, in consequence of the share that he personally experiences of the effect of social economic dynamics.

Movements of labor a sign of change in society and in its members.

We may keep in view, as the visible sign of this thoroughgoing transformation, the local shifting of labor and capital that dynamics involves. It is important to note that every such shifting of the work of production from group to group is an effort on the part of society to put itself into the new shape that static law *at the time* calls for. With population as it is at any moment, and with the other elements that determine the shape of society unchanged, there is a certain part of the working force that naturally belongs in each sub-group in the system. But with an accession of new workers, a new adjustment is called for; and labor will proceed to move toward the points at which, *under the conditions created by the enlarged population, static forces alone* would locate it. Capital must, to some extent, move also. If the dynamic changes were not again to take place, the labor and the capital of society would find their new places and keep them. They would so locate themselves that each unit of labor would create as much wealth as any other.

Society thereby takes the shape that static law *at the time* calls for.

Mere competition tends to equalize the productive power of what we may call units of labor in different occupations, and it has the same levelling effect on capital. If it were allowed to work without obstruction, competition would reduce the earning power of all units of either of these agents to uniformity, by apportioning them, in a natural way, among the producing groups.

Units of labor tend to be uniformly productive, and so do units of capital.

A skilled worker will, of course, always create more wealth than an unskilled one; for personal differences between men will always count in determining their social powers as producers. A good instrument will also produce more than a poor one. Such a good instrument, however, represents more units of capital than does the poor one; and all that we have claimed for competition is a tendency to put the different units of capital where their earnings are equal. This, of itself, requires that the better instruments — embodying, as they do, greater amounts of capital — should earn the larger incomes. In like manner, a laborer of a high grade embodies in himself more units of labor than does an inferior one. Precisely what such a unit of labor is, we must in due time ascertain; but provisionally we may use the familiar term, unskilled labor, and treat the work performed by a man with no exceptional skill or endowment as constituting the unit of which we are speaking. A superior artisan, however, represents more than one such unit, and a successful business manager represents many of them.

Unlike men tend to be unequally productive, and so do unlike tools.

Labor and capital tend to acquire each a certain producing power that is uniform in the different groups and sub-groups ; and it is movements caused by competition that cause this tendency. If we could think of dynamic influences as exerting themselves for a time and then completely ceasing to act, we should see society thrown out of one static adjustment and given time to assume another. If the dynamic influences were to act intermittently, with long intervals between their periods of activity, society would attain an endless series of perfect static adjustments, each of which would be unlike the one that preceded it. Thus, water in a quiet tank, to and from which there is no flow, is in a static condition. The pressure on each particle is uniform in all directions, and accordingly no particle is in motion. It is perfectly fluid, however, and the slightest excess of pressure in any one direction would make it change its place. Such perfect mobility without motion is the sign of a static state. Motion is prevented, not by friction, but by an equilibrium of the forces that press each particle in different directions.

Intermittent dynamic action would give a series of different static states.

Open now the valve that lets water rush into the tank. The equilibrium is destroyed, and there is movement everywhere. The surface boils, and currents are created throughout the body of formerly quiet fluid. A dynamic force has added itself to the static ones that were formerly in action, but those static forces are not annulled: they continue to act without any diminution of their energy. Stop the inflow; and though, for a time, the waves and the currents continue, in the end they subside. There is now attained a new static adjustment of the different particles of water in the tank. Each is where the equalized pressure will hold it under the new conditions. Repeat the whole operation at intervals; and after each inflow there will be a movement that will relocate every particle of water in the tank. Afterward there will come a period of quiet, when the particles will be held in a static equilibrium.

These facts illustrated by the action of water.

If we regard the individual laborer as the social

molecule, there is a force acting on him that is analogous to the pressure which acts on a particle of water.
This is the acquisitive impulse — the desire to go
where the largest earnings are to be had. If a man's
earnings in his sub-group are the same that he could
get elsewhere, the pressure on him is, as it were,
equal in all directions; and he keeps his place. If
the same thing is true of all other workers, society
is in a condition of static equilibrium. The movements of labor from group to group, which are the
visible signs of dynamic conditions, are then entirely
wanting. But if there is an influx of population,
corresponding to the flow of water into the tank,
there is a rearrangement of the social atoms. Some
groups come to have relatively more laborers than
they formerly had, and others come to have comparatively fewer. If the influx of population ceases
and other disturbing causes are absent, a new static
condition will ensue. The men will be in somewhat
changed positions, in which the earnings of laborers
of a given grade are again brought to an equality in
the different sub-groups. There are, however, some
dynamic influences that act more strikingly, as re-
arrangers of society, than a mere influx of population
would do. Machines, for example, have been rapid
transformers of the social organism; but, for illustrating the principle that we have in view, any one of the
five dynamic changes above specified will serve,
since each relocates the members of the industrial
society. If, after such a change, the dynamic influences cease to act, the static ones place the members
in natural positions and keep them there.

Let us now vary the illustration, by assuming that
the inflow of water is continuous. The static forces
are in action, as before; but they do not succeed in
placing each particle of the fluid in what would

Mobility of
labor and
capital,
without
motion, the
sign of a
static state.

be, if the water were undisturbed, its natural place.
They cause each particle to tend, at every instant,
to move toward what would be at that instant its
natural or static position, if the inflow were then
to cease; but there is a perpetual variation between
the actual position that the particle of water occupies
and its static place. Moreover, its static position at
one time differs from its static position at another
time. The addition to the volume of water in the
tank creates a change in the conditions under which
mere pressure, acting on the fluid material, has to do
its work; and the locating of the particles, under the
influence of this pressure, gives one result when the
tank is half full and a different result when it is full.

This corresponds to what is taking place in society.
There the five great dynamic influences are all constantly at work. The static forces do their full work
also; but the resultant of it all cannot be the shap-
ing of the group system exactly as static law alone
would shape it. At any one instant there is a particular place in the system which each man would
take, if the disturbing influences were altogether to
cease. At that instant the man is impelled toward

Continuous dynamic in-fluences cause soci-ety always to vary from its static shape.

the place, but he is not exactly there. Society
throughout shows an approximation to the natural
static arrangement of its members, but it can never
exactly realize it. A perpetual divergence from
the form into which the acquisitive impulse, acting
on each man, would bring society, if it worked without let or hindrance, results from the continuous
action of the dynamic forces.

These general forces of change also cause the static
shape of the society at one time to differ from its
static shape at another time. A variation from a
standard form is one effect of dynamic forces, and
constant change in the standard form itself is another

effect. A progressive society, as we have seen, has rising standards of wages, to which actual wages are always tending to conform. It also develops an endless series of ideal shapes, and strives to form itself after them. It approximates each of these shapes, but never exactly attains any one. The ideal model to which the group system is trying to conform at one time differs from the model to which it tends to conform at any other time. Society, in its growth, is pursuing the changes in its model, but it is perpetually behind time in the race.

They cause the static shapes themselves continually to change.

For static science the task is set of finding the natural condition of society at any one time. For dynamic science there remains the work of ascertaining the two effects of the forces of change: namely, the variation of the actual state of society, at any one time, from the static condition for that time; and, secondly, the difference between the static condition of society at one time and the static condition at another time.

One can hardly assert too emphatically the dominance of the static forces in real and dynamic societies. For example, a square mile of the ocean during a storm is not in a static condition. To the man in a ship dynamic forces appear decidedly to predominate; and yet it is the effects of weight, pressure and fluidity — the static forces — that keep the vessel afloat. They do what, even from the sailor's point of view, is the more fundamental work. It is these static forces that determine the effect of every blow that a wave strikes against the side of the ship; and it is these same forces that keep the waves from rising to abnormal heights and hold the general surface of the sea in a position that approximates its natural level. Projecting itself through the waves, in their most violent movement, there is

Static forces dominant in the midst of disturbances.

an ideal surface to which, at a particular moment, weight, pressure and fluidity, acting unhindered on the water, would make its surface correspond. The actual surface undulates above and below this ideal surface, but always tends toward it. Similarly, projecting itself through the group system of a progressive state, there is an ideal arrangement of the elements of society, to which the force of competition, acting on individual men, would make the society conform. The producing organism actually shapes itself about this model, and at no time does it vary greatly from it.

Ricardian political economy has distinguished itself by bold deductions concerning the values of commodities, the rent of land and the wages of labor. There are, it affirms, "natural values," to which the selling prices of different goods tend to conform, and to which they would accurately conform, if it were not

Ricardian theories of natural value, etc., based on assumptions. for "disturbing influences." There is also a "natural rent" of every piece of land; and, if there were no friction, the actual rent would equal it. Sweeping assumptions have been made, in order to create the conditions that the classical economists had in mind. The "economic man" has been created, and has been made to pursue his own interests remorselessly and intelligently. He knows what will increase his gains, and does it without hindrance. Mobility is his most marked characteristic. The slightest excess of pressure in one direction will cause him to change his place in the economic system. He drops one pursuit and takes up another without hesitation, and he encounters no obstacles in the transit. With such conditions given, prices, rents, wages and interest are supposed to be "natural." The prices of goods are in these older theories said to be "natural," when they equal the cost of producing them; and market prices are said to fluctuate about this standard.

The impression that classical political economy, where it has thus been most successful, has made on practical minds is one of doctrinarianism. The world that is under analysis appears to have been created in the study and to be unreal. All the con- These as-
clusions hinge on hypotheses which seem to be in- sumptions
unlike the
consistent with the facts of life. On the assumed facts of life.
premises, the conclusions are reasonable; but they seem inapplicable to any world but an imaginary one. In short, there appear to be so many disturbing influences at work that theoretical standards of value, rent, etc., cannot be realized. What the Ricardian theory unconsciously and imperfectly accomplished was the separation of static from dynamic forces. It was really studying a static world, but it studied that world with no complete idea of its nature. There was not in the minds of any of these early writers any conception of the two distinct sets of forces that are really acting together; and there could, therefore, be no systematic plan for studying them separately.

In reality, their "natural prices" were static prices. The Ricard-
They were those to which an actual market would ian study an
unconscious
conform, if dynamic influences were wholly to cease. attempt to
A heroic alteration of the mercantile world, a paraly- create a
static world.
sis of one set of nerves, an absolute stoppage of one set of activities — this would bring markets into the so-called "natural" condition. Stop all increase of population and of wealth, as well as all changes in the producing operation and in the character of its results, but let industry go on and perfect competition continue, and you bring the world into a state in which the standard theoretical prices will be the real ones. Also normal rates of wages and

interest will be realized. Had the Ricardians recognized the fact that they were trying to study a static world and then studied it consistently, they would have made even their own system more realistic.

It would have been realistic and complete, if it had first examined static forces alone and then dynamic forces.

Boldly suppressing in imagination one set of actual forces, in order to study more easily another set, must result in reaching conclusions that are partial but are not necessarily unreal. If these early students had later done what they never tried to do, and had completed their system by separately examining the dynamic forces, they would have attained a complete and realistic science.

The prices that conform to the cost of production are, of course, those which give no clear profit to the *entrepreneur*. A business man whose goods sell at such rates will get wages for whatever amount of labor he may perform, and interest for any capital that he may furnish; but he will have nothing more to show in the way of gain. He will sell his product for what the elements that compose it have really cost him, if his own labor and the use of his capital be counted among the costs. We shall see that this condition of no-profit prices exactly corresponds to the one that would result from the static adjust-

Cost prices really those that result from a purely static adjustment.

ment of the producing groups. We establish such prices, if we so adjust labor and capital in the different groups and sub-groups as to make the earnings of each of these two agents uniform in all parts of the system. The natural prices of the classical school are, therefore, static prices incompletely conceived. A no-profits régime is one of levelled gains for all units of labor and for all units of capital. If the classical study of wages had been, so far as it went, completely successful, it would merely have furnished a static standard of pay for labor.

A normal rate of interest early writers made no

attempt to explain. They referred to demand and supply, as the mechanism by which interest is adjusted, but gave no reason why these forces fix the earnings of capital at any definable rate. So far as it went in the direction of attaining natural standards, the classical political economy made an unconscious and incomplete presentation of the rates of interest that would prevail in a static society.

The impression of unreality that is made by these studies is removed by completing them, on the same theoretical plan upon which they have been started. We must use assumptions boldly and advisedly, make labor and capital absolutely mobile, and let competition work in ideal perfection. We must, in imagination, sweep remorselessly from the field the whole set of influences that we have called dynamic. In doing this, we remove all of that friction which vitiates the action of pure economic laws; for friction of this kind goes entirely with dynamics, and there is none of it in the static state. If we make the force that draws a man toward one sub-group equal to that which draws him toward another, — that is, if we bring his earning power in different groups to uniformity, — the man remains in his place. Then, of course, there is none of the friction that a transfer from one sub-group to another encounters; and it is exactly this kind of friction that vitiates the so-called natural laws of the classical economists. It is because labor and capital cannot go from group to group, instantly and without obstruction or waste, that actual values, wages and interest always differ from the normal ones that have figured in pure theory.

The unreality of the classical theories removed by completing them.

Since, then, it is dynamic changes that call for such local transfers of the producing agents, and since it is the transfers that cause the friction, the static condition is free from this disturbing influence. We

A static state frictionless.

have proposed to reduce the economic world to this frictionless state. We shall, in imagination, stop every one of the five organic changes that are actually moving and relocating the economic agents. Unlike, indeed, to real life is the economy that results; but it is unlike it only through incompleteness. The forces that in the imaginary world continue to act, are acting in the world as it is. Work continues and instruments are used; and these are substantial realities. Changes in the mode of working and in the forms of the instruments have been stopped; but the economy that is left is, so far as it goes, real. The standards of value, wages and interest that we get are those about which rates in the actual world are fluctuating.

We are next to try to make the economy that we are studying complete, as well as real. We are to give it the elements that are wanting, and make it, in its completeness, correspond accurately to the economy of the actual world. In the concluding part of our study we are to restore the dynamic forces that our earlier hypothesis removed and to note the special effects of their action. For the first time, we shall thus be able to understand and to measure these forces; for their effects will stand by themselves. We can make a science of the movement that is going on within the group system, and of the friction that it encounters. Whenever a theoretical world has been created, in which natural values, wages and interest prevail, that which has been banished is social economic dynamics. This ought not, however, to be treated as a mere disturbing influence: it is an element that science, as such, must include in its calculations. If we put it out of sight, with no intention of restoring it, we get a result that is unreal, because it is seriously incomplete; but if

Dynamic changes the cause of friction.

The introduction of dynamic elements

we first remove the dynamic movement and then restore it, we create a science that fully interprets economic life.

makes the assumed world like the real one.

In the preliminary study that is made in this legitimate way, population and capital are treated as neither increasing nor diminishing. Under the hypothesis adopted, inventions are not made and processes of production do not change. None of those consolidations of labor and capital, which are so striking a feature of recent times, are forming. The kinds of goods created remain perpetually the same. In consequence of all this, labor and capital remain constant, and values, wages and interest are, in the classical sense, natural. In the world of the completed study, on the other hand, population and wealth are increasing; processes and modes of organization are changing; new products are creating; and the flow of labor and capital from group to group, which is the outward sign of these changes, is going on. It is, in short, the real world that a completed hypothesis brings before us. Though theoretical throughout, the science thus makes itself real, by the completeness of its assumptions.

Economic dynamics has a striking relation to those recent historical economic studies which have been so attractive and fruitful. Progress is the fact that calls for such studies. The present state of the world, it is obvious, differs from the conditions of fifty years ago and from those of fifty years hence. Historical economics records and measures such differences, while the theory of economic dynamics accounts for them. Historical economics will note and measure the gains that have been made by a hundred years of migration and mechanical invention, while the theory of economic dynamics will refer these gains to their causes and furnish a philosophy of economic

Historical economics observes changes in the world; the theory of economic dynamics accounts for them.

evolution. As it shall become more and more nearly complete, this theory will, moreover, enable men to announce with increasing confidence the kinds of change that are to be expected in the future.

Economic dynamics will, in its entirety, incorporate into itself historical economics. The changes that are going on in the world will in future be studied inductively, as well as deductively; and it is the inductive part of the work that falls to the historical economist. In the long run, it is this part that will need to absorb the most scientific labor. The static laws of economics ought, consequently, to be known at an early date. Dynamic laws will not be known so early; but whenever they shall be scientifically established, there will remain to be done the work of measuring the effects of particular influences that act on society. *How great*, for example, is the effect of a mechanical invention or of the settlement of a new country on the rate of wages? Such a question, if it can be answered at all, will demand a far more difficult kind of research than does the question whether migrations and inventions naturally raise wages or lower them.

It is within reason to suppose that, before the twentieth century shall have passed, men will know what kinds of results follow an increase of population, an augmentation of capital, a new mode of organizing industry or the use of a new kind of consumers' wealth. What the pure theory of economic dynamics does, when it answers such a question, is in effect to make a qualitative analysis of the phenomena of change. It must go *seriatim* through the list of great movements that are transforming the face of the world, and ascertain the nature of the effect that each of them produces. It must analyze the process by which each effect is produced. Thus

[margin note:] Such a theory the deductive part of a complete science of economic dynamics; history the inductive part.

[margin note:] A theory of economic changes attainable.

far the study does not involve calculations of quantity: there is in it no computation of the *amount* of each effect. Purely qualitative as the study is, however, it will open to the theoretical economist an inspiring vista for future advances in his science. Does the law ensure the survival of what is best? Is humanity gaining by the changes that are going on in industry? If gains predominate, do they accrue largely to the laborers? What net result to a working-man has followed from the fact that farmer have cast aside the reaping-hooks of their fathers, and are using harvesting-machines? What will happen to workers of the future, as cheap motive powers shall be utilized, and as electric wires shall carry the power everywhere? What will be the effect of the automatic machines that will bring commodities out of non-existence at the cost of little effort beyond the touching of a button? How will the laborer fare as the world shall crowd itself with a dense population? What will befall him, if this teeming life is more than matched by the growth of productive wealth? If capitalists become inordinately rich, what will become of the class that is now poor? Will the ownership of capital ever be widely diffused? It is, in short, the *direction* that progress is taking that is the all-important question; and the laborer is the one whose fortunes, in the régime of progress, are of supreme consequence. Issues like this the theory of economic dynamics must decide.

There will then remain a work of verification and of measurement. If improvements tend to raise wages, statistics should prove it; and they should measure the rate of the gain. The most laborious study that economists will ever have to undertake will consist of such a use of comparative statistics as shall measure the separate effects of different dynamic changes that in real life are acting together. Thus, we may ask : How much, in the way of extra wages, can at this date be imputed to the use of electric dynamos ? With present means of information, this is an unanswerable question. The study of such problems can, moreover, never be completed, for they will forever present themselves in new forms. The mere theory of economic dynamics will enlarge by many fold the scope of political economy : it will lift theory to a new plane. The statement of the

Historical verification and statistical measurement the permanent work of economists.

pure laws of economic change will open, as it were, the vestibule of the science of the future. It will afford an approach to a larger area. But the largest and most permanent work of the future must consist of historical and statistical studies, directed by a full knowledge of economic law.

NOTE. — The statement made in the foregoing chapter that a static state excludes true entrepreneurs' profits does not deny that a legal monopoly might secure to an entrepreneur a profit that would be as permanent as the law that should create it — and that, too, in a social condition which, at first glance, might appear to be static. The agents, labor and capital, would be prevented from moving into the favored industry, though economic forces, if they had been left unhindered, would have caused them to move to it. This condition, however, is not a true static state, as it has here been defined. Such a genuine static state has been likened to that of a body of tranquil water, which is held motionless solely by an equilibrium of forces. It is not frozen into fixity; but as each particle is impelled in all directions by the same amounts of force, it retains a fixed position. There is *a perfect fluidity, but no flow;* and in like manner the industrial groups are in a truly static state when the industrial agents, labor and capital, show *a perfect mobility, but no motion.* A legal monopoly destroys at a certain point this mobility, and is to be treated as an element of obstruction or of friction that is so powerful as not merely to retard a movement that an economic force, if unhindered, would cause, but to prevent the movement altogether.

CHAPTER VII

WAGES IN A STATIC SOCIAL STATE THE SPECIFIC PRODUCT OF LABOR

THE value of a commodity might be called "natural," if it resulted from the action of the native impulses of men. There are impulses that cause men to do other things than to compete with each other in business; but competition is the activity that causes prices to be, in the customary sense of the term, natural. This process is, in reality, a rivalry in serving the public. The merchant who undersells his competitor is actually offering to the public a larger benefit than his rival offers for a given return. The motive is, of course, self-interest; and the action that results from it is a spontaneous and general effort to get wealth. One effect of it is, however, to insure to the public the utmost that the existing power of man can give in the way of efficient service; and another effect is to control the values of goods.

Competition the cause of "natural" prices.

A natural price is a competitive price. It can be realized only where competition goes on in ideal perfection — and that is nowhere. It is approximated, however, wherever prices are neither adjusted by a government nor vitiated by a monopoly. If a commodity were produced in a public factory and sold at a rate arbitrarily fixed by the state, with a view to getting a revenue or to attaining some ulterior end, the mode of adjusting the price would be the antith-

Legal regulation or monopoly would make prices unnatural.

77

esis of natural. If a private monopoly were created or fostered by the state, the price that it would put on its products would also vary from the natural standard. There is, in fact, always a trace of monopoly in the condition of an industry to which labor and capital tend to move, but cannot move with absolute freedom. Perfect mobility of the agents of production never exists; and hence prices are always varying, in greater or less degree, from the rates that the unhindered action of the competitive impulse in men would maintain.

A trace of monopoly due to imperfect mobility of labor and capital.

As we have shown, the terms "natural" and "normal," as used in economic literature, are other names for static. The assumption that removes all dynamic movement and all friction leaves prices normal. We shall see that this fact is in harmony with what we have just said — namely, that natural values are competitive values; for, if we stop all dynamic movement and also all friction, we enable competition to work in perfection. The standards of price that have figured in the older economic studies have been attained without any conscious reduction of society to the static condition; for, as we noted, the idea of separating the dynamic activities of society from the static ones did not occur to these writers. Their natural prices were attained by observing the tendency of actual markets to yield certain prices; and these standard rates they defined as those which would about repay to employers the outlay that they incurred in bringing the commodities into existence. It was a simple and preliminary study of natural or static price that the classical economists made, and it afforded an imperfect, rather than an incorrect, theory.

Early studies of natural prices were preliminary studies of static prices.

Cost prices are, of course, no-profit prices. They afford, in the case of each article, enough to pay wages for the labor and interest on the capital that are used in making it; but they give no net surplus to the *entrepreneur*, as such. Since dynamic changes cause the prices of this, that or the other commodity to yield such a surplus, they make prices, for the time being, unnatural, in the sense of being unlike purely competitive or cost prices. Dynamic changes themselves are, however, in another and a broader sense natural. Nature herself is continually disturbing the régime of natural prices, but competition is trying to restore it. At this moment many commodities are not selling at cost; yet in the case of all of them there are forces at work, which, if they were not counteracted, would bring the prices to the cost level. Ideally there is at this moment a natural price for everything; and if we could remove disturbances and friction, actual prices would reach and remain at this ideal standard. When we study economic dynamics, we shall ask how much an actual price may vary from such a theoretical price, without the introduction of a really abnormal force. In dynamics variations from standards have to be studied; and, in a broader use of terms, there is such a thing as a natural variation. Now, however, we are studying solely the standards from which variations are to be calculated, and we are following the classical economists in calling such standards natural. Natural, normal or static prices are cost, or no-profit prices. They are equalized-gain prices, for they cause the returns of different industries to be the same per unit of labor and per unit of capital. They enable the steel makers, for example, to pay as much for labor of a given grade as do the wagon makers; and they enable the two classes of employers to pay uniform rates of interest on capital. Natural or cost prices sweep away any special gain that an industrial group may enjoy.

Dynamic influences, which are in another sense natural, disturb static prices.

A normal variation from a static price gives a natural dynamic price.

No-profit prices natural under static conditions.

Under dynamic conditions perfect mobility of labor and capital would insure no-profit prices.

Such prices would prevail in practice, if labor and capital were absolutely mobile. If men in one industry could instantly leave it and betake themselves to another, this latter industry could not be favored in the amount of its returns. If we could at this moment remove everything that hinders a steel maker from becoming a wagon maker, we should preclude all chance that one class, as a whole, should be better paid than the other. Static prices would be realized at any one time, if we merely annihilated economic

Stopping dynamic changes would do this, even if the mobility of the agents were imperfect.

friction. They would be realized in another way, if dynamic changes were stopped and if friction were allowed to continue. Thus, let there be henceforth no improvement in methods of production, and let population, wealth, etc., remain forever unchanged. There is, then, nothing that will make the standard level of prices next year at all different from that which now prevails. Actual prices are not now at the standard levels; but they are tending toward them, under the influence of competition. Labor and capital are tending to move to the points where rewards are greatest, but this movement is obstructed by friction. With dynamic changes ended, this friction is slowly overcome. The transfers of labor and capital take place in spite of it. To stop the dynamic changes and wait for the transfers to take place is to bring industrial society slowly into the condition that static forces alone tend to impose on it. Henceforth the state will be an unchanging one. Once society has reached this shape, it will hold it forever. Each unit of labor and each unit of capital will remain forever in the group where it is, and prices will be unvarying.

Here, then, are two ways of conceiving a régime of static — or, in the Ricardian sense, natural — values. With dynamic changes in progress and friction absent, the standards of price change every day, but actual selling ratios conform every day to them: there is an endless succession of different actual prices, but there is never any difference between the prices that the market gives and those which theory calls for. With dynamic changes absent and friction continuing, the static or cost standard of price becomes an unchanging one; but actual values, which at the outset vary from the standard ones, require time to conform to them. In the end, they conform to them and remain thenceforth without change.

It is best to assume that both the dynamic changes and the friction which always obstructs competition cease. Under this hypothesis, labor and capital can instantly go wherever gains are large; and this movement brings prices at once to what is now their static level. As there are hereafter to be none of the changes that alter that level, prices — both actual and normal — must hereafter remain unchanged. No variation of actual prices from perfect competitive prices; no change in ideal competitive prices themselves; no change in price-making conditions — this is the conception that creates a perfect static state. There is mobility of labor and capital, but there is no motion. Here we may study static prices, pure and simple.

It is well also to see whether a theoretically natural rate of wages can be established in a similar way. Looking at the transactions between employers and employed, can we see in them anything that causes wages to fluctuate about a standard which is more or less akin to the natural prices of goods? We shall at once find that there is a similarity between what the classical economists distinguished as the market price of goods and the market rate of wages. Let us for the moment cease to look at standards of pay about which, through long intervals, wages fluctuate,

Dynamics without friction would insure change in standards of price, and absence of dynamics, changeless ones.

Excluding dynamic change and friction makes prices both natural and changeless.

Similarity between market rates of wages and market prices of goods.

and see how the rate for one short period is fixed. We shall find that it is fixed in a way akin to that in which the immediate selling prices of goods are determined. Later we shall find that, in both cases, the market rates fluctuate about permanent standards.

Let us use commercial terms, and speak of a "market for labor." Let us keep in view what is called the action of demand and supply, and say that they, in some way, put a price on men, as they do on commodities. There is much to be said as to the accuracy of such terms in this connection; but there is no great danger that by thus using the terms in a preliminary study we shall reach an incorrect result. We shall, in fact, be able in this way to establish a normal rate of pay for general labor, which will have a certain kinship to the normal standard of price with which we have long been familiar.

"The produce of labor," said Adam Smith, "constitutes the natural recompense or wages of labor. In that original state of things which precedes both the appropriation of land and the accumulation of stock, the whole produce of labor belongs to the laborer. He has neither landlord nor master to share with him." There follows in the same chapter the statement that modern industry has changed this natural condition, that wages are now paid out of employers' capital, and that they do not consist in the product of labor itself. It is, in Adam Smith's view, the presence of the landlord and the master that has made this radical change.

What we have claimed is that, in modern life as well as in primitive life, the identity of wages with the product of labor is, in a general and approximate way, maintained, and that this product furnishes the standard about which wages for short periods fluctuate. It is clear, indeed, that the whole product of

Adam Smith's identification of primitive wages with products.

industry does not go to the worker. If the entire joint product of labor and capital be what we have in mind, the men who furnish land, tools, buildings, materials, etc., get a share of it. If what we mean is the part of this total that is attributable to labor itself, it is not merely possible that the worker should get it all, but it is certain that he would get it all, if competition could do its work perfectly — that is, if the static standards of wages were realized. Moreover, it is the presence of the employer that helps to reveal what the product of labor is, and it is the action of employers that enables the laborers to get pay that approximates to that product.

Wages in modern life actually identified with the product of labor.

If we are accurately to express what takes place in simple types of industry, we shall say, not that " the whole produce of labor goes to the laborer," but that the whole produce of industry goes to the independent man who is both a laborer and a capitalist. Nowhere is actual economy so primitive that it uses absolutely no capital; and where there is any capital at all, a part of the product of industry is due to its presence. In the " original state of things," it is nearly impossible for a man to say how much of his product is due to labor only. The distinction between the whole product of labor and the whole product of industry is, however, all-important; for industry involves the coöperation of labor and capital.

The product of labor not separately measurable in primitive economy.

Let a man fish from a dugout, with the simplest line and hook that he can make. The fish that he will bring to the shore are the product of labor and capital. Effort aided by instruments has secured them. How much of the catch is due to the man, and how much to the canoe and the fishing tackle? Not for his life can the man himself tell. Can he put the fish into two piles, and say, " This pile is due to my effort only, and that pile to my equipment?"

Every single fish is a joint product — indeed, every fin or scale of a fish is so ; and the difficulty is that it is impossible to divide a single one of them into fractions due to the producing agencies. Hopelessly merged with the product of capital is the product of the labor of an independent producer. Instead of presenting the condition in which the wages of labor are readily distinguished from other incomes, and identified as the " produce of labor," such a primitive economy as actually exists is one in which it is impossible to say what the produce of labor itself is.

The illustration used by Adam Smith avoids this difficulty, indeed, by assuming that there is no capital in the case and that, therefore, whatever is produced at all is created by labor. The state that is referred to " preceded the accumulation of stock." If a man does, in fact, work without capital, as well as without a master, his wages will be what he creates. A physical law and not a social one will fix his pay. He will dig his wages literally out of the earth, fish them out of the sea, pursue and capture them in the hunting forest, etc., and he will not have to share them with any industrial partner. There are points in the industrial system where this condition, though it is not absolutely reached, is approximated ; and Mr. Henry George has advanced an interesting theory which makes the gains of men who are in this condition set the standard of general wages. A squatter may, for example, till land for which no rent can be obtained, using no appliance that is more elaborate than a hoe or a spade. He may live in a dugout, and have only a few dollars' worth of salable property of any kind. While this state of things lasts, the man has not capital enough to complicate the problem of wages ; and for the purpose of illustration he must not be allowed to own land. If he

Adam Smith's mode of isolating the product of labor.

is the owner of his farm, like a homestead settler in the United States, a complication arises which makes it impossible rightly to claim that his wages are the whole income that comes to him. This method not available where capital exists.

Mr. George has rightly said that, so long as land is so abundant as to be had for the asking, a man who is willing to work in a shop may demand and get from his employer pay that is large enough to make good to him what he gives up by not taking up a farm. In the period in which a great belt of country has been in the process of settling, and during which agriculture has been the dominant industry, the standard of all wages has, without doubt, been the gains that free farms always bestow on the men who not only till them but own them. These gains, however, are composite. They are not by any means the product of labor only. The fact that he owns his land gives to the homestead settler an income that is a large addition to the one that his bare labor creates. The situation is transitional and anomalous; for the men in the shops get pay that corresponds, in a general way, to the incomes of men who are getting wages and a large additional amount. The rewards of the men to whom the government has given homesteads consist, not merely in what they can get by raising crops, but largely in what comes to them in the form of increments of value that, from year to year, attach themselves to the land itself. The greater part of the income of the man who occupies a homestead, under American laws, consists at first in the so-called "unearned increment" of land value. The farm is worth, perhaps, a dollar per acre when the man enters his claim. It becomes worth five dollars an acre within a year or two, and ten dollars an acre very soon. It is for this reward that the man is willing to burrow under a Theory of Mr. Henry George.

A frontier settler's income composed largely of land value

hillside for a home, to clothe himself for a time in rags, to live on corn meal, etc. The direct product of his work takes the shape of turf turned over by the breaking plough or furrows cut by the cross plough. Very little of it is food and clothing. Mingled with wages is the larger element of gain that, with the growth of population, shows itself in the ten dollars per acre that the man can soon get for the land itself.

It is worth while to dwell long enough at this point to make it very clear that a man who is endowed by the state with a gift of land is not one the product of whose hands can furnish a standard of wages. It has been said that wages in America have been made to conform to the amount that homestead settlers can make by availing themselves of the offers of the government, and the statement is, on its face, not incorrect; but it is far from proving that wages conform to the earnings of unaided labor. If it be true, what it proves is that there has been a time when wages have equalled a large and composite gain, much of which comes from land. So long as a man can have a farm for the asking, he will not be willing to work in a mill or shop, except on conditions that afford a fair equivalent for a farmer's gains. During the transient interval in which an abundance of free land of good quality is to be had, the standard of pay in every employment within reach of that land may be said to be fixed in the belt of newly occupied wilderness that men are beginning to tame. This condition causes wages to vary from the permanent standard rather than to conform to it. The settler gets more than the income that comes to him in the shape of crops. The rising value of land enters directly into his gains; and it enters directly into the pay of the artisans and others who are held in the mills and shops by pay that is approximately

Transient interval in which increments of land value help to set the standards of general wages.

equal to settlers' gains.   Land values thus diffuse themselves everywhere.   To the right and to the left, through all trades and callings, they find their way.   The carpenter, the blacksmith, the cook, the hostler, the clerk, and even the doctor and the lawyer, find their earnings made larger by the values that the planting of a community on vacant land imparts to that land itself.   For a hundred years all American wages had more or less of this element in them.   They were sustained so as to conform, in an appr.ximate way, not to what could be made by tilling no-rent land, but to what could be made by tilling *and owning* the land.

As the larger of these sources of a settler's income is removed, the gains of an empty-handed laborer working on a farm are confined to what he can extort from the soil in the shape of a crop.   Make the man a mere occupier of no-rent land, and not an owner of it, and he will get wages with no increment of land value attached to them.   Farms that are worth anything cannot long be had for the asking. Of the fertile areas in America that were once considered boundless, not much remains unclaimed.   A law of wages, if it is to be permanently valid, must apply to this condition.

Gains from using no-rent land, without owning it, free from all admixture of land value.

It is possible to adhere steadfastly, as Mr. George has done, to the view that labor always tends to get what labor can create on such land as may be offering itself freely for use.   In an advanced state of industrial development, the only land that is thus offering is that which is too poor to command a rent; and the theory therefore claims that the permanent regulator of wages is the gain that labor can extort from marginal and rentless land.   There is, however, an element of truth in the theory, even in this form, for the man with capital in land and other instruments will not have to share gains with any one.   He will be in the same position as was Adam Smith's primeval worker, who labored "before the accumulation of stock," and who had "neither landlord nor capitalist to share with him."   His gains will be all his own, and they will be entirely the

The product of such labor separated from all other products.   product of labor.   The theory that makes them set the standard of all wages has the great merit of pointing out a method by which the product of bare work may be disentangled from all other products, and made to stand by itself and to be separately measured.

We are to try to prove that the product which is separately attributable to labor does set the standard of wages; but there is a grave difficulty in making tillers of valueless farms the ones whose returns thus regulate every one's pay.   If the theory is advanced that the general wages of labor are permanently fixed by the gains that men can realize by tilling no-rent

Theory that such gains furnish the general standard of wages.   ground, this theory must mean that the mere occupiers of pieces of land that cannot be let for any appreciable rent are the men to whose gains the wages of every one conform.   According to this, an artisan in any workshop in the country would have to keep his eye on the squatters' shanties and see what the occupants were earning, in order to know how much he could make his employer pay him. In its most reasonable form, this theory would mean that a worker in a Belgian mill must take about what a Belgian peasant of the same grade of ability gets by cultivating the sandy waste that

Weakness of this theory.   borders the sea.   It means that the watchmakers of Switzerland must accept pay that, with an allowance for differing personal power, tends to conform to the amount that their peasant countrymen can extort from patches of green among the crags.   It

means that, after all the free lands of America shall
have been allotted to owners, wage-earners in the
mills, shops, mines, etc., from the Atlantic to the
Pacific, will get, on the average, what a typical one
of them could produce, if he were to build a hut on
a piece of poor and untenanted ground, and proceed
to till it by the sufferance of the proprietor. This
is a theory of "squatter sovereignty" over the labor
market. It puts the man in the shanty into a position that is so strategic as to enable him to dominate
workmen of every class, to fix the amount of their
wages, and so to control the level on which they live.

With all its absurdity, this theory does at least appeal to the principle that wages tend to equal what
labor itself can produce. If the squatter has not
capital enough to count as a producing agent, his
entire crop can be attributed to his labor alone.
Putting a man into such a position is one way of
separating labor from capital, and of disentangling
the product of labor from the product of capital. It
seems to furnish a case in an advanced society, in
which we may see what Adam Smith saw in primitive
society — namely, labor getting the entire product
of industry and sharing gains with no one. Yet the
absurdity of making the occasional squatter dictate
the amount of every laborer's pay, is patent on the
face of the illustration.

A sound principle at the basis of it.

It is, however, desirable to seek for a no-rent
territory to which it is not absurd to look for the
standard that regulates general wages. It must afford
a larger field for labor than the worthless agricultural
land affords, if the men who occupy it are to have a
general wage-regulating power. Such an economic
field is at hand. The workers who occupy it come
into it empty-handed. They produce virtually without capital, and the whole of their own separate

A larger no-rent terri-tory to be sought, in which labor may get its whole prod-uct.

product is wages. They get the amount of this product as their pay, and all other workers have to take pay that is equal to it.

Looking first at market values, rather than natural ones, we noted that there is a commercial principle which causes the final or marginal part of the supply of anything to be strategic in its action on the value of the whole supply. The value of the whole crop of wheat, for example, conforms to that of the marginal bushel of it. If there are marginal laborers, in the sense in which there are marginal quantities of wheat, cotton, iron, etc., then these final or marginal men are likewise in a strategic position; for their products set the standard of every one's wages.

For the moment, we will adopt the mercantile conception of labor, as a thing to be sold in the market.

The final unit of the supply of a commodity the price-making part.

It is a familiar commercial principle that the last increment of the supply of any commodity fixes the general price of it. A common mode of stating this principle is to assert that English quotations gauge the price of American wheat — that the farmers of the Northwest must take for their entire supply of this grain what the surplus part of it brings when it is sent to Liverpool.[1] The statement that the price of our wheat is thus fixed in Liverpool expresses something that does not need to be disputed as a commercial fact. The price of grain on the western side of the Atlantic is actually equal to the price on

[1] This view may involve an imperfect conception of the law of value; for it is, of course, the final utility of that part of the wheat crop which remains at home that directly fixes the value of it here. England, however, represents the European market; and this, in its entirety, draws away enough of the American wheat crop to reduce appreciably the amount that has to be consumed here. The final utility of the part of the crop that is thus left at home is raised to such a level that it can be sold as advantageously here as in Europe.

the eastern side, minus the cost of carrying and handling. It is so, because Europe is a receiving ground on which the whole surplus of American breadstuffs may be sold. If we add fifty million bushels to the exportable crop, Europe will receive it at a somewhat reduced price, and English quotations will indicate the amount of the reduction. A small local market could not be a general price regulator. Iceland or Labrador may import American wheat, but quotations from there have no commercial significance. All that such a region can possibly take makes no impression on the American supply; and if, by reason of some calamity, the unusable part of the wheat crop of this continent had to be put on such a market, it would soon become there an encumbrance to be gotten rid of, worth less than nothing. The utility of the final unit of the wheat raised in this country fixes the price of all of it; but even though that last unit were sold entirely abroad it would be widely scattered. Labrador would have a small part of it, and the price of wheat there would correspond with the price of it elsewhere. Much effect in regulating the price elsewhere it could not have.

A large and elastic market necessary for the action of this law.

In seeking an outlet for surplus labor, it is necessary to look for some economic field in which an indefinitely large amount of it may find employment. Such an outlet is, however, not furnished by the bits of no-rent land to which men may betake themselves. The popular mind has not failed to see that, as an outlet for surplus labor, agricultural land at the margin of cultivation is more like Iceland than like Liverpool in the illustration just given, for it wholly lacks the capacity to receive any large overflow of the supply. Turn the whole overflow of the Belgian population upon the sands for a living, and calculate,

An elastic market for labor also needed.

if it is possible, how far below the starvation limit their earnings must, by a mathematical necessity, fall. The earnings of the men on the Belgian sands and on the American arid plains do, indeed, correspond with and, within limits, measure the general rate of wages; but this is because in the world as a whole there is a vast and indefinitely elastic market for surplus labor, of which the no-rent lands are certain to get only a microscopic portion. The final increment of the world's labor is the wage-fixing part, as the final unit of the supply of goods is the price-making part; but this unit scatters itself through and through the industries of the entire world. What it can everywhere produce, is the standard for general wages.

We not only admit, but positively claim, that there is a marginal region where wages are adjusted. It furnishes a large outlet for labor; and what men are able to get in this larger marginal field sets the standard of wages. This field is to labor what, in practical thought, the European market is to wheat: it is a place in which any possible surplus of labor may be disposed of at some living rate. If we find such a market, we definitely solve the problem of the law of wages.

At the very outset, we can find a market of this kind that is large enough to receive a very considerable amount of labor. An unlimited amount it cannot receive, but it is an important outlet for labor, and it is a factor that needs to be considered in a theory of wages. Men virtually work empty-handed, and get all that they create elsewhere than on lands at the agricultural margin. The true margin of cultivation — more accurately, that of utilization — is not wholly or chiefly agricultural, but extends throughout the industrial system. There are pro-

Wages fixed by the product of labor in such a market.

ductive instruments, other than land, that yield no rent to their owners, and may be had for the use of laborers for the asking. The workmen may not themselves be able to borrow them ; but the interest of the men termed *entrepreneurs* insures that they will be put into service, and that men will be set at work in connection with them, whenever wages, including pay for superintendence and for other labor, may thereby be secured. There is a margin of utilization in cotton-spinning, in iron-smelting, in shop-keeping, in transporting freight and passengers, and in every other possible occupation.

The marginal field for labor extends through all industries.

A part of the marginal field for labor is furnished by the waste lands that are available for raising crops ; but the part thus furnished is a nearly infinitesimal part of the whole field. A larger part is afforded by no-rent instruments of the other kinds ; and still a larger part is created by putting the entire stock of rent-paying instruments into uses for which no extra rent is charged. There may be a thousand men in a modern and profitable mill ; and out of the product that their labor and the mill itself create may be paid the rent of the mill. It may be that twenty more men might find places in this mill, and that their presence would result in a distinct addition to the daily product of it. It may be, also, that this entire extra product will go to the men as wages — that the owner of the mill will make no claim on it. If so, these marginal men will get their whole products and will be in reality as free from the claims of masters on their earnings as though they were tilling waste land by the sufferance of the owner, or were running an abandoned mill in which some proprietor might tolerate their presence.

No-rent lands furnish a minute part of this field, and no-rent instruments of other kinds furnish another part.

No-rent uses of good instruments furnish a still larger part.

Here, then, is a marginal fraction of the supply of labor ; and it would seem that it is in a position to set the market rate of pay for all labor.   Here, also, is a direct connection between the pay of this marginal part of the laboring force and the product that can

The product of labor in this enlarged field not the ultimate regulator of wages.

be specifically attributed to it.   Does this product of marginal labor set the standard of wages, as the price of a final increment sets the general standard of value of commodities?   If so, the law of wages would stand thus: (1) By a common mercantile rule, all men of a given degree of ability must take what marginal men of that same ability get.   This principle fixes the market rate of wages.   (2) Marginal men get what they produce.   This principle governs wages more remotely, by fixing a natural standard for them. In this formula we are, indeed, near to the law that we are seeking; but we have not yet reached it. The true law, when accurately stated, sounds much like the foregoing one; but between the two there is a vital difference.[1]

[1] For an early publication of the substance of this chapter and of much of the following one, the reader is referred to a monograph of the American Economic Association, containing a paper on "The Possibility of a Scientific Law of Wages."   The paper was presented at a meeting of the Association held in December, 1888, and was printed in March, 1889.   One qualification of the statement made in that monograph is to be found at the end of the eighth chapter of the present work.

The substance of much of the ninth and tenth chapters of this book was first published in May, 1888, in a monograph of the American Economic Association on "Capital and its Earnings"; and a further part was published in the *Yale Review* for November, 1893, in an article on "The Genesis of Capital."

CHAPTER VIII

HOW THE SPECIFIC PRODUCT OF LABOR
MAY BE DISTINGUISHED

IN that static condition in which competition would
produce its full effects and bring wages to a natural
standard, the pay of labor, as has just been shown,
would equal the product that could be separately
traced to it. We have discovered a limited field in
which whatever is produced is due to labor only;
but we need to find one that is larger and more
elastic. We have to look for an economic field to
which many men may go, and in which they will
be virtually rent-free and interest-free. They must *How labor-*
be able to work unaided and also untaxed and to *ers may be free from*
create a distinguishable product, all of which they *rent and interest.*
will then get. A few men may, of course, till
worthless land, and so make themselves free from
landlords' and capitalists' claims. Many more may
utilize instruments of other kinds that are too poor
to afford a rent to their owners. A larger number
still may get employment as additional workers in
establishments that have good working appliances,
and that pay no more for the use of them in consequence of the presence of the marginal men.

It does not follow that, because a man desires that
the product of his industry shall not pay tribute
to employers, he needs to take himself away from
them. Working near to the man who tills a waste
piece of land in an independent way, there **may**

be another man who works on similar land for the owner of it, and gets as wages the value of what he raises. This man is as free from a master's exactions as is the squatter. A man may have, as Adam Smith has said, "neither landlord nor master to share with him," though he work for a master. If he gives his employer no more in value than his employer gives to him, his product is intact, and it all comes to him as wages. It is in positions like these that most marginal laborers are found. They are not working in solitude, yet their products are distinguishable from all other products.

This condition possible under employers.

There are mills and furnaces so antiquated, so nearly worn out or so badly located that their owners get nothing from them; and yet they run, so long as superintendents can earn their salaries and ordinary workers their natural wages. There are machines that have outlived their usefulness to their owners, but still do their work and give the entire product that they help to create to the men who operate them. There are railroads and steamship lines that pay operating expenses only. There are stocks of merchandise so full of remnants and unstylish goods that it barely pays salesmen to handle them. Everywhere, in indefinite variety and extent, are no-rent instruments; and, if labor uses them, it gets the entire product of the operation. Let the general rate of wages rise, and many of these instruments will be thrown out of use. Let the rate then fall, and the utilizing of them will be resumed. Let a migration relieve the pressure of population in one country, and overcrowd another; and in the former country no-rent instruments of every sort will be abandoned, while in the latter such as are idle will be put into active use.

No-rent instruments abundant.

The advancing and receding of the no-rent line.

That no-rent instruments are not few in number

is made clear by the fact that every tool, machine, building, vehicle or other auxiliary of labor that wears out by use must, in the course of its deterioration, necessarily reach a point at which it yields no net gain to its owner. So long as an *entrepreneur* can keep such an instrument in his service, and gain anything whatever by so doing, he will keep it. When he loses something by its presence, he will abandon it. When he neither gains nor loses by the presence of the worn instrument, — that is, when the whole product gained by using it is required to pay for the labor that utilizes it, — the instrument is in the concluding or no-rent stage of its economic career. Everything that wears out in the using has such an old age period of service, preceding the moment of its abandonment; and the aggregate of things that at any one date are in this condition is enough to constitute a very large outfit of no-rent appliances, by which labor may be aided. The effect of an increase of population, if other things remained unchanged, would be to prolong the period of service of all such deteriorating capital goods. To make the existing stock of capital goods available for the larger number of men, it would be necessary to work the worn tool, the rickety engine, the unseaworthy ship, etc., somewhat longer than it would have been used under former conditions. When it is at the point of abandonment, however, the labor that uses it creates wages only.

The entire product that is created by utilizing the poorest instruments that are kept in action at all, goes to the men who work with them. The amount of this product corresponds with and expresses the rate of general wages, and it is an important element in regulating that rate. The men who use such instruments are a part of the final increment of

All instruments that wear out, have a no-rent period

Increase of population would prolong their periods of profitable use.

The product gained by the use of the poorest instruments goes to laborers.

labor, the market price of which regulates the price of all labor. They are, however, not the whole of this final increment; for there are in the field other marginal men who are not using valueless instruments of any kind. A man may be free from all claims of capitalist and landlord, without restricting himself to the difficult process of using only worthless land and tools.

If this were the only alternative open to an unemployed man, the wage law that our study is to reveal would be akin to that of Mr. George, which asserts that all wages depend on the product realized by tilling no-rent land. We should, however, have to offer one amendment to this formula, making it assert that all men must accept what any of them could produce, if they chose to utilize marginal land *and other valueless instruments.* The field that would thus be open to men seeking employment is, by one point, larger than the marginal territory that mere agriculture affords; but it does not comprise the whole field that is, in reality, open to them. We must consult facts to see where men may and do resort, when thus seeking employment.

This field for marginal labor not the only one.

Reverting to agriculture, we find an intensive, as well as an extensive, marginal field. For one man who finds work by pushing the boundary of the tilled area into no-rent territory, there are a number who find it by a harder tillage of rent-paying lands. Whenever one waste farm is brought into use, new men are likely to be set at work on many good ones. Indeed, the overcrowding of the good lands comes first in time; for it is the diminished returns that the workers get, as they till more and more intensively these lands of high quality, that cause an overflow of the working force to inferior lands. Men are, then, crowded outward from the intensive

centres of cultivation. The point at which it ceases The inten-
to be profitable to add to the amount of labor spent of cultiva-
on good land may be termed the intensive margin of tion.
cultivation. Such a field has received increment after
increment of labor; but the time has come when a
further force of workers can do better elsewhere.
Thus, one man may plough a rocky field alone, but
his ploughing is imperfect. For the best results a
spade must here and there be used; and the man
who uses it may be regarded as a marginal man.
Again, three men may plant a field; but their planting will be slow, and some parts of the land will not
have the benefit of a long growing season. Four
men, however, can plant the field more quickly, and
thus give to the part that is last reached a longer
time to mature its crop. In this case the fourth man
is the marginal one; and the value of the whole
additional produce that his presence causes may go to
him as wages. Once more, three men may be able
to reap a field; but four can do it more quickly, and
so save the crop from some of the danger to which
autumnal rain exposes it. Here, again, the fourth man
is the marginal one, whose whole product is his wages.
The value of the wheat that in a series of years
is saved from destruction through his presence may
be paid to him for his labor. There may be still
another man who gleans behind the reapers, and gets
just the value of his gleanings. Such an additional The product
man often adds to the perfection of the planting this inten-
process or the cultivating process. But if he created sive margin
less and received less than he actually does, he would wages.
betake himself to inferior land.
   It is by assuming perfectly free competition among
employers that we are able to say that the man on
the intensive margin of an agricultural force of
laborers will get, as pay, the value of his product.

When such a man offers himself to an employer, he is virtually offering an addition to the farmer's crop. If one farmer will not pay the market price of the additional produce, another will pay it, provided that competition does its work quite perfectly. Friction is, however, always an element to be taken into account; for adjustments like this are not perfect in any society. Our sole present inquiry is, nevertheless, to determine the standard to which wages *tend* to conform — the standard to which they *would* conform in a frictionless society. Our answer is that wages conform to the product that is attributable to marginal labor.

The hypothesis of perfect competition necessary.

We are also seeking to ascertain what such marginal labor is; and in agriculture much of it consists in the final increment of labor employed in the intensive tillage of good land. Such labor demands of a farmer no appreciable increase in his investment of capital. He does not need to buy more land or to put more permanent improvements into land that he already owns. In many cases he does not need to add a single tool to his outfit. He has only to add this man, empty-handed as he is, to his laboring force. Any extra produce is attributable to the man's labor, and to that only; and perfect competition tends to give the value of this produce to the man as wages.

Such an intensive margin of the field for labor is by no means confined to agriculture: it may be traced throughout the industrial system. Everywhere there is a line that it does not pay to pass in adding to the number of workers who are utilizing the really productive appliances of industry. Though a hundred men can sail a steamship, a hundred and five may sail it better. In that case, the five extra men are on the intensive margin of utilization of the steamship and are virtually rent-free. Whatever the ship itself

An intensive margin in all industries.

must pay to its owners, was paid when it was run by the original crew. The last five men that are taken on board, therefore, create a distinct product. They render the ship a more efficient carrier and put money into the owners' pockets; but they take this money out of the owners' pockets, when they draw wages. In mills, mines, shops, furnaces, etc., there is in this way often a chance to vary, within narrow limits, the number of men who are employed, without affecting the owners' incomes. If new men are thus taken, their whole product is given to them.

There are, however, some points in the industrial system at which there is no elasticity in the number of workers who can be economically employed. A given machine often requires one man to run it, and no more. It is not, then, at every point in a great establishment that the working force can be enlarged or reduced without any change in the character of the outfit of capital goods. Yet in commerce there is often an appreciable elasticity in the amount of labor that can be employed in connection with a stock of salable merchandise. In manufacturing and in transporting, too, the working force may often be varied perceptibly, with no change in the amount or in the character of the capital goods that are used in connection with it.

Such changes must, of course, be kept within comparatively narrow limits. At one point in the industrial system it may be that five men can be added to a gang of a hundred, without requiring a change in the amount of capital employed and without requiring any change in the form of it. Elsewhere only one man in a hundred can, in this way, be added or subtracted. If, in each of the general groups into which society is organized for the purpose of production, as many men as one for every hundred can be added to the working force or taken from it, without necessitating any change in the outfit of tools, machines, materials, etc., that they use, this fact is sufficient to furnish a certain theoretical basis for a law of wages. Any one man in a force of a hundred may, then, leave his own employer without injuring or benefiting the employer; and if he offers his service to another and demands, as pay, what he will produce for him, he will neither benefit nor injure this second master, in case he gets employment from him. There is, it thus appears, what we may

The zone of indifference. call a zone of indifference in the field of employment that each *entrepreneur* controls. Within this limit men may go or come without affecting the employers' pockets. Motives other than pecuniary interest may cause employers to accept new men that are offered to them; and there is a chance for a limited amount of labor to flow freely from group to group in the industrial system. If competition works in ideal perfection, wherever these marginal workers go, they get their exact products as their pay; though, in fact, as competition works imperfectly, what the men get is merely an approximation to their products.

How the product of labor on this zone is tested. When any man leaves his employer, the test that determines how much he has been worth is applied by ascertaining how much the employer loses in consequence of having his laboring force made, by one man, smaller. It may be that the identity of the particular man who goes is of no consequence. All that is important may be the fact that, somewhere in the mill, there are seven workmen in a gang that formerly had eight, or nineteen in a gang that had twenty. The man is, let us say, an average, unskilled workman; and he can change his occupation without that amount of waste and friction that is entailed when a man who has mastered a profitable specialty transfers himself from one group to another. One question to be answered is, How much does the former employer lose by the man's departure? Another question is, How much does the second employer gain by the man's presence?

So far as the men in an employer's service are thus interchangeable, it makes no difference to him which of them it is that leaves his service. If the man who departs has been doing some kind of work that is quite necessary in conducting the business, the employer has only to put in his place the man who has been doing the work that is least needed. The work that is left undone in consequence of one man's departure is always of the marginal kind. The men in a mill arrange themselves in different classes, in the order that expresses the importance of the work that they are doing. The first class does something that is indispensable, the second, something that is highly important but less so than that which is done by the first, etc. The last class does a kind of work that contributes least of all to the productiveness of the business. If a man belonging to the first class leaves his employment, the master has only to put into his place a man taken from the last class. It is the least needed work that will remain undone. The *effective* importance to his employer of any of these interchangeable men is measured by the *absolute* importance of the one that does the least necessary work. The principle of effective productivity.

Moreover, we shall find that, where men are not thus entirely interchangeable, something akin to this substitution of one for the other still takes place, when a superior man, performing an important function, deserts his employment. That function does not go unperformed. Another man is set to doing what the departing man did; and the work that remains undone is, as before, work of the marginal kind.

The substitutions that have to be made, in order to bring about this result, do, it is true, entail a special loss on the employer; for the important kinds of work are not so well done as they were formerly. The extra loss thus occasioned measures the special value of the superior man whose departure caused the substitutions. All grades of labor are, however, really measured, in the end, by marginal standards; and the entire process of measurement can be understood when we shall have reached a later point in the study of the marginal productivity of labor.

What we need now to note is that, so far as men are interchangeable, they are all alike in what we may call their *effective productivity*. One of them may actually be doing an indispensable work and another a work that is of slight importance; but it really diminishes the product of the establishment no more to take away the first man than it does to take away the second, for the second man is sure to leave his own work and do the more essential thing formerly done by the first. What we may call the absolute productivity of a particular man is measured by the importance of the particular work that he is doing. Let the man desert his place, leaving undone the work that he has heretofore done, and the loss that the establishment will thereby sustain measures the man's absolute productivity. What we have called a man's effective productivity is, then, measured by the loss that his employer suffers when the man departs, and when the employer rearranges his force so that the more necessary kinds of work are still done. The employer will put B into A's place, C into B's place, etc.; and the only work that goes undone is of the kind that is least necessary. If the men are quite interchangeable, the effective productivity of any one of them is equal to the abso-

Effective productivity the test of wages.

lute productivity of the final or marginal one, whose work can best be dispensed with. We shall find that all wages are naturally gauged by the effective, rather than the absolute, productivity of the men who get them. In so far as men can be freely substituted for each other, any man in a series of men is actually worth to his employer only as much as the last one in the series produces.

From an employer's point of view, the area within which he can set a few extra men working, without reducing their effective products, in amount, below those of men who are already in this marginal region, we have called the *zone of indifference* — on the ground that it is of no appreciable importance to him whether such men work or not. If he hires them, he will pay their products as wages, and will make nothing out of them. A small influence will determine whether an employer will hire such men or not. There is, of course, some friction to be overcome whenever a working force is enlarged or reduced. From a workman's point of view, this is evident. If I am a clerk out of employment, will you take me into your shop? Yes, if I can produce for you a bare tithe more than you will pay me in wages; no, if I can produce less. You may or may not take me, if I can add to your previous product exactly what I ask as wages. My labor will then lie within the zone of economic indifference, and humanity or other motives will determine your action. If I am in your employment, will you turn me off? Probably not, till the product that my labor adds to the other earnings of the shop falls short of my actual wages. If you have taken me into your shop at a time when business was unusually good, you doubtless realized, for the time, a small profit from my labor; and this sufficed to overcome the slight inertia that opposes an

How the test is practically applied.

enlargement of a laboring force. On the other hand, when you have once enrolled me among your men, inertia will work in my favor; for you will keep me till my presence involves a loss that is large enough to make you take the overt step of discharging me.

What we are seeking is, of course, the standard to which the pay of labor tends to conform; but inertia and friction are influences that, as we have asserted with all needed emphasis, have a place in all economic theories that aim to be complete. It is not, however, in that part of the theoretical statement which aims to establish the natural standard of wages **Friction not** that we have to measure the effects of friction. Even **considered** though, in the adjustment of wages, there were very **in fixing a** **theoretical** large disturbing influences to be encountered, yet, if **static stand-** competition caused the pay of labor to gravitate **ard of** **wages.** always toward the rate that is fixed by the product of the marginal part of the supply of labor, it would be enough for our present purpose to establish that fact; and this would be true, though friction and disturbance — the elements that are elsewhere to be studied — kept the actual rate of wages much farther from the theoretical standard than they do.

Summary.   The conclusions that we have now reached may be summarized as follows: *Wages tend to equal the product of marginal labor; and that part of the working force which occupies a zone of indifference is thus marginal.* The men who run no-rent machinery, or extort the last increment of product from better machinery, are within this field; and so are the men who till waste land, or give the final touches to the intensive tillage of good land. So, also, are the laborers who anywhere bring capital goods to the height of their efficiency, and so effect any of the final gleanings of the industrial field. All these men create a certain amount of wealth. Competition tends to give them the whole of it; and it also tends to make other laborers accept what these men create and get.   If the workmen within the zone of indifference constitute an appreciable force, and if they can be transferred freely from one position to another, it is clear that *the effective product of any workman must be equal to the absolute product of a man who is within the marginal zone.*   Let any man desert an employer's working force and, however necessary that man's labor may be, the employer will lose only what some man in the marginal area is now producing.   He will take this man, who is now doing some of the final gleaning work, and put him into the place where the more important labor is to be performed.   By *effective* standards all men's labor is equally important, provided that the men are interchangeable.   The friction that the interchange encounters is, again, an element for separate study. In the absence of friction, men who can be moved from place to place are of equal effective importance and get equal pay — that is, the amount that the marginal workers produce.

Another step may now be taken toward the attainment of a standard of general wages.   The product that is created within one employer's zone of indifference tends to equal what is produced on the corresponding part of another employer's field.   If the marginal machinery of some cloth-making firm is very poor, — consisting, perhaps, in antiquated and rickety looms in a remote mill in the country, — the men who use this machinery can produce only a little. If in a modern mill, elsewhere located, the marginal instruments are much better, the men who use them create more; and, under free competition, they tend to get more.   Here, let us say, is a situation that calls for a transfer of men from one field to the other.

Products on the zones of indifference of different employments tend toward uniformity.

The old and worn machines will be abandoned, and the men who used them will go to the good mills, and will there utilize poorer instruments than, in these mills, have heretofore been used; or they will make less productive uses of the good instruments that there abound. In short, they will press the margin of employment downward to a less productive level; and this movement will tend to go on till, in one employer's mill, marginal labor creates and gets the same amount of wealth that it does in the mills of his competitors.

This is saying that the zones of indifference in the several employers' fields, all taken together, consti-

A general zone of indifference in each industry.

tute a zone of indifference running through the whole group, or branch of industry, to which the men belong. Any man within this zone may leave one employer and betake himself to another, and he will produce for the second the same amount of wealth that he created for the first. This entire zone is an area of uniform productivity for labor and of equal pay for labor, if competition works without friction. The static adjustment toward which industrial society is at each instant tending is one in which the marginal men in all establishments belonging to one group are uniformly productive and are paid at a uniform rate.

Again, there is a similar tendency to uniformity of productive power and of pay in the marginal areas

A similar zone in industry as a whole.

in the different branches of industry. What is produced within the zone of indifference in one industrial group, tends to equal what is produced in the corresponding zone in another; and there is, in reality, a social zone of indifference that includes all the local areas. Thus, marginal labor in shoe manufacturing tends to be as productive and as well paid as is marginal labor in iron-smelting, in quarrying, in transporting, etc. If this were not so, there would be a steady flow of labor from the less productive to the more productive area. If in one occupation the marginal men create what is worth a dollar and a half a day, while elsewhere they create what is worth two dollars a day, the employers in this latter field are interested in hiring men entirely from that field in which the product and the pay are the lowest. This transfer of men from the one field to the other equalizes the productive powers of men at the several margins of employment. In the one field men will relinquish the poorest instruments and the least productive uses of good ones. The effect of this, in the branch of industry from which the men go, is to make better instruments become the marginal ones; and it is also to make more profitable uses of good instruments become the final or no-rent uses. It increases the absolute product of the marginal labor, and that raises the effective product of all labor. The result in the group to which men are going is the reverse of this. There the use of poorer and poorer instruments, and the making of less and less productive uses of good instruments, is the rule. There marginal labor is being forced into less and less productive fields. The inducement to move is withdrawn, and the movement ends when in farming, in cotton-spinning, in mining, in shoe-making, in cattle raising, etc., the final increments of labor are equally productive. Marginal social labor, in short, tends everywhere to be uniformly productive: labor of uniform personal quality is equally productive in all parts of the industrial system. The interchangeability of labor insures this. It is, therefore, all paid at the same rate; for the wages of a unit of labor anywhere in the working field tend to equal the product of a unit on the marginal part of it. The zone of indifference, then, extends through every group and sub-group into which industrial society is organized. The distinctive fact about it is, that it is everywhere a matter of indifference to an employer whether, within this area, he employs a man or not.

What "zones" represent.

The terms "zone," "area" and "field," are figurative expressions; and what they really signify is opportunity to labor. A fertile piece of land or a well-equipped shop offers to a certain number of men an opportunity to work in a highly productive way. This best opening for labor may be represented by the figure of a central circle in the universal field for employment. Additional men create less than did the original ones, because their opportunities are poorer; and this fact may be indicated by locating them, in imagination, on zones surrounding the central area. There is a series of such opportunities for labor, each of which is poorer than the preceding ones, and the last is the poorest of all. It is this most sterile of the fields, openings or opportunities for labor that we describe graphically as an outermost zone, within which men produce only their wages. This is the zone of indifference from an employer's point of view, because, if he sets men working within this area, he must give them all that they produce as wages. If one employer offers to them less than, by their productive power, they are worth, another will offer more, provided competition is perfectly free and efficient. Theoretically,

How the product at the marginal zone is secured by laborers.

there is competition between employers for every workman whose presence in an establishment affords to the owner any profit over what he pays to him; and the competition stops only when this profit is annihilated.

In this there is a parallelism of great importance

between the natural value of goods and the natural wages of labor.   It has been rightly asserted by early economists that the natural price of an article is one that yields only the cost of producing it, and this view is in harmony with common experience.   Normal prices are no-profit prices.   They afford wages for all the labor that is involved in producing the goods, including the labor of superintending the mills, managing the finances, keeping the accounts, collecting the debts and doing all the work of directing the policy of the business.   They afford, also, interest on all the capital that is used in the business, whether it is owned by the *entrepreneur* or borrowed from some one else.   Beyond this there is no return, if prices stand exactly at their normal rate; and the reason for this is that *entrepreneurs* compete with each other in selling their goods, and so reduce prices to the no-net-profit level.

It is through competition, which tends to carry prices of goods down to the no-profit level

Prices, however, seldom remain long at the exact cost rates.   There are fluctuations that carry them at one time above the rate, and then cause them to subside toward it.   The no-profit level of price is thus normal; because it furnishes, not the rate at which things continue to sell, but the one toward which prices are forever gravitating, where competition is free.   Wherever there is an *entrepreneur's* net profit, some article is, for the time being, selling for more than this normal price.   The tendency of competition is to annihilate the profit; and that is the same thing as bringing actual prices to what, in accepted economic theory as well as in common experience, is their "natural" level.   The friction that this movement toward the natural level encounters is a subject for later study; but we already see that the pure profit of an *entrepreneur* could never exist, if it were not for this friction.   If the price of everything could instantly take the level fixed by the bare cost of producing it, there would be nothing left for an *entrepreneur*, as such.

In employing marginal labor, competition, if it is free and efficient, has the same effect: it annihilates the profit that an employer might make on the last increment of labor that he hires. Employers have the same inducement to bid over each other for labor that will give them a net gain, as they have to bid under each other to secure a sale for goods that yield a profit. In the latter case, they run the prices down till no margin of gain is left for themselves; and in the former case they run the wages of the last increment of labor up, till no profit remains for them. The marginal wage rate is, then, naturally a no-net-profit rate; and it is employers' competition that tends to make it so. Here, again, there is friction to be encountered; for competition does not do its work with accuracy. Hence there are now and then profits or losses connected with marginal labor. The no-profit pay for such labor is, however, natural, for the same reason that cost prices of goods are natural: it is the rate toward which, under the influence of competition, the pay of marginal labor is everywhere tending.

Furthermore, as all pay for marginal labor tends to adjust itself to the product of that labor, so the pay for all other labor tends to adjust itself to that of the marginal part of the supply. What a man on the zone of indifference is getting, another man must accept, if the employer can substitute the one for the other. This principle would afford a sufficient regulator of wages, if the zone of indifference, as it has been described, were the whole marginal field of employment of labor; but it is not. Besides utilizing worthless instruments and bringing out the latent

and also to carry the wages of labor up to the no-profit level.

The zone of indifference not the whole marginal field of employment of labor.

possibilities of good ones — that is, by enlarging the whole field of labor in the extensive and the intensive ways that have thus far been described — an addition to the working force may in still another way find employment in which it will create a distinct product and get the whole of it. It is, therefore, not fair to say that the product of labor on the zone of indifference is the sole and adequate standard to which the pay of all labor conforms. It is the product of labor on a still larger marginal field, of which this zone is only a part, that constitutes this standard.

The opportunity for employment, which has been described by the term "zone of indifference," consists in the liberty to use capital-goods, or concrete instruments of production, in ways that make them yield more than they already do. Taking the working equipment of the world as it stands, we may get somewhat more out of it, if we spend more labor in using it. This is a different thing from getting more out of a given *capital* by a similar intensifying of labor. A mill with its machines as they stand can take more laborers than are now employed in it; but if the mill is worth a million dollars, that amount of capital is capable of employing a much larger number of marginal workers than the mill can use as it stands. The vast stock of working appliances that the United States possesses can enable more men to work than are now working ; but sixty-five billion " dollars " not confined to these appliances, but free to invest themselves in any other things, could give openings to a much greater number of additional workmen. There is a radical difference between the margin of employment that is offered by a particular stock of *capital-goods* and the one that is offered by a given *capital*.

In many parts of the industrial field a few more men or a few less might be employed, in connection

The margin of employment afforded by capital-goods contrasted with the margin afforded by capital.

with the amounts of capital that are there already in use, and *without any change in the form of that capital.* Thus, leaving a farm, with its buildings, live stock, implements, etc., exactly as they are, you may add a man to the working force or withdraw one from it without affecting the employer's gains.   This slight elasticity in the size of the laboring force that an industrial plant can receive is of great importance; but as an essential fact it is insignificant in comparison with the elasticity in the size of the force that a given capital can receive.   Though there are shops into which one or more men could be taken without loss, there are also shops that could not economically take another man.   There are, again, machines that must be tended all day by one operator. There are farms, gardens, mines, sailing craft, etc., to which the bringing of one more workman would mean an excessive and uneconomical supply of labor; but there is no such limit to the number who can work with a fixed amount of capital, *if the forms of it can be varied to suit the number of the men.*   If, whenever you added to the number of your workmen, you could instantly, and without waste, put your capital into any new shapes that you might select, you might double, quadruple or octuple your force of men without adding to the amount of your capital as a whole. If, therefore, capital is not limited in its forms, the labor that can use it is not limited in quantity.

This fact makes it ultimately possible for a far greater quantity of labor to move from group to group in the industrial system than could so move if capital were frozen rigidly into a fixed set of forms.   If this were the case, only men on the zone of indifference could be transferred without a disastrous amount of waste and disturbance.   If there were two industries, each of which employed a hundred thousand

Limited elasticity of the field for employment offered by a given stock of capital-goods.

Unlimited elasticity of the field offered by a given capital.

The mobility of labor largely dependent on this fact.

men and a hundred million dollars' worth of capital, it might be that one thousand men could move freely from one to the other without any gain or loss in productive power. If, however, it were desired to transfer ten thousand men or fifty thousand, this would be impracticable, so long as the forms of the capital in the two industries remained unchanged. Take half of the working men out of the one set of mills and put them into the other, and in the first set many machines will cease to run at all, while in the other mills men will be unable to do anything that is useful enough to make their company worth as much as their room. Yet a perfect mobility of labor is one of our primary hypotheses. Unless labor is thus mobile, it cannot be brought to an equality of earning power in different industries, and a general or social rate of wages cannot be established. It is clear that in thinking, in a practical way, of the manner in which a general rate of pay is established, we tacitly recognize the unrestricted power that *capital, as such*, has to employ varying amounts of labor. Because the capital of each group has this power, the groups are brought to an equilibrium, and their outputs are made normal. Because the capital of society, as a whole, has this power, labor, as a whole, always has, under normal conditions, an outlook for employment where its product will set the standard of its pay. An industrial society can, in some way, absorb any amount of labor. If capital is freely transmutable in form, labor becomes freely transferable and able to count on an indefinitely elastic field of employment. What a marginal unit of it can produce in this elastic field is the amount that can be specifically attributed to any unit.

The elasticity of the general labor market also dependent on it.

CHAPTER IX

CAPITAL AND CAPITAL-GOODS CONTRASTED

IT is now possible to state, in an intelligible way, the main thesis of the theory of wages: *The pay of labor in each industry tends to conform to the marginal product of social labor employed in connection with a fixed amount of social capital, as such.* That the full meaning of this statement may become clear it is necessary to present, in some fulness, the differences that science must recognize between "capital" and "capital-goods."

Necessity for contrasting capital and capital-goods.

Capital consists of instruments of production, and these are always concrete and material. This fact is fundamental. In claiming for capital a material existence, we go beyond many classical economists, since we do not consider acquired abilities of workmen as a part of the fund of productive wealth. Man does not add to his capital, when he spends money in training or educating himself for a useful occupation. He gets something, indeed, that increases his productive power; and in getting it he is obliged to practise abstinence. He deprives himself of pleasure, in order that thereafter he may produce more than he otherwise could. There is, it must be admitted, a certain similarity between the effects of money spent on a technical education and those of money spent in buying a tool. In using the term, however, we shall be strict constructionists, and shall insist that capital is never a quality of man himself,

Capital always concrete and material.

which he uses for productive purposes.   The capital
of the world is, as it were, one great tool in the hand
of working humanity — the armature with which
humanity subdues and transforms the resisting elements of nature.

The most distinctive single fact about what we
have termed capital is the fact of permanence.   It
lasts; and it must last, if industry is to be successful.
Trench upon it — destroy any of it, and you have
suffered a disaster.   Destroy all that you have of it,
and ou must begin empty-handed to earn a living,
as best you can, by labor alone.   Yet you must
destroy *capital-goods* in order not to fail.   Try to
preserve capital-goods from destruction, and you
bring on yourself the same disaster that you suffer
when you allow a bit of capital to be destroyed.   Stop
the machines in your mill that they may not wear
out, wrap and box them in order that they may not
rust out, and the productive action of your capital
stops.   What is more, the capital itself will also
ultimately perish; for your machines will, in time,
become so antiquated that it will be impracticable to
use them.

Capital-goods, then, not only *may* go to destruction, but *must* be destroyed, if industry is to be successful; and they must do so, in order that capital
may last.   Seed-wheat must perish that wheat may
abide.   It is this idea of permanence that originally
gave a name to the kind of wealth that is used for
productive purposes, for it is the kind of wealth that
is of such capital, or vital, importance that it must
always be kept intact.   It is, by its very name, contrasted with free income, which may be used up on
one's living or on one's pleasure.   Put your capital
out at usury and you may safely spend what comes
to you as the earning of it; but you may not safely

Permanence the most distinctive attribute of capital.

Capital-goods must perish in order that capital may abide.

spend the capital. The very policy, however, that preserves this essential element in industry is one that consigns to destruction nearly all the material instruments that embody it. The point of sharpest contrast between capital and most capital-goods is, indeed, the permanence of the one, as compared with the perishability of the other. Land is the only kind of capital-goods that does not need to be destroyed, in order that the fund of wealth embodied in it may continue.

Capital mobile, capital-goods not so.   Again, capital is perfectly mobile; but capital-goods are far from being so. It is possible to take a million dollars out of one industry and put them into another. Under favorable conditions, it is possible to do this without waste. It is, however, quite impossible to take bodily out of one industry the tools that belong to it and to put them into another. The capital that was once invested in the whale fishery of New England is now, to some extent, employed in cotton manufacturing; but the ships have not been used as cotton mills. As the vessels were worn out, the part of their earnings that might have been used to build more vessels was actually used to build mills. The nautical *form* of the capital perished; but the capital survived and, as it were, migrated from the one set of material bodies to the other. There is, indeed, no limit to the ultimate power of capital, by changing its forms of embodiment, thus to change its place in the group-system of industry.

The reason for describing capital in terms of money.   We now have the key to one scientific problem connected with productive wealth. Why do business men speak of capital in terms of money? Why, if you ask a merchant, "What is your capital?" will he answer, "It is the hundred thousand dollars that I have invested in my shop?" It is because what he means by the phrase, "a hundred thousand dollars," is an abiding thing, which he had when he went into business and still has, unless his business has been unfortunate. Yet he is usually under no delusions as to the character of the things that embody his capital; and, in particular, he knows that these things do not consist in coins or in any other currency. He would be a poor merchant who should keep more than a minute part of his capital locked up in safes or bank vaults, or scattered through his shop in cash drawers. His productive wealth consists in merchandise, in fixtures, in claims against customers for merchandise sold and delivered, etc. Yet he instinctively and unconsciously thinks and speaks of it as money. He can keep his "money," and he can move it from one investment to another. A value, an abstract quantum of productive wealth, a permanent fund — that is what the hundred thousand dollars in our illustration really signify. A value, a quantum of wealth, or a fund — if one of these be thought of apart from the concrete things that embody it, it is an abstraction; but if it be thought of as actually embodied in concrete things. it is not an abstraction, but a material entity. The business man always thinks of his hundred thousand dollars as thus embodied, and he can tell readily enough what things embody it. He knows that his investment is concrete and material; and yet he instinctively thinks and speaks of it through the medium of an abstract expression.

Guarding ourselves as carefully as we have done against the idea that capital ever lives in a disembodied state, we may safely use, for scientific purposes, the business man's formula. We may think of capital as a sum of productive wealth, invested in material things which are perpetually shifting — which come and go continually — although the fund abides. Capital thus lives, as it were, by transmigration, taking itself out of one set of bodies and putting itself into another, again and again. The more frequently it casts off one set of forms and takes on another, other things being equal, the more actively business operations are proceeding, and the more vitality there is in the fund itself. The life of such a capital is not torpid, like the life of a reptile having a sluggish circulation: it is rather like the life of a highly organized animal that casts off and renews its tissues at short intervals.[1]

[1] In a monograph of the American Economic Association on " Capital and its Earnings," published in May, 1888, I called attention to the distinction between capital and capital-goods, and applied the term *pure capital* to the permanent fund of productive wealth that in this chapter has been called simply capital. The word " pure " suggests freedom from some admixture, and the admixture that is excluded is a combination with concrete objects such as tools, etc. Yet it was not at all my intention to convey the idea that pure capital is something that can objectively exist without being in such a combination. It is, however, thought of in ways in which, *in the concept itself*, it has to be freed from the combination. " It lasts," as we say, and " it moves from industry to industry " ; but the tools do not last, and they do not change their places as working implements. The fund, the " dollars," or the pure capital does these things. When one set of bodies perishes and another one replaces it, we say that capital continues, and yet it is only an abstraction that has literally a continuous existence. The concrete embodiments of the abstraction have only transient existences. With this understanding, pure capital might be termed capital in the abstract, though it is never objectively an abstraction. It is value embodied in goods the identity of which is perpetually changing, so that any affirmation that may be made of the permanent fund applies to-day to one set of bodies, to-morrow to another, etc. Here is the kernel of the logical distinction. An affirmation that is made about capital-goods involves retaining the idea of the identity of the goods. We say " all capital-goods perish," and we mean by it, not that all matter belonging to the genus capital-goods perishes from the earth, but that the particular capital-goods that we identify in the affirmation do this. A literal description of what, in the monograph referred to, was called pure capital, and is here called capital, might term it a *quantum* of matter of the

Such an abstract formula as this for describing a concrete thing is common in every sphere of thought. We have already used the illustration of a water power. Power, in itself considered, is an abstraction, but power embodied in an endless succession of drops of falling water is not abstract, but eminently material and concrete. Life in itself is an abstraction, but life embodied in an endless succession of human beings is concrete. Productive power measured in units and expressed in terms of money is abstract; but when this power is embodied in an endless succession of capital-goods, it is concrete. We might designate capital, the permanent thing that we have described, as an endless succession of shifting goods always worth a certain amount. We mean exactly that, when we designate it as a certain amount of "money" permanently invested in a succession of perishable things.

Concrete things often described by means of abstract formulas.

It is because the idea of permanence is conveyed in the best and simplest way by this latter form of expression that, in this connection and in others, common thought adheres to it. It is a water power that the manufacturer buys, when he gets the right to have an endless series of particles of water flow through his flume. It is life that abides on the planet, as men come and men go. It is a fund, a sum of active and productive wealth, that continues in industry, as successive instruments of production live, as it were, their industrial lives and die. Here, as we have noted, there is one exception to be made: capital invested in land has no occasion to cast off

kind defined as producers' goods, measured in terms of value and having the characteristic of forever shifting its bodily identity. Nothing that is permanently true can be affirmed of the goods, as such: since the particular goods themselves do not abide. Such affirmations may be made only of the fund.

its present body and take another. This part of the general productive fund can live, as we have seen, without transmigration, but it is the only part that can do so.

Both capital and capital-goods must be studied. It is inevitable that both capital and capital-goods should be subjects of economic study. There are problems concerning each of them that have to be solved; and this fact appears, in an unfortunate way, in all those treatises on political economy in which the single term, capital, is used to designate productive wealth. Invariably does the application of this term shift from capital, as we define it, to capital-goods, and *vice versa*. This twofold meaning of one important word has made endless trouble and confusion. Are wages, for example, paid out of capital? That they are so paid is the essence of the wages-fund doctrine, which was for a long period scarcely questioned. What is meant by the term capital in this connection? Is it the abiding fund of productive wealth? If it is, then the statement that was so long current must mean that industry, as it proceeds, draws on this fund and reduces it. This vital element in business must, at least temporarily, dwindle; yet every one knows that it does not do so. Does the term capital, as thus used by early writers, really mean capital-goods? If so, their statement concerning it only asserts the fact that the real pay that a workman gets and shares with his family consists in goods taken from merchants' stocks. They have, it is true, been capital-goods heretofore, but they are consumers' goods now; and their places in the stock of capital-goods have been taken by other and similar commodities. There has been no reducing of capital, though there may have been a withdrawing and a replacing of the tissues of it. A statement that would have

made these facts clear would have precluded logom-
achies and confusions without number; and a definition of terms that would have distinguished capital
from capital-goods would have done this.

The early economists all defined capital as consisting in instruments of production, such as tools, buildings, raw material, etc. By a confusion of thought Confusions
they usually included, as one of the forms of capital, that have
food for laborers — a typical kind of consumers' been com-
goods; but otherwise they made it clear that capital
consists in tools, buildings, materials and other
things that assist labor. Yet, having defined capital
in this way, they were forced — as any one must be —
to revert to the common conception of it as a fund de-
scribable in terms of money, when they entered on the
consideration of the problem of interest; for five per
cent of itself per annum is something that a building
cannot earn, though the "money" invested in the
building may do so.

What, then, is interest? Is it not a fraction of
itself that a permanent fund of wealth annually
earns? It is five dollars annually earned by a hundred
dollars. It is usually expressed in percentages; and
percentages imply that both the capital itself and its
annual earnings are described in units of value.
Does a building, or an engine, or a ship literally
earn in a year a fraction of itself? Does it emerge
at the end of the year larger by one twentieth than
it was at the beginning? The *capital* that is embodied in the buildings, the engines and the ships
of the world does enlarge itself in this way. *It
earns interest; but what the concrete instruments themselves earn is not interest, but rent.*

A popular and accurate use of the term rent Rent the
makes it describe the amount that any concrete in- capital-
strument earns. Thus, a building earns rent, as does goods.

the land on which it stands; and so, in fact, does every machine or bit of raw material that the building may contain. Rent, then, is a lump sum and not a percentage. Let anything for hire, and whatever you get for it will, in common usage, take the name rent. Whether the thing that is let be a farm, a house, a vehicle, a ship, a tool or any other concrete capital-good, it earns rent; while capital, as such, earns interest. Make an inventory of all the concrete instruments of production that the world contains, including in the list every commodity that helps to produce other commodities and putting opposite the name of each article the sum that in a year it can earn for its owner. Add together all these sums, and the gross amount is the total income of the property-holding class, as this income is reduced to the form of rent. Now take a different course. Make the same inventory of capital-goods as before, appending to the name of each article the value that it embodies. Add together these values, and the grand total will describe the permanent capital of the world. Find what part of itself this fund will earn in a year, and you have the *rate* of interest. Find how many dollars this fraction of the fund of capital amounts to, and what you have is the absolute amount of interest. It is, again, the entire income of the property-holding class; but this time it is in the form of interest, conceived as the product, not of perishable instruments, but of an abiding fund of invested wealth. In a use of terms which harmonizes with practical thought and which, as we undertake to prove, is entirely scientific, rent and interest describe the same income in two different ways. *Rent is the aggregate of the lump sums earned by capital-goods; while interest is the fraction of itself that is earned by the permanent fund of capital.*

Mode of reducing rent to the form of interest, or earnings of capital.

These terms describe the same income in two ways.

It will be noticed that, in computing the rate of interest, we first ascertained the absolute amounts, or lump sums, earned by all the several instruments. In a sense, interest depends on rent: it is total rent, reduced to a percentage of total capital. In another and a deeper sense, rent is governed by interest: the amount that any one instrument earns depends on the number of such instruments that are in use. Increase the number of tools of any one kind, and the earnings of each of them will grow smaller; diminish the number, and the earnings of each will grow larger. The number of each kind of instrument that is naturally brought into use depends on the law of interest. The *capital* in one kind of tool, machine, building, etc., is made to earn as large a percentage of itself as does the capital in another; and the number of each kind of capital-goods is so adjusted as to make it do so. This equalizing force determines the number of capital-goods of each kind; and this, again, governs the rents that they severally earn. If there are at work so many turning lathes that another one will not earn as large a fraction of its cost as will some other tool, the other tool is produced and set working, in preference to the lathe. *Proximately, rent fixes interest.* Given a certain number of capital-goods of each kind, and what they earn is the amount that, by an arithmetical reduction, is converted into interest. *Fundamentally, interest governs rents.* Given a certain permanent fund of capital, and it is put into such forms that the rent secured by one concrete form, or capital-good, is as large a fraction of its value as is that secured by another. A fuller statement of the laws of rent and interest will later make this clear.

Among those statements concerning capital which Mr. John Stuart Mill classed as fundamental is the

The dependence of interest on rent, and the more fundamental dependence of rent on interest.

assertion that it is all destined to destruction. Raw materials, he says, will transform themselves into finished goods and will then be used up, tools will wear out, buildings will go to decay, etc. Here is a naïve reversion to the original idea, expressed by the definitions of capital that were then current — the idea, namely, of capital-goods. These do perish; but the fundamental fact about capital — the fact that originally gave it its name — is that it cannot perish except by disaster.

Unlike relations of capital and capital-goods to abstinence. Another of Mr. Mill's fundamental propositions is, that capital originates in abstinence. In this assertion it is permanent capital that is referred to. Not a little care needs, however, to be used, if we are to have a clear idea of the function termed abstinence; for concerning it there are current many old confusions and some modern ones. We abstain from something when, as a man would say, we "save money." We do, indeed, get something by abstaining; but what we abstain from is very different from what we get. That which we keep our hands off from — that which we put away from ourselves and do not consume — is not capital-goods: it is the consumers' goods, the articles for personal comfort, that we should have bought and used, if we had not saved our money. We do not abstain from using and destroying a machine or a building; we use them and wear them out. In getting them, however, we abstain from pleasures and articles that give pleasure. Abstinence is nothing more than electing to take our income in the form of wealth-creating goods, instead of in that of pleasure-giving goods. It is on these latter goods, which we elect not to take, — and which are, therefore, not produced for us, — that we practise abstinence. We let alone things that do not exist, though they would exist if we called for them.

What we get by abstinence is true capital; and this means that the capital-goods which come to us are not merely for the replacing of other capital-goods that we are wearing out. They are new goods, embodying a net addition to our fund. In every case an instrument that is gained by genuine abstinence signifies that the man has more permanent capital than he had before. In due time this instrument will wear itself out; and it will be followed by another instrument. Virtually, though not literally, it will have created that other instrument; and the second instrument in the series, as well as all following ones, will have come into existence without further abstaining acts. When a loom in my cotton mill shall be discarded by reason of age and infirmity, I shall not be forced to replace it by trenching upon my income and denying myself goods that I have been accustomed to consume; for, in addition to the net income that the loom has earned for me, it has provided a sinking fund which replaces itself without imposing on me any further burden. Not all the creating of capital-goods, then, calls for abstinence. The starting of an entirely new series of capital-goods does so; and the abstinence exhausts itself in calling the first one of the series into being, for the later ones are virtually made by the first one. This is saying that abstinence always calls a new bit of permanent capital into existence.

In modern economic literature there is a disposition to divide continued production into periods, and to connect these periods with capital. Every bit of capital is, according to one form of analysis, supposed to thrust itself between the labor of production and the beginning of consumption. This, however, is, as we have seen, what capital-goods do. They separate labor, in time, from the enjoyment that will

Periods of production connected with capital-goods.

be afforded when the particular thing with which labor is now engaged shall be fully ripe for use; while capital, on the contrary, synchronizes labor and its fruits. We may measure a period of production by the interval which a particular capital-good thrusts between labor and its fruits. This is measuring it by the lapse of time between two different subjective experiences — namely, the sacrifice from making a thing and the personal gain from using it. In another way, we may measure the period by the duration of the instrument itself; and, if it is a tool for aiding labor, we have to divide the life of it as we divide the life of a human being, into a period of growth and a period of maturity. There is a time when it is taking shape under the hands of workmen; and there is a later time when it is fulfilling its destiny by helping other workmen to produce.

Capital-goods follow one another in an endless succession, and each one has its day. Capital, on the other hand, has no periods. It works incessantly; and there is no way of dividing its continuous life, except by using arbitrary divisions, such as days, months or years. There is nothing in the function of it that can make a basis for such a division as we can trace in the life of capital-goods. Capital, as such, does not originate, mature and then exhaust itself, giving place to other capital. Goods do this, but funds do not. No permanent capital ever ripens and begins to minister to direct wants: immaturity is of the nature of capital. Some raw materials, which are now capital-goods, do mature in this way; though in doing so they cross the division that separates producers' wealth from consumers' wealth; for when they are ripe and in use, they embody capital no longer.

Capital works without such periods.

In the reservoir that we have lately used as an illustration, every particle of water, separately considered, has its period of production. It enters the pond at one end and slowly flows through it; and here its function is to help in keeping the surface of the pond at a certain level — to keep what is called the head of water, that drives the wheel, at a certain height. In the end, it passes quickly through the wheel pit, and in an instant its productive function is over. That particular water has thus reached the end of a period. On the other hand, a water power, as such, has no periods, unless we make them arbitrarily by shutting the gates and stopping the mill at a certain part of the day. If the power be used to drive dynamos that work day and night, there are not even such arbitrary periods traceable in its action: the power is perpetual.

There has lately appeared in some discussions a use of the term "waiting," as a synonym for abstinence; and the waiting that is referred to connects itself with the periods that define the life of particular capital-goods. It is as though, when a man abstained, he began making for himself some instrument of production that would have its day and would, in the end, exhaust itself in the operation of giving to him consumers' goods. It is as though the man measured the length of time that it would take for the instrument to run its course, and then weighed and counted the cost of waiting for his consumers' goods through such a period. It is as though he could not have the consumers' goods till the period should be ended. After the instrument should have worn itself out, it would then be necessary to make a new one; and in doing this the man would again measure the period of its duration and would count the cost to himself of so much waiting. According

to this view, if the periods were long, there would
be a great deal of abstinence, or waiting, to be done
in connection with a particular bit of capital; while
if the periods were short, there would be comparatively little.

This resolving of abstinence into waiting for
consumers' goods, through the economic lifetime of
particular instruments of production, would be reasonable, *if* consumers' goods actually came in that
periodic way; but they do not. They come continuously; and they begin to come from the moment when
the instrument begins to act at all. From the moment when a gallon of water flows into the upper end
of a reservoir, the wheel at the lower end is made to
move by the overflow that there takes place. It is
wholly unnecessary for the owner of the mill to watch
the inflow, note the time of it and calculate how long
it will be before the particular gallon of water that
then flows in will reach the wheel pit. He is, in
fact, relieved from the necessity of doing any waiting
whatever, in connection with the career of that particular bit of capital-goods. At the beginning of the
period he has no occasion whatever to look forward to
the end of it, since nothing will happen at the end
that is not happening at every moment. There is a
perpetual shifting of the identity of the drops of
water in the pond, and there is a perpetual working of
the wheel; but, granting that the rate of the outflow
is given, the time that it takes for the water to get
through the pond signifies nothing.

A'''	B'''	C'''
A''	B''	C''
A'	B'	C'
A	B	C

When the raw material, A, starts on its economic
career, there is no occasion for calculating how long

Abstinence
is not wait-
ing through
such periods.

it will be before that particular material will become A''' and pass into the hands of consumers, to render the ultimate service for which it was designed. The moment that this A appears on the scene, some A''' has been released from the capitalist's hands and has entered the realm of consumption as an article of use. There has been an outflow of usable wealth. There is, then, no need of calculating at the outset the ripening time of A. The consumer has not to wait for it; and, even if the ripening were very remote, this fact would subject him to no inconvenience. It is an actual fact that the length of periods of production defined by the life of capital-goods is a matter of entire indifference, so far as the time at which consumers begin to get enjoyment out of the production is concerned. If a reservoir is large, it will take a certain gallon of water a long time to make its way through it; if the reservoir is small, it will get through more quickly, but it will do its work of moving the wheel, by causing an overflow, as soon in the one case as in the other. *The comparative length of the periods does not affect the time when the enjoyment of the fruits of labor begins;*

Let us, for another example, plant a forest of such slow-growing trees that it will take fifty years to bring one of them to the point of maturity, at which it will be ready for cutting. Let us arrange the trees in rows, and plant one row each year. During this part of the process there is waiting to be done; though this does not mean that we must wait for any return whatever. The young and growing trees have *value;* and this repays us for our labor, and does it promptly, as the labor proceeds. This return, however, comes in a form in which we cannot use it for consumption. We must at least wait for our firewood. After fifty years the cutting begins; and now all waiting is over. We may cut every year a row from the ripe end of the forest and plant a row at the

since capital makes the work and the ripening of its virtual product synchronous.

opposite end.   From this point on, the long period involved in the ripening of the trees loses its importance.   The setting out of a new row of trees is now a very different thing from the planting of the original row fifty years ago; for in a sense the present planting yields firewood at once.   It replaces the row that we now cut, and prevents this cutting from trenching at all on the capital represented by the forest; and it would have this effect if the trees required five hundred years for maturing instead of fifty, provided only that there were, in that case, five hundred rows in the forest.   As tree planters, even in that case, we should have no more waiting to do than we should now have if we could sow acorns, and, by magic, cause them instantly to become oaks five centuries old.   The time that will be required for the ripening of the particular trees that we are now setting out has lost its importance, since we are not dependent on those particular trees. If the forest will yield us any other mature trees in equal number, it is enough; and it will do this so long as we keep unimpaired our permanent capital, in the shape of the forest; and the planting of the new row and the ripening of the older ones, as they take place each year, have the effect of thus preserving the forest.   If the process goes on, it will continue to the end of time in the same condition — as a forest arranged in graded rows of different degrees of maturity.   So far as the industry that is spent on them is concerned, it is every year the same — planting one row, cutting one row, with no waiting for the newly planted trees to ripen.   All the waiting that was done was involved in getting this bit of arboreal capital into the condition in which it should perform its function.

If the industry represented by the column of A's,

in our recent table, were of such a kind that it took
fifty years for an A to become A''', and if, on the other
hand, a B could become B''' in one year, the first
industry, when once it should be in running order,
would impose no more waiting upon any one than
would the second. There would be daily a creation
of a new A and a new B; and there would be daily a
yielding up of an A''' and a B''' to consumption.
It is, in short, the *genesis of new capital* that requires
abstinence. The maintenance of it, the mere renewal
of the wasting tissue of it, does not require abstinence. The duration of particular tissues has no
effect on the amount of the abstaining. We have
seen that the making of a new instrument, to take
the place of an old one, imposes on the owner no such
sacrifice as that involved in making the original one;
for the reason that the instrument virtually, though
not literally, makes its own successor. The loom in
the factory that is worn out and is about to be replaced has, during its career, earned its share of
dividends for the stockholders of the mill and,
besides this, has earned for them a sum that will buy
a new loom. It is not necessary, therefore, to take
the cost of the new loom out of the stockholders'
incomes. That would impose on them the necessity
for a genuine act of abstinence, and that only would
do so. If the loom had not done what well-selected
machines always do, — if it had not created a fund to
replace itself, — then it might have been necessary
to assess the stockholders for the cost of new machinery. That would have made them abstainers;
for it would have caused them to trench upon their
incomes and to forego some consumers' goods.

Abstinence, then, *originates* new capital: it di-
verts income in money from the expenditure that
would secure goods for consumption to that which

secures instruments of production. This is the same thing as saying that abstinence consists in taking one's income in the form of producers' goods — electing to take draft horses instead of driving horses, trading vessels instead of steam yachts, factories instead of pleasure palaces, always as a part of the income of the men who do the abstaining. The effect of this is to put such a series of coördinated capital-goods as the trees, the gallons of water and the A's, etc., of our illustrations into working order.

since none of it is involved in maintaining a series of capital-goods. Once the abstaining is done, no further diverting of income is involved. The keeping up of the series of capital-goods is, in a sense, automatic. The mill, the ship, etc., virtually replace themselves as they are worn out; and these facts signify that, in a static condition, capital-goods would be created forever in limitless variety and number, but that no capital would be created. No net addition to the fund of productive wealth could then be called into existence. This takes place wholly under dynamic conditions, and it is a typical and important part of what constitutes economic dynamics.

Abstinence relinquishes an enjoyment forever. It causes an increase of capital, and is entirely a dynamic phenomenon. Abstinence is the relinquishment, once for all, of a certain pleasure from consumption and the acquisition of a wholly new increment of capital. The particular enjoyment that the man might have had, if he had spent his money for consumers' goods, he will never have if he saves it. He has abandoned it forever; and, as an offset for it, he will get interest. In the absence of disaster, the new capital will create its outflowing product thenceforth forever.

It is not, in economics, to be treated as morally meritorious. It has been customary to regard abstinence as an "economic merit" and to justify interest on the ground of it. In our view, such an argument is not necessary. If we reduce society to a static state and keep it so, every bit of capital that society owns will have inherent power to create wealth. If the men who own the capital keep it in their own hands, they will get the product of it; but if they loan the capital, they virtually sell the product of it, and they may ask for an equivalent, as they would do in making any other sale.

To every one who has a larger income than is necessary to sustain life, is presented the option of taking, as part of his income, something that will give pleasure for a time and then utterly perish or, on the other hand, of taking something that will never in itself give any pleasure, but that to the end of time will create, every year, a quantity of other things that will do so. It is nature, and not human institutions, that offers this choice. It is not a government that says to a solitary hunter, "You may pursue game on foot and catch what you can of it, or you may make a bow and thus secure more." It is the nature of the bow to add something to the hunter's product; and, moreover, it is the nature of it to add enough to the product to enable him to take time to make another bow, when the first one is worn out, and still have more game for his own use than he could have had otherwise. The laws of matter, in short, make capital productive. Being productive, it may make over its product to the owner directly or it may make it over to some one else, who will pay the owner for it. Paying interest is buying the product of capital, as paying wages is buying the product of labor. *The power of capital to create the product is, then, the basis of interest.*

The fact that the product of capital is salable, is of great importance in furnishing a motive for abstinence. There will come times when the owner cannot use it. Men perish, but capital remains; and, though it may pass into the hands of young children

Loan interest a payment for a product.

or of others who cannot personally use it, the inheritors will still get the value of the product, if they loan the capital and thus sell the product to others. This reveals the motive for accumulating productive wealth. It is to get an income that will never cease; and it is, therefore, to get an income of which all but a minute part will go to others than the one whose abstinence has created the capital. A fraction of itself the capital will earn every year; and, in the absence of disaster, it will do this to the end of time — infinitely longer, that is, than any man's life.

The salability of the product of capital a motive for abstinence.

In assuming the static condition of society, we assume also the absence of those disasters which would destroy capital; and we likewise assume a fixed amount of the capital itself and a fixed earning capacity. If this static condition continues, the rate of interest will stand forever at the rate current at the outset. This fixed condition cannot exist, however, unless the motive for saving something from men's incomes is not equal to the motive for spending it. In the static state there is no abstinence or creation of new capital; because, with the capital now on hand, men would lose more by foregoing pleasure and making their fund larger than they would gain by doing so. The whole subject of creating capital belongs, as has just been said, in the dynamic division of the science of economics. The process involves a perpetual comparison between present pleasures and an endless series of smaller pleasures, accruing mainly to the heirs of the man who abstains.

The static hypothesis excludes abstinence.

A recent and brilliant theory [1] connects the rate of interest with the length of what is called the period of production, or with that interval which, as we have noted, thrusts itself between the labor and the

Professor v. Böhm-Bawerk's theory of interest as dependent on periods of production.

[1] See Professor v. Böhm-Bawerk's *Positive Theory of Capital.*

concrete fruits of that particular labor, whenever a
man makes an instrument of production. When the
man begins to sharpen a stone for the making of a
rude hatchet, one of these periods is said to begin;
and when the tool has completely hacked itself to
pieces, leaving no other result than firewood for the
owner's comfort, the period is supposed to end. The
longer the average period becomes, the smaller becomes the interest. In reality, however, there is a
successor of this first hatchet to be considered. It is
the virtual product of the first one; and it continues
to embody the same bit of permanent capital that the
first one embodied. The period of production of this
capital is not bounded by the life of any one concrete
instrument. If the first hatchet was made by labor,
without any capital created still earlier, then the life
of the unit of productive wealth has a beginning; but
it has no end. Its existence is bounded on one side,
but not on the other. When we create a bit of new
capital, we start another endless period: we do not
lengthen any period that has already begun. We may
thus go on adding tool after tool to our equipment,
till we create the complicated mechanism with which
society is now working; we may continue the process,
and elaborate the mechanism without limit; but we
shall have added not one day to the period that inter-
venes between the abstinence that created the first tool
and the enjoyment that will mark the virtual end of
its economic career or, rather, that will mark the end
of the productive action of the true capital that the
first crude tool represents. There is, in fact, no such
end: with a single bit of permanent capital launched
upon its economic career, the lifetime of the capital,
in the static state, is endless.

The periods
virtually
limitless and
so incapable
of being
lengthened.

The one thing that we can do is to bring new bits
of capital into existence and to start them on similar

New bits of capital may be created and started on endless periods of existence.

endless periods. After the hatchet we may make a spade; and it, in turn, will have furnished us with another spade by the time its work is done. We shall thus find that we have started a second endless series of capital-goods; and this is saying that we shall have doubled the amount of our contribution to the capital in permanent existence. It is, in short, possible to add to the units of capital that are to exist through the ages; but it is not possible to add to the ages through which capital exists.

Limited periods defined by the duration of particular capital-goods;

If we disregard the action of an instrument of production, in virtually creating its own successor, and say that the period of production connected with such an instrument commences when some one begins to make it and ends when the owner throws it away, then we have periods of finite length to deal with; but now we encounter the difficulty that adding to the length of such periods does not necessarily add to the amount of capital in existence. If it does not do that, the increase in the average length of the periods does not have the effect that the brilliant Austrian economist attributes to this lengthening; for it does not reduce the rate of interest. This might, indeed, be high when the periods were long, and low when they were short. It is, however, when the *quantity* of permanent capital increases that interest falls. Many instruments that last a short time may embody as much capital as do a few that last a long time. If we were to substitute a dozen ferry-boats for a single bridge of solid masonry, we might have the same amount of capital that we had at the outset; and if all adjustments were quite natural, we should get the same rate of interest. Yet the periods of production — as defined, not by the lifetime of capital, but by that of particular capital-goods — would have grown appreciably shorter.

Professor v. Böhm Bawerk's view is that short periods are highly productive, that longer periods are less so, and that every addition to the average length of the periods adds less to the products of industry than did the preceding additions. In our view, every addition to the quantity of permanent capital in existence adds less to the product of industry than did the preceding additions. In our view, also, the average length of such periods as we are now considering might conceivably be made either longer or shorter, without affecting either the quantity of capital in existence or the rate of its earnings; for the period connected with the duration of capital itself cannot be lengthened. Here is a dilemma. If we measure productive periods by the duration of true capital, they are endless. If we measure them by the lifetimes of particular capital-goods, they may be lengthened or shortened without affecting the rate of interest. The deeper fact in the case is, that the periods which are measured by the duration of capital-goods have no significance as affecting the amount of waiting for the pleasures of consumption that a capitalist is supposed to do. Once the series of capital-goods is created and set working, there is no futher waiting to be done. In its permanent static function, capital does not make any one wait, although in its origin it causes its creator and owner to begin a period of endless waiting. Abstinence, in short, means a perpetual surrender of something, and not a mere deferring of it.[1]

[but their average length may be changed without affecting the rate of interest,]

[and without changing the amount of sacrifice incurred by capitalists.]

[1] The bringing of a new coördinated series of capital-goods into existence takes time. The original planting of the forest, in our illustration, involved waiting for fifty years before the cutting of the first row of trees could take place. This, however, is not the kind of waiting that is supposed to be involved in the use of capital. If no new capital were ever to be created, the vast fund that now exists would do its work forever. Interest would still be created;

and, if capital were loaned, interest would still be paid by one person to another.   In this there would, of course, be no waiting that would be like that which the original maker of the forest had to do ; and we have seen that this is the only waiting that is involved in the process.

Moreover, this waiting that takes place in the creating of a new coördinated series of capital-goods, like the forest trees, or the A's, the B's, and the C's of our more general illustration, is not a waiting for *income*.   The capitalist, even here, gets his income every year ; but he is forced to take it in the form of more capital.   The forest, when it has reached the degree of maturity at which cutting begins, is worth more than fifty times the amount that has been spent on it each year.   It is a bad investment if it is not then worth enough to pay interest on all the capital that has been sunk on it in the making.   The owner has had to forego dividends, in the shape of firewood, and to take what, in the case of corporations, are rated as additions to a surplus of real capital.   The capitalist who makes up his mind to secure such an instrument of production as a growing forest, a canal, a tunnel, or anything that takes time in the making, has to forego getting *an income in the form of consumers' goods*, while the instrument is making.   He does not, however, wait for his true income even during that time ; and after that he does not wait for consumers' goods or for anything else.   The instrument will, of itself, virtually create a new instrument to take its place when it is discarded : the series of capital-goods will be self-perpetuating.   All the while it will yield a net income, in goods for consumption, to its owners ; and this creation of income in this form will go on day by day, as the capital does its work. To-day's work will bring to-day's income, and to-morrow's will do the same.

It is worthy of notice that, so far as the periods which are bounded by the beginning and the end of particular instruments are concerned, a certain slow increase of their average length takes place, as capital increases, because this increase makes it desirable to substitute durable things for more perishable ones.   Some marginal capital may substitute a steel bridge for a wooden one.   But the duration of the *series* of steel bridges, which embodies the true capital, is not different from that of the wooden ones ; and the duration of any one bridge in the series, on the supposition that it replaces itself by special earnings, is a matter of indifference to the capitalist.   Moreover, the lengthening of the average period is not in proportion to the increase of capital.   On the quantity of this capital depends the productivity of the final unit of it.

In connection with the definitions of rent and interest given in the foregoing chapter, see Chapters XIX and XXII.

CHAPTER X

KINDS OF CAPITAL AND OF CAPITAL-GOODS

CAPITAL has been classified as "fixed" and "circulating." These terms properly describe two distinct parts of the permanent fund of true capital, rather than two kinds of capital-goods; and in proper thought and speech the terms are more frequently employed in this way. Thus, a merchant is said to have fifty thousand dollars in fixed capital and two hundred thousand in circulating. In scientific usage, however, these terms have been made to describe two varieties of capital-goods; and here again there has resulted some of that confusion which never fails to result where the two different conceptions that attach themselves to the term capital are used vaguely and interchangeably. It is particular kinds of instruments that, as economists have told us, are fixed capital, and certain other kinds that are circulating. Buildings, machinery and the like represent the former genus; and raw materials, unfinished goods, etc., the latter.

In a rude way, these terms describe the behavior of two different kinds of working instruments; and the scientific nomenclature has something to justify it. The plane that is in the cabinet-maker's hand may be fixed there, in that it does not need to leave the man and betake itself to another owner, in order to do its productive work. But the board that the

141

carpenter is planing may have to change ownership, since the chances are large that the man is working on an article for another person. In this way it comes about that some of the working instruments seem to do what may be rudely described as circulating, and others do not. In reality, however, there is no true circulation in the case of any of these instruments. A table, when it has been finished in the cabinet shop, may go straight to the house of the man who is to use it and stay there. All the circulating that it will have done is thus reduced to a single movement from one proprietor to another. Capital-goods, in fact, with a single exception, do not truly circulate. The exception is money; for coins, bank-notes, etc., necessarily pass from hand to hand indefinitely in performing their functions. A commodity of any other sort circulates as little as it can. There is, indeed, a waste in having it pass from hand to hand: the more directly it can go from the man who makes it to the man who is to use it, the better it is for society. It may be necessary for it to pass through a few changes of ownership in the making — and rather more of such changes are likely to be required where industry is highly organized than where it is not so; but in a given stage of social organization we have given methods of production. With the methods thus given, the less the article circulates the better.

Capital-
goods do not
truly circu-
late.

Another distinction — one that was once used by Mr. John Stuart Mill and is still common in economic treatises — asserts that fixed capital, meaning fixed capital-goods, can be used many times; while circulating capital can be used only once. Thus, the carpenter, it is said, may often use his hammer for a while and then lay it aside. He may keep it day after day, year after year, and drive countless nails with it; but, on the other hand, when he has once nailed together the boards that are to make a chest for some customer, he will part with the boards in their new form and will never see them again.   The materials are, then, said to be circulating capital, and the hammer, fixed capital.

This distinction is a vague one.   What constitutes a "time" — as the term is above employed — in the using of a tool?   It is obvious that a man can take a hammer, use it and then lay it aside as many times as he will; but he can treat raw materials in the same way.   He can begin working on a board, cease and begin again.   To have any value this definition should complete itself — as, in some forms of statement, it does — by saying that goods which constitute circulating capital cannot be used more than once *without undergoing a change of character.* Under the successive manipulations of the carpenter the rough board becomes, first, a smooth one, and then a part of a chest; while the plane and the hammer remain unchanged, except by unavoidable wear, however often they may be used.   If we thus define the "time" that a capital-good is used by some change that takes place in the condition of it, we shall have attained a measure of truth.   The goods that embody fixed capital can, in fact, be used repeatedly without any change in their economic status, while those that embody circulating capital acquire a new economic status at every use.   If we describe the character of this change of condition that such goods undergo, we shall make the essential and clear distinction between the one genus of capital-goods and the other.

There are two opposite ways in which capital-goods aid production.   Some things, like artisans' tools, help to fit for use the matter furnished by

An incomplete definition based on the number of times a thing can be used.

This definition completed.

nature. They have an active, rather than a passive function to perform, for they impart utilities to other

things. Machines that transform matter, vehicles that move it and buildings that protect it — all come in this category; and so do all appliances that, in the war between man and nature, range themselves on the side of man and help him to subjugate resisting elements to his use. These instruments constitute the active variety of concrete capital.

The materials on which implements work, on the other hand, are mechanically passive. They receive utilities, instead of imparting them ; they undergo modification, and themselves modify nothing. In the contest between man and nature, they range themselves on the side of nature and maintain a receptive attitude toward man and his active appliances. Cotton is thus passive, while the spindle is active ; bar iron is passive, while the roll and the hammer are active ; and thus throughout the field of industry the character of the process itself draws a line of demarkation between actively working instruments and passive materials — between man's weapons of offence and nature's subjects for defence, or her elements that are undergoing subjugation. The class of passive instruments includes not merely the crude matter with which industry begins, but the products that pass, in an unfinished state, from one working group to another. It includes not only ore, but iron, and not only wool, but yarn, cloth and even ready-made garments awaiting purchasers. It includes all the stocks of merchandise that, in the hands of dealers, are awaiting the minor utilities of form, place, etc., that are necessary in order to make them entirely ready for final consumption.

This distinction underlies the one usually made between so-called " fixed " and "circulating " capital.

Instruments that have been rated as fixed capital — buildings, tools, etc. — have active industrial functions to perform; while those which have been rated as circulating capital have passive ones. Practical thought, however, does not usually apply the terms fixed and circulating to capital-goods, but applies them to different portions of the permanent fund of true capital; and here, again, common usage bears the test of careful analysis. Concrete things, as we have seen, do not circulate in any true sense. They go through a series of hands into the possession of users, and remain there. There is, however, something that truly circulates. True capital passes through an endless series of outward forms. We have called it a permanent fund, and it is so; but it perpetuates itself only by passing continually out of one body into another. It lives by transmigration; and its movement must be as perpetual as its life.

True capital is fixed or circulating.

It should be noted, and in current discussions of this subject has often been noted, that the raw materials which enter into a tool make a transition from one variety of concrete capital to the other. The hammer that goes from the hardware merchant's shop to the blacksmith's forge is said to become fixed capital, after having been circulating capital. What is clear is that it thus takes on an active economic function, after having had a passive one. It pounds hot iron and imparts utility to it. The steel that is a capital-good of the passive kind when it is in a bar becomes active when it is in a hammer. At any particular time it is easy to see on which side of the line a thing belongs, for its function distinguishes it — it is either imparting utilities or receiving them. We shall, then, always designate the two kinds of capital-goods, according to their functions, as active and passive.

The case of materials that are destined to become tools.

Some idea of this distinction is probably present in the mind of nearly every one when, keeping the old nomenclature, he makes an effort to say what particular things are "fixed capital" and what things are "circulating capital." Instinctively he selects as an illustration of the former an engine, a tool, a building or something else that is not getting ready to be worn, or eaten or otherwise consumed in the direct gratification of wants. The essential thing about such an article is that it will never "ripen." It will never be like mature fruit, which is good for nothing but to delight a consumer's palate and replenish the wasting tissues of his body. Goods of the active kind never grow any riper in the performing of their functions. At the outset of their careers they are well removed from the possibility of being directly consumed, and they never get any nearer to it. They are always man's active auxiliaries in the onerous operation that he undertakes when he reduces the passive materials of nature to a serviceable condition. The mill will never be eaten, but it will always help a man to get something to eat.

The terms fixed and circulating, however, are not to be discarded, for there is an exact way to use them. We have said that they properly apply to two portions of the fund of permanent capital. There are, in fact, three parts of this general fund, each of which is unlike the others in the matter of circulation. There is one part of the fund of capital that is destined to circulate forever, as rapidly as its owners can make it circulate; there is another part that circulates as slowly as its owners can make it; and there is still another part that does not circulate at all. These two latter portions we may group under the term fixed capital, and call the first part circulating capital.

Goods that are "ripening" distinguished from those that are not.

A practical use of terms that is accurate.

If a business man were to say, "I have a circulating capital of fifty thousand dollars," he would mean
that the fifty thousand dollars are in the shape of
goods that he is interested in selling as quickly as
he can — finished goods in his warehouse or unfinished ones in his mill. He must put his particular
touch on them, thus imparting to them a certain
utility, and then make haste to be rid of them.
When he is thus rid of them, the capital that they
represented will have taken the shape of new goods
like them. The oftener this capital shifts its forms,
the better it is for the owner. The so-called "nimble sixpence" is profitable. If the man has a fixed
capital of fifty thousand dollars, this sum is in forms
in which it will stay as long as the man can keep it
there. The sooner the shoes in the factory are finished and sold, the better; but the machines that are
finishing them are not better for having to be quickly
shifted. The "sixpences" that are in them do not
gain by being nimble: it is the "slow shillings" that
are here the best.

Of the fixed capital of fifty thousand dollars some
is, perhaps, invested in land, and this will never wear
out; some is in buildings, and these will wear out
slowly; and some is in tools and machines, which will
wear out more rapidly; but the essential fact about
them is, that it is not good for production to have
them wear out at all. This sum of fifty thousand
dollars may be forced to change many of its forms of
investment; but the change is unwelcome to the
owner, and he will put it off as long as he can. He
must, however, come to it in the end. All capital, except the part that is invested in land, lives by transmigration. It must eventually cast off one set of
bodies and put on others. Not even in a massive
building will capital stay forever, since even this will

*Fixed capi-
tal changes
its forms by
incidental
wear; while
circulating
capital
changes
them by
doing its
productive
work.*

perish by degrees. It may be replaced by degrees, so long as the structure is kept in repair; but even this involves a shifting of the substance of it, and ultimately it will be destroyed and replaced altogether. Capital, then, does some circulating, even when it is embodied in substantial and active tools of production. The thing that separates fixed capital from circulating, it thus appears, is not the absolute length of time that the fund stays in one set of bodies: it is the fact that, in the one case, the operation of circulating is productive, and the man causes the movement to go on as rapidly as he can; while in the other case the circulating is not productive, but wasteful. The fact that a mill wears out, and has to be reconstructed or altogether replaced, does not, of itself, contribute to production. It is not a welcome fact in the experience of the owner of the mill, and he permits it to occur only so far as it is unavoidable.[1]

We are now prepared to test the relation of capital of every kind, as well as of capital-goods of every kind,

[1] The pure fund of capital may even stay longer in some kinds of passive capital-goods than it does in some active instruments. Emery, for example, is an active agent for polishing metals. While doing its work, it imparts utilities and does not receive them ; but it does not last long, and the metal that it is polishing may continue for a much longer time in the condition of a passive instrument. Coal, too, is an active instrument : it is not in the mill for the purpose of receiving any additional utility, but is there for the purpose of helping workmen to impart utility. It transmutes itself into power, and saves muscle ; but it perishes quickly. The essential fact is that it is for the interest of the owner to have his emery-wheels last as long as they will, and to have his coal keep up a fire as long as it will. Capital may stay for an instant in steam, and for an hour in the fuel that generates it ; but it also stays for weeks in unfinished products. It remains for years in machines, for decades in the buildings that house them, and forever in the land that the buildings now stand on. Fixed capital will always keep its forms as long as it can ; while circulating capital will change its forms as quickly as it can.

to wages. The separation of these two problems will save us from encountering difficulties that have often baffled inquirers and made absurdities plausible. In particular, we shall avoid all difficulty connected with either the wages-fund doctrine itself or any of the collateral fallacies that have attached themselves to it.

Is there any capital that is simply a "fund for the maintenance of labor"? Is it true, as Adam Smith said, and as a hundred others have repeated, that the natural way to originate capital is to heap up food enough to live on for a long period and then, during that period, to make something useful, like a boat, a hut or a tool? Is stored food the original capital? By our test, capital, if it is in what can be called food at all, must be in food-stuff that is really a raw material of industry. Wheat is a capital-good of the passive kind, for it receives utilities; and so do flour in the grinding, bread in the kneading, meat in the baking, etc. If it is not raw materials, but food in the full sense of the term, — something which neither receives utilities itself nor imparts them to other commodities, and which has nothing further before it but to be eaten, — it is not capital at all. The traditional way of studying the subject of capital has put before the mind, as the first and most typical form of it, something which has nothing to do but to exhaust itself in satisfying consumers' wants. If such a thing is to be rated as a capital-good at all, this can only be by that curious and perverse conception of the laborer as an engine, and food as the fuel that keeps it running. Meat is as coal for this wealth-creating machine. *Storing food a supposed method of originating capital.*

One obvious difficulty here is on the teleological side: What is the end of the whole economic process? We have said that it is utilization. It is the gratifi- *Defective teleology implied by this view.*

cation that shows itself in the nervous sensations, and the higher sensibilities of the consumer. If, afterward, the consumer works, this labor is not to be considered as impelled by the food that he has eaten; it is induced by the further food that he will afterward obtain and eat, and by very much besides mere nutriment that he will otherwise enjoy. The food that is to follow labor is one of the lures to labor and, in that sense, is the cause of it. The food that precedes the work is, in any normal teleology, the cause of nothing except an effect in the person of the eater. With the eating, one economic cycle ends; for the activities that have fallen within that cycle have produced their consummate effect. When, with the opening of another day, more labor begins, it is the starting of a new cycle; and this will end, as the former one ended, when the man consumes the fruits of it.

This, however, is not the most conclusive reason why food, as such, should not be regarded as a capital-good, or as a form of investment of any part of the permanent fund of capital. It may, indeed, be possible to carry through an entire study of economic science the conception of phenomena arranged in an abnormal order; and it may even be possible to do something in the way of solving practical problems, while one is working under the disadvantage of having his theories colored by an illogical teleology; but the conclusive objection lies in the fact that no such store of food for laborers anywhere exists. The recurrence of the winter season makes it necessary, indeed, to store raw materials for food during the time when the earth does not produce them. The material so stored belongs to the passive variety of capital-goods: in other words, it embodies some of the circulating variety of permanent capital. It

The supposed store non-existent.

receives utilities until it is finally made into food proper and served on the table. Wheat gets "time utility" by being stored in the elevators until it is wanted for grinding; and its value is all the while increasing, as it is when it gets form utilities in the grinding, place utilities in the carrying and further form utilities in the baking.

Wherever there is intermittent production, a store is, of course, needed to insure continuous consumption. The tank that is pumped full once a day may disc'.arge an unbroken stream during all the day; and in this way a store of such goods as are produced only at intervals may, in felicitous words suggested by President A. T. Hadley, "translate an intermittent flow of production into a continuous flow of consumption." In a similar way, a store of such goods may be accumulated by a slow and continuous production, and may then be used up by one quick act of consumption. The reservoir may be filled by a constant trickling stream, and may empty itself once a day in a single rush through the flood-gate. Fireworks may be made during the year and used on the Fourth of July. Here a continuous flow of production is translated into an intermittent consumption; and many kinds of goods that are usable only during one part of the year illustrate this process.

There are other stores for enabling consumption to go on continuously.

It is a store of a different kind to which the theory under consideration refers. Independently of any question as to whether production is continuous or intermittent, the view has been presented that capital is originally and typically a store to be drawn on for the sustaining of labor. With production and consumption going on steadily and at uniform rates from day to day, this feeding of men from a store must, as has been said, take place.

These not the stores referred to in the theory under consideration.

The storing that raw food-stuffs undergo, by

reason of the periodicity of agriculture, is, in its nature, in sharp contrast with that different kind of storing which Adam Smith and many others have cited as a typical mode of originating capital. This supposed store is made distinctly for "laborers," and it is made only by capitalists. The object of it is the using of the laborer as a piece of productive machinery. It is supposed to take place not at all because of the periodicity of the harvesting season, but because of the relation of capital to labor. Some one gets capital in the form of food, in order that he may feed a day laborer and thus obtain capital in some other form. The laborer is a transmuter of capital-goods; and such a storing of food as this, if it were necessary at all, would be necessary even if the season were such that we could plant wheat every day of the year and harvest some of it every day in the year.[1]

The relation of capital to labor in continuous production involves no such storing.

[1] Professor Cairnes, in his latter-day effort to galvanize the wages-fund doctrine into life, classified all capital as consisting in raw materials, fixed capital and the wages fund. If his terms be understood in the natural way, this classification involves adding together two qualities and one pure quantity in order to get a sum total. The wages fund is a quantitative fraction of all the capital in existence; while raw materials and fixed capital, in the sense in which Professor Cairnes uses the terms, are material forms of it — are kinds of capital-goods.

If, however, we interpret all three terms as referring to kinds of wealth, and not to quantities, we encounter another difficulty that is equally fatal. Let us make the term, wages, found in this connection, mean the kind of goods that laborers consume; and we now have, as the three varieties of capital-goods, raw materials, fixed capital (meaning active instruments of production), and, finally, the commodities that laborers consume. The third kind of capital-goods, however, nowhere exists. Instrumental wealth is all included in the first two classes. Every bit of it is either in the category of active instruments of production, or in that of passive instruments; it is either among the tools that transform, or among the matter that is in the transforming.

It is clear that Professor Cairnes could not have intended by the

A'''	B'''	C'''
A''	B''	C''
A'	B'	C'
A	B	C

Illustrative table.

Let A, again, be the raw material that will become successively A', A'' and A''', and in the last-named condition will be ready for consumers' use. Let the B's and the C's represent other articles in parallel stages of the producing process. There are men, both laborers and capitalists, who make the raw material, A; there are other men who transform A into A'; and each one of the transformations that follow is effected by one class of producers, with the needed tools, buildings and other appliances.

term wages fund to designate goods in retail shops ; for many of these are destined for the use of other persons than laborers. If they are neither raw materials nor fixed capital, they cannot find a place anywhere in Professor Cairnes's classification ; yet obviously they represent a part of the merchant's capital. A list of varieties of capital that was intended to include the whole of it, could not well omit those parts of the stocks of retail merchants that are designed to be sold to those men who are not laborers. If they are not raw materials, they are not forms of capital at all, according to Professor Cairnes's classification ; and if they are raw materials, then the parts of the stocks that workmen will buy come in the same class, and should not be counted a second time as the "wages fund."

Retail stocks are, in fact, passive capital-goods, receiving utilities. Thus, the shoe that is in a box on a merchant's shelves has by no means acquired its full service-rendering power until a foot is found that it fits, and the fabric that lies in a roll upon the counter will not develop its full utility until a customer comes whose taste it shall accurately gratify. All goods that are waiting to be parcelled in proper quantities and delivered at customers' houses, are waiting to have producers' finishing touches put upon them — are consumers' goods in the making, like any other raw materials.

An article by Professor S. N. Patten, in the *Quarterly Journal of Economics* for January, 1889, discusses admirably the case of food storing that is compelled by the intermittence of agriculture, and makes an acute study of the element, time, in connection with capital and its function.

There is a series of productive establishments, organized in a similar way, engaged in producing B and in transmuting it successively into B′, B″ and B‴. There is a similar series of producers creating and transforming the material, C. Each group consists of laborers, capitalists and *entrepreneurs*. A‴, B‴ and C‴ are goods in their final forms, quite ready for consumers' use; and this, in logical consistency, requires that they shall be at the very last point in their economic careers at which they are capital-goods at all. They are now in the retail shops waiting for purchasers. If they take one step more, they will cease to be capital-goods altogether and will become consumers' goods. Society, as the great producing organism, will have given them up, and individuals, as consumers, will have them. There is, then, no form of capital that is not an instrument in the hands of producing society. When the A‴, the B‴ and the C‴ are taken by individuals, as such, they thus become consumers' wealth.

If we adhere to our static hypothesis, and suppose that the quantity of capital and the quantity of labor remain unchanged, that the methods of industry remain the same, etc., all income must be regarded as ripened capital-goods of the passive variety. No one gets any income except what comes in the form of A‴, B‴ and C‴, fully ripened; for taking capital-goods as a part of one's income would be merely adding to capital, and this would be a dynamic process. Things which up to the point at which they become income have been receiving utilities, and so have been embodiments of circulating capital, make up every one's returns. Where, then, is the independent and specially stored food-fund for laborers? Nowhere; the difficulty in recognizing it as a variety of capital lies in the fact that it does not exist. The food, clothing and other income goods, for laborers as well as for other persons, consist in the ever-ripening A''', B''' and C'''. The material tissue of circulating capital wastes, as some of it ripens into income, but it is at the same time replenished by industry.

It is most remarkable that the theory which assumes that goods are somewhere stored for the use of laborers should not notice the fact that, if this were indeed true, there would have to be a similar storage of income goods for the use of capitalists. The capitalist who is helping to make the raw material, A, must have his daily income in the shape of A''', etc. He is making raw goods and using ripe ones every day; and his position is exactly analogous to that of the laborers who are working with him. Neither he nor they can eat, wear or otherwise use the crude stuff that they are getting out of the ground. Three distinct productive periods must elapse before this identical material will be usable, yet they must live in the interim. They must all, capitalists and laborers alike, have a supply of A''', B''' and C'''. Must it be stored for them, to supply their needs until their own raw stuff shall be ripened? We have answered that question. Of the constantly emerging A''', B''' and C''', a share goes instantly to the capitalists and the laborers at A. In neither case is any waiting necessary. The point that we are now insisting on is that, if a store were needed to supply the wants of the laborers in the sub-group that makes A, it would be needed, for precisely the same reason, to supply the wants of the capitalist at A. The static hypothesis that capital is not increasing means, as we have just said, that the whole net income of the capitalist class is used up daily in the form of consumers' goods. It means, also, that capital is not diminishing; and that, therefore,

If the store existed, it would be for capitalists as well as for laborers.

only the income of the capitalist, and not his permanent fund of productive wealth, is available to supply his wants. He has, indeed, an ultimate safeguard against starvation, which the laborer lacks; for by changing his plan of life he can use up his capital. But naturally he does not do this, and the static hypothesis requires that he shall not do it. In this condition, he needs a store of subsistence goods, *if the laborers need one.* For the reasons that have been fully stated, however, neither of them needs such a store.

Goods that are receiving utility, on the one hand, and goods that are imparting utility, on the other, exhaust the entire class of capital-goods. As they come and go in their endless succession, they perpetuate the entity to which is here given the distinctive name, capital.

CHAPTER XI

THE PRODUCTIVITY OF SOCIAL LABOR DEPENDENT ON ITS QUANTITATIVE RELATION TO CAPITAL

THROUGHOUT this work the thing described by the term, capital, will be what a business man understands by that word. It is a permanent fund of productive wealth, and is what is commonly meant by "money" invested in productive goods, the identity of which is forever changing. The articles that embody the fund are, like particles of water in a river, vanishing things; while the fund itself, like the river, is the abiding thing.

It is a striking fact that labor also is a permanent force — a fund of human energy that never ceases to exist and to act. Men are as perishable as are capital-goods, but labor is as permanent as is capital. The problem of wages has to do with the continuous earning power that the imperishable agent, labor, possesses and will possess. The question is, What will labor create and get during this year, next year and all the following years? If the rate of wages is hereafter to rise, this means that labor will acquire, as the years pass by, an increasing power of production. The attention of practical men is directed to the interests, the rights and the struggles, not of particular laborers, but of labor in its permanence.

This enduring agent is not an abstract or an immaterial thing any more than is capital. We do

Labor a permanent force.

157

not view it as an action apart from an actor, for it consists of men in action. Moreover, the men, in their capacity of consumers, get the benefit of their work, and they have the privilege of deciding what forms their work shall take. Just as a capitalist determines what kinds of goods shall constitute his productive wealth, so the laborer decides into what kind of productive action he shall put his bodily and mental powers. He decides, that is, whether he will make of himself a farmer, a miner, a weaver or a printer. The man as a consumer is the owner of the man as a producer. He will put his powers into the particular kind of activity that, in his view, gives a promise of yielding the largest product.

As the generations come and go, the forms that labor takes steadily change. The conditions of the year 1800 demanded certain kinds of labor; those of 1900 demand different kinds. There are youthful laborers coming continually on to the industrial stage; and, when the conditions of their time are akin to those of their fathers' time, they may learn their fathers' trades. Even then, however, they usually practise the trades in new ways; and where the conditions require it, they master wholly new acts. Labor, the permanent personal agent, is as changeful in its forms as is capital, the permanent material agent. As a worn-out instrument may be succeeded by one of a different kind, so may a retiring laborer be followed by one who will do a different kind of work. Men come and men go, but work continues forever. Because the men are changing, however, the kinds of work change also.

There are, then, two permanent entities combined in the industry of the world. The one is capital, or the wealth that continues forever by casting off and renewing material bodies — capital-goods. The

Forms of labor changeful.

other is labor, which continues in a similar way. It is represented to-day by one set of men, and to-morrow by another. Both of these permanent agents of production have an unlimited power of bodily transmutation: they are changing their embodiment every year and every day.

What has here been termed economic dynamics compels both labor and capital to go through this change. With new wants to be gratified, men must make new kinds of consumers' wealth; and they must do this by working in ways and with instruments that are unlike the old. Mechanical inventions alter the forms of labor and of capital. The centralizing process that supplants many small shops by one great factory, and then gathers many such factories under one management, does the same thing. Labor, as such, never stops; but certain forms of it stop and are succeeded by others. Capital never goes out of existence, but certain forms of it perish and are followed by others. These permanent producing agents are in endless self-transmutation. *Dynamics compels both labor and capital to change their forms.*

What has already appeared, and what greatly concerns us at this point, is the fact that any increase or diminution in the amount of labor that is employed in connection with a given amount of capital causes that capital to change its forms. Where there is a capital of five hundred dollars for each worker, that fund is in one set of forms; and where there is a capital of a thousand dollars per man, it is in a different set. Now, the labor changes its forms in the same way. The men who are working with the smaller capital perform one set of acts, and those who have the greater capital in their hands perform another set. Arts are always practised in new and changed ways, when capital multiplies itself and takes the shape of costly and elaborate machinery. That

A change in the relative amounts of the two agents causes changes in the forms of both.

the relative *amounts* of labor and capital should change, means that the *forms* of both should change: it means that each agent must fit itself to the other's requirements. Mutual adaptations are the rule, wherever the two agents are combined.

We are now prepared to test the productive power that resides in the final increment of each of these permanent agents. With a force of a thousand men, working for decade after decade, with neither diminution nor increase, and with a capital of a million dollars, sustaining itself also without deduction or enlargement, how large is the product that a unit of labor will produce? The answer to this question, which furnishes the law of wages and

The final productivity test is to be applied to labor and capital as permanent agents.

interest, is: *These incomes are fixed by the final productivity of labor and of capital, as permanent agents of production.*

There is a formula which has been used to explain the rent of land that we may well apply in a new way. We may have a simple illustration, by disregarding, for a moment, the existence of that auxiliary capital which labor needs in tilling the soil. We will suppose each worker to carry with him a simple tool, of which the cost is too small to represent any appreciable amount of wealth. Practically empty-handed, then, this labor applies itself to a piece of land, and creates an income in the shape of a crop. This reduction of the auxiliary capital to a practical zero, be it noted, affects no principle that we are studying; for the thing that we have to prove could be established perfectly well, if we used a

The principle illustrated by applying empty-handed labor to land.

more cumbersome illustration, by assuming that the workers were supplied with a complicated outfit of tools, seed, live stock, etc. The product that can be traced to the last unit of labor applied to land affords, however, the most available, because the most simple, illustration of the principle of the final productivity of labor.

It is a static standard of wages that we are now seeking. The field and the working force are assumed to remain unchanged, while methods and environment also remain constant. What permanent income are we, under these conditions, to attribute to the final unit of labor? We apply the simplest test that can be made, when we take one man from the force and so dispose of the remaining men that no appreciable disarrangement of the industry results from this withdrawal. The field is still tilled in its entire area; but it is tilled less completely and the crop is, by a certain amount, reduced. On the other hand, we may add a man to the force and rearrange the company so that no misadjustment is occasioned by the addition. A more intensive cultivation of the field now results, and in consequence there is a definite enlargement of the product.

A man may be added to a working force or taken from it without wasteful disarrangement.

The amount that is taken from the crop, when one cultivator is withdrawn from the force, measures the effective productivity of every laborer of like personal capacity. It makes no difference which of such laborers is selected for the test. The withdrawal of any one makes the force by one unit smaller; and what we wish to measure is the reduction of the crop that the taking of a unit from the working force occasions. No man can get more than his presence adds to the product that the land and the labor could create without him.

The effect on the crop measures the effective productivity of every man.

It may be that there are differences in the kinds of work that different men do; and one man may do what is indispensable to the securing of any crop whatever, while another does what is of far less consequence. The man who drops seed cannot be dispensed with; but the one who gives to the land the

Kinds of work that are unlike in absolute importance are equal in effective productivity.

final touches that prepare it to receive the seed can be spared with less loss. Yet the one laborer is of no more effective consequence than the other, so long as they are interchangeable. Let the seed sower depart, and the other man will be put in his place. The crop will be the same as it would have been, if the worker in the less important place had been the one to depart. In effect, the products of all men who are personally equal and interchangeable are alike. The product that can be attributed to any one, as due solely to his presence, is tested by taking him out of the force, rearranging the remaining workers and letting only the least important kind of work go unperformed.

Now, if we can assume, for a moment, that this territory is a state by itself, and that workers do not come to it from other industrial fields and do not go from it to others, the rate of wages is fixed by what one man on this isolated plantation is effectively worth. A man can claim, not what men are paid somewhere else, but what he virtually gives to his employer here. Only under such circumstances are wages fixed by the product that is attributable to a final unit of labor.

These principles illustrated in a self-contained field.

If the assumed reduction in the working force be permanent, so that the force forever continues smaller, the crop will amount to less, year by year, by reason of the reduction. A similar test might have been made by adding a unit of labor, instead of taking one away. In that case, if the addition be permanent and the force always continues by one unit larger, the average crop will be greater. This enables us to measure the permanent income that is imputable to one unit of labor.

It is the "final" productivity of labor, as thus measured, that fixes wages. This term, final, implies an order of succession: it signifies that there is a first, a second and a last unit of labor to be distinguished. By the common method of illustrating the law of value, there is a final unit of a kind of commodity consumed by one person. We give to him one article of a kind, then another and after a while, a last one; and we discover that they are less and less useful to him, as the series is carried toward completion. The last unit has less of utility than any of the others. By a law that Austrian studies have made familiar, the value of any article in this series of goods of one kind is fixed by the utility of the final one — final utility universally gauges value.

The term final productivity implies an imaginary series.

This principle we have undertaken to apply to the productive powers of different agents of production, and just now we are applying it to labor. We may, if we wish, arrange in a similar imaginary series workmen who are of like personal capacity and can be changed, the one for the other. We shall then introduce the men into the field one at a time, and see what product is virtually created by each of them. With one man in a field of a given size, a certain crop will, on the average, be secured. With two men, however, the crop will not be doubled; for the second worker will create less than the first one. This reduction in the productivity of successive units of labor, as they are set tilling a field of fixed extent, furnishes the basis for a general law.

A series of laborers would get diminishing returns.

It is, of course, true that, if two men can combine their labors so as to assist each other in essential ways, such a diminution of their specific productivity may not appear. Two men make possible a rudimentary organization of labor; and this is a new influence, of which a full study must take account. If we start with one man quite alone on a very large tract of land, he may work at a certain disadvantage; and a second man may so far remove this disadvantage as to insure more than a double crop. A third, a fourth and a fifth man might contribute to the perfection of the organization, and so hold somewhat in abeyance the law of diminishing returns that we have cited; but in the end the law would assert itself. When there are twenty men in the field, for example, the addition of a twenty-first will have no appreciable effect in improving the organization; while, on the other hand, it will overcrowd and overwork the land. The mere effect of this crowding is what we now have to study. We may disregard the gain that would come in the earlier stages of the process, through the organization of labor; for in a large force it is the last unit which fixes by its product the standard of wages; and what this unit does is not needed for the perfecting of the organization.

Improved organization may at first counteract or conceal the diminution.

In studying the mere effect of crowding the land with laborers, it is better at first to disregard the gain that comes by organization. This gain we have to study by itself, in that division of the theory which is to be devoted to economic dynamics. Organization, like mechanical invention, simply improves the conditions under which the successive units of labor are applied. It is as though the new men brought better tools with them. If we are to isolate and measure the mere effects of overcrowding the land, we must, however, assume that this and all other conditions remain for the time being unaltered.

Land crowding of itself reduces returns.

We will, then, assume that one man goes into a large field, then another and another, till in the end there are twenty. We will assume that their methods of tilling the soil remain unchanged, and we will disregard the enlarged power that, in the early stages of the growth of the force, they may derive from coöperation. The whole process of thus building up a working force is, of course, imaginary: it represents an unreal and one-sided process in economic dynamics. Nowhere can we ever find such an experiment. A farmer would never actually place one man on two hundred acres of land, leave him there for a year and measure the crop; and then, putting an additional man there in the following year, measure the increase of the crop. He would certainly not continue such an experiment for twenty years and so make of his farm a laboratory where the economist might see, in complete operation, the law of diminishing returns from land under tillage. Having twenty men at work on the two hundred acres, the farmer would, indeed, ascertain in some experimental way how large a product is imputable to the twentieth one. He would test the final productivity of labor; and he would find that the product due to the twentieth man's presence is less than would be the product that one man would have called into existence, if he had entered the field when it was less crowded. This fact is amply attested by experience, is confirmed by deductive reasoning and is one of the undisputed truths of economic science. Land of a given area and quality yields less and less per man, as more and more men are set tilling it. The simplest and most natural mode of illustrating this law is to imagine the men placed in a field, one at a time, till there are twenty of them at work. Each of them is thus seen to add less to the crop than did his predecessor. The product that can be attributed to any one man grows steadily less, as the force is thus built up to its full complement; and the amount that is due to the twentieth man is least of all. If

The actual building up of a working force by units impossible.

all men must accept as pay what this man produces, we have the solution of the problem of wages.[1]

In a static state the working force continues forever, without addition or diminution; and methods and conditions of production remain forever the same. The *personnel* of the force undergoes the change of identity that must occur as one man dies and another replaces him; but the laboring force, as such, suffers no change. The processes and the environment of the labor are fixed. There is no building up of the force from a small beginning, and no change in its *per capita* product. Yet the earnings of the men are fixed by the law of final productivity. This means, in reality, that every laborer gets what would be lost to the employer if any one man now in the force were to stop working. One way of measuring this final product of the labor, and at the same time presenting to the mind a principle that governs the amounts of it, is to imagine that the force grows, unit by unit, to its present size. Each unit, when it adds itself to the force, is for the time being the final one; and it transiently sets the standard of pay. But when the last unit comes, its product becomes the permanent standard; as the force is not further enlarged, and the pay of the men is not again changed. The whole process is imaginary; but it illustrates two principles that together control the fortunes of laboring humanity, namely : (1) At any one time wages tend to equal the product of the final unit of labor; and (2) this product becomes smaller or larger as, other things remaining the same, the force

The force unchanging in a static state; its pay subject to the law of final productivity.

Two actual laws illustrated by the imaginary force that grows from a single unit.

[1] The possibility that in the early stages of the growth of the laboring force, the diminution of the returns might be counteracted by improved combinations among the men, or by improved methods of tillage, needs to be considered, as do other dynamic influences, in a separate division of economic theory.

becomes larger or smaller. The former principle is static, and governs wages in each period; while the latter is dynamic and, with other dynamic principles, controls the future of the laboring class. Mere growth of population, without further change, is an impoverishing influence.

How is it, now, that the product which is attributed to the last man fixes the pay of all the men? Here we must be careful to make the conditions of our illustration conform to the facts of life. A farmer hires his men in a general market, and pays a rate of wages that the market has in some way established. He then puts the men into his field until, by the law of diminishing returns, the product of the final man has become so small that it yields wages only. The rate of pay, be it noted, is fixed in the main outside of this farm; and the final productivity of labor on the farm is made to conform to this rate of pay. *On a single farm the final productivity of labor conforms to the general rate of wages.*

What if there were no outside market in which the rate of pay might be fixed? What if the farm were the whole industrial field? This supposition would simplify industry, so as to make it grotesquely unlike the actual world; but it would place in the clearest light the law of wages that is at work in the actual world. If the farm were an isolated society, not selling its products and buying others, and not importing labor at a rate of pay that was fixed outside of its confines, then the rate of pay would be fixed within the farm itself, and by the final productivity of the labor there employed. *In a society as a whole, the rate conforms to the final productivity of labor.*

Let there, for example, be an island of the sea not reached by ships, and having a fixed amount of land and an unchanging population; and let it have no industry that needs to be considered except agriculture. We need no one to tell us that this state is imaginary and grotesquely unlike the world as it is.

It is, nevertheless, like the world in this vital particular, that what is produced by the final man in such an isolated population sets the wages of all men there. The effective value of any man to his employer is what would be lost if he were to cease working. That amount — the effective product of any man in the force — sets the standard to which the pay of labor generally conforms. There is now no consulting an outside labor market there is no importing into this community a rate of pay that in some way is fixed in an environing world. We have made the community on the island to be a world by itself, and have found that any such society gives to all laborers, as their natural reward, what the final laborer produces.

We will next, to complete our illustration, make our plantation resemble the world in this essential respect, that it is a completely organized society. We will make it vast in extent and will cause the occupants of it to carry on, not agriculture only, but every industry. We will give to the community its complement of smiths, carpenters, weavers, shoemakers, miners, printers, etc. We will supply the needed capital and see that it takes the needed forms. We will make sure that each particular industry has its proper part of the whole social fund, and we will carefully retain the condition originally assumed — that the community is isolated from all others. It is a world in itself, and there is no other accessible

This rule prevails in the economic world.

world from which it can derive its standard of wage. What, then, fixes the rate of pay for labor? Clearly the final productivity of labor, as it is employed in connection with the total fund of productive wealth in all the affiliated groups and sub-groups, or specific industries. The product created by a final unit of social labor sets the standard of wages.

There is, in fact, no other standard to which pay can conform. When we were speaking of a farmer who obtained his laborers from an environing region of shops, railroads, etc., we found that he would pay to his men what the shops, etc., pay; and he would employ so many of them that the last one set working on the limited piece of land in the farmer's possession would earn his wages only. Here the last man's product does not set the rate of wages, but simply conforms to the rate that is imported from without. Other standards for general wages impossible. In a society that is a world in itself, the rate of wages cannot be a borrowed one. The men cannot be lured into society from without and paid enough to induce them to come, since there is no *without* in the case. The men are in the society from the first, and must stay there; and all of them must be employed. Every one of them who offers himself to an employer has something to offer to that employer, since he can increase the output of goods in any establishment to which he may go. At some rate the employer will take him; and if competition is perfect, the rate will actually conform to the amount that the man's presence adds to the product of the mill, farm or shop in which he may be set working. If the man gives to an employer more than he gets from him, an inducement is offered to other employers to take him at a better rate of pay. Men in other occupations are in the same strategic situation, and the wages of social labor equal the product of a composite final unit of it.

How is this product to be measured? Take away one social unit of labor, and see what is lost by the withdrawal of it; or add one such unit, and see what is gained by the addition. In either case, it is possible to note the amount of product that is separately due to a unit of labor and to no other agent. Let us, then, withdraw what we have called a social unit

Character of the final unit of social labor.

of labor. This is a composite unit, consisting of some labor from every industrial group that the community contains. We will take away cultivators of the land, smiths, carpenters, weavers, etc., in carefully adjusted proportions, causing a final unit of labor to vanish from every specific industry.

As we take away laborers, we leave the capital everywhere unchanged in amount; but we change the forms of it in every one of the industries, so as to make it accurately fit the needs of the slightly reduced working force. There must be, if our test is perfect, no disarrangements caused by the withdrawal of the unit of social capital. The whole of that capital must continue to be utilized; and, therefore, when the departing men throw down their tools, these must not be left on the ground, as representing so much wasted capital. If this were done, the departure of the men would mean, not only loss of the product of a unit of labor, but the further loss of so much of the products as was attributable to the tools that the men were using. The remaining men may have no need of the abandoned tools themselves, but they do need the capital that these implements embody. That we must save, and we do it by the transmuting process already described. The abandoned pick and shovel become, by a miracle of transmutation, an improvement in the quality of a horse and cart. There are fewer men digging; but they have as much capital as ever, and they have it in a form in which, with their reduced numbers, they can use it. Similarly, in the mill there are abandoned machines, and the remaining workers cannot set them running. The capital that is in them can be utilized, however, if it will transform itself into an improvement in the machinery that the remaining workers use. Everywhere there are fewer in-

The withdrawal of it causes forms of capital to change.

struments, but better ones; and the capital, as such, is not reduced by a jot or a tittle.

This hypothesis it is that tests the productive power of a unit of empty-handed labor — that reveals the actual standard of wages. If a hundred men constitute the unit of social labor that we have described, and if their departure reduces the product of all industries by a total amount that can be stated as two hundred dollars, then that is the product that can be attributed solely to the work of the hundred men. If they are typical men of equal working powers, two dollars a day make one man's natural wages. *The withdrawal then tests the productivity of labor itself.*

How ultra-imaginary is such a test of the productive power of labor! How far beyond possibility is the actual creation of such a microcosmical society as our assumed plantation would constitute! It would, indeed, be impossible to apportion the labor rightly among all the different industries that, in a laboratory test of the wage law, would have to be represented, or to withdraw exactly the right number of men from each of the industries, when the final unit of social labor should be taken away. How nearly unthinkable is that essential part of the test, the prompt transmuting of the capital into the forms that the reduced working force would require!

Yet all this is done in actual industry: the world daily accomplishes this miraculous thing, automatically and without observation. By forces that run through its economic system, it gives to each industry its due portion of the whole social capital. It puts that portion, in every case, into the forms that the men of the group require. Wherever men become scarcer or more abundant, it alters the forms of the capital to fit their needs. It makes an unconscious but real test of the final productivity of labor; *The law thus illustrated is real.*

for it reveals what the world would lose, if a unit of labor were to withdraw itself and if the capital were still to be fully utilized; and it makes the pay of labor conform to this standard. In this process is involved a permanent fund of social capital, a permanent force of social labor and an automatic adjustment of wages in each particular part of the industrial system, to conform to the final productivity of labor as a whole.

NOTE. — If in this static study we could allow the eye to range forward and take in a view of the part of the field where changes are going on, we should see that the very formula that describes the present natural standard of wages reveals one of the cardinal influences that cause this standard to rise. If capital becomes abundant, while the supply of labor remains stationary, the same effect is produced as if the supply of labor diminished, while that of capital remained unchanged. It is the reverse of the effect that comes from crowding an environment with workers, and it makes the efficiency of one man grow larger, instead of smaller. The richer the world is in capital, the richer the worker is in productive power. Into this region of thought we may not now go ; but what we may properly note is that at every point in the period of growing wealth, labor will find its natural rate of pay fixed by the law that we have now before us. Fifty years hence wages will be higher than they are to-day ; but they will be fixed by the final productivity of labor in that later and more fruitful industrial state.

CHAPTER XII

FINAL PRODUCTIVITY THE REGULATOR OF BOTH
WAGES AND INTEREST [1]

INSTEAD of the plantation in our late illustration,
we will think at once of the world, with its innumerable industries and its complete outfit of agents
and appliances. It is, of course, isolated, since
neither products, workers nor instruments can migrate to it or from it; and the rate of wages that it
affords must be determined entirely within itself.

We can now derive an advantage from the imaginary process of supplying the labor for this community, unit by unit, provided that we can do this
without getting the impression that the action of the
law of final productivity depends on it. This is
only one way of illustrating the action of that law.
The actual and practical test of the productive power
of one unit of labor is made, if one unit only is taken
out of a complete force and if the ensuing reduction
of the product is noted. This test we have already
applied. It is for the sake of having a more complete
view of the action of the law of final productivity
that we now build up a working force, unit by

[1] The theory advanced in this chapter and the two following
ones was first published in the *Quarterly Journal of Economics*,
in two articles entitled, respectively, "Distribution as Determined
by the Law of Rent" (April, 1891), and "A Universal Law of
Economic Variation" (April, 1894).

unit, leaving capital unchanged in amount, though changing in its forms with the arrival of each new unit of labor. We will let a thousand workers constitute each increment of labor, and let farmers, carpenters, smiths, weavers, printers, etc., be represented in it in carefully adjusted proportions. Every occupation must have its representatives, and the comparative number of them must be fixed according to a law that it will soon be our duty to study. All that we now need to know about this law is, that it so apportions labor among the different groups and sub-groups that the productive power of labor is brought to a certain uniformity in the various occupations. Common and adaptable labor is made to produce as much in one sub-group as in another.

An illustrative society created by a succession of composite units of labor.

Give, now, to this isolated community a hundred million dollars' worth of capital, and introduce gradually a corresponding force of workers. Put a thousand laborers into the rich environment that these conditions afford, and their product *per capita* will be enormous. Their work will be aided by capital to the extent of a hundred thousand dollars per man. This sum will take such forms as the workers can best use, and a profusion of the available tools, machines, materials, etc., will be at every laborer's hand. If we were to try to imagine the forms of productive wealth that such a condition would require, we should bring before the mind a picture of automatic machinery, of electrical motors and of power obtained from cataracts, tides and waves. We should see chemical wonders performed in the preparing of materials, the creating of soil and the like. We should place the worker in the position of a lordly director of natural forces so great and so varied that they would seem more like occult powers of the air than like tools of mundane trades. All this, how-

Forms taken by a vast capital used by few workers.

ever, is only a picture of what would be slowly and remotely approached, if capital were quietly to outgrow population and were to reveal its power of taking the forms that the needs of the relatively few workers would require. Something like this is the goal of natural economic tendencies.

Add, now, a second thousand workers to the force; and, with the appliances at their service changed in form — as they must be — to adapt them to the uses of the larger number of men, the output per man will be smaller than before. This second increment of labor has at its disposal capital amounting to only half a hundred thousand dollars per man; and this it has taken from the men who were formerly using it. In using capital, the new force of workers goes share in share with the force that was already in the field. Where one of the original workers had an elaborate machine, he now has a cheaper and less efficient one; and the new workers by his side also have machines of the cheaper variety. This reduction in the efficiency of the instrument that the original worker used must be taken into account, in estimating how much the new worker can add to the product of industry. His presence has cheapened the instruments used by the first set of workers and has taken something from their efficiency. His own share of the original capital, as it is made over to him by the workers formerly in his immediate part of the field, consists also in the cheaper and less efficient instruments. For two reasons, therefore, he brings into existence less wealth than did one of the first division of laborers.

All over the field the hundred million dollars has, as it were, stretched itself out to meet the needs of a double force of workers. Of some kinds of tools there are now twice as many as before; but they are

Nature of the changes in these forms caused by additions to the number of laborers.

all less costly and less efficient. Cheaper buildings and more of them, is the rule. Railroads have more curves and grades, less durable bridges and, in general, less substantial plants. There are two sailing vessels, where there was formerly one steamer; and there are two wooden ships, where there was one of steel. The capital of the community, without changing in amount, has taken a form that is more extended than its earlier one — the instruments are everywhere multiplied and cheapened.

We must be careful as to the arithmetic of the change. The product that can be attributed to this second increment of labor is, of course, not all that it creates *by the aid of the capital that the earlier division of workers has surrendered to it;* it is only what its presence adds to the product previously created. With a thousand workers using the whole capital, the product was four units of value; with two thousand, it is four plus; and the plus quantity, whatever it is, measures the product that is attributable to the second increment of labor only. There is a minus quantity to be taken into account in calculating the product that is attributable to the final unit of labor. If we take, first, all that it creates by the aid of the capital that is surrendered to it, and then deduct what is taken from the product of the earlier workers and their capital by reason of the share of capital that they surrender to the new workers, we shall have the net addition that the new workers make to the product of industry.

With the vast capital utilized, the product that the new unit of labor adds to the product that could have been had without it will be very great, though it will be less than was created by the first unit. Every man in the new working force produces enough to rival a fortunate gold hunter. Add increment

The product of the final increment of labor not all that it creates with the aid of its share of capital.

after increment of labor, till the force is decupled; and the product that is due to the last of the additions is still great. Continue to add to the force till it numbers a hundred thousand, having still the hundred million dollars' worth of capital, but in changed form. The workers are then about as well equipped as are those of the United States at the present day. The last increment of labor may be supposed to add to the product that the society would have realized without its aid about as much as a working force of the same size, in this country, could separately create, by adding itself to the force already employed.

If, now, this hundredth increment of labor is the last one that the isolated society contains, we have the law of wages. We have set the population working till no reserve exists from which we can get more. The last composite unit of labor — the final division of a thousand men — has created its own distinguishable product. This is less than the product that was attributable to any of the earlier divisions; but, now that this section of the laboring force is in the field, no division is effectively worth any more than is this one. If any earlier section of the working force were to demand more than the last one produces, the employer could discharge it and put into its place the last section of men. What he would lose by the departure of any body of a thousand men, is measured by the product that was brought into existence by the last body that was set working.

Each unit of labor, then, is worth to its employer what the last unit produces. When the force is complete, no one body of a thousand men can withdraw without lessening the product of the whole society by the same amount that we have attributed

The final product of labor only the test of all wages.

to the one that we last set working. The effective value of any unit of labor is always what the whole society with all its capital produces, minus what it would produce if that unit were to be taken away. This sets the universal standard of pay. A unit of labor consists, in the supposed case, of a thousand men, and the product of it is the natural pay of a thousand men. If the men are equal, a thousandth part of this amount is the natural pay of any one of them.

We are seeking, of course, a static standard of wages; but the process that gradually builds up a force of laborers from a thousand to a hundred thousand, and causes capital to modify its forms as the increase of the force goes on, is not a static process. It is a dynamic operation which brings the working force up to its static complement. From the time that the force is complete, however, we leave it unchanged: we let the static condition thus attained continue forever. The importance of going through the illustrative dynamic process, and making up the permanent force unit by unit, lies in the clear view that this gives of the product that can be attributed to the "final" unit.

No unit of labor final in point of time.
Actually, no unit is last in time. The hundred thousand men, with the hundred million dollars' worth of capital, work on year after year, and no one division of a thousand can be singled out as constituting the particular division whose product fixes wages. Any one such body of men is always worth to its employers what the final division would produce, if we were to set them working in such an order of succession as, for illustration, we have described. That the men will get this amount, is insured by employers' competition. The final division of a thousand men has in its hands a certain potential

product, when it offers its service to employers.   If one set of *entrepreneurs* will not give them the value of it, another will, provided that competition is perfect.   With an ideally complete and free competitive system, each unit of labor can get exactly what a final unit produces.   With an imperfect competition, it still *tends* to get that amount.   The final product of labor sets a standard for the pay of labor; and actual wages tend toward it, with variations.

We have noted the fact that an *entrepreneur's* net profit is an incentive to competition.   Such a profit is mercantile, and means that employers are selling their products for more than they are paying out in wages and interest — that the price of the goods exceeds the cost of the elements that compose them. We noted the fact that "natural price," as defined by economists, is really a wages-and-interest price; for it equals the sum of these two outlays.   A profit-giving price exceeds that sum, but the competition that tends to annihilate the profit cuts it off at both ends.   By bidding against each other in selling goods, employers make the prices smaller; and by bidding against each other in hiring labor and capital, they make wages and interest larger.   There is a profit on labor, so long as the men in a working force are paid less than the final one produces; but competition tends to annihilate that profit and to make the pay of labor equal to the product of the final unit of it. *Profits cause competition that secures to labor its product.*

As has again and again been said, we have constructed an ideal society in which disturbing facts are omitted, and we have so far described none of the obstacles that pure law encounters in real life. We have made no estimate of the amount of deviation from the final productivity standard that the pay of workmen actually reveals.   All such studies have

Variations to be treated in the dynamic division of the theory.

a place in the dynamic division of our work. As real as gravitation is the force that draws the actual pay of men *toward* a standard that is set by the final productivity law. This law is universal and permanent: everywhere it will outlive the local and changeful influences that modify its operation. We are to get what we produce — such is the dominant rule of life; and what we are able to produce by means of labor, is determined by what a final unit of mere labor can add to the product that can be created without its aid. *Final productivity governs wages.*

Summary of conclusions.

We may now summarize the conclusions that we have thus far reached, concerning the natural standard of wages, in the following series of propositions: —

(1) Labor, like commodities, is subject to a law of marginal appraisal. The rate that the market puts on the final unit of the supply of each of them, it puts on the entire supply. As the last unit of consumers' goods is a price-making one, so the last unit of labor is the one that fixes wages.

(2) The term *final* does not designate a particular unit that can be identified and separated from others. There is not, for example, in the elevators of the United States a special lot of wheat that is in a strategic position and has a price-making power that other wheat does not possess. Any unit whatever of this commodity is final in the economic sense; inasmuch as, by its presence, it brings the supply to its present actual magnitude. Similarly, the *final*, *marginal* or *last* unit of labor does not consist of particular men. It is especially necessary to guard against the idea that the final men, whose products fix the general rate of wages, are those who would naturally be employed last, because they are the poorest. We have been careful to say that it is units of labor, as such, that are the basis of the law of wages;

and a body of men must be of the average quality of
ordinary laborers, if it is to constitute such a unit.

(3) In presenting the law of final utility, it is
customary to arrange the units of a commodity in an
imaginary series, to present them one at a time and
to ascertain how important each one is to the consumer. Yet commodities never come to the market
in such an order. The whole present supply of a
commodity is offering in the market; but the price
that it is bringing is fixed by the importance that
wou'd attach to the final unit, *if the supply were
offered in such a series of units.*

In like manner, we may find it useful, in presenting the law by which wages are fixed, to go through
an imaginary operation of setting men at work, one
man at a time or one company of men at a time, and
thus to find what importance the market places on
the last one. This reveals the operation of a law of
diminishing productivity; and whether we take a
single man or a body of men as the unit of labor, *any
unit can get, as pay, what the last one would produce,
if the force were set working in this way.*

(4) The standard of wages thus attained is a static
one. So long as the labor and the capital continue
unchanged in amount, and produce the same things,
by the same processes and under an unchanging
form of organization, wages will continue at the
rate that this test establishes. Setting men at work
in succession is a bit of imaginary dynamics, but
what it reveals is a *static law.*

Let the number of units of labor be measured, in Graphic
the following figure, along the line AD. Let them statement of
the law.
be set working in a series, in connection with a fixed
amount of capital. The product of the first unit of
labor, as aided by all the capital, is measured by the
line AB. What the second unit of labor adds to this

product is the amount expressed by A'B'. The third
unit enlarges the output by the amount A''B'', the
next by A''' B''', the next by A'''' B'''' and the last by
DC. DC measures the effective productivity of any
unit of labor in the series and fixes the general rate
of pay. If the first unit of labor claims more than
the amount DC, employers will let it withdraw, and
will substitute for it the last unit. What they lose
by the withdrawal
of any one unit in
the entire force is
the amount DC.

A fact of great
importance now
appears. We may
reverse the appli-
cation of this law,
and by so doing get
a law of interest.
Let the labor be
the element that
is unchanged in
amount, and let

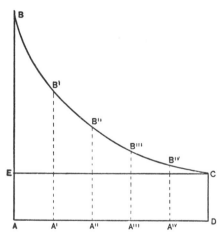

capital be the one that is supplied in a succession
of increments.

AB is now the product gained by using one increment of capital in connection with the whole working
force. A'B' is the additional product that is created
by a second increment of capital. A''B'' is the
product of the third increment and DC is the amount
produced by the last. This amount, DC, fixes the
rate of interest. No one of the series of units of
capital can secure for its owner more than the last
one produces. If the owner of the first increment
asks more than this for the use of it, the *entrepreneur*
will relinquish this bit of capital and will put the

last unit in its place. What he will lose, in the way of product, is measured by the amount DC, the direct product of the final increment of capital. This expresses the *effective* product of every increment, since it is the amount that would be lost if any one of the series were withdrawn.

All that we have said about the change that must take place in the forms of capital, when the amount of it is fixed and the working force is increasing, applies here, where these conditions are reversed. The steady increase of the capital, if the amount of the labor be fixed, compels a similar change of forms. With one unit of capital and ten units of labor, the instruments will be simple and cheap. Hand tools will generally prevail; and buildings, roadways, bridges, vehicles, etc., will be of a makeshift kind, which will, at a small cost for each instrument, enable the men in some way to work. With two units of capital, a better type of instruments begins to prevail. Every increase in the amount of the capital shows itself primarily in transmuting poor appliances into better ones. There are, indeed, more tools, and there is more raw material; but the striking fact is that all the tools, etc., are costlier and more efficient. With the addition of the tenth unit of capital, the condition may be thought of as approximating that of our own country at the present day. There is much costly machinery, many durable buildings, a good supply of large ships, efficient railroads, etc.

Character of the changes in the forms of capital caused by increase in quantity.

At the cost of what may be a tedious repetition, we have now described the series of changes that an increasing capital undergoes, because this is what is actually taking place. Capital is the element that is outgrowing labor. We may take the world that exists instead of an imaginary one, as our illustration.

As the accumulation of capital actually goes on, it shows itself more and more in qualitative changes of existing instruments. Society pulls down its barns and builds others, better as well as larger; it carries its mercantile buildings farther into the air, and makes them fireproof and durable; it substitutes steel ships for wooden ones and steamers for sailing craft; it takes the curves and grades out of its railroads, and makes bridges and viaducts of the kind that defies time and strain; it bores tunnels through mountain ranges to avoid climbing over them and cuts canals across isthmuses to shorten the voyages of ships. As capital grows very abundant, there are made longer tunnels and canals; and they have, as their purpose, the avoiding of climbs that are easier and voyages that are shorter than were those that were avoided by the earlier engineering works. They thus represent a greater outlay incurred for a smaller gain. Society also makes all its machinery as nearly automatic as it can, so that one laborer's guidance shall keep much machinery in successful motion. Everywhere there are taking place such adaptations of capital as fit a large amount of it to the needs of a relatively small amount of labor.

The changes that have to be made in the forms of the capital, as the amount of it increases, reveal a reason for the decline in the rate of its earnings. The rudest hatchet that can be made may vastly increase the owner's power to get firewood. It may wear out in a year; but in that period it may save enough of time, that would otherwise have been devoted to a slow and painful mode of wood gathering, to enable the owner to make six new hatchets. Though he will probably not use the liberated time for this particular purpose, whatever he does secure by it represents an interest of five hundred per cent

The most productive form earliest in the series.

on the capital invested in this first and most productive tool.   A second tool may liberate labor enough to replace itself only five times.   The owner will actually replace it once, and will employ the time that could give him four duplicates of it in making other things for his own use; but the fruit of the spare time that the second tool makes available is now four hundred per cent of the cost of the tool, as computed in terms of unaided labor.

Tools are, of course, employed in the order of their productivity, so far as men judge their several powers of production correctly.   It soon ceases to be possible to add to a working equipment anything that produces a multiple of its own cost in a year, and the interest on the final increment of capital becomes a fraction of that capital itself.   This fraction steadily diminishes, as the productive fund grows larger, and as improvement in the quality of tools, etc., becomes one form of investment for the growing accumulations.   The difference between the cost of a rude and poor hatchet and that of a better one represents an increment of capital; but it has less power to reproduce itself, in amount, than had the investment that was made in the original tool.

As accumulation proceeds, there are always made costlier machines, representing more capital; and the product that comes from using them is a smaller fraction of their cost.   The straightening of the curves in railroads is one of the ways in which capital may find investment.   This may cost as much as the first making of the corresponding parts of the road themselves; but it does not liberate as much labor, in proportion to its cost, as did the building of the old and crooked road.   The boring of a long tunnel, to avoid a short climb over the mountains, does not result in as large earnings for the capital that is thus invested as did the making of a short tunnel to avoid a higher climb. Everywhere do the forms of the capital show differences in earning power; and the owners choose first the most productive forms, and later the less productive. To this fact is due the present low rate of interest. We are utilizing the opportunities for investment that stand late in the series and are low in the scale of productivity.

We have said that no increment of capital can get for its owner more than the last increment produces. We may state this in another way by saying that no form of capital can claim and get for its owners in a year a larger fraction of its cost than the least productive form produces. Under modern conditions, if the man who lends " money " for the procuring of a highly necessary tool demands the whole amount that is secured through the use of it, the *entrepreneur*, who is the borrower, will refuse the money and will use, for the procuring of the tool which is so much needed, the money that formerly went into the tool that was last and least important on the list. In terms of more primitive life, if the man who performs the labor of making a very necessary tool demands the whole product that it creates, the *entrepreneur* will decline to utilize this tool-making labor and will divert to the making of the needed instrument that labor which has been used for the making of the least important part of his working equipment. Capital is, it thus appears, completely transmutable in form. Society can quit making one kind of instrument and make another. Capital-goods are, then, interchangeable; and while this is so, no increment of capital can ever secure for its owner more than the final increment produces.

It is, of course, true that labor also has to change its forms, as capital accumulates. The man who

The least productive form the one that sets the standard of interest.

watches a complicated machine is going through a set of movements very different from those executed by a man working with a hand tool. Every time that we change the form of the capital, we change, by that very fact, the character of the labor. Mutual adaptation in form is the general rule for these two producing agents. Change the merely quantitative ratio of one of them to the other, and you make it necessary to transform both of them in character. As with ten units of capital for ten units of labor there will be one grade of instruments and certain kinds of work performed in connection with them, so with eleven units of capital for ten units of labor there will be somewhat different kinds of instruments and different modes of working. This double transformation must, moreover, theoretically extend through the whole mass of capital and the whole process of labor. Everywhere there are to be seen new and improved kinds of capital-goods and new modes of using them.

Corresponding changes in the forms of labor.

With this qualification, we may represent the law of interest by the process of building up, increment by increment, the fund of social capital and measuring the product produced by each unit of it. In this imaginary process we have revealed a true law of varying productivity. As we have said, the addition to the product caused by the last unit of capital fixes the rate of interest. Every unit of capital can secure for its owner what the last unit produces, and it can secure no more. The principle of final productivity, in short, acts in two ways, affording a theory of wages and of interest.

Two-fold action of the law of final productivity.

CHAPTER XIII

THE PRODUCTS OF LABOR AND CAPITAL, AS MEASURED BY THE FORMULA FOR RENT

IT has been customary to define rent as the income derived from land. In attempting to solve problems of distribution, furthermore, it has been customary to eliminate from the earnings of society the element of ground rent, and then to try to find principles that will account for the division of what remains. That ground rent is entirely unlike wages, interest or *entrepreneurs'* profit, has been the most prevalent theory. According to this view, the income from land is a differential gain fixed by a law of its own, which does not apply elsewhere. The rent of a particular piece of ground is measured by comparing its product with that which can be had from the poorest piece that is utilized by the application of the same amount of labor and capital. When, by this independent reckoning, the part of the income of society that is derived from land has been disposed of, it is thought that one step has been taken in the direction of solving the really difficult problems of distribution. Wages, interest and net profits, it is believed, can be accounted for the more readily when the product of land has been put out of sight.

It has become obvious, however, that wages are fixed by the final productivity of the labor that is used in connection with a fixed amount of total capital; and in computing that total capital, we make confusion, if we do not take all kinds of capital-goods into account. It is the whole fund of productive wealth, in every form that such wealth takes, which constitutes the complex agency that coöperates with labor. When the amount of productive wealth in its entirety remains fixed and the quantity of labor increases, the law of diminishing returns that we have stated operates. The final unit of the agent, labor, — coöperating, as it does, with land and every other instrument, — produces less and less, as the units of labor become more numerous; and thus the standard of wages falls. When the increase in the working force ceases, the rate of wages remains fixed.

Land a part of the productive wealth that figures in the theory of wages.

It may be alleged that the same result will be reached by assuming that capital in artificial forms remains fixed in amount, while the working force grows larger. Land, it may be claimed, is fixed in amount by nature; and, if we can measure the productive wealth that exists in the shape of buildings, tools, materials and the like, and keep that also unchanged in amount, we shall have the condition that we have described. The total amount of productive wealth will then be a fixed quantity; and we can let the labor increase, unit by unit, testing its final productivity as we have done.

This method of statement would tell the truth about the decline in the productivity of labor, but it would not assign that effect to its true cause. What the labor combines itself with is not merely the artificial capital: it is that *and the land*, as they are combined in one and make a general labor-aiding agency. As the working population has grown larger, some of it has betaken itself to hitherto rentless ground — the enlargement of the laboring force has pressed outward the margin of utilization of land.

During the same period of growth, moreover, new labor has constantly added itself to the force that has tilled good land. More and more intensively has land everywhere been cultivated and otherwise used. The artificial capital, as such, has received, as it were, only its own fraction of the increasing force of labor. It has aided the land, and together they have received all of the new workers. Wages fall because such capital and land together cannot make the tenth unit of labor as productive as they made the first.

It is, therefore, the whole economic environment of the growing population that has to be considered, if the cause of the decline in the final productivity of labor is to be understood. Land and artificial goods are blended in an intimate mixture; and the last unit of labor produces what this whole composite agent enables it to produce. There are only two generic members in the combination by which the rate of wages is determined. Indeed, as we have noticed, the variations in the comparative amounts of these two agents, labor and all capital, determine both wages and interest.

No controversy need arise over the question of mere nomenclature. It is necessary to find some term to designate the whole permanent fund of productive wealth, and the natural name for it is capital.[1] It is also necessary to have a term for all kinds of concrete goods in which this permanent fund consists; and we shall call these things, including land.

[1] It will be seen that this is not calling land capital. When land is referred to, it will be called by its ordinary name. There is a constant necessity for referring to the total fund of permanent productive wealth that is embodied in land and in artificial instruments. When this is thought of, in practical life, as "money invested in business," it is designated by the term capital; and in this work it will be so called. The objection to calling land one variety of capital-goods vanishes, if it is admissible to call all productive wealth,

All capital-goods constitute one element in adjusting wages.

capital-goods. As our analysis of the process of distribution proceeds, we shall hope to justify this nomenclature by its fruits. In any case, it is important to note that it is the quantity of labor, on the one hand, and that of all productive wealth, on the other, that fix the natural or static standards of wages and interest.

Ground rent we shall study as the earnings of one kind of capital-goods — as merely a part of interest.[1] We are now able to see that wages and interest, though they are determined by the law of final productivity, are also capable of being measured exactly as ground rent has been measured. That is to say, the Ricardian formula, which describes what is earned by a piece of land, may be used to describe what is earned by the whole fund of social capital: all interest may be made to take the form of a differential gain, or a surplus. Again, the Ricardian formula may be employed to describe the earnings of the whole force of social labor; for wages, in their entirety, are a differential gain. It is one of the most striking of economic facts that the income of all labor, on the one hand, and that of all capital, on the other, should be thus entirely akin to ground rent. They are the two generic rents, if by that term we mean differential products; and the earnings of land constitute a fraction of one of them.

All wages and interest may be regarded as differential gains akin to ground rent.

Let us now simplify the law of ground rent, by disregarding the auxiliary capital that, in advanced

"in the abstract," capital. Any objection that may arise to this usage is less serious than is the objection to using through a long discussion such a phrase as "permanent fund of productive wealth," or some equivalent and equally inconvenient expression. The nomenclature that we adopt guards not only against confounding land with this fund, but against confounding any other instrument, as concretely regarded, with it. In this, at least, it is a strict constructionist nomenclature. [1] See Ch. XXII.

agricultural states, is applied in large quantities to land. Let the ground that we use as an illustration be worked by labor that is practically empty-handed. Every laborer brings with him a simple tool, but the interest on the capital that the tool represents is so small a part of what the man earns in a year that it may be disregarded. We have, then, only two pro-

Differential gains of labor applied to land, a type of all rents.

ducing agents to deal with, and they are the land — which now embodies all the capital that needs to be considered — and labor. The neglect of auxiliary capital affects no principle that we are studying; for what we have to prove could be established as completely, though less clearly, if we made our illustration more complex by taking all kinds of capital into account. The differential gain of labor as applied unaided to fertile land, offers the clearest illustration of the different incomes that can be measured by the Ricardian formula. It is the type of all the rents.[1]

Labor, as thus applied to land, is subject to a law

The law of diminishing returns here operative.

of diminishing returns. Put one man on a quarter section of land, containing prairie and forest, and he will get a rich return. Two laborers on the same ground will get less per man; three will get still less; and, if you enlarge the force to ten, it may be that the last man will get wages only. We must, however, be very careful to make sure of the reason why the tenth man gets only his wages. If the men are hired by the owner of the land at the prevalent rate of wages, what has happened is that the force has been enlarged till the last man produces only what is paid to him. In this case, as was said in the tenth chapter, wages fix the intensive margin of cultivation of this land. The rate that we must pay to the men decides for us how many of them we can employ on our farm. If, however,

[1] These are (1) the rent of all capital, (2) that of all labor, (3) that of particular capital-goods, and (4) that of particular laborers.

our farm is isolated and the workers are a society by themselves, and if there are ten of them to be employed, we shall set them all working and pay to each of them as much as the last one produces. Here it is the product of the marginal labor that fixes the rate of wages, as we noted in the chapter referred to; and here, also, the situation illustrates the true law of rent.[1]

All the earlier men in the series create surplus products, over and above the amount created by the last man. They get only what the last one produces, and the farmer-landlord gets the remainder. What goes to the owner of the land is the sum of a series of remainders that are made by taking, in each case, the product that is attributable to one of the earlier men as a minuend and the product that is imputable to the last man as a subtrahend.

Call the product that the single worker creates, when he has the whole field to himself, P^{1st}. Call the additional product that the second man is able to bring into existence P^{2d}, etc.; call the enlargement in the output made by the last man P^{10th}.

Surplus products created by the earlier men.

---

[1] The law of rent, as commonly stated, has the defect that is illustrated by the former of these cases, where it is applied to the reward for labor. The farmer who figures in the current statement of the law hires his men at the wages that prevail in the various industries that are carried on about him; and, when he finds that more men will not produce their wages, he quits enlarging his force. Each of the earlier men creates a surplus above his wages. When we are considering the rent of a limited piece of land devoted to one use, the scientific way to calculate the rent is to use as the subtrahend wages, rather than the final product of labor; since it is wages that fix final product. If what we want is a genuine differential product, we must isolate our working society, count the laborers, set them all at work and let the last produce what he can. There will then be a difference between what each of the earlier men produces and this final or standard product. This is, in each case, a true differential product. It is measured by comparing, not products created for the farmer and wages paid by him, but one product with another product.

$P^{1st} - P^{10th}$ = surplus created by the first worker.
$P^{2d} - P^{10th}$ = surplus created by the second worker.
$P^{9th} - P^{10th}$ = surplus created by the ninth worker.

If we complete the series of such subtractions and add the nine remainders, the sum of them all will be the rent of the piece of land. This is the amount that the owner can keep, from the total created by the different workers aided by the land.

The sum of $P^{1st} + P^{2d} + P^{3d}$, etc., to and including P^{10th}, is the whole product of the field and the labor that is spent on it. It is the sum of all the minuends in the foregoing series, with the product of the final man added to it. $10 \times P^{10th}$ equals the total subtrahend; and the total rent of the field is the difference between these amounts. It is, in other words, the whole product minus ten times the product of the tenth and last unit of labor.

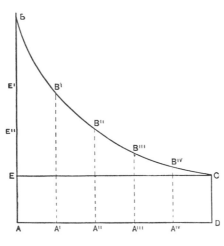

Let us, again, measure the number of laborers by the line AD, and the product of successive increments of labor by AB, A'B', etc. If we give to these lines an appreciable width, so that a series of them will fill the entire figure, ABCD, that area will measure the product of all the labor and all the capital in our illustrative agricultural community. The capital is virtually all in the form of land; and we are now able to attribute to the land that part of the product which, in effect, it creates.

The last unit of labor creates the amount of product that is expressed by DC; and, accordingly, each unit of labor is effectively worth just that amount to the employing farmer, and each unit gets that amount as its wages. AECD measures total wages, and EBC measures the entire rent of the land. This amount we have spoken of as composed of a series of surpluses, or differential products, and we have measured them in each case by subtracting from what we have called the product of one of the earlier increments of labor the product of the last increment. AB minus DC gives such a surplus, and it is a part of the rent. It looks, at a careless view, as though land had the capacity to cut off and claim for itself a part of the product of labor—that is, the surplus part of the product of all the earlier increments of *labor* appears to be the *rent* of the *land*. Rent the sum of a series of surpluses,

In reality, this surplus is the fruit of the aid that the land affords, and is attributable to the land only. A correct conception of the nature of any rent makes it a concrete addition which one producing agent is able to make to the product that is attributable to another producing agent. Land makes its own addition to the product of each unit of labor except the last one. When there was available only a piece of land, with no labor to till it, the product was *nil*. When one unit of labor combined itself with the land, the product was AB; and in this form of statement we impute the whole product to the labor.[1] A each of them attributable to the land.

[1] In the case of the first increment of labor, we might, by different dialectics, attribute the whole product to the land. Labor by itself creates nothing, and the addition of the land brings the whole product into existence. Again, by subdividing the one unit of labor into a series of smaller units, we might attribute the product partly to the labor and partly to the land. The product of the last frac-

second unit of labor now comes, unaided by capital, into the field and adds itself, empty-handed, to the working force. Whatever it produces, it brings into existence by adding to what the field yielded to one man's cultivation. The product thus created by an addition to labor, with no addition to capital, is A'B'. The difference between AB and A'B', which is the line E'B, measures the surplus that a man can produce when he has the whole field to aid him above what he can create when he is unaided. The last man adds labor and no land to the productive combination; while the first man had land, and the addition that the land itself made to the bare product of labor constitutes the differential quantity which is the rent of the land. The science of rent is a science of economic causation, which traces products to their sources. The rent getter is a product creator.

The third man, also empty-handed, creates the amount A''B''; and E'B + E''E' measures the contribution that the land has thus far made to the joint product of land and labor. Extending the vertical lines and giving to them width enough to make them

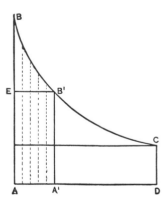

tional unit of labor would then set the standard to which wages, or the effective product of all fractional units of labor, would conform; and the figure that would express this fact would be the one in which A'B' is the amount that is attributable to each fractional unit of labor, AA'B'E is the amount that is attributable to all the labor, and EB'B is the amount that is attributable to the land. It is when there is more than one unit of labor at work that it becomes clear how much should be attributed to all the labor and how much to the land.

fill the area of the entire figure, we have AECD as the product of all the labor, when it is taken unit by unit and made to work virtually unaided. ABCD is what it creates as it is aided by the land, and EBC is the amount that the land contributes to the product of the combination. This measures the difference between the product of ten units of aided labor and ten units of unaided labor.

We can now make the really important application of the principle of diminishing returns, which fixes both marginal productivity and rent. This is the application that is actually making everywhere in the business world. The isolated farm, with its whole capital in land, is an illustration only; while the real field for labor, to which the farm corresponds, is the world, with its whole circle of industries and its complex equipment of capital.

For a fixed area of land read, now, a fixed fund of permanent social capital. It is at this moment an exact sum; and it will, as it were, prolong the conditions of this moment, remaining at exactly its present size. The artificial instruments are, of course, perishing and renewing; but, if there is no need of changing the form of the capital, a worn-out instrument will be replaced by another that is exactly like it. A hoe will replace a hoe, and a ship will succeed a ship; and the new instruments of production will be exact duplicates of the old. This would be clear in a completely static condition. We are, however, to introduce labor, increment by increment, into this general field of industry; and this, of course, compels such a change in the forms of the capital as we have already described. The amount of the capital remaining fixed, the instruments become more numerous and cheaper, as the force of labor enlarges.

The product attributable to capital tested in a similar way.

Labor, applied to the whole fund of capital, in land and all other instruments, is now subject to the

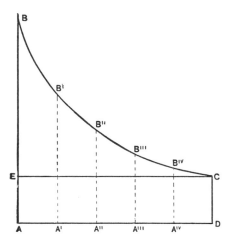

law of diminishing returns. The first unit produces the amount AB, the second produces the amount A'B', the third creates the quantity A''B'' and the last the quantity DC. This last amount sets the rate of wages, and the area AECD measures the amount of wages.

It leaves the amount expressed by the area EBC as the rent of the fund of social capital. All interest is thus a surplus, entirely akin to the rent of land, as that is expressed by the Ricardian formula: it is a concrete product, attributable to the agent that claims it as an income.

This rent is, moreover, made up of a series of genuine differential gains. It is not like the rent of the farm, in our former illustration, which, as we found, really depends on the rate of wages that pre-

Interest the sum of a series of surpluses attributable to capital. vails elsewhere. The rent of the whole fund of social capital is the sum of a series of differences between certain products and a final, or standard, product. True differentials lie between different products, and not between products and wages. The line DC, which sets the rate of wages, expresses primarily the product of the last unit of labor. We have set all the men in the society working, we have measured the amount created by the last addition to the force, and we have measured the surplus that each earlier unit of labor creates above this amount. The surplus is, in each case, a true differential product; since it is not merely a remainder that is left after paying wages, but is a difference between one product and another. It is the difference between the product of aided labor and that of the labor that is virtually unaided, and the sum of all these differences is the rent of the social fund of capital.

Reverse now the situation. Let labor be the fixed element and let social capital enlarge, changing its forms of course, in the enlarging.

ABCD is the total product. AB is the product of the first unit of capital, A′B′ the product of the second, A″B″ that of the third and DC that of the last. A unit of capital, adding itself with no new labor to the productive combination, enlarges the product by the amount DC. So much can be attributed to any unit of capital, separately considered. The effective importance of every one of the units of capital is the same. While capital-goods are not interchangeable, true capital is completely so; and all parts of it are, therefore, on a plane in their earning capacity. A merchant, a manufacturer or a farmer, if he can offer good security, can hire all the " money " that he needs at the rate that the least necessary sum which he invests

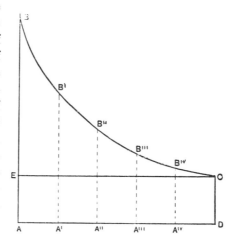

in his business will earn for him.   Does this imply
an exploitation of the earlier units of capital?   Does
the borrower of these sums rob the lender?

If the final unit of capital produces the amount
DC, it will get that amount as interest; and certainly
no other unit can get any more.   AECD will be the
total amount of interest, and EBC will be a surplus;
but it will be a surplus that is causally attributable
to labor, and to labor only.   The difference between
the product that is solely due to capital and that
which is due to capital and another agent in combination is the effect of the presence and the work of
that other agent.

If we were to apply the term *rent* to all such surpluses, we should say that EBC is the rent of the
force of laborers that is at work in connection with
capital.   This amount is made up of a series of
differential products.   Apparently AB − DC is the
difference between the product of the first unit of
capital and that of the last, A'B' − DC is the difference between the product of the second unit of capital and that of the last, etc.   *The rent of the labor*, if
we use that expression, is the sum of the surplus products connected with the earlier units of capital but
not attributable to them as a cause.   The laborers
seem to get a part of what the earlier units of capital
produce; whereas, in reality, this is the difference
between what capital and labor jointly produce and
what capital alone contributes to the product of the
combination.   EBC is, therefore, the amount that is
imputable to labor only.

One law governs wages and interest — the law of
final productivity.   By one mode of statement of the
law (Fig. 1), we get wages as an amount directly
determined by this principle: it is the area AECD of
our diagram.   Arithmetically stated, the earnings of

Wages the
sum of a
series of
surpluses
attributable
to labor.

all labor equal the product of the final unit of labor multiplied by the number of the units.   In Fig. 1, in which wages are thus determined, interest is a

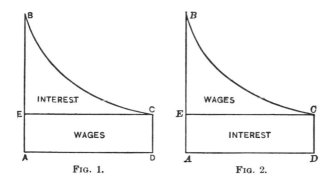

FIG. 1.   FIG. 2.

surplus that is of the nature of rent.   By another mode of stating the law (Fig. 2), we get interest as the amount that is positively fixed by the final productivity law, and wages are now the surplus that is akin to rent.   These amounts together make up the whole static income of society.

Profit has no place in such static conditions.   The two incomes that are permanent and independent of dynamic changes are the products, respectively, of labor and of capital.   Each of them is directly determined by the final productivity law, and each is also a remainder — a surplus or a differential quantity.   In one use of terms, it is a rent made by subtracting the other income from the whole product of social industry.

Does such a remainder ever go to the persons who naturally get it, merely because it is a remainder and is not claimed by others ?   In Fig. 1, where EBC, representing interest, is a surplus governed by the law of rent, does the capitalist get this amount merely because labor cannot get it ?   The whole

Wages and interest both directly and residually.

product is ABCD, and labor can have only AECD.
If there is no profit, capital must get the remainder.
Do the capitalists, then, come into the possession of
this income merely because it is thus left for them
by the laborers?

This point is of much consequence. The question
at issue is nothing less than whether any static income is determined residually. Clearly it is never
so determined. No static income is what it is merely
because the deducting of another income from the
social product leaves a certain remainder. Any income that is nothing but a remainder must go to
the *entrepreneur*. Because EBC, in Fig. 1, is not
claimed by labor, it is left in the hands of the *entrepreneur*. Thus far it is a residuum. It is, moreover,
important that this amount should thus be left in
the employer's hands, for by this means he is made
able to pay the interest that the capitalist will claim ;
but there is in the mere fact that he has this sum
nothing that makes it necessary for him to pay it to
the capitalist. What the owners of capital can force
entrepreneurs to pay them, is determined by the final
productivity of capital. Employers of capital must
pay for the final increment of it just what that increment produces, and they must pay for all other
increments at the same rate. If this necessity takes
from them the whole amount, EBC, which labor
leaves in their hands, then EBC goes to the capitalist. It does so, however, only because the capitalist
can claim and get it, by the direct action of the final
productivity law. What the capitalist can get under
this principle is expressed by Fig. 2. AECD is
here the amount of interest, as directly and positively fixed. This amount must pass, in any case,
from the *entrepreneurs* to the capitalists.

The *entrepreneur*, then, after paying wages, as in-

dicated by AECD in Fig. 1, has left in his hands
EBC, out of which he can pay interest. What he
must pay as interest, is *AECD* in Fig. 2. If the
area EBC in Fig. 1 were larger than *AECD* in Fig.
2, there would be a remainder left for the *entrepreneur*. This would be a pure profit, the only kind
of income that is ever residually determined.

Profit a
residuum
only.

It is clear, on the face of the facts, that the two
static incomes — those, namely, of the laborer and of
the capitalist — are paid to them by the *entrepreneur*,
who receives and sells the product of their joint industry. In the cotton mill, it is the hirer of capital
and of labor who puts the goods on the market and
from the proceeds pays the workmen and the owners
of capital. If he pays first to the capitalists what the
final productivity law, as applied to capital, calls for,
he has a remainder out of which he must pay wages ;
and now it is the final productivity law that decides
what he must pay as wages. If there is anything
left on his hands after the two payments are made,
it is a profit ; and the terms *profit* and *residual income*
are thus synonymous.

This truth we may demonstrate by using our dia-
grams in a reversed order. In Fig. 2 *AECD* is
interest, as directly determined, and *EBC* is the
remainder, which is left in the *entrepreneur's* hands
for the payment of wages. What the *entrepreneur*
must pay to the workmen is AECD of Fig. 1. If
that is less than *ECD* of Fig. 2, there is a residuum,
or profit, for the *entrepreneur*. Static conditions,
however, exclude such a profit by making these two
areas equal.

We have, then, established the following propositions : —

Summary of
conclusions.

(1) Wages and interest are both determined by
the law of final productivity.

(2) When, in an illustrative case, one of these incomes is so determined, the other appears to be a residuum.

(3) As a residuum, such an income would be left in the *entrepreneurs'* hands; but it is actually taken from them by a further action of the final productivity law.

(4) *Entrepreneurs'* profit and residual income are synonymous terms.[1]   The static conditions assumed in the present study preclude the existence of such *entrepeneurs'* gains.

[1] The above theses appear sharply to contradict the theory of wages advanced by the late President Francis A. Walker, in which wages are called the residual share in distribution.   It is an aid in removing causes of confusion from the discussion, and in giving to the theory of this eminent economist what is due to it, to notice the fact that his study was essentially a study of a subject in economic dynamics.   If the total product of industry becomes larger than it has been, and if interest, rent and profit do not become any greater than they were, wages must absorb the whole increase. In this view, the residuum may be regarded as a remainder that is left when the former product of the whole industry is subtracted from the present product.   Such a view of the power of labor to get all the increase that dynamic changes create would be consistent with the view that, in the merely static adjustment that takes place at all times, wages are determined directly by the law of final productivity, as are other shares of the total product.   We might claim that the progress which makes industry, as a whole, more productive makes labor, separately considered, more so, but leaves the productivity of other agents unchanged.   Laborers would then, in each static adjustment that takes place, force *entrepreneurs* to give them their product, just as capitalists would do. Statically, wages would be determined directly ; while dynamically they would consist partly in a residuum, made by deducting the former product of industry, as a whole, from the present product.

In our view, progress in methods of production makes both labor and capital more productive ; and the fruits of progress are thus shared by the two agents, according to the degrees of specific productivity that the progress gives to them.   Labor, then, does not get the whole difference between the former product of industry and the present product.   What we are trying to make clear is that, in a merely static adjustment of shares in distribution, both wages and interest must be determined directly, and not residually. After paying interest, the *entrepreneur* has wages left in his hands ; but he is forced to pay it to labor *because it is the product of labor.* In making his bargain, the worker has the benefit of free competition. He is virtually selling his forthcoming product, and can resort to another employer, if the present one refuses to give him the full value of it. The capitalist, in making this contract for the payment of interest, is in the same way selling a product, and can exact the value of it. Without this power, neither laborers nor capitalists could get their shares from the *entrepreneur's* hands. For an early statement of the principles presented in this chapter, the reader is referred to an article by the present writer, in the *Quarterly Journal of Economics*, for April, 1891, on " Distribution as Determined by a Law of Rent.''

CHAPTER XIV

THE EARNINGS OF INDUSTRIAL GROUPS

WE have not yet exhausted the applications of the principle that is at the basis of the familiar law of rent. It has been customary to apply it to the product of land; we have made it govern the product of all capital; and, in thus applying the principle, we have put out of sight particular instruments of industry and have treated capital in its entirety as a permanent agent of production. Interest, the product of this agent, can be translated into a form that is akin to rent. Capital constitutes a social fund; and, if economic law be not obstructed, the suitable amount of it is to be found in each one of the affiliated industries that constitute the producing organism, society. This apportioning of the social fund among the different industrial groups helps to fix the amount of goods that each group shall produce; and that, again, controls the value of the goods. Values, as we have seen, control the comparative earnings of different groups; for the one whose product is selling at a high price is getting a relatively large group income, and the one whose product is cheap is getting a small one. Values themselves are governed by the same all-embracing law that fixes rents, but it is that law in another sphere of action. We have to examine the special way in which this law acts in fixing values, which is the same thing as adjusting

The principle of rent applied to social capital.

The mode of apportioning this fund among different groups.

206

the comparative earnings of groups. Group distribution and that final distribution which fixes wages and interest are controlled by one law.

We have seen that the law which has been made the basis of the rent of land really governs the earnings of labor; and, in studying labor, we have ceased to think of particular men and have considered labor, in its entirety, as a permanent agent of industry. Work continues, though particular workers pass from the field and are replaced by others. Labor is a social agent of production; for, like capital, it has to apportion itself in certain quantities among the groups and sub-groups of which industrial society is composed; and a free play of economic forces decides how much labor each industry shall have. We presuppose this apportioning and locating of labor, when we speak of it, in its entirety, as a second generic agent of production, and one that is combined with capital in a proportion that determines the earnings of both of these producers. It is by the combination of all the labor of society with all the capital of society that the general rates of wages and interest are fixed; but the combination runs through all the groups, and a play of forces that is simple in principle, though minutely detailed and complex in its practical working, tends to give to each occupation that men pursue a definite amount of the laboring force of society, as well as a definite part of the social capital. It is, again, by this apportioning process that group products, values, and group incomes are controlled. Each industry tends, under a perfectly free competition, to get that share of the social laboring force which will make its output of goods and its collective income, as derived from the sale of the goods, normal.

By a wonderful social mechanism these results are brought about. The production of the world is car-

The principle of rent applied to labor as a permanent social force.

The apportionment of labor among the groups.

ried on by a network of affiliated groups or industries, which are so interdependent that a change in any one of them carries a series of resulting changes through the whole complex system. It is this dependence of industrial occupations on each other that makes it possible to speak of labor and capital as having, in each case, a unity, a social character and a general rate of earnings.

We have already gone far enough to get a view of one very general law. So all-embracing, indeed, is it that it dominates economic life. Classical studies afforded a glimpse of the working of it, within a very limited field, by their study of the so-called diminishing returns from agriculture. As they pointed out, labor and capital, when applied to land in a series of increments or "doses," produce less and less per dose.

Modern studies of value afford a glimpse of the action of this principle in a wholly different sphere. They show that doses of consumers' goods, given in a series to the same persons, have less and less utility per dose. The final utility theory of value rests on the same principle as does the theory of diminishing returns from agriculture; and this principle has a far wider range of new applications. One law, therefore, governs economic life, and theories old and new contain partial expressions of it. The theory of value rests upon one application of the general law, and the theory of rent on another. As this law may be traced in consumption, where the "final increment" of a particular article is less useful than earlier increments, so it is observable also in production, where the final increment of an industrial agent is less fruitful than earlier ones. As value depends on final utility, so shares in distribution depend on final productivity. Thus, interest is fixed by the product of the final increment of capital, and wages are deter- mined by the product of the final increment of labor. The value of goods, on the one hand, and the productivity of the two agents, labor and capital, on the other hand, depend on the same general law. It is value, however, that controls group incomes in their entirety; and it is the action of this law in the sphere of consumption that ultimately fixes values. Opposite in kind, indeed, are consumption and production. Nature spends itself upon man in the one process, and man spends himself upon nature in the other. Yet the same law governs the results realized in each of these cases. It may be called a law of variation of economic results ; and, if it were stated in its entirety, it would give unexpected unity and completeness to the science of economics. It would explain at the same time values, wages and interest.

Consumption is a process that yields subjective returns, which are measured in the sensibilities of men and are the ultimate objects of the production itself. The immediate objects of production, on the other hand, are the material things that affect the consumer's sensibilities. These things are objective, but they are valued only for what they do for man. Man acting on man through matter—such is the whole economic process. How much can be gained by the whole of it? is the practical question to be answered. The gain depends on the benefit that a product will afford to a man when he gets it, and also on the number of products which he can get. This, however, is merely saying that it depends on the utility of the goods, and on the productivity of the agents that create them. It depends, then, on the two variations that are governed by this law.

Final utility itself has been studied in a way too narrowly limited. In the case that is usually cited,

Recent application of the principle to series of similar commodities.

one commodity is taken and, in imagination, is given in increasing quantity to one consumer. The successive units of it then do less and less for him. Bread given to a man in a succession of slices nourishes, and pleases, but ultimately gluts him. The nth slice, if he must eat it, is worth nothing to him, and the following slices less than nothing. Coats of one kind bestowed on a man, one after another, soon lose their power to benefit him. The fourth may be of so little use that a tramp can have it for the asking. Duplicate copies of the same book or of the same picture encumber the shelves and walls, and their room is better than their presence. Very abrupt, in short, is

Abruptly descending utility curves thus gained.

the descent of the "utility curve" which, in graphic representation, expresses the lessening services that successive units of things of exactly the same kind are capable of rendering.

Vary the articles in kind, and you have a different result. Change the weight, the color and the cut of the successive coats, and the man will be glad to have more than four of them. Give him books that differ from each other, and he may strain the storage capacity of his house to accommodate them. By changing the quality of the articles offered you appeal to different wants; and so long as there are in man's sentient nature wants still to be satisfied, there is no reason why he should cease to accept what you offer.

Increasing wealth in varied forms shows gradually diminishing utility.

If two coats are alike in all respects but weight, the thicker garment satisfies just one want that is not satisfied by the other. It will be purchased, perhaps, for the sake of that single utility. Clothing in general, not confined to garments of any kind, shows a utility curve descending gradually. Food in general diminishes in utility far less abruptly than does a single article, like bread. Duplicate nothing; to potatoes add bread, then meat, pastry, fruit and the refined products of the French cuisine, and you will find the diminution of the utility of successive increments far less rapid than is the diminution of the utility of any one thing. Where we thus vary the quality of the second increment of an article offered to a consumer, we virtually offer him a different article, which renders a new and distinct service.

The theory of value has not taken due account of the abruptness in the decline in the utility of an article, when successive units of it, wholly uniform in quality, are offered to one consumer. The gently descending utility curves of the ordinary graphic representations tell what is true of a genus of articles rather than of a single one;[1] and a correction, therefore, needs to be made in the theory of value.

Corrections needed in the theory of value.

This is not the only correction that needs to be made; for we have undertaken to generalize the law that is at the basis of the theory of value. In reality, it is all-comprehensive. The first generalization to be made consists in applying the law, not to single articles, but to consumers' wealth in all its forms. The richer a man becomes, the less can his wealth do for him. Not only a series of goods that are all alike, but a succession of units of wealth itself, with no such limitation on its forms, becomes less and less useful per unit. Give to a man not coats, but "dollars," one after another, and the utility of the last

The law of diminishing utility, as applied to general consumers' wealth.

---

[1] These curves tell, also, what may be true of raw material that is capable of being put into many kinds of finished goods. Oak lumber offered for sale, foot after foot, may have a utility that diminishes quite gradually; for it can be wrought into tables, chairs, mantels, bookcases, doors, etc. But if, on the other hand, its use were confined to the making of dining-tables of one pattern, the utility of the lumber itself would soon be slight. Raw materials, however, are not consumers' goods and should not figure at all in this part of the study. They have productivity, but none of the utility of which we are speaking.

will still be less than that of any other. The early dollars feed, clothe and shelter the man, but the last one finds it hard to do anything for him. A dollar, as thus used, means command of a quantity of consumers' wealth indeterminate in its form; and wealth, as such, loses its specific utility, if you give it, unit after unit, to a single consumer. To apply the law of diminishing utility only to series of similar goods is to get only one of the facts that are at the basis of the law of value; but to apply it to the largest genus of usable goods that can be made — that is, to consumers' wealth in general — is to take a scientific step in advance. The more wealth, then, that a man has for personal use, the less is its value per unit to him.

The composition of different increments of consumers' wealth.

Very many and very diverse, it should be observed, are the articles that constitute the last increment of general wealth that a consumer devotes to his personal use. In the consumption of any person for a year, for example, an article or two for food may constitute the first or most necessary element. Plain clothing may constitute the second. Rude shelter, an improvement in the food, and some fuel for heat and light may compose the third. Every later element, however, will include qualitative changes in the articles already possessed; for the man wants, not only more things, but better ones. He improves and diversifies the material that he uses, and the later increments of his year's stipend of consumers' wealth take on a very heterogeneous character. The composition of the several increments of wealth consumed is of scientific importance. In the statements that are current, it is said that the final increments of different commodities purchased for consumption at the same cost are, with certain allowances, of the same utility to the purchaser. With the last hundred dollars of the year's income, the man in the illustration will buy some particular things that he did not have before, and he will add quantitatively to his supply of things of which he has already had a certain amount.   If each distinct article on the list costs a dollar, they are all supposed to be of equal utility ; but their degrees of utility are, in fact, very unequal. If the modern theory of value, as it is commonly stated, were literally true, most articles of high quality would sell for three times as much as they actually bring. It is well, at this point in the discussion, to make the needed correction of the law of value ; inasmuch as group incomes depend on that law, and inasmuch as the distinction on which the correction rests is of cardinal importance in connection with wages and interest.   When we undertake the more detailed study of the productivity of final investments of capital, we shall find that success depends on keeping constantly in view this essential distinction.

Error concerning final increments of wealth.

In careful statements of the law of value, allowance is made for the fact that, as an income grows larger, there is not a continuous quantitative increase in the consumption of all the articles that are early secured. Some articles for consumption are never duplicated at all ; and others which are duplicated have, after one unit has been supplied, a comparatively slight utility. Thus, one watch may be nearly indispensable, while a second would be of very little use. Another correction of the current form of statement of this law is of much more importance. What is the final increment of wealth consumed? It is not complete articles, *as such :* it is almost entirely composed of *utilities* of articles. These can be mentally distinguished from other qualities that compose the entire articles, but they cannot be separated from them. A man's final increment of consumers' wealth

They actually consist in utilities in articles.

consists mainly in certain elementary qualities that help to constitute the articles that he uses. It is a literal fact that one can scarcely find on the dining-table of a rich man a single article that, in its entirety, enters into the final increment of wealth that he consumes; yet some component element of almost everything there found does so. Something in the meat, the prepared vegetables, the pastry, etc., is bought with the man's final dollars and constitutes his final increment of food.

In pure theory, the statement of the vital fact of consumption should be this: Every article that a man buys for personal use contains a composite of elements, some one of which enters into his final increment of consumers' wealth. What a man does, as his means increase, is, before anything else, to demand new qualities in the articles that he uses. Often he does not add at all to their number; but he causes them to be made of finer material or to be larger or handsomer. He adds to his wealth for

Goods improved in quality as consumption increases.

consumption, not new things, but new utilities; and these are mainly attached to things of the kinds formerly consumed. As he cannot literally buy a cheap article and afterward improve it, he buys the improved article at a single purchase. The literal effect of spending his last dollar consists in the substituting of a good article for the cheap one, with which he would have contented himself if his available means had been smaller.

Shelter, for example, is one of the prime necessities of life, and there is something in the rich man's mansion that satisfies this primary need. His present house may be the last house that he builds, and in point of time the whole of it is final; but, in its entirety, it is not included within the final increment of his consumers' wealth. The element of simple

shelter that the building contains represents one of
the earliest increments. Some of the dollars that he
has spent are paid for shelter, some for comforts and
conveniences, and some for the final elegances that
the owner adds to his list of consumers' goods. It is
these last elements of cost in the dwelling that, in
this man's case, constitute the final increment of
wealth consumed. The same thing is true of simpler
articles. As the man sits at his breakfast table, he
recognizes, if he thinks, that the very chop on his
plate, by virtue of its different utilities, spans the
entire range of his consumption, from the first increment to the last. It contains nourishment which is
bought with what is logically the man's first dollar.
It also has qualities that are imparted to it at great
cost. Skilled and expensive culinary labor has done
much for it; and it would not be precisely what it
is, if it were not for the last dollars that are expended
in securing an accomplished cook. Simple as this
article is, it contains, in effect, a composite of qualities, some of which enter into the final increment of
wealth consumed, while others distribute themselves
through the series of increments to the very last. If
he can isolate one of these qualitative elements, he
can locate it in the series. But the chop, as a whole,
is bought with a sum of which some part enters into
each increment of the "money" that the man spends
on his own gratification.

It is clear that what is called a "final" unit of
consumers' wealth is not the one secured last in point
of time. In the case of the house in our illustration,
the first and the last increments of consumers' wealth
were bought at the same time, and so were all intermediate increments. This, moreover, is the usual
rule. Even if we were actually to dole out to a man,
unit by unit, the money that he is to spend on him-

[margin note:] Only the
least neces-
sary ele-
ments in
goods
are final
utilities.

[margin note:] Utilities
of different
grades
secured by
purchasing
one article.

self in a year, and let him try to buy the supplies for the year in the order of their importance, he could not do it. Let him have, for example, a yearly income of ten thousand dollars. Give him this amount, in a series of sums of a thousand dollars each, and let him try to buy with the first thousand dollars what is actually the first increment of consumers' wealth for a man on a ten thousand dollar income. With the second of the units of income, let him try to buy what is actually the second increment of consumers' wealth for a man in his status; and with the last thousand dollars let him try to buy what is the true final increment of consumers' wealth for such a man. How could he do it? With the first unit of income he would have to buy the cheapest food; and with later increments he would be obliged to transmute such material into that which is of finer quality. But he does not, in fact, try to accomplish this impossibility. Knowing the extent of his income, he buys the fine food in one purchase. That which, in logic and not in time, constitutes the first increment of consumers' goods is that economic element, or utility, in goods consumed which in some form would have been secured if the man had had only one unit of income at his disposal. A man does not, with the first unit of his income, build a shanty, and with later units transmute it successively into a house, a mansion and a palace: he builds the palace at one operation. Somewhere within it there is what, in an economic sense, is equivalent to a shanty; for there is in it, above all else, a power to afford some shelter to its occupants; and this single utility, merged and lost in the great structure, constitutes an early unit of consumers' goods. Logically, this unit stands near the head of the list, since it precedes most others in importance. In time, however, it accompanies other utilities that stand late in the list. Some quality in the house and similar qualities in the other goods that the man uses constitute the logically final increment of his goods for consumption. A mass of utilities — the group of logically last and finest qualities imparted to articles used for consumption — constitutes the true final increment of the wealth that he consumes. This is an obvious and practical fact, and it demands — what we shall soon consider — a somewhat radical amendment of the theory of value.

Men add to their consumers' wealth, then, more by improving the grade of the goods that they use than by multiplying them. They infuse wealth, as it were, into their goods. They give to these goods new service-rendering powers, and cause articles that in their cheapest forms embody one unit each of consumers' wealth to take a form in which they embody two, three or ten such units.

Capital increases in the same way.[1] New units are added to producers' wealth more by improving capital-goods than by multiplying them. We infuse new wealth into the instruments in our hands by imparting to them new productive powers. We substitute a better tool for the one that we have been using, and it is the difference between the two tools that constitutes a final increment of capital. Parallel facts concerning capital.

The conclusions so far reached may be summarized as follows : — Propositions concerning all wealth.

(1) Wealth, as such, whether it be used for consumption or for production, may be arranged in a series of increments, in the order in which they would be selected by a user, if they were purchased one at a time.

(2) This series is imaginary, since it is impossible to separate and buy singly these increments.

[1] See Ch. XVII.

(3) The several increments of consumers' wealth, on the one hand, and of producers' wealth, on the other, consist rather of elements in goods than of goods in their entirety.

(4) The utility of the final increment of consumers' wealth grows smaller, as the number of the increments in the series increases.

(5) The productivity of the last unit of producers' wealth in a series grows less, as the number of units increases.

Value not fixed by the utility of entire articles. Two further assertions that we now have to prove are: (1) Market values are fixed entirely by the utility of the final increments of consumers' wealth, as we have just defined them, and not, as a rule, by the utility of entire articles.   (2) Interest is fixed **Interest not fixed by the productivity of entire instruments.** by the productivity of final increments of capital, as we have just defined them, and not by the productive power of instruments of production, taken in their entirety.   The usefulness of the final commodity of a given kind seldom fixes the values of such commodities ; and the productivity of the final instrument of a given kind seldom fixes the rate of interest.[1]

---

[1] The law of variation that we have stated in this chapter is so comprehensive that, in another mode of action, it fixes wages. The pay of labor is governed by the final productivity of labor, as such, and not merely by the productive power of a final or marginal laborer.   We can add to the supply of labor by making workmen more efficient, as well as by making them more numerous. Educating and training men adds new increments to the supply of human productive energy.   We can arrange increments of labor, as such, in a series, in the order of their importance, and define the successive increments in the same analytical way in which we have defined the increments of consumers' wealth and those of producers' wealth.   In the series of increments of labor, as thus defined, there is traceable the law of diminishing productivity ; and it is the productive power of the final increment of labor, thus defined, that in reality governs the rate of wages.

CHAPTER XV

THE MARGINAL EFFICIENCY OF CONSUMERS' WEALTH
THE BASIS OF GROUP DISTRIBUTION

VERY practical is the correction that has to be made in the accepted theory of value. If we were to go through the shops of a city, selecting at random articles of high quality and learning the prices at which they are actually sold, we might multiply all these prices by ten, without bringing them up to the figures at which, according to the final utility theory as it is usually stated, these goods ought to sell. If this theory in its uncorrected form were true, a man would pay five hundred dollars or more for an overcoat for which he actually gives fifty, and a thousand dollars for a watch for which he actually pays a hundred. A very rich man would give ten million dollars for a dwelling instead of one million, etc. The final utility theory of value, when it is thus applied to commodities in their entirety, gives results that are grotesquely at variance with the values that the market establishes. It exaggerates the prices of all goods, except the poorest and cheapest.

The final utility theory applied to entire commodities calls for a great marking up of actual prices.

Here we record a charge of some gravity against a modern theory. We assert that the so-called Austrian teachings concerning value rest on a perfectly sound principle, — that, namely, of final utility, — but that the mode of applying this principle needs to be changed. *It is final increments of wealth in*

*commodities, and not, as a rule, commodities in their
entirety, that furnish those test measures of utility
to which market values conform.*

The difference between the last commodity of a
given kind that a man buys for his own consumption, and the last addition that he makes to the consumers' wealth that he uses, is a very real one. As
we have seen, the man adds the last increment to the
wealth that is embodied in his wardrobe, when he replaces a coat that cost forty-five dollars with one that
costs fifty. The last five dollars that are spent on the
coat are represented by some quality that this garment
possesses. It is a final utility in the coat; but the
garment in its entirety is far from being a final utility, even though it be the last one of its class that
the owner procures. It is only what the man pays
the last five dollars for that acts directly in adjusting the value of the coat; and what he gives the
forty-five dollars for consists of elements that get
their value in another way, and a way that is not
directly connected with this action.

In a few cases, however, commodities in their entirety are final units of consumers' wealth. There
are some goods that cater to no wants except the
last and least intense ones that a consumer satisfies.
In these cases, the entire articles figure directly in the
adjustment of values. But in most cases there are elements in the goods that do not figure directly in
the adjustment of values; and these elements often
constitute almost the whole of the goods. Very
analytical is the test that the actual market applies
to the goods that are offered for sale. Very subtle
is its process of resolving goods into their economic
elements, and of putting an appraisal on each of the
separate utilities that compose them.

Here we forecast the correction that has to be

Mode of
detecting
real final
utilities.

made in the theory of value, for the distinction between final commodities and final units of wealth in commodities is equally important in the theory of wages and interest. The earnings of all capital, in fact, are gauged by the product of the final increment of capital; and this final increment consists, not mainly of entire instruments of production, but of elements in these instruments.

Wages and interest are the chief subjects of our present studies; but they depend on a general law of economic variation which, in another application, adjusts also the market values of goods. In all the applications of this law, the distinction between final goods and final wealth-elements in goods is of primary consequence. The so-called Austrian theory of value — with which our readers are assumed to be familiar — gives a psychological basis for the commercial fact that the more goods of a kind there are to be sold, the lower must be the price, in order that all may be purchased. As the classical economists said, the price must be reduced, in order that men who have not as yet bought goods of this kind may take some of them, and also in order that those who have already bought some may take more. For this result the Austrian theory accounts. It furnishes the philosophy of the adjustment of what may be called, in the case of each kind of goods, the consumers' purchase limit. It tells why a man who has bought three units of the commodity A, when the price of it was a dollar, buys four units and no more, when the price falls to ninety cents. The purchaser, it shows, simply obeys the rule of getting the largest obtainable utility for each dime that he spends.[1]

The general law of economic variation best known in its action on prices.

---

[1] The money that the man spends really represents some sacrifice on his own part; and a full statement of the theory of value would take us into a psychological region whenever we speak of

Single articles that are exactly alike grow, as is usually said, less and less important to a user, as he comes to have more and more of them. The commodity A may be the most necessary thing that the man uses; and the first unit of it, if indispensable to his life, has an indefinitely great utility. A second unit of this article will be much less needed, and it may be that a first unit of the commodity B will now be preferred. We may for convenience define, as a unit of each kind of goods whatsoever, what is offered in the market for a dime. The man will buy, with the dimes that he can spend each day, a series of things that arrange themselves in the order of their importance to him; and the law that determines what he will actually buy is that of the diminishing utility of the successive units.

Graphic illustration of the law of final utility, as usually stated.

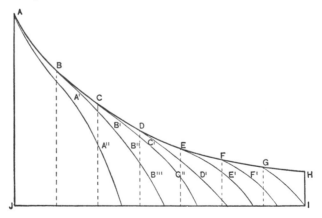

Let A, B, C, etc., represent different kinds of consumers' goods; and let the utility, to the same con-

cost, as it does whenever we speak of utility. Cost is, in the last analysis, pain inflicted, just as utility is pleasure conferred. So far in the study we do not now need to go. It is enough, for present purposes, that the man, as a result of his sacrifices, has dimes to spend and is studying how to make the most of them.

sumer, of a dime's worth of each of them be measured by the vertical distance of the letter that represents it from the line JI. The first unit of A has a utility amounting to AJ, and the first of H has a utility of HI; while B, C, D, etc., have the utilities that are severally measured by vertical lines descending from them to the line JI. A, B, C, etc., are first increments of the several commodities; while A′, B′, C′, etc., are second increments of the same kind of goods; and A″, B″, C″, are third increments. In like manner, we may designate fourth and fifth increments, etc.

We will say that the man arranges in a series the dimes that he can spend in a day, and buys with the first dime what is of most importance to him; with the second dime that which stands next in the order of importance; and so on, till with his last dimes he buys things that are needed least of all. The first increment of his day's purchase of consumers' wealth is, then, one dime's worth of the article A. The second unit is B. As a return for the next dime to be spent, there are two articles offering themselves which have equal degrees of utility. They are C and a second unit of A, here designated as A′. The man will spend two dimes and get these two articles. D and B′ are next in importance, and they have equal utilities. The man's fifth and sixth dimes will get them. With the seventh dime he buys C′, or a second unit of the article C; and with the eighth, ninth and tenth dimes he buys E, B″ and A″. When he reaches H, he finds that that article and B‴, C″, D′, E′ and F′ are on a par in importance to him, and he spends his last six dimes on these things. In all, he has spent twenty-one dimes and has exhausted the free income of a day.

The last increments of each commodity that this man buys are price-making increments. The sale of them is secured by bringing the price down to such a point that nothing else that the man can buy with the money has for him a higher degree of utility. In other words, the lowering of the price of the article brings this increment of it within the man's purchasing limit and within the purchasing limit of other men who are in the same economic condition. If the price were higher, no one of these men would take what is now his final increment. If the whole supply needs to be sold, the price must be reduced to the point thus defined. If, for example, in our diagram, the article H were costlier than it is, the article I would be preferred to it by all of this class of purchasers. As it is, the increment of H indicated in the diagram is sold ; and the price that insures this sale is also the price of all other units of this commodity.

Final increments, then, are commercially strategic. Their utilities count in price making; while the excess of utility in the earlier increments does not, in this connection, have any influence. In fixing the prices of these things the great usefulness of the earlier units of A and B counts for nothing. These units would be purchased, even though the prices were higher than they are ; and there is, therefore, no need that the venders should bring the price of A and B to the present level, in order to insure the sale of these highly serviceable units of them. This is saying that, in the case of each kind of goods, all increments except the last one give net gains to the purchasers. They insure to them what has been called "consumers' rent." The utility of final increments to the men who buy them, however, gives no surplus benefit, since it is fully offset by the cost of them. What the man sacrifices in order to get them is worth to him as much as they are. The extra utility of the earlier

Final increments the price-making ones.

increments, on the other hand, is uncompensated. Consumers
It is a differential amount of personal benefit, or an surplus
illustrated.
amount of good that is done to the consumers by
certain units of a commodity, in excess of the benefit
conferred by the last unit.

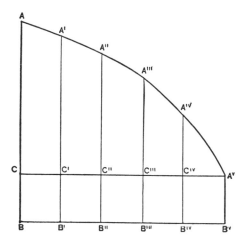

If, for example, the utility of successive increments
of A declines along the curve AA^v, and if AB measures the utility of the first increment, $A'B'$ that of
the second, and A^vB^v that of the last, the differential
benefit conferred on consumers by the earlier increments of this article is measured by $AC + A'C' +$
$A''C'' + A'''C''' + A^{iv}C^{iv}$. If we suppose that the
lines are contiguous, having width to fill an area,
then the area CAA^v measures the whole of what
has been called the consumer's rent, derived from
the article A by one purchaser.   Such consumers' It does not
rent, differential benefit or uncompensated utility count in
price
cannot enter into the adjusting of prices. This is a making.
principle that everywhere holds true.

Final increments of different goods, then, are supposed to compete with each other for the favor of

purchasers — with the result that final utilities secured at equal expense are equal; that the earlier utilities in the series are unequal to each other, and are always greater than the final ones; and that the amount of this excess has no effect on prices.

What if even the final increments themselves do not always count in the adjusting of market values? Careful statements of the law have already shown that this is sometimes the case. There may, indeed, be a large difference between the utility of the first increment of a commodity and that of the second, and the utility curve for such an article may show a series of considerable gaps. It is not a continuous downward curve, but a series of points more or less widely separated. The points in the diagram on page 222 that are marked by the letters A', A'', B', and B'', etc., constitute such a series. In cases of this kind, the last increment of a commodity that a particular man gets may not figure in the adjustment of values. He would pay more for it rather than go without it. The last units of many articles that the consumer buys have a degree of usefulness to him that exceeds the utility of the really marginal things that he buys for the same price. The prices of A and G might go up considerably before he would cease to buy these articles; and the prices might go far down without inducing him to buy more. The articles B''', C'', D', E', and F' in this diagram are really in the strategic or price-making positions. If you raise the price of any one of these, the consumers of this class will cease to buy it, and will take another article in place of it.

In seeking for the reason why the article A is sold at the price that it actually commands, we must, of course, find the reason why some part of the supply will remain unsold at a price that is in the least degree

Final units of goods usually do not count.

higher. With this adjustment the men whose consumption is represented in the diagram on page 222
have no connection. There are, however, other men
in whose cases an increment of A is a part of the true
final increment of consumers' wealth. To them this
commodity is on a plane, in usefulness, with other
things that are bought with their final units of available income. If you raise the price, those men will
cease to buy some of A; and then some of this product will remain unsold. Thus far we have stated,
in outline, the accepted theory of value, and have
added nothing that is not already contained in careful presentations of it. The discontinuity of successive units of some commodities, as they are arranged
in a series joined by a utility curve, is a part of this
theory. In this there is enough to show that, if we
understand the philosophy of value, we must take
all society into view as the purchaser of things.
If you raise the price of an article, you will find,
somewhere in the consumption of the public, a
point where purchases of this article will cease.
The action of raising the price singles out the particular men, in the strategic position, whose action
fixes the value of this commodity for all other
men. They are the social price makers for this
commodity.

It is not enough, however, to say that this principle
merely introduces a refinement of the theory of value,
as that theory stood before the discontinuity of successive units in the utility curve of a particular article
was recognized. It is not final commodities, but final
units of wealth, that figure in the adjustments of
values, and articles in their entirety are seldom final
units of wealth in any consumer's scale. Search
through the whole of society, and you will probably
not find a man in whose estimates the commodity

Articles that
enter into
the final
social incre-
ment of
consumers'
wealth are
price
makers.

C is a final or price-making utility. There are, as we have seen, a few cases in which whole articles are included in the last social unit of consumers' wealth, and the utility of these things is a factor in price making. As, in most cases, only one element in an article is a part of this test increment of consumers' wealth, only that element is a factor in price making. There is no class in all society to whom the last unit of C does not afford a surplus of utility. If C is a house, it affords shelter; but it also caters to the more luxurious wants. In the house, merged with other qualities, there is something that is a true final utility. This quality acts on prices, and the other utilities that the house contains do not.

Few articles in their entirety do this.

What is essential in a theory of value that shall account for prices, as they actually exist, is contained in the following propositions. We state them here, because something akin to what they assert is true of capital, and is essential in a theory of distribution that shall account for the rates of wages and interest that actually prevail. The universal law of economic variation must be stated with accuracy, if it is to account for either values, wages or interest.

(1) It is the final increment of consumers' wealth, as such, and of that only, that figures in the adjustment of values.

Propositions concerning the law of value.

(2) Commodities in their entirety are seldom included in the final or price-making increments of consumers' wealth.

(3) A commodity for consumers' use is a service-rendering thing, and is valued according to the amount of service that, at certain test points in social consumption, it is able to render.

(4) Most commodities render several different kinds of service at the same time. A thing of this kind is to be regarded as a bundle of distinct utilities,

tied together by being embodied in a common material object.

(5) The tests of the actual market measure these utilities separately, and the value of the article results from all the measurements.

(6) Only one of the utilities that constitute a commodity is a part of one man's marginal unit of consumers' wealth. The other utilities in the thing are intra-marginal. They are higher utilities and do not, in the case of this consumer, have an influence in fixing the price of the article.

(7) Only as the final utility principle is applied separately to each of the utilities or service-rendering powers in goods can it account for the values that goods have in the actual market.

If the principle of final utility be applied to entire articles, it will give values that are, in most cases, many fold greater than are the actual values that the dealings of the market establish. If, on the other hand, it be applied to value elements in goods, it will give results that the market will confirm. Here we are bringing theory into harmony with life. The modern theory of value analyzes the psychological process that lies back of the phenomena of the market — that is, it traces the phenomena of the market to their causes, in the mental operations of those who buy goods. In every market there are measuring operations going on, and the things measured are personal benefits. If a commodity has embodied in itself the power to render several distinct kinds of service, — if it is a composite thing, having a number of distinct utilities, — there is no escaping the fact that a true valuation must find a way to appraise each of these qualities by itself.

If we were not to push the analysis of this process to the end, we should do well to adhere to the older and more simple theory of value, and to keep altogether clear of the psychology of market dealings. Mr. John Stuart Mill has told us that, if the tentative price of an article is too high to insure the sale of the whole supply, the price is lowered till new purchasers take some of the goods and old purchasers take more than they

Old theories of value more accurate than recent ones, if these are left incomplete.

formerly did. This statement is, in any view, a correct one; and unless we want to understand the mental operations that determine the action of consumers and bring their purchases to a stop at certain definite points, it is enough. But if we do wish to understand that operation, we must find how each utility in that composite thing, an average commodity, is actually measured, and how the measurement controls the market. We shall, therefore, now examine the manner in which utilities, as such, are tested in commercial dealings. Only thus is it possible to perceive how values and the group shares that depend on them are actually adjusted.

CHAPTER XVI

HOW THE MARGINAL EFFICIENCY OF CONSUMERS
WEALTH IS MEASURED

THE simplest condition in which the law of value could act would be a state in which each article in the stock of consumers' goods was able to render one kind of service, and that only, to the man who used it. Let us, then, at first assume that this is the fact, and later let us modify the assumption, by taking into account the different kinds of service that a commodity can actually render.

It is a psychological fact that a person cannot receive, at any given time, more than one service of a particular kind. If at this moment you can confer on him one particular benefit, you cannot, at the same moment, confer on him a second benefit that is the exact duplicate of the first. There is a difficulty encountered, in appealing to a consumer with two services that are quite alike, which is akin to the physical difficulty that is experienced if one tries to make two material objects occupy the same space at the same time. Two utilities that are absolutely alike need, as it were, to get access to the same spot on the consumer's sensorium ; and they cannot do it at once. There is no enjoying two absolutely similar pleasures together. They must come in turns, if they are to be enjoyed at all.

Hypothesis that each article renders one service.

Impossibility of receiving at once two services exactly alike.

231

If any commodity were able to render only one service, then, for use within a particular period of time, a first unit of it would have a positive utility and a second unit would have a negative one. Any unit after the first would be in the way, and the possessor would take some trouble to get rid of it. Having a coat of a certain kind, he would have no immediate use for another made of the same goods and cut in the same pattern. If he possessed such a coat and had to use it at once, if at all, and if there were no secondary use that he could make of it, any tramp might have it for the asking.

Under such circumstances, there is no utility curve for this commodity. The line that expresses the usefulness of successive units of it will show an abrupt drop from a point that indicates a plus quantity to a

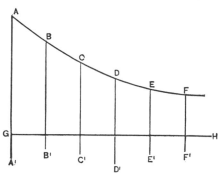

point that indicates a minus one. Let positive utilities be measured upward from the line GH, and let negative utilities, usually called disutilities, be measured downward from that line. The line descending from A to the line GH measures the amount of service rendered to a consumer by one unit of the commodity A, and the line ascending from A' to the line GH measures the disutility of a second increment of it. In like manner, the lines from B, C, D, E and F measure the usefulness of the first increments of these things; and those ascending from B', C', D', E' and F' measure the disutility of the second increments. The curve that descends through A, B, C, D, E and F is the only utility curve that the case affords. It describes the diminishing amounts of *different* utilities arranged in a series. The line from each of these letters to the horizontal line GH measures the importance of each single service, which is the only one of its kind that the man is receiving. Here we have the primary law of value. Of a series of utilities that are exactly alike, the first is measured by a positive quantity and all following ones by negative quantities. These negative quantities, moreover, grow larger as the number of similar utilities is multiplied : a second superfluous A is somewhat more in the way than is a first one, and a third is a still more annoying incumbrance. The same is true of successive B's, C's, etc.

We may, however, often get secondary services out of goods, by devoting them to uses so distinct from the services which they primarily render that we can use two similar commodities at once. The case of the rolls of bread cited by Professor von Böhm-Bawerk [1] is an instance of this kind. Some of the bread is there used as food for the man who possesses it, and the remainder serves to feed his dog. There we obviate the psychological difficulty which arises from the impossibility of rendering two services to the same consumer at the same time by introducing a second sentient being, a four-footed consumer, for whose welfare the man is concerned.

We can usually get secondary services from goods, by ceasing to limit the time in which they must be rendered. One might, for example, have furnishings,

[1] See *The Positive Theory of Capital,* by Professor von Böhm-Bawerk, page 146.

decorations, equipage, etc., at a city residence and similar things at a country house. The owner would then use the two sets of commodities in turn, the real utility of one set consisting in saving the cost of transportation of the other set. In all cases like this, the second unit of the commodity is virtually a different thing from the first one. It may be commercially the same article, but it is a different consumers' good. It appeals to a different want, and may be of some use to the person who is already enjoying the first unit of the commodity.

If we assume that our commodity renders only one service, we do not vitiate the principle on which value is based, and we make a gain in simplicity of statement. In making such an assumption, we put out of view the subsidiary services that a thing can often render — we forget that the roll of Professor von Böhm-Bawerk's illustration can feed the dog, as well as the man. This is separating, in a bodily way, the utilities that the market actually appraises separately. The primary fact about such isolated utilities is that we can use only one of them at a time, for a second one is worth less than nothing. The figure on page 232, then, shows what goods have a part in fixing market prices — namely, those only which are indicated by the letter F of the diagram. Each article, let us say, costs a dollar. Since all of them except F afford consumers' surpluses, or "rents," they are not on the margin of consumption, and you may ask somewhat more than you do for any of them without losing this customer; but if you raise the price of the last thing that is within his purchase limit, he will stop buying it. A, B, C, D and E are not, in this man's case, price-making articles.

How, then, do these commodities get their market value? Somewhere in society there obviously must be a point at which the sale of these things will stop, if the price becomes higher than it is. There are, in fact, a number of such points. There are men in whose scale of consumption E, for example, is a marginal article. The price of E is made to be what it is, in order that these men may buy it, for their purchases are needed to carry off the supply of it. There are, again, other men to whom D is a marginal commodity; and there are those to whom, respectively, C, B and A are marginal. For each commodity, separately considered, there is a group of purchasers who will cease to buy the article, if it becomes more costly; and this group of men is, therefore, the social price-making class for this commodity. It is to insure the patronage of this class that the makers of the article put the price where it is. *Certain units of the other articles are final in the scales of other consumers, and they are their price makers.*

Now tie these articles together, in different combinations, and sell the entire bundles. Let one combination contain all the utilities; let another contain A, B, C, D and E; let a third contain A, B, C and D; let a fourth contain A, B and C; and let a fifth contain A and B. Let A stand alone and be separately procurable. How is the law of value affected by this bunching process? Does the selling of A, B, C, D and E in the same bundle with F give to these things any power over prices that they did not have before? Not at all. F is still the sole price maker, in the case of the men who buy it. The man whose scale of consumption already contained all the articles, to and including F, will buy them all, as he did before; and of them all only F will, by the amount of its utility, act in adjusting values. *This fact not changed by combining the articles in various ways, and selling entire combinations.*

If F becomes dearer, this purchaser will not buy the bundle of goods containing it: he will buy only the bundle that contains the other articles, and E will now be the thing procured by his marginal purchase. All the men in his economic status will do this; and the demand for the combinations of goods terminating with E will be quickened, while that for the bundles which have F, in addition to these things, will be slackened. Production will adapt itself to the changed demand. More combinations without F and fewer with F will be the result. The net effect is precisely what it would have been, if each article had been sold by itself. A rise in the price of F has caused the men with whom F was a marginal article to cease buying it. A return of the price of F to its former level would cause them to resume their purchases of it. The price of F, in fact, adapts itself to the utility that this article has in the want scale of this class of men.

The price of E is regulated in a similar manner, but the regulating is accomplished by a different set of purchasers. There is a class of men to whom E is the marginal article; and a rise in the price of it would cause the members of this class to stop buying it. They do this in the way already described, by ceasing to take the bundles of goods containing E and taking instead those having D as the least needed or marginal article. Restore the former price of E, and this class of consumers will renew their habit of purchasing the combination containing it. This class, then, is the one whose estimate sets the market value of E. Another class of men similarly do the price making for D, since this is their marginal commodity. For each article, in short, one class of persons is in the strategic position, at the point in the economic society where values are determined. The estimates that members of this class may make of the utilities of other articles have no direct influence on values.[1]

The prices of the different articles still determined by different sets of purchasers.

[1] A full study of value would, of course, notice many things that we here omit. One of them is, that a rise in the price of any

Now we are ready to see how values are in reality adjusted. Every article, except one of the poorest and simplest kind, is a composite of different utilities, and can render various unlike kinds of service at once. It is only for the sake of these services that it is wanted or bought. Utilities, as we have said and as we cannot say too emphatically, are all that the market takes account of in fixing values. Commercial dealing has its way of measuring the importance of each specific service that an article can render, and of fixing the value of it so as to make it express these measures. In every such commodity there is a marginal utility, and this is the only one that counts in fixing the price of it. Every commodity, except the poorest and cheapest that can be made, is, in effect, such a bundle of service-rendering elements as we have just described. The marginal element in the bundle has a direct influence on prices, but the other elements have none.

Commodities are bundles of unlike utilities, which act as distinct articles in the fixing of values.

Only one of the utilities is marginal in the case of each purchaser, and only marginal utilities influence prices.

For example, let A, B, C, D, E and F represent, not separate articles, of which each can render one service, but separate utilities in one article of a high grade. There are six different things that this article can do for a man who uses it; and, as the services are dissimilar, they can be rendered at the same time. A is the most important of these utilities, or service-

article in the list would cause purchasers of the class first mentioned, if their incomes in money remained unchanged, to cease buying F. The demand for the marginal goods of each of the classes of purchasers is thus checked, wherever goods that are not marginal become dearer. Moreover, when a rise in price, either of F or of one of the other things, throws F out of the purchasing list, some article — say, G — may take its place. There is in this, however, nothing that calls for a modification of what we here affirm — namely, that each class of purchasers has its marginal article, that the utility of that article to them has a direct influence. in the adjusting of the price of it, and that the utility to these persons of other things has no direct influence on values.

rendering powers, and F is the least important. F is, then, for the time the only price maker. If this article, with all these qualities, becomes more costly, buyers will cease to take the article which has that quality and will content themselves with the one that is of the next lower grade. They will, in other words, cease to buy a bundle of utilities including all from A to F and will buy instead the bundle that includes the list ending with E. The demand for the utility, F, is thus slackened, and the price of that particular value element tends to fall.

That this is no bit of pure imagination, may be seen by examining the workings of the market for any kind of goods of high quality. Our illustration is, in fact, far from making our theoretical statement actually as subtle as is the working of demand and supply in the commercial world. Unerringly does this process single out the value elements in goods and adjust prices, in all cases, by appraisal of the marginal element in them.

A practical illustration. Here, for example, is a canoe that a man keeps, for his recreation, in a lake in the wilderness. It is a composite article; and, if we were to analyze it into the elements that give it value, we should find that, for all economic purposes, it virtually consists in a series of utilities. This series of economic qualities, named in the order of their importance, would stand somewhat as follows: —

(1) Power to keep a man afloat. A dead tree would have this quality.

(2) Power to carry a man across stretches of deep water. A smooth log could render this service.

(3) Power to keep an occupant dry and comfortable, and to carry his effects. A dugout would do this.

(4) Power to move swiftly and to ride waves safely. A well-made sailing canoe would do this.

(5) Power to gratify the owner's taste. A gracefully shaped vessel, with appropriate colors and fittings, does this.

Here are five distinct services that the sailing canoe renders, and of them all the first is the most important. A means of floating is what the man absolutely needs, if he is to entrust himself at all to the waters. The capacity to sustain the man on the surface of the lake is, then, the primary utility of the canoe. If the man embarks on the water at all, there is no limit to the "subjective value" that he would assign to this quality in the thing that he uses to sustain him. Though this thing were only a dead tree rolled into the water, the one utility that it has is· greater than is any other utility that the best canoe can possess. Nothing whatever in the finished and graceful craft is as important to the owner as that element in it which is nothing more than the equivalent of a floating tree. The quality that is next in importance is power to move, and this a smooth log possesses. The third is the increased commodiousness afforded by the dugout, the next is the speed possessed by the well-shaped canoe with its sail, and the last is the elegance of the handsomely shaped and decorated vessel.

Figuratively speaking, in a very good canoe there are a dead tree, a log, a dugout, a convenient sailing boat and an elegant one ; for the qualities of all these things are massed in the one craft that a sportsman actually procures. We need, however, to see clearly that only the last of these qualities is, in the economic sense, a final utility and that the whole boat cannot be such. The boat in its entirety includes utilities of every grade. For them all the owner may have given seventy-five dollars; but he would, perhaps, have given a thousand, if he had paid what would measure the individual importance of the various utilities. The power of the canoe to keep him afloat would be worth five hundred dollars to him, if he could not have it for less. The power to move to and fro would be worth three hundred. Carrying power counts for one hundred dollars, speed of movement for seventy-five and decoration for twenty-five. These sums represent what he would give, if he had to do so, for the various utilities in this commodity. If this man were the marginal purchaser of this whole commodity, a thousand dollars would then be the price of it.

How the market analyzes goods and appraises their elements separately. The last quality that the boat possesses is a final utility in the true sense. If the decoration of this vessel cost thirty dollars, the fisherman would buy a less ornate canoe. The demand for decorated vessels would thus be reduced, and the demand for vessels of the less ornate type would be increased. More canoes of the inferior kind would be made, and there would be fewer of the superior kind. The net result would be a reduction in the output of that product which consists in utility number five in the series. As many canoes would be made as before, but they would be without the special decoration that constitutes the final utility in the canoes of the highest quality. In canoes costing seventy-five dollars, this utility is clearly the only one the measure of which is a gauge of price.

How, then, do the other utilities in the boat get their market valuation? There is a class of persons to whom the fourth utility in the canoe, its speed, is **A different set of purchasers appraises each element.** the final one. They buy boats of the fourth grade instead of those of the fifth, doing without the decorations. The amount that these men spend, in order to insure a boat that will sail by some points faster than another would do, yields to them, in pleasure, a result that is worth just what it costs. The float-

ing power of the boat and its other intra-marginal
qualities are, however, worth to them more than
they cost—they yield a "consumers' rent," or a gain
that exceeds the gain that can be had by a marginal
purchase. To this class of men, therefore, only the
fourth utility in the canoe is a price-making one.
In consequence of the demand of this class of persons, this utility may bring twenty dollars in the
market.

There is, likewise, a class of persons to whom the
third utility in this composite article is marginal;
and these men are the consumers whose demand sets
the market value of this third utility. They sacrifice speed, contenting themselves with comfort; and
their demand may make this utility worth fifteen
dollars. There is, again, a class of buyers who fix the
price of the second utility — say, at ten dollars —
and another of those who fix the price of the first
utility — say, at five dollars. If there are five distinct services rendered by such a pleasure craft as
we have selected for illustration, it takes five distinct classes of persons to fix the value of it in the
market. The law of final utility works as it would
if each service-rendering power possessed by the boat
were a distinct article. To all intents and purposes, the different utilities are different articles tied
in bundles, some of which contain all five of the
articles, some four, some three, etc. To no one consumer are all these virtually different things final
utilities. A bundle, *as a whole*, is never a final unit
of any one's consumers' wealth; but each element in
it is a final utility to some class, and it is that class
only whose mental estimate of it fixes its price. There
are, then, five prices in the canoe. Expressing the
values of the five different services which the canoe
renders, they are, respectively, twenty-five, twenty,

fifteen, ten and five dollars. The entire canoe, then, brings seventy-five dollars in the market.

Make watches dearer than they are, and the man who pays a hundred dollars for a watch will not go without one. He will buy one that formerly sold for ninety dollars, and will forego something in the way of ornamentation. Another class will take the grade that lately sold for eighty dollars, and will forego something in the way of accuracy. Each class will give up, not watches, but something in watches. A certain class that formerly bought dollar watches will, however, give them up altogether, since there is no cheaper pocket timepiece to be had. To these men the lowest grade of watches, taken in their entirety, may be rated as final utilities. Their demand fixes the price of watches of this first and lowest grade.

Although this statement may seem to take us into a region of theoretical subtlety, there is no doubt of the substantial fact that the market acts in this analytical way, and that the commerce of the world takes a character which is the result of this action. Over the whole world the mills would be turning out different goods from those that they are now making, ships and railway cars would have different contents from those that they now contain, shops would everywhere have different goods in their windows and on their shelves and counters, if the law of final utility, as applied to goods in their *entirety*, determined the values of the goods. If we could make the theory of value, as it is commonly stated, rule actual markets, we should radically change the prices of all kinds of goods; and in doing this we should change the quantity of goods of each kind that is produced and used — we should effect a radical transformation in the economic life of the world.

Goods of fine quality would then be, as a rule, many times dearer than they are.

If we were here undertaking to present at length the theory of value, we should lay great stress on the fact that value is a social phenomenon. Things sell, indeed, according to their final utilities; but it is their final utilities *to society*. In the social body as a whole, every utility in a costly article is somewhere in the position of a final utility. The shanty that, in an earlier illustration, we found was virtually contained in the palace, is a final utility to some members of society ; and it is their valuation that fixes the market rate which that element in the palace commands. This quality in the palace we may call the first of the *value elements* that compose it. It is the lowest and cheapest of the economic constituents that compose the royal dwelling, and may be had for a hundred dollars. The difference between the shanty and a cottage may be regarded as the second value element ; and this also has its marginal purchasers. If it were possible to make the shanty and then to transform it into a cottage, the two value elements would be produced at different times. What is actually done, however, is to build the cottage instead of building the shanty ; and the second class of purchasers gauge by their demand the value of this substitution. It is in this way that a distinct class of buyers has the fixing of the actual price of each value element that enters into a palatial dwelling. If there are ten grades of watches, and if, therefore, it takes ten classes of purchasers to fix the value of a watch of the highest grade, each of these classes may be regarded as the social valuers and appraisers of the particular value element that, in the consumption of its members, is a final utility. In general, then, when fine articles — composite things, bundles of distinct elements — are offered to society, the great composite consumer, each element has somewhere in the social organism the effect of fixing a part of the total value. In no other way can the article, as a whole, get a valuation. To no individual are all its utilities final.[1]

[1] A point of much consequence is the fact that many articles have secondary uses, besides those for which they are primarily intended ; and so more than one such article may be useful — but for different purposes — to a consumer at one time. The roll, in Professor Böhm-Bawerk's illustration, already cited, can be used to feed a dog as well as a man ; and, if we regard the dog, not as a consumer, but as a commodity for his owner's consumption, the roll that appeases the dog's hunger is put to a distinct and subordinate use. Again, the sportsman whose hunting lodge is on one of the Adirondack lakes may keep boats on several others, for the sole purpose of saving the trouble involved in carrying boats from place to place. None of these boats, of course, except the least useful of them, can, in its entirety, be a marginal and price-making commodity. If the owner, for economy, relinquishes any of his boats, it will be this marginal one ; and he will give for no one of them more than the marginal one is worth to him. Does that change the principle that we have just stated, that values rest on marginal utilities in goods rather than on goods in their entirety ? Let us see.

If the prices of the boats rise, the man who is about to purchase an outfit of them has the alternative of getting on with one less than he had intended to procure, or of keeping the proposed number intact and somewhat reducing the quality of all. If he had intended to buy five boats, for use on five different bodies of water, he may content himself with four ; and, in lieu of the fifth, he may submit to the inconvenience of carrying one of the others occasionally to the lake where the fifth would have been kept. If this is a smaller sacrifice than is involved in reducing the quality of (say) three of the less important boats, it is conceivable that we have here an exceptional case, in which an entire marginal article of a high grade figures as a price-making increment of consumers' wealth. The man may buy no boats but those of the quality that he had intended to buy before the price was raised, but he may take fewer of them. The utility of the final one, consisting solely in its power to save to the owner the trouble of having a boat transported, will furnish a gauge for the price that this man will pay for all boats of this kind. It is the fortuitous fact that the article has secondary uses which makes this mode of adjusting the price of it possible.

The line of conduct that the owner of these boats is here supposed to pursue is, be it noted, not the line that consumers usually pursue. In a vast majority of cases, a rise in the price of goods of a particular kind throws, not entire goods, but marginal qualities in goods out of use. Even in the case — not over-frequent — of the man who is about to buy several exactly similar boats, the chances are ten to one that a rise in price would cause him to forego something in the quality of one or more of them. If he does this, — if he takes cheaper boats for the less important uses, — the principle that we have stated applies.

Goods of the very poorest grade may, indeed, be marginal in their entirety. If there is no cheaper kind to which one may resort, he must take this grade or nothing. Even then he will doubtless seek 'or some article, of a somewhat different kind, that will serve as a partial substitute for what he foregoes ; and, when he does this, the effect is much the same as if a still poorer grade of the article that is foregone had existed.

It should be noted that most articles deteriorate in the using, so that the only way to keep one's self supplied with perfect or nearly perfect goods of this kind is to get new ones often. Wear a coat a few weeks only before discarding it, and be equally liberal with the remainder of your wardrobe, and you will always be clothed in garments that are stylish and free from traces of wear. You must, however, buy many coats, etc., in order to do it ; and, by thus increasing the quantity of such garments, you really improve the quality of those that you use. This, indeed, is the sole object of the increase. Quantity in goods for consumption may thus really insure quality. It is only the last and least utility that has gone out of a coat that has been used for a short season ; and it is only for the sake of restoring that marginal utility that the man buys another. The principle that we have stated operates here. Increasing the amount of consumers' wealth always means improving the quality of consumption, for new qualities are thus added, in an all-around way, to the things that every one uses. There is a social increment of utilities — a vast and composite addition to the service-rendering qualities of things — that appears at every step in the increasing wealth of the world. These are the strategic elements which rule the market. The measure of them fixes values. The men who, in each case, do the measuring are the agents of society controlling their respective parts of the whole market for consumers' wealth.

CHAPTER XVII

HOW THE EFFICIENCY OF FINAL INCREMENTS OF PRODUCERS' WEALTH IS TESTED

WE are now ready to apply to the fixing of wages and interest the principle which we may term that of analytical valuation. Everywhere does the market have a marvellous power of resolving concrete things into their elements, and of measuring separately the efficiency of each element. Consumers' wealth and producers' wealth alike it treats in this way. If we are to understand its procedure in fixing prices, we must seek out and identify not, as a rule, certain whole commodities, but certain elements in commodities; and so, if we are to understand the adjusting of interest, we must find in instruments of production, in a like way, certain elements that are in a strategic position and control the gains of all capital.

The earning power of capital is fixed by the productivity of the final increment of it; and this final increment of capital does not, as a rule, consist of instruments of production in their entirety. It consists of *elements* in such instruments. Just as we add to our consumers' wealth by procuring for personal use better articles than those which we have been using, so we add to our producers' wealth by procuring better instruments of production. When, for a machine that has worn itself out, we substitute one that is by a single point more efficient and more costly, we are adding a final increment to our capital. It is final increments of capital, as such, the productive power of which fixes the rate of interest. As *entrepreneurs*, we must pay for any capital that we hire what a final increment of it will produce; and that is what we and others can get, as a net addition to our products, by making our buildings by one degree larger or more substantial, our machines by one degree more rapid or more nearly automatic, our engines or our water-wheels by one degree more powerful, our raw materials by one grade finer, etc. *Its action in the case of capital.*

We have seen that in a limited number of cases final increments of consumers' wealth consist of goods in their entirety. When, for example, we procure the plainest and cheapest article of its kind that is anywhere made, as an addition to our stock of goods for personal use, the whole article is a part of our final unit of consumers' wealth. In such a case, the article, as a whole, helps to set the standard price for all goods of exactly that kind. Nobody gives for a duplicate of this final article in our supply of consumers' goods more than we give for this one. So there are cases in which entire instruments of production are final increments of producers' wealth ; and in these cases what these instruments produce, in their entirety, helps to set the standard of interest. If there is a hammer, a shovel or a cart, so poor and cheap that one of a lower grade cannot anywhere be found, then we add a final increment to our capital, whenever we procure one of these instruments.

These cases, however, play only a small part in the general adjustment of interest; for the enriching of the industrial world shows itself by a steady upward trend in the grade of its capital-goods. Better things of every kind come to constitute the world's working

equipment: buildings are taller, ships are faster, engines are more economical, railroads are straighter and more nearly level, locomotives are more powerful, trains are longer, etc. It is what we gain, in the form of more products, by making these perfecting changes that determines what we can afford to pay for the last capital that we hire. Society as a whole pays for all its capital what these *last productive elements* in goods are worth to it.

This truth is not affected by the fact that, as the wealth of society increases, capital-goods become more numerous, as well as better. It is true, indeed, that we are building more engines, at the same time that we are building better ones; but the new ones are mainly of a grade so high that, in their entirety, they cannot be treated as final increments of producers' wealth. Here, for instance, is a new locomotive. It has not been secured by the railroad that owns it to take the place of one worn out, but is an additional engine, made necessary by an enlarged traffic. Is it a final increment of capital? Not unless that engine would be dispensed with, in case any reduction of the capital of the road were necessary. The actual fact is that the quality of the new engine is determined by that of the roadbed, the rails, the bridges, the cars, etc., with which it is used; for it would be uneconomical to combine one poor engine with an equipment of good cars, good rails, etc.

This complementarity of producers' goods must always be considered; since a poor machine introduced into an equipment of good ones has the effect of taking something from the productive power of the other parts of the equipment. The good cars, etc., cannot develop their full wealth-creating power, if they have to coöperate with a poor engine. With a given number of cars, there needs to be a proportionate number of engines; and for the best results the entire equipment of cars, engines, track, freight houses, etc., is maintained at a uniform standard of quality. In a commercial form of statement, therefore, the " money " which is spent in bringing the equipment to the point of perfection that it has reached represents the final increment of capital " invested " in the railroad.

In a more scientific view, money is a means of moving real capital from hand to hand, and there must somewhere exist capital-goods that embody capital. The cars, engines, tracks, buildings, etc., are these goods. They embody the whole capital of the railroad; but when we try to find and identify the part of it that is " final " and interest-determining, we cannot single out such parts of the equipment as particular cars, engines, etc. We must try to find what is the final productive element in the whole equipment, and in each of the instruments that constitute it. What outlay would the company forego if, in the building and equipping of a railroad, it found that its real capital — its concrete and material outfit of instruments for carrying passengers and merchandise — must be made smaller than its original plans had called for? If it proceeded in a natural way, it would slightly reduce in quality nearly everything in its proposed outfit. It would forego putting the final perfecting touches to cars, engines, roadbed, buildings, etc. It might relinquish a few instruments altogether, but these would be things of the poorest and cheapest kinds.

The final productive element in the plant governs interest.

There are, of course, facts to be considered which, in a practical case, would modify this policy. If the railroad in the illustration were a connecting link in a great system, it would have to carry the cars of other railroads, and it would have to make its gauge broad enough, its rails heavy enough and its bridges strong enough to do this. This case, however, confirms, instead of contradicting, the general fact which we are stating — namely, that it is uneconomical to reduce, in a disproportionate way, one part of the equipment of an industry. The small road is, in this case, not a complete industrial plant. The larger system, of which it is an integral part, is the complete industrial establishment that has to be considered. If the great system, as a whole, were to reduce its capital, and if it had the power to reduce it by cheapening things as well as by reducing the number of them, it would prefer to make the equipment of every part of the entire system poorer, and so preserve the coöperating power of all the constituent parts, rather than to leave most of the system untouched and take out parts of the equipment of some railroad that is only one link in the system. It must be remembered that we are seeking to identify the final increment of the capital of a complete industrial establishment; and, in the case of a railroad system, that is not the fraction of the great plant that happens to belong to one small corporation. The system must be considered in its entirety.

Moreover, if, when the road was about to be built, the owners found themselves able to use a larger capital than they had expected to use, would they lay the same track and procure the same rolling stock that they had planned, with some extra cars or engines? Would they build depots of the form and quality that the first projects called for, merely adding a building or two to the list? It is clear that, in adding a few things outright to their equipment, they would improve many things — that they would add everywhere what we have called productive elements. The final increment of the capital of this railroad corporation is, in reality, a difference between two kinds of plants for carrying goods and passengers. One of these is the railroad as it stands, with all its equipment brought up to the highest pitch of perfection that is possible with the present resources. The other is the road built and equipped as it would have been if the resources had been by one degree less. A difference in all-around quality between an actual and a possible railroad — is, in reality, the final increment of capital now used by the actual corporation. The product of that last unit of capital is the difference between what the road actually earns and what it would have earned if it had been made by one degree poorer. This element really the difference between two kinds of plants.

It is clear that this final increment of the capital of this industry is not one that can be physically taken out of it, as it could be if it consisted of a few locomotives or a few cars that could be sold to another company.[1] It is in the plant to remain. It runs through the whole tissue of the complex instrumentality that engineers, trainmen, superintendents, etc., make use of in the carrying of goods and persons. If we wished to make a good test of the productive power of this particular bit of capital, we should have to invoke a magic that would at once shrink the whole plant into inferiority. The final increment of capital not physically separable from the other increments.

[1] If one part of a symmetrical equipment for carrying on an industry were taken away bodily, this would have such a deranging effect on the remaining parts that it would reduce their own separate power of production. Removing all the locomotives from a railroad would, of course, paralyze all the cars, the tracks, the freight-houses, etc.; and removing even one of them might, in a smaller degree, have the same effect. Reducing the quality of the whole equipment by one degree would, however, have no such effect. This method of taking out an increment of capital takes from the product of the whole industry only what is attributable to that one unit. It does not reduce the productive powers of the remaining units.

In a long period we might make such a practical test. We might let the plant deteriorate, letting the engines become worn and weak, the passenger cars shabby, the buildings dilapidated, etc. If, in the interim, the other circumstances that affect the productive power of a railroad remained absolutely unchanged, we might compare the earning power of the plant before it had deteriorated with its earning power afterward. Two difficulties are, however, encountered in the making of such a test. First, the other circumstances that affect the productive power of capital do not remain unchanged. Secondly, the qualities that wear and tear take out of instruments of production are not the same qualities that would have been left out of them if, in making them, it had been decided to "invest less capital in them"—that is, to make them by one degree less costly and efficient. No one is ever willing to waste a part of his fortune by making in cold blood such a laboratory experiment for testing the productivity of capital; yet actual experience enables employers to form such judgments as to the productive powers of final units of capital.

Could not an *entrepreneur*, however, test the productive power of his final increment of capital, as embodied chiefly in the final qualitative element in his working equipment, by reducing the quality of one thing at a time? Here, let us suppose, are two machines side by side, and alike except in the extent to which they have suffered the effects of wear: one is new and perfect, and the other is old and worn. Cannot the owner form a true conclusion as to the difference in their productive powers? Here, again, are two machines, both new, of which one is costlier and better than the other. Cannot the *entrepreneur* tell how much one exceeds the other in its earning capacity? If he can make such a test as this at all,

A possible mode of testing the productivity of the final increment.

why cannot he make it in connection with all parts of his equipment? He can take his plant and outfit by sections, and find, in the case of each section of it, how much he would gain by making it better or how much he would lose by making it worse.

The difficulty to be encountered in making such an experiment consists in the deranging effect that a reduction of the quality of a single instrument may have on the general plant. This effect could, however, be made small, by taking great care in making the change. Moreover, in making experiments of this kind, an owner could avoid all the more serious deranging effects that would follow if he took bodily from the equipment some instrument that is needed to make the whole an efficient complement of capital goods. He does not even need to let the machine that he is testing wear out to such an extent as greatly to mar the efficiency of anything else. If the test is to be made by buying and using a machine of an inferior grade, the owner does not need to make it so greatly inferior that the other machinery will not work well in connection with it. Little by little, a man could undoubtedly test in this way the productive power of the final increment of his capital. Though his calculations would be difficult and liable to error, he could form some opinion of the difference between the earning power of a part of his capital, as it is embodied in one set of instruments, and the earning power that it would have if it were by one point better or by one point worse.

Some such tests are, beyond doubt, constantly making. Men must form business judgments as to the exact grades of instruments of every kind that will "pay the best" in their several places. As the equipment of a mill and the mill itself wear out, the owner has constantly to decide what grade of instru-

The practical necessity for making such tests.

ments he shall procure to replace the discarded parts
of his outfit. He must know — approximately, at least
— how large is the difference in productive power
between a tool of one grade and a tool that is above
it or below it in the scale of quality. This is a part,
and a vitally necessary part, of the complicated process by which society puts its productive fund into
the most judicious shapes. Conscious mental estimates are constantly being made of the productive
power of such final increments of capital. It is not,
however, this conscious measuring which makes it
certain that the instruments which are either too
cheap or too costly will be discarded, and that those
of the right kind will be retained.

The decisive
tests made
by competi-
tion.

Competition makes the test in another and an in-
exorable way. It causes establishments that are so
equipped as to get out of their capital the utmost service that it is capable of yielding to survive, and incapable ones to fail. If, in a certain mill, every machine,
every tool and every other working appliance is so
judiciously selected that the final productive element
in each yields, as net income (let us say) five per cent
of its cost, and if that is the prevalent rate of interest
on loans, the owner of this mill is, in so far, in a condition to stand competition. The rate of interest on
capital that he borrows will, moreover, be five per
cent, if that is what the final increment of capital
in properly equipped establishments generally yields.
This is saying that a man's outfit of capital-goods
must be so selected and so combined that the final
productive element in each part of it shall yield the
same rate of interest that is yielded by the final element
in the outfit of capital-goods used by competitors.
Competition acts as a leveller, by reducing the earning power of the final increments of different men's
capital to equality. This it does by putting out

The survival
of well
coördinated
equipments
of capital-
goods.

of the field the competitor whose last increment of capital — consisting in the final productive element in his various capital-goods — creates less than the standard amount of product. With the final unit of capital generally earning five per cent, interest is at that rate. With interest at five per cent, the borrower whose last unit of capital earns only four must take each year the one per cent that is needed to make up the deficit out of his capital. This is a procedure that cannot be long continued; for the man must change the forms of his capital and bring the fund up to the prevalent standard in its earning power, or he must go to the wall.

We are here making assertions that will bear a more extended examination than it has thus far been possible to make. We affirm that interest is fixed by the earning power of the final increment of social capital; that that increment consists mainly of qualities of instruments of production, rather than of instruments in their entirety; that competition acts as a leveller, causing the earning power of such final productive elements in capital-goods to tend toward a certain normal level; and that any kind of instruments in which this element earns less than the standard amount must be thrown out of use.

With the final products of different capitals brought to equality, the earning power of the final increment of social capital fixes interest.

In the interpretation of these statements there are cautions to be observed; and one of them connects itself with the assertion that, as capital increases, the new parts of the fund embody themselves in new qualities imparted to goods. It is here assumed that labor remains unchanged in amount, and that it is a *per capita* enlargement of capital which forces *entrepreneurs* to procure better and better working instruments. Indeed, with workmen doubled in number and with capital doubled in amount, there would not need to be the qualitative improvement of the capital-

A *per capita* increase of capital insures the improvement, rather than the enlargement, of working plants.

goods of which we have spoken. If we could give to the new men exactly the same outfit of working appliances that the former workers possessed, the capital would be doubled in a more or less natural way. There would, it is true, be a difficulty in doing this, owing to the relation of land to other capital-goods. We could duplicate every part of the outfit except the land; and, because we could not duplicate the land, we should still be obliged, in enlarging the capital, to make changes in the quality of the goods that embody it. What we desire now to make clear is, that our assertions concerning the natural way in which capital increases have reference to an increase that is not accompanied by a parallel enlargement of the working population. With ten units of capital in the hands of ten men, that fund is in certain concrete shapes; while with twenty units of it in the hands of ten men, it takes different shapes. The improvements in the instruments, much more than such increase in the number of them as may also take place, embody and measure the new capital. The final increment of capital is mainly, though not wholly, qualitative.

If this is so, it is clear how far from being true is the conception of capital as existing, in bodily shape, — a stack of concrete instruments, — in the midst of competing *entrepreneurs*, and as ready in that shape to be drawn to this one or to that one, according as the one or the other offers the most for it. Capital is, in just this way, the subject of competition; but capital-goods are not. The capital that is competed for does not consist in instruments — concrete, visible, movable and ready for any one of a dozen different uses: there is no stock of capital-goods that has such adaptability that all *entrepreneurs* are anxious to get shares of it. Yet there is a universal competition for

Capital and not capital-goods, as such, competed for by employers.

capital, and the effect of it is to fix the rate of interest. Any *entrepreneur* in the entire system of social industry is a possible demander for any capital existing in the system. If he can make more with it than the present holder of it can make, his natural course is to bid higher for it than the present holder will bid and thus to secure it. No *capital*, as such, is fastened to one user or to one place in the system. Yet the goods that embody the capital are as fettered in their movements as the capital itself is free. A's tools are often useless to B. If we were to take one of them bodily out of A's shop and put it into B's, we should render to B no service. We should injure A's operations and benefit no one else. A furnace is valuable to a smelter, but not to a cotton spinner; a ship is useful to a carrier, but not to a miner, etc. There is, in short, only a very limited competition for *capital-goods* between employers in different kinds of business.

If tools of trade are not very mobile, what is to be said about productive elements in the tools? Can we take out of the smelter's blast-furnace the last of the qualities that give it efficiency, and impart this quality to the spinner's mules? Can we speak the magical word that will reduce the quality of the furnace and improve that of the mules? This is exactly what would need to be done if the smelter were to surrender the final increment of his capital and the spinner were to get it.

Here it seems expedient to enumerate some of the facts that are to be reconciled with each other if a final-productivity theory of interest is valid: —

(1) Interest generally conforms to the earnings of the final increment of social capital.

(2) This increment consists mainly of qualities in instruments of production, rather than of instruments in their entirety.

Summary of facts that involve a seeming contradiction.

(3) Instruments are limited in the range of their productive action, and are often useless in any kinds of business other than those for which they were designed.

(4) Qualities in instruments are, of course, not literally transferable to other instruments.

(5) The final increment of the capital of each kind of business consists in an element that is literally tied to that business.

(6) Capital is absolutely mobile: it can go anywhere. It can leave any business and betake itself to any other; and it is therefore the object of a competition that is universal. Any single unit of capital is desirable for use in any productive process that is going on; and it is by the general competition for it that the rate of interest is fixed.

We have said, moreover, that the capital which is the object of this universal competition does not exist, antecedently to the bidding for it, in any bodily shape in which the men can see it and carry it to their several shops. There is nowhere a central heap or stock of instruments of production waiting to render service to some one. Such stocks of merchandise as those which are in shops are already in use, doing their productive work. There is no accumulation of food, clothing, houses and other subsistence goods, waiting to be doled out to laborers, in order that the laborers may make capital-goods and so, virtually but not literally, transmute the subsistence goods into capital-goods. We have noted the several reasons why this entire feed-and-work theory of the origin of capital is untenable, and we have seen that the chief of them is the fact that there is no stock of subsistence goods anywhere accumulated and capable of being used in that way.[1] Competition for capital is, there-

[1] See Ch. X.

fore, not a competition for capital-goods that already exist.

The most comprehensive of the paradoxes concern- ing capital and interest is, that the competition for capital, which is constant and universal, is an all- around struggle to get concrete things that *are about to be*. The capital of society has no existence till it is in the shapes in which *entrepreneurs* use it. Till it is raw materials and tools for the manufacturer, merchandise for the retailer, vehicles for the carrier, etc., capital has no existence at all. Of the hundred billion dollars' worth of capital-goods in the United States practically all will be in use as instruments fitted for certain purposes and actually doing the things for which they are fitted.

When the *entrepreneur* bids in the market for an extra unit of capital, he is asking for something the presence of which in his business means a readjust- ment of his plant. He is virtually saying: "I offer five per cent a year for a certain amount of produc- tive wealth that cannot come to me, except as I change the shape of the plant I am using. I must make that plant better; and the improvement that I propose to make in it will constitute the new unit of my work- ing capital. Moreover, whoever surrenders to me a unit of capital must do it by a similar change. He must make his business equipment worse."

Bidding for capital, then, is bidding for something which does not antecedently exist and which, when it exists, will consist mainly in a change of quality of working equipments. When we offer interest for capital,[1] we virtually ask for the power to trans-

---

[1] It is employing new labor without new capital that makes capi- tal-goods more numerous. Extra men can go into a business in which the capital is not enlarged, but they can do this advantage- ously only where tools are cheapened and multiplied.

mute our shops and tools. This transmutation is possible, because the things that are about to be, and for which we are bidding when we offer to borrow " money " for the enlarging of our business, are wanted for the replacing of things that are about to cease to be. In the place of a tool that is worn out and on the point of being discarded, we may put a new one of superior quality. In this condition lies the possibility of adding a new *capital element* to our plant, without adding a new tool in its entirety. When we tender interest for the loan of new capital, we offer something for the power to substitute new tools containing a certain complement of capital elements for old ones containing fewer of such elements. Machines of grade number one are in demand at many points, because machines of grade number two are about to be discarded; and new productive powers are thus everywhere adding themselves to the social stock of capital-goods.

Not one of the employers who is making such a change as this is making it for the sake of applying a scientific test to a final increment of capital and of registering the rate of its productivity; yet, as the many changes are actually made, the test is applied, and the rate of productivity of final units of capital is registered. What the man finds he has gained, when he has infused a new capital element into his plant, becomes a guide for himself, at least, in bidding for further capital, since it tells him how much he can

Unconscious testing of the final productivity of capital.

In saying that competition tests the productivity of final capital elements, by driving out of business the men in whose plants these elements earn less than a normal amount, we do not deny that the survivors, who fix the rate of interest, must have ways of ascertaining what the final capital elements in their own plants earn for them. By comparisons of various kinds they manage to ascertain what these elements produce, and this knowledge is the basis of the offers that they can make for loans.

pay for it. Similar experiences tell other employers what they can afford to offer; and, when new capital is to be had, the men whose experiences reveal the fact that new capital elements will yield large returns will bid for and get the new capital, rather than any employers whose tests have proved that new capital elements are worth less to them. All such tests take time, but social evolution has time enough at its disposal. Slowly, but surely, it comes to be known what value elements are worth the most to each employer, and also what employers can, on the basis of the amounts that the best capital elements will in their hands earn, overbid others in the competition for loans and thus get such new capital as may be offering. Slowly and surely, the whole capital of society disposes itself in the way in which it can produce the most. It leaves the men in whose hands it creates the smaller products and goes to those who can make it create the larger ones; and in a perfect static adjustment it would attain a state of *locally equalized productivity*, as well as one of *maximum total productivity*.

There is, as we have seen, a zone of indifference for labor. There is a limited marginal region, within which a few men may be taken out of one employment and put into another, with no appreciable change in the character of the capital that is, in either case, used. This fact has much importance in the practical adjustment of wages. There is, in connection with capital also, a fact that is rudely parallel to this. A few instruments are usable in different industries. We may take a hammer from one shop and put it into another; and we may do the same in the case of a number of things, without causing a change in the nature of the work that is done or in the character of the remaining equipment. There is,

A zone of indifference in the field for capital.

then, something resembling a zone of indifference for capital.

These zones, however, are not the whole marginal fields in which wages and interest are adjusted. Those fields are much larger. Wages tend to conform to the product that an additional unit of labor can create anywhere in the industrial system, provided the *entrepreneurs* will make an advantageous place for it, by changing the shapes of their plants and equipments. Interest tends to conform to the product that an extra unit of capital can nearly everywhere create, by embodying itself in an advantageous change in the outfit of capital-goods. When these more general dispositions of capital have been made, the product of capital on the zone of indifference becomes an available indicator of its productive power in the more general marginal field.

From the first, we have remembered that capital is material. It exists only in goods that can be seen, touched and handled; and yet it now appears that final increments of capital cannot be thus manipulated. We cannot, in any literal and physical way, take out of a machine such a final capital element as we have just defined, leaving the rest of the machine intact. There is no mechanical process that can take out of a tool of the first grade that which makes it better than one of the second grade and even preserve for use the element that is thus withdrawn. Increments of capital may be arranged in an imaginary series, in the order of their productive efficiency, so that the final unit is the least efficient one; but it is utterly impossible to take the working plant of any employer and separate it bodily into such increments. Assorting the different machines into classes would not do this, and taking them to pieces certainly would not do it. If we let them all wear out and then replace them with inferior appliances, using what is saved by the buying of inferior tools in improving the quality of some other general plant, we indirectly separate the final increment of the capital from the other increments; yet, when the process is completed, we still have that increment inseparably tied to others in a new combination. All the increments, taken together, constitute a stock of capital-goods, or appliances of trade, that can be handled bodily; but increments of capital, separately viewed, are abstractions, for they are mainly nothing but qualities of material things. We are, in fact, in a realm of such abstractions, when we reason about the productivity of successive " doses " of capital applied to a farm, a mine or a manufacturing plant. By reducing capital, for purposes of study, to a series of increments, we are able to analyze a concrete thing into qualities; but, while these together may constitute the thing, separately they have only an ideal existence.

Such increments resolvable into qualities of things.

It is, therefore, blended increments of capital that are embodied in capital-goods; and the phrase "literally separated increments of capital" would involve a contradiction, for any literal separation would mean the ruining of the capital-goods and the annihilation of the capital.[1] Increments of *capital-goods* may, however, exist separately. Having built one ship, we can build another and another, till we have a fleet; but each ship will span the whole range of our increments of capital, if these be arranged in the order of their productive power, and will contain some part of every increment of our capital, from the first to the last.

Moving goods contrasted with moving capital.

[1] In the case of some of the very cheapest tools that are used, an exception to this rule is to be made. They constitute *first* increments of capital. It is the later increments that cannot be separated from combinations.

We can, of course, move the ships literally and bodily; but we cannot move the final increment of the capital, in the economic sense, from group to group, except by the method of gradually replacing the ships of the fleet with poorer ones and raising the grade of capital-goods elsewhere.

In spite of all this, it is possible — and, indeed, absolutely necessary — to measure the productive power of the final increments of true capital. The *entrepreneur* who cannot successfully do this will be eliminated from business. In the hypothesis of a static state, in which competition works with ideal perfection, the whole field is possessed by men who have made the tests successfully and have so developed the power to use the agents of production with the maximum of efficiency.

CHAPTER XVIII

THE GROWTH OF CAPITAL BY QUALITATIVE INCREMENTS

THE outline of the law of interest and wages has now been filled in by the addition of some important details. The diagram that has already been used presents the law of interest in its simplest form; and it is now clear that the capital which increases along the line AD is a permanent fund, consisting of instruments every one of which, except land, perishes but virtu-

Details that have now been added to the outline of the law of interest.

WAGES

INTEREST

The capital consists in self-renewing goods,

ally creates a successor to keep the series unimpaired. The increments that come to the fund, as the line AD lengthens, are mainly new qualities infused into the capital-goods already in the working outfit. If we were to try the experiment of making a capital grow from a small beginning to the size which, in view of the amount of labor that was to use it, it was naturally to take, we should need to have a magical power of transforming and improving every instrument of production ; and we should have to

and the increments consist mainly in new qualities in these goods.

265

exercise this power with every addition that we might make to the productive fund. At a touch, nearly everything that labor uses would then become by one grade better; and the difference between the old grade of everything-in-the-stock and the new grade of this miscellaneous aggregate would constitute the new increment of true capital. It is composite in the highest degree, and it is mainly an aggregation of new qualities imparted to old things. We have next to see by what mechanism this is done. In the group system of production, we shall see, lies the alchemy that accomplishes this difficult thing.

The new capital, as thus composed, is under a very composite control. It is all, indeed, the property of the social organism; but this means that a certain foreordained part of it is in the hands of each *entrepreneur* in the system. A social law governs this apportionment; and, if the law could work without friction or disturbance, it would make the apportionment unerringly. If, under such conditions, a million dollars' worth of capital were injected into the working fund of an entire society, a definite fraction of this amount would go to every sub-group in it; and a law that it is possible to trace would determine how large each of these fractional amounts should be. Interest, under such conditions, would conform to the product of this widely distributed increment of true capital, consisting mainly in qualities newly infused into old appliances. Before us, then, is the further problem of tracing the manner in which society, by no conscious act but by what is clearly a collective or social act, makes this apportionment, assigning to each group and to each sub-group its determinate share of the whole fund of capital, as well as of each new increment that adds itself to the fund.

The same law that apportions the capital among

The incre-
ments are
apportioned
among dif-
ferent in-
dustries by
a social law.

the sub-groups apportions the whole laboring force Labor apportioned by the same law. among them, and thus gives to each specific industry a certain share of the whole number of workers. The increments of labor are social, and are apportioned among the groups and sub-groups by an unconscious act of society. These increments are not mainly qualitative, for a working force is not to be thought of as gradually built up by making a given set of men more efficient. Improving men does, indeed, add to Increments of labor not mainly qualitative. the laboring power of society; but the addition to labor that economics has first to deal with comes from an increase of population. The chief qualitative transformations that the enlargement of the working force occasions are still in the capital-goods; but they are opposite in character to those which take place when labor is fixed in amount and capital increases. Enlarging population, with a fixed *quantity of capital*, means, as we have seen, an increasing quantity and a deteriorating quality of capital-goods. With two men working where one worked before, there are, perhaps, twice as many tools as before, each costing a half of what a tool for the same purpose formerly cost. Quantitative increments are, in this case, adding themselves to the working force, while qualitative elements are leaving the capital-goods, and quantitative additions to the stock are making and are keeping the true capital intact.

With these interpretations of the terms of the general law in mind, let us see, first, how qualitative additions to capital are actually made and, later, how capital apportions itself among the sub-groups. The mechanism by which capital-goods are improved is the same as that by which they perpetuate their kind. We noted that each perishable instrument of production virtually creates a successor for itself. The table that represents the group system of production reveals how this is done and also how, as true capital grows larger, the goods that embody it become better.

Let us, then, complete the table representing groups and sub-groups, in an extremely simple form but in a way that will completely reveal the law by which the apportionment of labor and capital is affected.

A'''	B'''	C'''	H'''
A''	B''	C''	H''
A'	B'	C'	H'
A	B	C	H

The A's in the table now represent an article of prime necessity in process of completion. Let us say that A''' is food ready to be eaten, and that A is the rawest material that enters into it. Possibly A may be standing wheat, A' threshed and winnowed wheat stored in the granary, A'' flour and A''' bread. B may represent the material for clothing, in the shape of wool on sheep's backs; B' may be wool washed, sorted and stored in the warehouse; B'' may be cloth and B''' clothing. The C's may represent, successively, forest trees, saw-logs, lumber and houses. Severely simple, indeed, would be the wants of a society that should content itself with this list of articles. It is, perhaps, heroic theorizing that creates such a society, even in imagination; but what we said before, about the creating of an imaginary static society, holds true here. We are putting a myriad of facts for the moment out of sight, in order that we may isolate and clearly understand certain other facts. The law that would apportion the labor and capital of a very simple society is, as we shall see, the one that actually apportions them in the most complex society that anywhere exists.

In every one of these sub-groups there is labor and capital; and, as we have seen, the material tissues of

the capital — the concrete things that compose it —
are in a perpetual process of destruction and renewal.
How are the destroying and the renewing effected?
The stock of passive goods wastes, whenever an A''',
a B''' or a C''' is withdrawn for use ; and it is replenished by the industry that continually goes on in
all the sub-groups. So much we have already seen.
The stock of active capital-goods — the tools, machines, buildings, etc. — wastes by wearing out and by
falling into natural decay. How is this stock replenished? There is, obviously, no power in the group
of A's directly to restore the active capital-goods
that are used up in making A''', for the whole power
of this group exhausts itself in making A'''.

How the
tissues of
circulating
and of fixed
capital are
replenished.

Somewhere, however, there is another group, which
we may represent by a series of H's. Its function is
to make tools, machines, etc. In our highly simplified table, we will let this group of H's replenish all
the waste of tissue that fixed capital suffers in the
whole series of groups. H, H', H'' and H''' now represent the materials that go into active instruments
of production, and they represent them in four stages
of advancement. H is the rawest material that goes
into tools, etc., while H''' is the assortment of instruments ready to be used. This succession is kept
up, as in the case of the other groups : every evening
finished H''''s are taken away, and every day the
stock of H''''s is replenished by the transmuting of
H'' into H''', H' into H'' and H into H', and by the
creating of a new H. Forever intact is the series of
H's, and this means that the true capital in the instru-
ment-making group remains unchanged in amount.

The table
representing
groups com-
pleted by
the addition
of a group
of produc-
ers of active
capital-
goods.

Where do the H''''s go, and what do they bring to
the man in the H group? They go everywhere
throughout the system replacing instruments that
are worn out. Some of them go to A, some to B',

some to C'', etc. Some of them go back into the different sub-groups of the H series itself, to replenish the stock of instruments that are worn out in the making of instruments. The income which comes to the men in the sub-group H''' must, it is clear, come in the form of A''', B''' and C'''. The men in the last group in the table cannot eat the looms, the threshing-machines, the flouring mills, etc., that they are themselves making; but they must eat the bread represented by A'''. They can not wear their machines or dwell in mills ; but they must have clothing and dwelling-houses. These they must get by taking some part of the product of the first three groups.

What is the source of that part of consumers' wealth which goes to supply the wants of makers of instruments? Is it gained by taxing the other groups ? Does it come out of other men's wages? Is it, in truth, produced by labor or by capital in the former groups? Here we must be careful ; for here, if anywhere in the analysis, there is a temptation to say that labor is creating " capital," by feeding the men who make the capital. The laborers in the A group are certainly working for the laborers in the H group, and getting capital-goods as a return for it. Yet, as a matter of fact, the food for the men in the H group is no part of the net product of any of the men or of any of the tools in the A group. It is, however, a part of the gross product of the tools in these groups. Every instrument that is wo-th having creates a product that makes good its own wear and tear, besides the further product that is a dividend for its owner. The cloth that a loom weaves, to make good the waste that it undergoes itself in the weaving, is what it passes over to the H''' group. The men of H''' are virtually eating flouring machinery, since they are eating the flour that the mill

The sources of the incomes of tool makers.

makes in wearing itself out, but they are eating only
that part of the flour which is reserved to make good
this waste.

There are, then, quantities of A''', B''' and C'''
that are regularly making their way to the H'''
group. If they constituted deductions from the
wages and the interest of the men in the first three
groups, the makers of H''' would be pensioners
of the men in the other groups. In fact, however,
the men in H''' make their own income goods, in an
indirect way, just as the men in the first three groups
make their own active capital-goods, also in an indirect
way. The men in H''' are not pensioners, but self-sus-
taining men, eating their own wages and interest. In
concrete form, their incomes consist in goods that are
of the kinds that support other men and that come
from the same sources. The A''', B''' and C'''
groups make the things that maintain the men in
H'''; but the quantitative part of these products
that goes to the men in H''' is solely that special
amount that is produced by the machines, etc., in
the first three groups for the replacing of the worn
parts of the plant. In quantity, it is entirely distinct
from the product of labor; and it is equally distinct
from the net product of true capital, as such.

The men of the first three groups, then, in maintaining the men in H''', do not tax themselves in any
way. The first task that is imposed upon a tool is
to create wealth enough to buy another like itself,
when it shall be worn out. This is a part of the
gross product of the instrument, but it is no part of
the net product of the capital in the instrument.
Only where an endless succession of instruments does
more than to maintain itself — only where such a
series of capital-goods creates a net surplus for its
owner — is capital. as such, productive.

The tool-
making
group self-
maintaining,
because
tools in use
are so.

We have noted the fact that capital tends to be everywhere equally productive. It is true capital, however, that is so, not capital-goods. The net product from an endless succession of working instruments in the sub-group A tends to be as great as that of an endless series of working instruments in the group C'', or as that of one in B''' or elsewhere. This tendency requires that every instrument which is anywhere used shall, under a normal adjustment, create a product just large enough to pay for a duplicate of itself, besides yielding to the man who uses it a net annual income that is the same fraction of the cost of the instrument as is the income yielded by other capital-goods. This is the literal and concrete fact that is involved in the law of uniform interest.

Surpluses for self-renewal distinguished from interest.

The instruments of the H''' kind that are scattered through the general groups, A, B and C are thus besides providing for their own successors, paying uniform interest. Every one earns a sinking fund during its lifetime, and the goods that constitute this sinking fund maintain the men in H'''; but entirely distinct from this fund is the interest on the true capital embodied in the instruments, which tends, under static law, to be uniform in rate. The goods that feed the men in H''' are the material forms into which, in a figurative sense, the tissue of the fixed capital has converted itself; while the goods that feed the men in A''', B''' and C''' are the true product of the labor and the capital in these groups.

Active capital-goods, or the tissues of fixed capital, are, then, self-maintaining; and, over and above this, true capital maintains its owners.[1] What this

[1] In the foregoing discussion, the statement has been made that capital-goods, virtually though not literally, make their own successors and thus keep capital unimpaired. Active instruments do this by

capital bestows on its owners they can afford to use up, without at any point impairing the integrity of the series of capital-goods that is to embody the permanent capital.

creating a special income for the group that replaces them. Passive instruments, or raw materials, such as the A, A' and A'' of our table, do it by becoming, in the end, consumers' goods for the men in this series of sub-groups, whose activity keeps the series of A's, etc., intact. The active instruments perish in the using, but the passive ones do not perish while being used as capital-goods. During this process, they receive accretions of value and lose nothing. Only when they cease to be capital-goods and begin to serve consumers do they begin to go to destruction. It is when they are ready for consumption that they are ready to replace themselves by making it possible for the men in the lower sub-groups to replenish the tissue of the circulating capital.

Saying this is not falling into the old error, which has been criticised in an early chapter of this work, of calling a store of food for laborers the primary form of capital. In the view here advanced, (1) there is no such store in existence, (2) the goods of the A''', B''' and C''' type cease instantly to be capital-goods when they are devoted to consumption, and (3) they are not " food for laborers," but income goods for all laborers and capitalists. Further, the way in which they keep the tissues of capital intact is by substituting themselves for capital-goods that laborers and capitalists have already created and that constitute their incomes in the original forms which those incomes take. Products of the type A''', B''' and C''', as they go through the sub-group system to be used, merely transmute incomes already existing into available forms. The A that is created in the lowest sub-group is entirely income to that group; for it is not a constituent part of its capital or of the series that that sub-group must keep intact in its own hands. It represents the amount that this lowest sub-group can afford to spend on its living. In a static state this group will spend the whole amount. To society, these goods, as they are passed on to the A' sub-group, are a constituent part of capital ; since society cannot afford to trench on the amount embodied in the complete series of A, A', etc. Society can, however, spend the A''' that has just emerged from the last steps in the series. This it does by substituting the A''' for the unfinished goods that, to the men who now have them, are income in amount but not income in a usable form. In the forms in which they first exist these incomes keep social capital intact.

More capital, as has been shown, means better cap
ital-goods; and we can now see how they are secured.
In terms of our table, this improvement signifies that
the H group becomes larger and that, in this way, a
larger amount of productive energy is available for
replenishing the tissues of fixed capital, as they perish in the using. Either more tools or better ones
can now be made; but the conditions require that,
in the main, it shall be better ones. The fixed
number of workers in the A, B and C groups get improved appliances, and they turn out more of the A''',
the B''' and the C''' than they formerly did. The
improved tools maintain themselves, as the original
ones did; and the special surplus of consumers' goods
that goes to the H group is sufficient to maintain
that group in an enlarged state.

An incidental result of the existence of more capital is higher wages and a larger grand total of interest. This signifies a greater output of A''', B''' and
C'''; but it involves an improved quality of these
consumers' goods, rather than a greater number
of them. The studies that we have made of the law
of value make this clear. Consumers' wealth, like
producers', enlarges itself mainly by qualitative increments; and it follows that the difference between
A, B, C and A''', B''', C''' becomes greater than
it was. Each transmutation that takes place in a
raw material that is "refining" under the workers'
manipulations becomes a more decided transformation, and the finished product is a finer and better
thing than an equally ripe product formerly was.
This is possible without any addition to the number
of laborers in the A, B and C groups, by virtue of the
increased power that more capital — that is, better
capital-goods — gives to them.

How the original enlargement of the capital is

Mode in
which capi-
tal-goods are
improved.

caused is a question of economic dynamics. It may even seem that we have been outside of the strict limits of a static science, whenever we have traced the process of increasing the social capital. Throughout this volume, however, we have allowed ourselves to observe changes that directly bring about static adjustments. We have followed the growth of capital from a small beginning to a natural size solely for the purpose of placing by itself the product of the final unit of the capital. The fund is used by a complex society composed of groups and sub-groups, the sum total of the fund is fixed, and the growth of it to its existing size is an imaginary and illustrative process. The illustration, however, is the more valuable when it respects the facts of life and keeps before the mind so much of the action of groups and sub-groups as suffices to reveal the mechanism by which, first, the material tissues of each kind of capital can be maintained and, secondly, the grade of each kind of capital-goods can be improved. What is a mere substitution, when a new and improved tool is put into the place of an old one, becomes a transformation, when the permanent series of such tools is viewed in its entirety. Here permanent capital transforms itself for the better, — leaves inferior bodies and enters better ones,— when the amount of it increases, while the laboring force remains unchanged. But it transforms itself for the worse, when it remains unchanged in amount, while labor increases. Both transformations are effected by the agency of the branches of industry that in our simplified table are designated as the H group.

How substitutions of new goods for old ones become transformations of permanent capital.

CHAPTER XIX

THE MODE OF APPORTIONING LABOR AND CAPITAL AMONG INDUSTRIAL GROUPS

WE are now prepared to state the law by which the entire capital of society at each point in its growth apportions itself, in certain natural quantities, among the different groups and sub-groups. That conception of social capital which we have carried through our entire study implies such an apportionment as this; for capital does not act as a completely socialized agent unless society, in some way, controls it all and disposes it so as to secure the best results. This requires that an economic force shall put into each sub-group in the system a definite and normal fraction of all the capital that society possesses, much as physical force levels the surface of a pond by putting into each part of it a definite fraction of all the water that it contains.

It is clear that there is a normal apportionment. In the static state, there must be a given number of units of capital at A, a given number at A', a given number at B, and so on throughout the system. What is it that makes these numbers normal? We have said that, in a general way, the apportionment is normal, when both labor and capital are uniformly productive at all the different points within the system — that is, when a unit of labor produces as much in one sub-group as it does in another, and when a

How a normal apportionment of labor and capital among the sub-groups is distinguished.

276

unit of capital has everywhere the same producing power. Labor moves to and fro, seeking the points where it can produce and get the most wealth. What capital may get at the different points is not an influence that appeals to labor, for wages only are what labor is seeking. Capital, likewise, moves to and fro in the group system, seeking out the points where it can get the most interest. So far as motives are concerned, each of these agents is independent of the other.

Yet neither of these agents can move without affecting the productive power of the other. If any labor departs from the sub-group A', the capital that remains there will lose something of its own productive power — will produce per unit fewer goods than before. As yet we say nothing about values, although they constitute a second element that must soon be considered. The first consideration is : How much power has a unit of labor, on the one hand, or a unit of capital, on the other, to create goods ? If labor departs from one group, the power of capital to create commodities is there reduced ; and there is, to this extent, an influence that tends to make capital move also. As a matter of fact, neither of these producing agents can move from group to group without exerting an influence that tends to make the other agent also move. The action of these influences in actual life is highly complex, because different industries are related to each other in very detailed and complex ways ; yet the principle that governs the movement is in its nature simple. It is not difficult to understand what share of the whole capital of society is the normal amount for the group A to possess, or what is the natural amount for B or for C. When an abnormal amount of capital is found at one of these points, an influence that is not hard to detect

A movement by one of them affects the productive power of the other.

sets itself at work to move capital to or from it, as the case may require.

Capital is moved from group to group by the same agency which brings about the transformation in its quality. Both kinds of changes involve the intervention of the H group. If there is an instrument in the A group that is not to be replaced, and if it has earned its sinking fund by creating enough of A''' to pay for the replacement of it, then this A''' goes to pay for another instrument that is capable of being used in (say) the B group. The men in the H group make, for example, a tool that will help to make clothing, instead of one that would have helped to create food. The *entrepreneurs* at A thus relinquish a certain quantity of capital, and the *entrepreneurs* at B receive it. The mechanism by which this transfer is effected we have just traced, for the self-replacing fund created by one instrument has been used to pay men for making an instrument of another kind. There are, of course, cases in which tools may be taken bodily out of one industry and put into another; but there are few in which this can be done without some waste of capital. The regular method of moving capital, without wasting any of it, is the one that we have just described. Together with this moving of fixed capital, there are, of course, local changes in the amounts of raw materials used, and these are equivalent to moving circulating capital.

The function of the tool-making group in the moving of capital.

It is to be noted that labor is moved in the same way. Men can be taken out of one industry and put into another more easily than can material instruments, since they are more adaptable; and yet the cases are few in which a workman can change his occupation with absolutely no waste of productive energy. If he has learned to work at one occupation, it requires some time to enable him to work at another equally well. Old workmen in highly skilled occupations can, as a rule, never develop in a new employment the facility which they have possessed in the old one. The regular way of moving labor without wasting any of it is to let the son of a workman learn a trade that is unlike his father's. The permanent force of social labor maintains its own tissue in a way that is quite analogous to the way in which social capital does so. Besides earning a living for themselves, men must rear successors who will take their places in the working series. The moving of labor from group to group means, then, that the successors of certain laborers do new kinds of work. Labor, as a permanent force, may be said to be perfectly mobile; and yet the transfers, if they do not reduce the amount of the force, must be made without actually changing the places of the men.

A parallel way in which labor is moved.

Being, then, quite sure that it is perfectly possible to move both labor and capital without sacrificing any part of either of them, we may put before our minds a society that fulfils the condition of the static state. The elements are perfectly fluid, but they do not flow. The condition is like that of a pond, where the dropping of a pebble into the water would ultimately move every particle of it, and yet not one particle stirs. The static group system is one in which a slight disturbance would cause many transfers of labor and capital from group to group, and yet not a single transfer takes place. There is, in other words, a perfectly normal amount of labor and of capital in every group and sub-group in the series. How did it get there? It is equalized pressure that brought the surface of the pond to a level; and it is *equalized inducement* that produces the static adjustment of labor and capital in the group system.

We have described, in an earlier chapter, the law

that controls the apportionment of labor and capital among all the groups, and have called it the universal law of economic variation. It acts in consumption; and when it operates upon a fixed number of persons, it causes an increasing amount of consumers' wealth to have less and less specific utility. That law thus regulates values; for goods bring smaller prices, the more there are of them. The law acts also in production, causing an increasing amount of one industrial agent, when it is used in connection with a fixed amount of another agent, to have per unit less and less productive power. Labor, for example, in connection with a fixed amount of capital, produces fewer and fewer goods per unit, the more there is of it. The law has to act in both these ways, in order to apportion labor and capital, in natural amounts, throughout the industrial system. The general law that, on the one side, fixes values and, on the other side, fixes power to produce goods thus has a twofold effect; and the outcome of it all is that a unit of labor tends, under perfect competition, to have as large a power to produce *value* in one part of the system as it has in another. A unit of capital shows the same tendency.

The movement of labor tends to give to it a uniform value-producing power; and that of capital does the same.

Let us apportion labor and capital somewhat at random throughout the group system. In some places we shall have more of both agents than a static adjustment calls for, and in some places we shall have less of both. In some sub-groups we shall have more of one agent and less of another than a normal adjustment would give. If the proportions of labor and capital within a group are normal, and if there is an excess of both of these agents within the sub-group, the effect will show itself simply in the low price of the product of the industry. The respective products of labor and of capital, as these products are measured in kind, will be normal. Each agent creates the right amount of goods *within* the group.

Where, on the other hand, there is too much of one agent and too little of another, a unit of the agent that is present in excessive quantity will create fewer goods than it should, and a unit of the agent that is present in deficient quantity will create more goods than it should. It is possible, under these conditions, that the price of the goods may still be normal; since, whatever their respective productiveness, the two agents together may produce a normal quantity of the goods. In apportioning labor and capital among different employments, we can seldom secure to a group, as a whole, the exact amount of productive power that static law calls for; and we can still less hope to secure for the labor and the capital that go to each sub-group the right amounts of specific power to create goods in kind. Nearly every sub-group will, then, produce either too much or too little of its commodity; and the price of its product will be either too low or too high. In nearly every sub-group there will be too much labor, as compared with the amount of capital, or too little. The specific power of one of these agents to create goods will be larger, and that of the other will be smaller, than static law requires. Under such circumstances, there will be movements in many directions; as there would be in a pond, if water were in some way put into different parts of it in an equally haphazard way. Nevertheless, the principle that governs such currents of water as would result is simple, though the currents themselves may be too complex for tracing; and the same thing is true of the movements of labor and capital.

Two causes that may throw the productive power of labor or of capital out of uniformity.

Labor and capital move from separate impulses, since each agent seeks its own interest, and not the

Interde-
pendence of
the move-
ments of
labor and of
capital.

interest of the other. The motives of their movements are independent; but their movements are
interdependent, since neither of them can move without changing the productive power of the other. As
the result of all this, each one goes where it can produce the most. Whenever one is placed in such a
position that any movement would diminish its productive power, it is under an inducement to stay
where it is. Such an agent, however, may enjoy
for the moment a productive power that is abnormally great; and, if that is the case, it is bound
to lose this excess of productivity by reason of the
movements of other agents. We shall see how this
occurs.

Let us, at first, confine our attention to movements between the general groups, whose incomes
are clearly derived from the sale of completed products. When the price of A''', for example, is high,
the whole group that makes it is well off; and
when the price falls, this body as a whole becomes
worse off. This change affects the product and the
income of the group as a whole; but there is another
change that affects the product and the pay of labor
within the group; and that, as we have seen, is a
diminution in the amount of this labor or an increase
in the amount of the capital that is used in connection with it. In general, the returns obtainable by
an agent of production depend, first, on the relation
of the group in which it works to other groups and,
secondly, on the relation of this agent to other

Local points
of highest
produc-
tivity.

agents within its own group. The agent that has
the largest productive power of all is in a group the
total output of which is abnormally small; and,
further, this agent is present in the group in an
unnaturally small quantity. Labor would have its
largest wealth-creating power, if it were employed in

making an article of which the demand exceeded the supply, so that the value of the article should be great, and if it were working in shops in which capital was over-abundant, so that the part of the product that could be traced to a unit of labor itself would be large. A single workman might virtually make, in a year, many pairs of shoes, because of the profusion of instruments placed in his hands; and yet the price of the shoes might be high, because of a shortage in the total supply. Here is the condition of an abnormally large productivity for this kind of labor.

It is clear that labor would rush to such a point from groups where opposite conditions existed. This influx would have two effects. It would first reduce the specific power of labor to create goods; for, as soon as there were more laborers in the shops, — supposing that the capital were adapted, in form, to the needs of the larger number of workmen, — a particular worker would be able to make a smaller number of them than he could make when labor was scarcer. Moreover, the influx of labor would mean a greater sum total of these goods for sale, and the price would fall. The goods attributable to a unit of labor would, then, already have been reduced in quantity; and they would now also be reduced in price. The specific product of the labor, as counted in value, would thus be reduced in two ways. Each man would produce fewer goods than he did before, and each unit of the goods would sell for less.

Two cumulative effects on its own productive power of the movement of one agent to such a point;

What, now, is the effect of such an influx of labor on the productive power of capital in this group? In one way it reduces it, while in another way it increases it; and it may end by leaving it not greatly changed. The more labor there is in the group, the greater is the specific power of capital there to produce goods. In this respect, capital steadily gains by the influx of labor. On the other hand, this influx means the enlargement of the total output of the industry, and a reduced price for its product. Here the capital loses. While there are more goods, the origin of which is traceable to a unit of capital, these goods sell for less than they previously sold for. Capital loses by the fall of the price of its product, though it gains in the quantity of its own specific product, as measured in kind.

It may be that, after the influx of labor, the capital of this sub-group is slightly more or slightly less productive than it is in other industries. The variation from the normal productivity will, however, probably be far less than it was in the case of labor. The original hypothesis assumed that capital was abundant in the group and also that the price of its product was high, by reason of a small total output. Under these original conditions, a unit of capital would produce few goods; but, as the price of the goods would be high, possibly the power of a unit of capital to produce *value* might not be very abnormal. When the new labor came into the group, the power of the capital to create value might not greatly change, for it would be diminished by one influence and increased by another. The enlarging power to create goods might, therefore, allow a unit of capital, in the end, to create about as much value as it did at the outset.

The power of labor to create value would, then, have been lessened by two influences working together, since a unit of it would create fewer goods, while the goods would bring smaller prices. The specific power of capital to create value would, on the other hand, have been reduced in one way and raised in another. If, as we have said might be the case, the value-producing power of capital, after the transfer of labor had been completed, were either more or less than it was elsewhere, there would be a slight movement of capital to or from this group. This movement would quickly make the productive power of this capital about normal. If capital were flowing into the sub-group, this movement would reduce the productive power of capital in the two ways that we have described — by diminishing its power to create goods, and by bringing down the price of the goods. It would, however, have very little effect on labor; for, while it would slightly increase the total output of goods and would reduce the price of them, it would increase the quantity of goods specifically traceable to labor. Slight secondary movements induced.

It is clear that movements of this kind have the power to correct disproportions in the quantities of labor and capital existing within the groups. We selected for study an industry in which the productive power of labor was at its maximum — where labor produced much in goods and goods were high in price. Such a group exercises the largest attractive power over labor. The group from which labor would be most strongly repelled would be the one in which these conditions were exactly reversed — one, namely, in which there should be much labor relatively to capital, a large aggregate of goods produced and a low price for the goods. Here one man would produce few goods, and the goods would be cheap; so that the men would be under the greatest inducement to move away. Local point of minimum productivity of labor.

In noting the manner in which a disturbed pond of water acquires a level surface, we do no harm by supposing that the identical water of the highest wave flows into and fills the deepest trough. So, in the case of the disturbed sub-groups, we may suppose that labor rushes from the point where it has the smallest productive power to the point where it has the greatest. If, for local reasons, some of this particular labor stops on the way, it does not fail to cause an equal amount of labor to move to the point where the great deficiency existed; and the effect is the same as though the identical men in the group where the labor had the smallest productive power made their way directly to the group where it had the largest.

In the group from which the labor moves the effects are, of course, exactly the opposite of those which are seen in the group to which it goes. We said that at first the group where labor was in excess created a large output of goods and got low prices for them. The productive power of a single unit of labor was low, however, because it produced few goods and because the goods did not sell well. With every unit of labor that departs from this group, the remaining labor becomes more productive of goods and the goods sell better. The labor thus gains doubly in its specific power to produce value. The capital in this group loses power to produce goods, but the goods gain in value; and, although these influences may not accurately offset each other in quantity, and some small movement of capital to or from the subgroup may still take place, the amount of this movement, as compared with the movement of the labor, is slight. The changes that take place in this subgroup are, in short, the antithesis of those which take place in the group that we first described.

Two influences, then, determine the specific productive power of labor and of capital in a group. One of them is the price of the product, and that depends on the total amount of it. Another is the fraction of the product that is attributable to a unit of labor or to a unit of capital, and this depends on

Effects of the movement of labor from such a point.

the relative amounts of labor and capital within the group. Where one agent — say, labor — is in excess, the two influences work together to reduce the amount of it; while, in the case of the other agent, capital, the two influences work in opposite ways.

Three possible conditions render an agent comparatively unproductive in the group where it is located: (1) It may have a low power to create goods, while the goods are of normal value; (2) it may have a normal power to create goods, while the goods are abnormally cheap; or (3) it may have a low power to produce goods, while the goods have a low value. The first condition is corrected by a change in the relative quantities of the labor and the capital in the group, leaving the gross output of goods unchanged. If labor is the agent that is poorly paid, some labor may move out of this group and some capital may come into it. The second condition is corrected by a change in the absolute quantity of goods produced, leaving the relative amounts of labor and capital essentially unchanged. Both labor and capital may move out of the group, and the price of the product may rise. The third condition is corrected by changing the proportionate amounts of labor and of capital, and also the total amount of goods produced. If labor is the poorly paid agent, some of it may migrate from this industry to others, while no capital migrates to it. The whole output of this industry will then be smaller, the price of it will be higher, and the contributory share of a unit of labor, as compared with that of a unit of capital, will be larger.

Three opposite conditions make an agent exceptionally productive: (1) It may have a large power to create goods, while the goods are of normal value; (2) it may have a normal power to create goods,

Three possible conditions of abnormally low productivity.

Mode of correcting each.

Three conditions of abnormally high productivity.

while the goods are abnormally dear; or (3) it may have an exceptionally large power to create goods, while the goods are unnaturally dear. Movements the reverse of those just described correct these conditions. Whenever the price of goods is normal, while one agent is abnormally productive, the other agent must necessarily be abnormally unproductive. The one agent will, therefore, move to the group and the other will move from it at the same time. One influence tends to raise the price of the goods, while the other tends to lower it. These influences in time neutralize each other, and the only effective change is in the specific powers of each of the agents to produce goods. This is the adjustment that the conditions required, and it ends by making both of the agents normally productive. Where the value of the goods needs to be changed, with no change in the relative powers of labor and of capital to produce goods, the adjustment is effected by an influx or an efflux of labor and capital moving together. Where value and comparative productivity have both to be changed, in order to bring the value-creating power of labor and of capital to a natural level, the adjustment is effected by the process that we described at the outset. One agent is moved out of or into the group by two forces which work together, while the other agent is affected by two forces that work against each other. If the two forces work concurrently in the case of labor, the sum of them expresses the amount of force that is impelling labor to or from the group. If the two work against each other in the case of capital, the difference between them measures the resultant force that acts on that element.

If we were actually to apportion labor and capital at haphazard among the different industries, there

Mode of correcting each.

would be a few of them into which both labor and capital would flow, in quantities that would be about uniform ; there would be a few industries from which labor and capital would flow, in about uniform proportions; and there would be a few into which only one agent would go, and others from which only one agent would go. A great majority of the industries would require some compounding of these adjustments — would demand that one agent should go to them or from them in large quantites, while the other should go from them or to them in small quantities. Every movement that would thus take place would be brought about through the action of the universal law of variation that we have described. The greater the amount of one agent that cooperates with the other, the smaller is the power of a unit of it to create goods; while the greater the amount of goods produced, the smaller is their value. Agents that are perfectly mobile would quickly reach a state of uniform productivity in all industries, by the action of these influences.

All the movements referable to one law.

We have spoken of the movement of labor and capital as though it were spontaneous, and as though labor, for example, went of its own accord from a place where its productive power was small to a place where that power was greater. But it is, in reality, *entrepreneurs* who do the moving, and it is competition that makes them do it. Our theoretical assumption makes the competition of one employer with another active and certain ; and unerring, therefore, are the transfers of labor and capital that result from the competition. In every group in which the productive power of labor is slight, low wages only can be paid ; and labor can be lured away from this group by the offer of the slightest advance over the rate that it gets. In our ideal hypothesis, there is -no

Entrepreneurs the movers of labor and capital.

friction to be overcome: five cents a day of extra wages will take labor out of one employment and into another, and a tenth of one per cent in interest will move capital.

In the industry where the productive power of labor is great, the actual pay that the men are getting depends, however, on the productive power of labor, not in that group, but in society as a whole. There is a general rate of wages; and employers in this group can have laborers for what it costs to get them out of the other groups, in which their productive

Wages fixed by the final productivity of social labor, and an *entrepreneur's* returns by that of labor in a sub-group.

power is smaller. By doing this they can make a profit. For an interval they can hold the difference between the pay of labor in the general market and its earning power in the industry into which they bring it. This is, however, a vanishing difference; for, as competition does its work, it slips through the employers' fingers. The eagerness of different employers to get a part of this profit makes them strive to anticipate their competitors in enlarging their working forces; and the enlargement goes on till the local product of labor is equal to its pay, and there is no further profit to be gained from this source.

Movements of capital caused by a similar influence.

The movements of capital are brought about in the same way, by the action of *entrepreneurs*. Competition does it all; profit is the universal lure that makes the competition work; and the ultimate goal of the whole movement is a no-profit state. As the movement proceeds, each bit of *entrepreneurs'* gain dwindles to nothing. A static state offers no inducement to further movement; and that is saying that it offers no profits, for profits are always an inducement to such movements.[1] When, therefore, we say that the

[1] It is clear that one group cannot keep its profit-making position in the system, if *entrepreneurs* who are making no such net

productivity of labor is high in one industry, and that other labor flows into it, what we mean is that the *entrepreneurs* in that sub-group are getting the benefit of the high productivity. They are making a profit; and the competition of other *entrepreneurs* moves the labor into this sub-group, till labor produces here no more than it gets — that is, till profit is annihilated.

Any unbalanced state of the group system gives profits to some one. Too much labor here and too little there, or any other of the unnatural conditions that we have just described, means that somewhere labor creates more than, for the moment, it gets. Its pay is fixed by its general or social productivity, but here and there its productive power is above this general standard. The profit that is here to be had is the lure to the movement that adjusts the local productivity of the labor to the general standard.[1]

gains are at liberty to enter it. May not all *entrepreneurs* be making the same rate of net profits, and making them at the same time? May there not be a condition of equal and universal profit? Clearly not; for this would be a universal invitation to capitalists to become *entrepreneurs* and, as such, to bid against each other for labor and capital till the profit should everywhere vanish, by being made over to laborers and capitalists in the shape of additions to wages and interest. The pay of each of these agents, therefore, under perfectly free competition, is bound to stand at the productivity level.

[1] A difficulty may seem to arise from the fact that a particular *entrepreneur*, in changing the amount of labor or capital in his establishment, is not greatly affected by a slight change in the value of the product that may result from his action. A concurrent increase in the capital of a whole sub-group would lower the value of its product, but an increase made by one employer might not do this in any appreciable degree. It might chance that the entire capital of a sub-group would be normal in amount, and that some employers would have too little and others too much. An employer who had too little capital, in proportion to the labor that he employed, would not be deterred from keeping all his men and hiring more capital by the fact that he would make his product

The adjustment that determines how many units of capital are to be used in one general group, in connection with a given number of units of labor, is not the only one that has to be made, since every sub-group needs to get its normal share of the labor and the capital of the general group to which it belongs. This secondary adjustment is made by the same play of forces that makes the more general apportionment between the groups in their entirety. In every completed commodity there is a distinct element that constitutes the specific product of each of the sub-groups that have contributed to the making of it. The product of the A' sub-group is, indeed, merged and lost in the finished article, A'''; but it is a definable element in that completed article. It is the difference between A and A'. A itself is the product of the lowest sub-group in this series; and the product of the second sub-group is the utility

cheaper; and one who had too much capital and too little labor might not be deterred by the same consideration from keeping all his capital and hiring more men. If this happened often, the whole sub-group would suffer from lowered prices and would reduce its labor and capital in an all-around way. It is clear, however, that it would not happen; since, with prices normal, the man with a relative excess of labor would find his marginal labor not earning its pay, and would discharge some part of his force; and the man with an excess of capital would, for a similar reason, part with some of that. The labor discharged by the first employer should, in theory, go to the second; and the capital released by the second employer should go to the first. Such adjustments within a sub-group are more easily and surely made than are adjustments between the different groups and sub-groups. The practical fact is that each sub-group attains, by experiment, a knowledge of the normal ratio of labor to capital which in its own specific industry will give the best results. This ratio then tends to remain more or less fixed. Enlargements and reductions of output are afterward made by increasing or reducing labor and capital together, and the motive for the increase or diminution is the state of prices. When the product of the sub-group is dear, its facilities for production and its operative force are enlarged together.

that it imparts to A in converting it into A'. So the specific product of the A'' sub-group is, not the article A'' in its entirety, but the single utility which, when imparted to A', converts it into A''. With this understanding of the nature of the specific products of the different sub-groups, we may apply to them the whole statement that has been made concerning the more general groups. The term sub-group may, in fact, be substituted for the term group in the entire foregoing argument.[1]

In movements that take place within one general group a certain steadying effect is secured by the necessity of preserving a uniform flow of the passive capital-goods that are ripening into the completed products. A nice adjustment of the raw materials in different stages of advancement is always needed. There is a relation to be maintained between the quantity of A and the quantity of A', and between that and the quantity of A'', etc. For every A''' that leaves the series in a day, one A'' must become A''' in a day; also one A' must become A'', one A must become A', and one new A must be created. This does not imply that there are necessarily in the series as many A's as there are A''s, as many A''s as there are A'''s, etc. On the contrary, unless it takes the same number of hours to prepare an A as it does for that A to become A', the number of units of these different passive goods that are constantly to be found in the series will be unequal. If it takes ten days to make an A and twenty days to convert an A into an A', then a

The coördination required for a uniform flow of ripening goods.

---

[1] The movements of labor and capital to or from one sub-group are not necessarily from or to another in the *same* series. There is nothing to prevent labor or capital moving from A' to B'' or to C'''; and, if it does so, it is under the twofold influence of price- and goods-producing power that has been described in the foregoing pages.

uniformity of rate in the general onflow requires that there shall be constantly in the stock twice as many A''s as A's. Let there be ten A's in the stock, with a new one added every day; and let one that has had ten days of ripening be passed on to the A' group. Here it requires twenty days for further ripening, before it can be passed on to the A'' group. If there are twenty A''s constantly on hand, one of them can be passed on every day, in the shape of A', to the following group; but, if there are only ten of them, taking one away daily must mean taking it away in an unripened state.

If, for example, trees in the forest require twenty years to fit them for cutting, and if one row is planted and one row is cut every year, there must be twenty rows in the forest. The same amount of cutting could be done from a forest consisting of ten rows, if the trees ripened in ten years; and even a single row would do, if the maturing took only one year. Again, along the course of a river which is flowing steadily, the same amount of water passes each point in a minute; but, where the movement of the water is rapid, the stream may be narrow and shallow; while, where the flow is slow, it has to be broad and deep to give a uniform flow. Accordingly, it is clear that, if converting A into A' takes ten weeks and converting A' into A'' takes twenty weeks, there must be twice as many units undergoing manipulation in the A'' group as there are in the A' group, in order to give a constant product.

The very existence of circulating capital, or of that which is in the form of passive capital-goods, is, in the strictest logic, the result solely of the time that the transformations of matter require. If we could conceive of them as instantaneous, there would be none of this capital; if, the moment that a raw element in nature were touched by a worker, it passed through all the steps of its ripening and emerged as a finished product, it would be impossible to find passive capital-goods on hand. If the ripening, without being instantaneous, were very rapid, there would be few of such goods. But with slow ripening there are many.

Economy, then, in the use of capital requires that there shall be an accurate adjustment of the relative quantities of passive capital-goods in the different groups of each series; and this adjustment is primarily determined by the comparative rapidity with which the ripening process takes place in the different sub-groups. When the correlation is complete, all the labor and capital of each entire group exactly replenishes the waste of tissue of circulating capital that takes place when a finished article — say, an A''' — passes out of the hands of organized society and goes to some individual to be used up. There is then no industry wasted in making things to be stored, for there is just enough of the A'' made to replace the A''' that is taken for consumption.

With such coördination, industry replenishes at every point the wasting tissue of circulating capital.

This concerns only the different quantities of circulating capital in the different sub-groups of one general group, but there must be at every point a similarly nice adjustment of fixed capital to circulating capital. It is uneconomical to whittle two blocks of wood at a time with one knife, and it is equally bad to use two knives at a time whittling one block. Increase the quantity of circulating capital used in connection with a given amount of fixed capital, and the former variety will create a smaller and smaller product per unit. Having plenty of tools to work with and no material to work on, the product is nothing. With very little material and a profusion of tools, the material is worked up very quickly; but the gross amount transformed in a year is small. Every

The mode
of adjusting
the relative
quantities of
fixed capital
and circulat-
ing capital.
part of this little stock of raw material is, under such conditions, of great consequence. Reduce the stock by one-tenth, and you take much from the daily product of the industry, as a whole; add a tenth to the stock, and you add much to the output. The *specific productivity* of a small amount of circulating capital thus used in connection with a large amount of fixed capital is very great. It is possible, evidently, that a shop may have on hand too little raw material to give adequate scope to its machinery; and then the machines produce too little, while the materials produce relatively too much.

The product of the circulating capital per unit grows smaller, as the quantity of it is increased. At first, it is as though there were one log waiting to be squared into timber by the axes of a dozen workmen, who work at a great disadvantage for lack of free play for their tools. A second log, drawing off six workmen with their tools, would effect a very large increase of the product. Though the six men cannot hew one log into shape quite as rapidly as can twelve, they can do it nearly as rapidly; and so the advent of the second unit of raw material, the second log, may very nearly double the product of the entire industry. This increase in the output represents an enormous proportion — several thousand per cent a year — of the amount of capital embodied in one log.

In this condition, any increase of general capital, if it is to have its best effect, must take the shape of enlarging the quantity of passive capital-goods in use. Doubling the amount of them the second time will vastly increase the general product; though, in the nature of the case, it is not likely to increase it as much as did the former doubling. The active tools now have much freer play; but, if we continue increasing the raw materials, there will certainly

come a time when a further increase of them will
do less in the way of enlarging the product than
will some enlargement or improvement of the active
tools. This means that capital embodied in passive
goods, on the one hand, and that embodied in active
goods, on the other hand, will have reached an equality in their specific productivity. A unit of circulating capital will then be worth as much to the
entrepreneur as a unit of fixed capital. No more
material in the left hand than can be profitably manipulated by the tool in the right hand, and no more
tools in the right hand than can work advantageously
on the stuff that is held in the left — these are the
principles of adjustment. The organized worker,
society, follows the common-sense rule that a man
would follow in fixing the amounts of the two kinds
of capital; but, in the case of society, this means a
delicate and elaborate adjustment through all the
minutest details of the production of every article.
Ore and mining machinery, wool and the mills that
are to manufacture it, logs and the saws that are to
cut them — all must be proportioned in quantity;
and these are only a few simple and crude cases of a
coördination, the minute and delicate details of which
we cannot stop to indicate, which runs through every
occupation that men pursue. In the different sub-
groups of each series, the circulating capital, in the
shape of materials in different stages of advancement,
must be present in certain well-adjusted proportions;
and the fixed capital must also maintain a certain
relation to the circulating capital. Crowding the
shops at A′ with tools and stinting those at A″,
would obviously be uneconomical. But within the
general groups these apportionments are easily made.
Land is one of the active goods, and it must be
adjusted in quantity to the other goods of the same

general class. There must not be in any industry so much land that it cannot be advantageously used in connection with the buildings, tools and machines that are there combined with it. Grant, for example, that in the production of A in our table there is much land, in proportion to the other capital-goods, while in the sub-group at A′ there is comparatively little. The specific productivity of land itself will then be larger in A than it is in A′, and there will be an inducement to use less land in the creating of A and more in the transmuting of A into A′.

The natural and accurate expression for the method by which land apportions itself among different groups and sub-groups of the economic system is, that land shifts itself freely from point to point in the system, until it attains equalized productivity. The meaning of this term, equalized productivity, will require special attention, when we reach the point at which we shall study the rent of land.[1] It does not mean that one acre is as productive as another, or that one man will produce as much as another, for there are differences between men and likewise differences between acres. Yet there is such a thing as a unit of land, just as there is such a thing as a unit of labor.

The quantity of land in each combination adjusted by a law of equalization of specific productivity. As the apportionment of labor throughout the groups and sub-groups of industrial society gives a uniform productivity per unit, so the apportionment of land gives uniform productivity per unit of land. We shall see in time just what this means, in the way of the adjustment of land to various other producing agents. What we wish now to note is, that land is economically mobile. It is the exception to the rule that capital-goods, as such, cannot be taken out of one industry and put freely into others. Capital, as we have seen, is absolutely mobile, while capital-goods

[1] See Ch. XXII.

are usually not so. Land, however, is mobile ; and what we have been saying about it shows that it cannot develop its full productive power, unless it moves freely from industry to industry till exactly the right quantity of it is found in each one. There is not the full and normal amount of permanent capital in the form of this capital-good, land, so long as one industrial group has more and another has less than it ought to have. The starting-point in a really scientific study of land and its rent looks upon this agent of production as a universal producer, and thus as helping to create every kind of commodity. It looks upon the land as apportioning itself, by a nice adjustment, among all the sub-groups in industrial society. Unscientific is that limited view which, in the study of rent, holds within the field of vision only so much land as, in some mysterious fashion, is given over to creating one particular kind of product. The rent of land is not the result of the price of wheat: it is the result of the power of land to create wealth in a myriad of different forms.

Land mobile and to be treated as a universal producer.

The general law of varying productivity that we described in an earlier chapter determines, first, how much circulating capital shall be combined with a given amount of fixed capital. With the amount of fixed capital given, more and more units of the circulating kind will produce less and less per unit; while, with the amount of circulating capital given, more and more units of the fixed kind will produce less and less per unit. This law operates in so apportioning the whole amount of capital, as between the fixed and the circulating kinds, that a unit of one is as productive as a unit of the other. Within the fixed capital, too, an adjustment has to be made. Land is one form of such capital ; for it contains a portion of the entire fund that is embodied in active

General action of the law of varying productivity.

instruments and operates to impart utilities rather than to receive them. This part of the fund is subject to the law of varying returns. If you combine more and more land with a given amount of fixed capital in other forms, you get less and less product per unit of land. If you combine more and more fixed capital in other forms with a given amount of land, you get less product per unit of the other capital. These two principles, if they have their full effect, result in combining everywhere the right relative quantities of land and of fixed capital in other concrete shapes.

When we study the whole amount of capital in one industry, as compared with the whole amount in another, we have on our hands an elaborate adjustment that introduces considerations of value. What any one kind of business produces, depends on the price of its product. The law of varying productivity, to which we have just referred, does not, however, primarily involve questions of value. In considering it, we were talking about the power of different kinds of capital to produce *goods*, as such. With a certain total amount of capital in one industry, that total amount has to be apportioned among the different kinds according to a law of productivity. Too much fixed capital, combined with a given amount of circulating capital, means that the power of a unit of fixed capital to produce *goods* is less per unit than it should be. If a shoe manufacturer, for example, has made such a misadjustment of his working funds, he is getting fewer shoes in a year than he might get, and he can increase the output by correcting the error. The law of varying productivity, in all its applications, means primarily that, if we put one productive agent in increasing quantities into combination with another, the increasing agent will produce, in commodity, a smaller and smaller product per unit. If, then, within any particular sub-group — say, A' — we add land, unit by unit, the land will produce less and less per acre in the way of concrete things. Thus far no consideration of the value of the goods is introduced. We said, however, that land apportions itself among the different groups and sub-groups, until it is as productive in one as it is in the other. It has to be moved freely from sub-group to sub-group until this equality is attained, and the same is true of artificial capital and of labor. When we are studying the combination of these things within a sub-group, the only thing that we have to note is, what part of the sub-group's product — estimating the product only in kind — is imputable to each agent. An *entrepreneur* in the shoemaking business, for instance, has occasion to know, first, how many more cases of shoes he can make in a year if, without changing his capital in quantity, he gets a few more men in his mill. Again, he has occasion to know how many more shoes he can make in a year, by adding a few thousand dollars to his general capital. Also he needs to know whether he can the better increase his product, counting the product always in shoes, by using more fixed and no more circulating capital, or *vice versa*. When the fixed capital is to be increased, he needs to know whether he will turn out more shoes in a year, if he uses more land without enlarging his buildings, machinery, etc., than he will if he keeps his present area of ground and enlarges his mill. Within the sub-groups, or specific industries, productive agents have to be coördinated with each other — the quantity of each kind has to be determined; and the first thing that determines this coördination is the specific power of each agent to produce goods.

The productivity of an agent first estimated in terms of commodity.

302 THE DISTRIBUTION OF WEALTH

The value of the commodity a further element.

In the end, the whole social supply of the several productive agents has to be apportioned among the different industries, so that the right quantity of each one of them may enter into each sub-group. Into this adjustment, moreover, value enters; for the value of the shoes that are attributable to a final unit of land helps to determine how much land shall be used in the shoe-business. The power of each agent to produce a commodity is one factor and the value of the commodity is another factor; while the working of the two together determines how much of each agent

The productivity of an agent made uniform in terms of value.

there shall be in each sub-group. Each general agent of social industry is, in short, subject to a law of uniform final productivity — measuring products in value, and not merely in kind — in all the different uses to which it is put.

CHAPTER XX

PRODUCTION AND CONSUMPTION SYNCHRONIZED BY RIGHTLY APPORTIONED CAPITAL

THE law of final productivity that the familiar diagram presents is not yet translated into concrete and literal terms. We know that, when the agent which is increasing along the line AD is capital, it is the productive fund of true capital, rather than the mere number of capital-goods, which is thus increasing; also, that the increments are mainly qualitative improvements of the general stock ; also, that at any point in the growth of the fund, it is all apportioned among the sub-groups according to a certain law ; and, finally, that the forms of it, in each sub-group, are determined by an equally nice adjustment and by the action of the same law. There are further general statements, suggested by the same figure, that need to be expanded into detailed and literal descriptions of the phenomena of business life. CD, for instance, measures the rate of interest on capital, and AECD expresses the total amount of this income. In a static adjustment of society, no one is "saving money" and adding to his capital ; and therefore the whole income of capitalists, as a class, comes to them in the shape of goods that are ripe for consumption. These are goods of the type of A''', B''' and C''' of the table that we have often used to illustrate the system of groups and sub-groups and the mode of producing

wealth of different kinds. Capitalists in all the different sub-groups get a uniform rate of income, in
proportion to their several capitals, and get it in
a uniformly ripened state; yet capitalists in the sub-

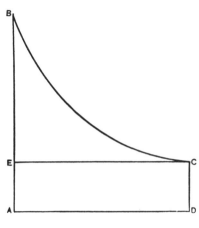

groups, A, B, C —
and, indeed, in all
the sub-groups ex-
cept those in the
uppermost tier in
the table — are pro-
ducing things to-day
that will not them-
selves be ready to use
for some time to come.
Weeks or months may
elapse before the cap-
italists in A can use
any of the things that
they are at this moment working on. But during
the interim they must live. May they not, therefore,
have to borrow commodities from capitalists at A'''?
May not the element, time, make trouble, disturb the
simple action of the law that the diagram expresses,
and make it necessary for capitalists in the lower
sub-groups to get advances from men in the upper
ones and to pay for these advances? May not such
payments disturb the equality of the earnings of
capital at different points in the system?

The same question arises in connection with the
laborers in the different sub-groups. Those at A''', B'''
and C''' are making finished goods; and, if they can
divide their gross products with the capitalists in
their several industries and carry away from their
mills their own shares of the joint output, they have
only to exchange with each other, in order that each
may at once get his income in the forms in which he

The ques-
tion whether
incomes are
advanced by
one class to
another.

needs it. Laborers at A, B and C, however, are apparently not in so favorable a position. May not they have to get and pay for advances from the workmen in the uppermost tier of sub-groups, just as the capitalists in the lower tiers seem obliged to get them from the capitalists in the uppermost tier?

The whole question, whether goods are advanced by one class of persons to another, in order to tide that other class over an interval of waiting, clearly has reference, not to the relation of capitalists in general to laborers in general, but to the relation of certain sub-groups to other sub-groups in the producing series. It is the sub-group A''' that must advance the stock of the article A''' to all the sub-groups that are below it in the series, if any advances at all are needed; but does it actually make any advances? If this term be used in any true sense, it must mean that a stock of passive capital-goods is drawn upon at one date and replenished at a later date, and that it stands reduced in size during the interval. Nothing of this kind, however, takes place. The stocks of A''', B''' and C''' are drawn upon and replenished simultaneously, like water in a full pipe, with an inflow at one end and an outflow at the other. *If advances of consumers' goods are made, they must be made by the highest sub-groups to the lower ones.*

Let us try the experiment in a simple and practical way, and see whether advances of this kind are necessary, either by capitalists to laborers or by one sub-group to another. Here are three households needing water for daily use. Two have capital to use, while the third has only labor. One establishes a pumping plant which raises the water to a high level; the second furnishes a settling tank and a filter, which, as it were, " ripens " the water, or makes it fit for use; and the third family, having labor only to put into the combination, does the pumping for all. The tanks are full, pumping is going on and *Illustration showing that advances are not required either by labor or by the lower sub-groups.*

the outflow of pure water is continuous. Does the
man who furnished the settling tank advance water
to the man who furnished the pump and to the other
man who is using it? He gives to them to-day, it is
true, water that is in a more advanced state than the
water they are pumping to-day, but he does not de-
plete his tank in doing it. A true advance would require that he should drain his tank and let it fill again,
but this he does not do. The apparent storage of
water is only a means of improving the quality of it:
the man imparts a utility to the water, but he does
not change the quantity of it.

Intermittent production, with constant use, of
course, demands storage. Where production is, for
natural reasons, periodic, as in the case of agriculture,
a special store is obviously needed. If the pumping,
in our illustration, could not take place except in the
early morning, it would be necessary to have a reservoir of pure water, in addition to the settling tank.
This kind of storage, however, raises questions entirely apart from the problems that arise from the mere
relations of labor to capital, or from those of sub-
Irregular- groups to sub-groups. Where production is constant,
ities in pro- there are laborers to be provided for, and there are
duction and whole sub-groups that of themselves produce only
consump- whole sub-groups that of themselves produce only
tion not to raw materials. These all get finished products for
be con- use, and that without imposing on any one the neces-
sidered use, and that without imposing on any one the neces-
in solving sity of making a true advance.
this general
problem.

Does the *amount* of A''' on hand at any one
time have anything to do with the *rate* of wages?[1]
The *form* of wages it affects in a certain way. If the
demand for this kind of finished goods were to be,
not continuous and uniform, but intermittent and
irregular, workers might chance at some time to

[1] For an early discussion of this subject see Chapters vii and viii
of *The Philosophy of Wealth*, by the author of the present work.

exhaust the stock of it. In that case, they would have to take their pay in some other form. In a static condition, this could occur only in consequence of the changing seasons. The production of winter clothing, for instance, might go on through the year; and there would then be, at the beginning of a cold season, a stock of it large enough to meet the demand arising at that time. In the absence of such an intermittent demand, the A''' would be taken for use as fast as it ripened, and no faster. With the sub-groups properly balanced, the A''' would be brought to completion as fast as would the A'', the A' and the A. There would be no accumulation at any part of the line. If more of A were made than could in the same time be converted into A', there would ensue a glut of A, a falling of the price of it, and a quick transfer of labor and capital to the other sub-groups. Static law thus keeps the sub-groups balanced in point of size and productive power, keeps the passive capital-goods in a continuous flow and makes every one's pay depend on the rate of the flow. Passive capital-goods are, however, never a fund, in the normal sense of the term. They are not kept in storage, except as irregular demands require this. It is on the *rapidity* of the flow of ripening commodities that income depends. It is all a question of velocity — of the quantity of A''' that ripens in a given time.[1]

Incomes depend on the rapidity with which goods ripen

[1] The amount of A''' which ripens in a given time is the product of quantity and velocity, since the quantity of unfinished goods on hand, in connection with the rate at which each piece moves toward completion, determines the gross amount completed within a given period. In so far as the quantity of unfinished goods varies directly as the number of units of labor and of capital that are at work on them, the quantity of income goods *per unit of labor and of capital* depends on mere velocity of movement. The gross *quantities* of wages and interest are the products

Capital, apportioned in the ways that have just been traced, is a requisite of *synchronized production and consumption.* Labor and time are the only absolute requisites of production not thus qualified. If the existence of the natural world and of human wants and powers be assumed, man has only to work and to wait in order to create wealth. But, with capital already on hand and rightly coördinated, labor and its fruits become synchronous. Coördinated capital is, then, a requisite of that production which is instantly followed by a ripened and consumable income. By means of a permanent fund of capital, adjusted in the ways in which the play of forces that has just been described would arrange it, men in all the sub-groups may produce at the same time and consume at the same time; and the consumption of all of them may closely accompany their production.

Effort and time the universal requisites. In the natural sense of the term, then, the universal requisite of production is effort; but the production that comes by effort only is certain to cover a period of time. It separates by an interval the beginning of the productive operation from the enjoyment of the first fruits of it. If the man is collecting tree trunks for a raft, it will be some time before he can float on it across the stream; and if he is making a hut, in the same primitive way, it will be still longer before he can get shelter within it.[1] It is, however,

of the two factors, quantity and speed of flow; but the *rates* depend mainly on speed. How quickly can an A be made and transformed into an A'''? This is the chief question to be asked, in this connection, if what we want is the rate of wages and that of interest.

[1] An unfinished raft is wealth, though it is not yet a consumers' good. It is a capital-good. The first log that is put into position for the making of the raft is a bit of wealth of this kind. It follows that for the creation of the beginnings of wealth effort *without time*

practically certain that the man will not build a hut in this simple way. He can do better by first making a rude hatchet; and this making of the hatchet is the "round-about" method of making goods, of which Professor von Böhm-Bawerk has spoken, as the typical fact in capitalistic production. By spending some time in making a tool and more time in using it, a man can get a larger and better house in a month than he could have secured by working empty-handed for the same time. The tool adds to his product; and indirectly, therefore, the time spent in making it does so.

Tools are productive, but time is the condition of getting tools — this is the simple and literal fact. The round-about or time-consuming mode of using labor insures efficient capital-goods. Granting that time be used for this purpose, we may say that "time is productive"; but we must be careful to keep in view the fact that it is the tools secured by time which do the producing.

Time productive because tools are so.

When the hatchet has worn itself completely out, and the fruits of using it are before the man in the large dwelling, he may look backward to the beginning of the process, when he faced nature empty-handed, and say: "Labor has done it all. Work and waiting

is all that is requisite. We have, however, been careful to keep in view finished goods, in condition to render their services to the men who make them. For securing these, an amount of time that is at least appreciable is requisite. Yet one cannot work on raw material through any period of time without having a bit of capital-goods in his hands undergoing manipulation. The full statement, therefore, is that, with only man and nature in existence at the outset, production is initiated by labor only, and the simplest kind of capital-goods is brought at once into existence. Further effort, extending through time, insures consumers' goods, but not without manipulating the materials that are in the interim capital-goods. Capital is requisite for the creation of wealth in the forms in which it can satisfy direct wants.

have given me my goods." The working and the waiting have, indeed, insured the hatchet, as an incidental result of this way of working. Production that plans to put its fruits into the future will create capital-goods as an immediate effect, but labor and time are enough to make the ultimate effect certain. Let the man work intelligently through an interval of time, and the production of consumers' wealth is sure. The thing, then, that is ultimately essential for production is labor. But if time is to intervene between the labor and the enjoyment of its fruits, the work may be first spent on capital-goods, which are a requisite of an accelerated rate of production. What they insure is an added quantity of product. They are not, however, a requisite of production, *as a process*, for wealth may be created without them.

An essential fact concerning capital-goods.

What, on the other hand, are the requisites of that production which does not put its fruits into the future? What must be given, in order that effort and the emerging of the product of effort may be simultaneous? When a savage contents himself with gathering sticks by hand and throwing them into his fire, he consumes very little time on each armful of wood; and an industry conducted on this plan is conceivable ; yet even in this case the wood that is in transit from the forest to the fire is not warming the man. The labor and the enjoyment are not quite synchronous. It would seem that working with any elaborate outfit of instruments must put the bringing together of work and enjoyment out of the question. Capital-goods would seem to be retarders of enjoyment; though, when the enjoyment comes, it is clear that they have increased the amount of it. If this is their effect, it is certain that enjoyments will always be so retarded. Working without tools is physically possible but practically impossible.

Capital-goods seemingly retarders of enjoyment.

Men can do it, but they certainly will not: they will invariably make the instruments that aid later work. The first tool that is made separates work from its fruits — makes the men wait for what they want, and every added tool means more waiting. Every addition in days of labor to the cost of a tool extends the interval of time that thrusts itself before the enjoyment that is to come. The mass of raw material and enginery by which a modern society produces is the enormous wedge that civilization has driven between labor and products. It is solidified time, or the material result of waiting on a vast scale. It is the visible testimony to the fact that some one's labor for present fruits began far back in the past.

Capital-goods imply waiting for the fruits of labor. Capital, on the contrary, implies the direct opposite of this: it is the means of avoiding all waiting. It is the remover of time intervals — the absolute synchronizer of labor and its fruits. It is the means of putting civilized man in a position which, so far as time is concerned, is akin to that in which the rude forester stood, when he broke off limbs of dead trees and laid them on his fire. The very appliances which, in their extent and complexity, seem in one view to mean endless waiting, in another view mean no waiting at all but the instantaneous appearance of the final fruits of every bit of labor that is put forth. *Capital the synchronizer of labor and fruits.*

What, now, are the requisites of production in which time intervals do not figure? Labor, capital and organization. Grant these, and the fruits of to-day's effort appear to-day, in the shape of the myriad things that civilized men need. Society is an organism. Let it work as an organism, with the proper instruments in its hands, and out of every day's labor will come in their completed shapes the consumers' *Three requisites of production without the interval between it and consumption.*

goods that civilized life will at once use. Given collective labor and not individual labor, and you may
put out of view all those separations of work from its
fruits that appear when we take a different look at
the world as it is. Into the shops go workers, and
out of the shops come goods. The work and the out-
coming of the goods are synchronous.

This synchronization — this bringing together in
time of work of every kind, and the complete ripening
of its virtual product — is the function of what we
have termed capital, in distinction from capital-goods.
Watch a bit of capital-goods — say, a lump of iron
ore just broken off from the bed of similar mineral in
the Mesaba range. It will make its way to the ships,
traverse the Great Lakes, reach a smelting furnace,
and become, first, a piece of steel and, later, a knife

The action
of capital-
goods con-
trasted with
that of
capital.
blade. There is a long interval between the beginning of its career as a capital-good and the beginning
of its service as an article of consumption. But watch
the entire capital of the steel-making and the cutlery-
making industries, and you will see this period vanish.
There is always ore in the mine and in the ships, and
steel in the furnaces and in the mills. If society is in
a static condition, there is always the same amount
of it in each department of the extended industry.
As some is withdrawn from each department, more
takes its place; and a fixed amount of "ripening" metal
maintains a continuous existence. As labor goes on
in the department farthest removed from the cutlery
shop, — as the picks break off lumps of ore in the
mine, — knives ready for use emerge from these
shops; and the essential fact is that some of these
knives are the virtual, though not the literal, product
of the work that is done in the mine. All this results
from the maintenance of a fund of permanent capital.

Let us take the simplest of illustrations. The water

that is now flowing into the reservoir of a mill is a
good in the raw state. It will take its turn in moving the machinery of the mills, but some time will
elapse before it does this. The drops that are at this
instant entering the upper end of the pond will require time for their passage to the wheel pit. It
takes many days for one of them, which is now in
its raw state near the inlet, to "ripen" into motion
imparted to a turbine wheel. The drops, separately
regarded, have periods of production, but the pond
as a whole has no such periods. The water that at
this moment flows into one end of the pond causes an
overflow from the other end, and the overflow moves
the wheel. There is an instantaneous result from the
coming of the "unripe" water, and this is assured by
the full reservoir. It is this permanent quantity of
hydraulic capital that enables the water which to-day
is far from the wheel virtually to move the wheel.
Forget all about the identity of particular drops of
water and the time that each one will take in trav-
ersing the pond, and what you see is an inflow which
at once causes an outflow that moves the wheel.
Capital in the shape of a pond full of water — of
which the constituent drops, indeed, are forever
changing — synchronizes the flow from the inlet
and the moving of the wheel.

Again, let a forest twenty acres in extent suffice to
furnish fire-wood for a family. A tree will mature
in twenty years ; and the forest must be kept intact,
in point of size and maturity, or the supply of wood
will fail. Each year we plant a row of trees along
one side of the forest, and cut a row from the other.
The planting and the cutting are, in a way, simultaneous. We do not burn to-day the tree that we
plant to-day ; but we do burn a tree, the consuming
of which is made practicable by to-day's planting.

The tree that is just set is, then, an enabling cause of
the consuming of one that is twenty years old. To
plant a sapling and wait for it to mature would be a
slow way to make a fire ; but to plant one and, *by
means of this planting and the maturing of the forest*,
to get at once another tree for use, is a quick way to
make a fire. The forest is a synchronizer of labor
and its virtual fruit. The fact that is of practical
consequence is, that if we have once secured the
permanent forest, we need do no waiting for fuel.
The identity of the tree that we burn is of no consequence. To plant one and to burn another, which is
at once made available in consequence of the planting
of the former, is to annihilate the interval that would
have existed, had it been necessary to depend on
one particular tree. The key to success in the effort
to make to-day's work yield to-day's fuel is the surrender of the identity of the thing that we are now
working on and that of the thing we at once use.

If, as consumers, we were so made that only the
particular thing which is beginning to takè shape
under our hands to-day could satisfy our wants,
then the wants of the present would have to go
unsatisfied. There would be an interval of painful waiting between industry and its fruits. Again,
if industry were conducted on such a plan that the
work that to-day begins to fashion a bit of raw material had no influence in causing a finished article at
once to emerge at the other end of the line of operations, then also we should have to wait. As it is,
we wait not at all. It is, in practice, immaterial to
us whether we consume one thing or another that
is exactly like it. Our plan of working enables
the labor that is done on a raw article to cause a
finished one to come into our possession. In the
hydraulic illustrations, the full pond is the condition

Conditions
that would
make wait-
ing neces-
sary.

that causes water at the inlet virtually to move the machinery of the mill. The full pipes furnish the condition that causes water among the remote hills virtually to satisfy the wants of the people of the city. In the case of the forest, the fixed number of trees maintained in the different stages of maturity is the condition that enables the planting of a sapling to furnish fuel. Capital it is, in each case, that does the synchronizing work. This is a cardinal function of this social agent of production.

On the ranches of Montana cattle are breeding, among the forests of Pennsylvania hides are tanning, in the mills of Brockton shoes are finishing; and, if the series of goods in all stages of advancement is only kept intact, the cow-boy may have to-day the shoes that he virtually creates by his efforts. This result is attainable because of the existence of a complete stock of capital-goods. We must have growing cattle, hides, tanned leather, partly made shoes and finished shoes, all maintained in a constant quantity, in order that a certain number of shoes may each day be taken for use. With sheep in the pastures, wool in the mills, cloth in the tailoring shops, and ready-made garments on the retailers' counters, the labor of the people can, as it were, instantaneously clothe the people. With a series of capital-goods of the right kinds once established, the work of to-day yields its result to-day in the shape of completed clothes.

Illustrations of the mode in which capital abolishes waiting.

A   A′   A″   A‴

Let the letters in the above horizontal line represent such a series of goods in various stages of completion. A is the raw material, A′ is that material somewhat transformed, A″ is the same material farther advanced toward completion and A‴ is

The position of workers in the different sub-groups of a series.

the completed article ready for consumption. Thus stands the series at the beginning of a working day. At the end of the day the series stands thus : —

$$(A) \quad A' \quad A'' \quad A''' \quad (A''')$$

The A' here is the A of the former series, which has been advanced to its present state by ten hours of industry; and at the same time a new A has been created, as is shown by the letter in parenthesis that is now prefixed to the series. A'' is the A' of the former series, which has also been advanced toward completion. A''' is the earlier A'', which has now been made ready for final use. The A''' in the parenthesis represents the former A''', which has been taken away to be distributed among all the workers and the capitalists whose agency has made the consuming of it practicable.

There is enough of this A''' to satisfy the claims of all the workers and all the capitalists in the series ; and each of them gets his share, and gets it without waiting. All have been applying their powers to the stock of capital-goods, in order to keep the series of goods intact. The withdrawal of the A''' is called for by the wants of all of them, and it is foreordained to take place. In itself alone, it would have made an inroad on the stock of capital-goods — an inroad that had to be neutralized. A''' must never be lacking, and the industry insures that it never shall be. The creation of a new A and the ripening of each of the remaining articles of the former series leaves, at the end of the day, a new series that is the exact duplicate of the former one. At the opening of the second day of industry, there are the same conditions that existed at the beginning of the first day. A is waiting to be made into an A', A' is waiting to be made into an A'', A'' is waiting to be made into an A''' and A''' is ready to be taken for consumption. At each point in the series there is a distinct set of men ready to make the needed transformation, and all these groups will now act again. Each will do its appointed work, and at the end of the second day all will again receive their pay.

This is a picture of organized industry. All the farms, railroads, mills and shops of the world are doing exactly what we have described, and doing it on a vast scale. What stands for A''' in the economy of the world is a vast mass of consumers' goods of every kind that humanity uses. It is all in process of creation, by the method that our simple illustration describes. Each finished article has its series of uncompleted articles of its own kind behind it. When one such thing is taken for use, another replaces it. Coats are bought from the retailers, and other coats come from the workshops to take their places. Cloth goes to the workshops; wool goes to the mills; sheep are growing up on the Western ranges and yielding their fleeces to the shearers. Bread comes from the bakeries for this evening's use, and other bread replaces it. Flour comes from the mills; wheat from the elevators, and ultimately from the soil. Everywhere there is the series of capital-goods in various stages of advancement. Everywhere industry is applied to this stock of goods, to ripen it, thus making good the waste of its tissues which results from the withdrawal of the consumers' goods and keeping the series intact.

For the immediate creation of wealth for consumption, then, there is needed: (1) A series of consumers' goods in various stages of advancement; (2) workers and tools at each point along the line; (3) simultaneous work. Out of this organization comes consumers' wealth, yet the supply of pro-

The relation of permanent capital to work and to enjoyment.

ducers' wealth never fails. The men keep the stock of capital-goods from failing. The permanent stock of shifting capital-goods — the true capital — keeps the men from waiting.[1]

[1] For an earlier statement of these principles see an article on "The Genesis of Capital" in the *Yale Review* for November, 1893.

CHAPTER XXI

THE THEORY OF ECONOMIC CAUSATION

IF a society is static and capital is not increasing, both wages and interest consist in goods of the type A''', B''' and C''' of the illustrative table. They come into existence in a steady flow that is synchronous with the productive action of labor and capital in all the sub-groups, and they go simultaneously to the men in all of these groups for consumption.

It is capital, as such, which earns the interest that is embodied in these goods; and the earnings of it are made to be uniform — that is, they are made to secure as much of A''', B''' and C''' to the men in A as they do to the men at A''', at B''' or elsewhere. The products of labor are, in a like way, uniform. Is it certain that capital, as a whole, gets exactly what it produces? Obviously, what the last unit of capital gets is what it produces, and that is what every other unit must take; but is there not a chance that the earlier units may be exploited? The same question arises in connection with labor: The last unit of labor gets its product, it may be admitted; but do the earlier ones get their full product? Does the income of the whole body of laborers tend at all, under natural law, to equal what they produce? Is there not an exploitation of all early increments of labor, if the law of final productivity works in perfection?

Restatement
of the law
of final
productivity
as acting on
a social
scale.

With this question in view, let us revert to the familiar graphic statement of the law of final productivity.

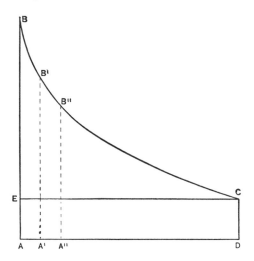

Letting the amount of capital remain fixed and causing the amount of labor to be measured by the line AD, we will go through the imaginary process of supplying this labor, unit by unit. The first unit, then, so long as it remains alone, has a vast amount of capital to coöperate with it. For simplicity, let us say that each unit of labor is a tenth of the whole force and that, while the first unit is alone, it has a profusion of appliances, all of the costliest grade, to coöperate with it. It is, in fact, aided by ten times the amount of capital that a single unit will, in the end, have to aid it. If we are to think of an actual society in which labor is thus, as it were, over-satu-rated with capital, we shall have to imagine costly materials, buildings of the most solid and enduring kind, motive power in abundance, and automatic machinery of a degree of costliness and perfection that is far from having been attained as yet, even in the departments of industry in which invention has done its best. With all that machinery to aid it, the product of the one unit of labor will be enormous.

In our figure, we measure the amount of a unit of labor by distance along the line AD, and indicate one unit by a tenth of this line, or the distance AA'. We may measure the amount of the product of the first unit of labor by the area of the figure ABB'A'. This area measures the amount of wealth that is called into existence by one unit of social labor, assisted by a nearly inconceivable profusion of social capital; and the wealth measured by this area consists in consumers' goods of every kind, destined for the use of a whole population.

Let us now add a second unit of labor, the quantity A'A'', measuring the quantity that it produces by the area A'B'B''A''. Here we must be careful. The quantity that this second increment of labor produces is, as we have said, measured by the area of this second figure. This statement may easily bear an interpretation that will make the entire theory lead to an erroneous conclusion — to one, in fact, which is the direct opposite of the truth. With a certain interpretation, the statement that the second increment of labor produces less than the first may lead to the inference that, — so long as all are paid at the same rate, — nearly all labor is robbed of a part of what it produces, and that too by the action of competitive law. This is a natural inference from the law of final productivity, when it is left incomplete. If one man produces the value of a dollar and a half a day, while another produces the value of a dollar, and if each gets a dollar, there is a clear case of exploitation of labor.[1]

An imperfect final productivity theory of wages, implying an exploitation of labor.

[1] The most brilliant of early German economists, Von Thünen, offered a theory that applied a final productivity test to both labor

The surrender of a share of capital by the first division of the working force is the important fact

The element needed for correcting this theory. here to be considered. With the coming of the second increment of labor, tools are multiplied; but they are so cheapened that all of them together

and capital, and made wages and interest depend on the result. In his work, *Der isolirte Staat*, he said that, when new men are taken into an industry, — the tilling of a farm, for example, — they produce less than did the men who were earlier employed. What the farmer gets by means of the labor of the last man, is what he pays for the work of every man. Von Thünen also asserted that a final unit of capital, tested in the same way, shows a similar reduction in its productive power, and that the product of the unit last applied sets the standard of interest.

It is a startling fact that the statements of Von Thünen did not lead directly to the solution of the problem of wages and interest. With such a brilliant beginning of a true theory before them, why should economists still account for the rate of wages, by saying that it depends on the amount of capital that is foreordained to be divided among laborers in the form of wages ? Why, also, should they account for the rate of interest merely by saying that it depends on demand and supply ? It is doubtless true that Von Thünen himself attached far less importance to his final. productivity formula than he did to that entirely different formula by which, in his view, the socially desirable and rightful rate of wages is expressed ; yet it would seem that his statement of the principle of final productivity should have put investigators on the right track.

The explanation is to be found in the incompleteness of Von Thünen's actual theory. It was left in a shape in which it not only fails to reveal the most important fact about wages and interest, but seems actually to contradict it. This fact is that, under the influence of perfectly free competition, the pay of all labor tends to equal the product of all labor, and that interest on all capital tends to conform to the product of all capital.

Von Thünen's theory of wages is apparently a theory of the exploitation of labor. In his illustration, there is a certain force of laborers working on a farm and a man is now added to the force. His presence enables the farmer to glean his fields more closely. As Von Thünen suggested, he can now gather a smaller grade of potatoes than it was formerly profitable to gather ; and if the new man is taken in the harvesting season, his product is embodied in the addition that, in such ways as this, is made to the crop. This

embody only the original amount of capital. How
do we estimate the specific product of the new increment of labor? The essential fact is that the new
working force and the old one share alike in the
use of the whole capital, and with its aid they

man, however, produces distinctly less than the men who are before
him in the order of the series ; and their pay is scaled down to his
product. There are expressions in Von Thünen's discussion which
seem to imply that, in his own view, the law of final productivity
is a law of exploitation of labor. There are also indications that
his theory of the final productivity of capital involved a similar
exploitation of the earlier units of capital.

What is first needed, in order to make Von Thünen's statement
cover a principle that is of cardinal importance in connection with
wages, is a theory of what has been called " imputation," or of
what, in the foregoing chapter, has been called economic causation. At any one time, all units of labor tend to be equally productive. There is, then, no class of workers who are degraded and
virtually robbed, because of the pressure of others who produce
less than they do and who set the standard of their pay. The
excess of pay that the men on the illustrative farm *formerly* got is
attributable to the greater product that they *formerly* created ; and
that is solely due to the excess of capital which they had in the earlier period. The theory needs to trace to capital, and not to labor,
that extra product which an overplus of capital insures to the men
who, in the assumed case, are made to come early in the series.
It needs, also, in studying the products that are attributable to a
series of units of capital, to use the same discrimination and to
show that the earlier units of this agent are not exploited.

As between a theory which asserts that every unit of labor naturally tends to get, as its pay, its entire product and one which says
that the great mass of laborers are, by competition, regularly robbed
of a part of their product, the difference is radical ; and yet these
theories may use identical language, in telling how the pay of all
labor is directly determined. Both may apply to labor the commercial principle of final valuation and say, in effect, that there
cannot be two prices of the same article in the same market — that
what the last unit of labor brings, all labor brings ; and that the
last unit brings what it produces. If it produces less than do other
units, these others are sufferers by their connection with it, for
they lose a part of their products. If, however, all units *under
present conditions* produce the same amount, there is no robbery
involved in fixing the pay of all by the product of the final one.

now create equal amounts of product.   The earlier
men have relinquished a half of the capital that they
formerly had; and in making this surrender, these
men of the earlier division have reduced the pro-

Von Thünen's theory is a final productivity theory; but it needs to
become, in addition, a *specific productivity* theory, which makes
the pay of each unit of labor conform to its own specific product.

A theory that is to explain the adjustment of wages and interest
needs to make clear what is the nature of that "last dose" of capital, on the product of which interest depends; and this involves dis-
criminating between capital and capital-goods.   Particularly, also,
does the study need to enlarge its scope, so as to include, not
one industry merely, but the whole system of groups and sub-
groups that make an economic society.   The final increment of
labor, the product of which fixes wages, is a social increment,
some of which is found in every sub-group in the series; and the
same thing is true of the final increment of capital.   The law of
value is active in making these apportionments, and it needs to be
included as a part of the theory of distribution as a social phenomenon.   With Von Thünen's work before us, no one else can claim
as his own the application to labor and to capital of the principle
of final valuation and the basing of valuation on productivity.   A
prospector in a mining country may, indeed, independently discover
and re-occupy an abandoned claim; and this is all that one would do
who should re-discover the single principle of final valuation of labor
and capital and should stop where Von Thünen stopped.   Going
farther and discovering laws that tend to bring the products of
different units of labor at any one time to an equality, to bring
the products of different units of capital to an equality, and to
make wages equal to the entire product of labor and interest equal
to the whole product of capital — this is attaining the essential truth
in the theory of wages and interest; since it establishes the fact that
natural law, so far as it has its way, excludes all spoliation.   Such
further study reveals the fact that what are apparently surplus parts
of the products of early increments of labor are really products of
capital.   This result is gained by following the line of study in which
Von Thünen took the initial steps; and it may, perhaps, give so
much of a title to the final result as a miner secures when he
strikes a new vein of metal by using, as an entrance way, an
abandoned shaft that had led only to a deposit of ore of a different
kind.   As Von Thünen did not suspect, the natural law of wages
gives a result that would satisfy his own requirement, as being
desirable and morally justifiable.

ductive power of their industry, by the amount that
the extra share of capital formerly imparted to it.
This reduction measures the amount of product that
is attributable to the relinquished capital. Of prime
importance is this fact that the product which is now
attributable to the first section of the working force,
with its tools and other appliances, has now become
smaller than it formerly was, solely by reason of the
capital that has been taken from it. The excess of
its former product over its present one is not attributable to labor; and no exploiting of labor takes place,
though each of the two units now receives less than
the first one formerly received.

Two facts are now clear; and we may state them
briefly in two propositions which include a whole
theory of economic causation — a theory that tells
to what agency each fraction of a composite social
product is to be traced. (1) The difference between
what the first division of workers created by the use
of the whole capital and what they now create is an
amount that is solely attributable to the extra capital
which they formerly had. (2) The difference between
what one increment of labor produced, when it used
the whole of the capital, and what two increments
are now producing, by the aid of that same amount
of capital, is attributable solely to the second increment of labor. We have, in this way, tested the
specific productivity of a certain amount of capital,
and we have also tested the specific productivity of
one unit of labor.

Surpluses connected with early increments of labor attributable to capital; the whole product connected with the final increment attributable to labor.

It is with the latter test that we are immediately
concerned; and what we have been careful to guard
against is the notion that, at any one time, there is
a difference between the products of different units
of labor, as such. Each of them, with its share of
the capital, produces one-half of the whole present

All units of labor at one time uniformly productive.

output of the industry; but a half of the present output is less than was the whole output, when only one man was working with the aid of the entire capital. This reduction measures the product of one-half of the capital, as used by one unit of labor. On the other hand, the whole product, now that the two units of labor are working, is greater than was the whole product with one working; and this addition to the product is due solely to an accession of labor. The amount of the addition measures the product of that labor and of all labor under the present changed conditions.

If C stands for the amount of capital that is used in the industry and if L stands for one unit of labor, the difference between the product of $C + L$ and that of $\dfrac{C + 2\,L}{2}$ is the amount that is attributable to one-half of the capital. The difference between the product of $C + 2\,L$ and that of $C + L$ is the amount that is attributable to a unit of labor. In the first of these formulas, the minuend is what one man can produce with the whole capital, and the subtrahend is what one man can produce with a half of the capital. In the second formula, the minuend is what two men can produce with the whole capital, and the subtrahend is what one man can produce with the whole of it.

In the following diagram the amount of capital is not represented, but it remains fixed. The product that is imputable to one-half of the capital is the area ABB'A', minus one-half of the area ABB''A''. The product that is traceable solely to one unit of labor is the area A'B'B''A'', and this is now the amount that is specifically attributable to either of the two units. It will be seen that here there is no unnatural cramping of the productive power of the second man — there is no limitation of his produce to the gleanings of any field, agricultural or other. Each man gets what one unit of labor, under fair

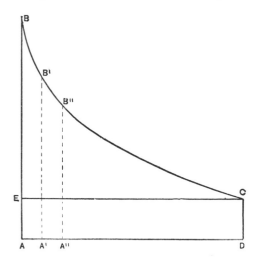

conditions, creates; while capital gets what is imputable to it.

Let us now revert to our graphic statement of the law of specific productivity. Keeping the original capital intact, and changing only its forms, let us add a third unit of labor to the force. The product of it is the area $A''B''B'''A'''$ in the figure on the following page; and, if we continue to make similar additions to the force till it is complete, the product of the last unit of labor will be the area $A^{ix}B^{ix}CD$. This is the standard of wages. It is the specific product of any one unit of labor, at the time when there are ten units of it. All that we have said about the product of the second man, when he was the last one, applies here. Before the arrival of the tenth man there were nine in the field; and they were utilizing the whole of the capital,

The product of all labor separated in detail from that of capital.

having it, of course, in forms adapted to the use of
that number of workers. Each produced an amount
that is measured by the rectangle the sides of which
are $A^{viii}A^{ix}$ and $A^{ix}B^{ix}$. All of them together produced the amount that is expressed by the area
$AE^{i}B^{ix}A^{ix}$. A narrow strip between the lines EF
and $E^{i}B^{ix}$ measures the difference between what nine
men of themselves produce at the time when they
are working in connection with the whole of the

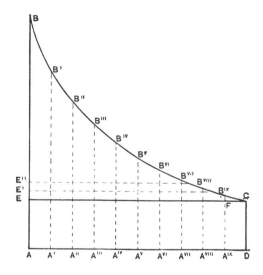

capital and what the nine men produce when they
are working in connection with nine-tenths of the
capital; for it is fair to consider that, when ten men
are using the whole of the fund, each of them virtually uses a tenth of it. The area $AEFA^{ix}$ represents
nine-tenths of the product that is specifically attributable to the whole working force when it has the
entire capital coöperating with it, and of course adding its own further share to the joint product. The
area $EE^{i}B^{ix}F$ represents, not the entire addition that

a certain amount of capital makes to the output of the industry, but only the addition that an increment of capital makes to that part of the output of the industry as a whole which is separately attributable to labor.

So, when there were eight men at work, each one produced the amount of $A^{vii}B^{vii}B^{viii}A^{viii}$; and all of them together produced the amount $A E^{ii}B^{viii}A^{viii}$. A second narrow strip, between the horizontal lines $E^{ii}B^{viii}$ and $E^{i}B^{ix}$, measures the difference between what eight men of themselves produce when they have all of the capital coöperating with them and what they produce after they have shared the capital with the ninth man. They give him one-ninth of the entire capital, and the strip between $E^{ii}B^{viii}$ and $E^{i}B^{ix}$, therefore, measures what the eight men lose in their own productive power by this surrender. In like manner, when the working force is enlarged from seven to eight, there is a surrender of one-eighth of the entire capital and a reduction in the distinctive product of the labor of the seven men ensues. Every *per capita* reduction of the productive fund takes something from the amount that is specifically traceable to the labor of each man.[1]

[1] In all the foregoing graphic representation there is a slight mathematical inaccuracy, due to the fact that the upper boundary of the figure is made to be a curve with a continuous downward trend. Strictly, the whole figure should have been made of rectangles, and the upper boundary should have been the tops of the contiguous rectangles. With ten units of capital one man produces the amount that is expressed by the first rectangle in the following figure ; while, after he has relinquished one-half of the capital to the second man, he produces only the amount indicated by the smaller rectangle on the right of the figure. The difference between these areas, or the space above the dotted line in the larger rectangle expresses the product of five units of capital in the hands of one man. If we continued thus to build up the figure,

Another
mode of dis-
tinguishing
the product
of all labor
from that
of all
capital.

Knowing that the area $A^{ix}B^{ix}CD$, in Fig. 1 below, measures the product of the final unit of labor, we may be sure that no unit in the working force produces less than this amount. Brief statements of the law of final productivity may raise the question, whether the earlier units of labor in the series do not produce more than does the last one; but that they produce as much as does this one cannot be doubted. AECD, then, is the smallest amount that can be traced to labor as the cause of its existence.

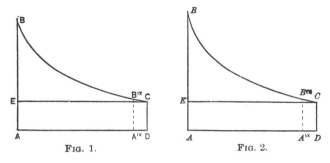

Fig. 1.   Fig. 2.

In Fig. 2, let the line AD measure capital instead of labor, let the amount of labor be a fixed quantity, and let the product of successive units of capital decline along the curve BC. $A^{ix}B^{ix}CD$ is, then, the product that the last unit of capital brings into existence. No other unit of capital produces any less; and the area $AECD$ is the least that can be attributed to the entire ten units of capital.

Now, in Fig. 1, EBC is all that is left of the entire product that is not produced by labor. If $AECD$, of the second figure, is as large as EBC, of the first, this amount, EBC, is the product of capital; since the rectangle $AECD$ is certainly the

we should avoid the small inaccuracies just referred to; but we should have a somewhat cumbersome mode of description to contend with, when we should describe the figure by letters.

product of capital. We know that, by our hypothesis
of perfect competition and a complete static adjustment, there is no profit realized by the *entrepreneur*,
as such; and the figure ABCD cannot contain more
than wages and interest. The amount EBC is, therefore, not larger than is *AECD* of the second, and
all of EBC is the product of capital.

Again, *EBC* is shown, in the same way, to be
the product of labor. It is not larger than AECD,
of Fig. 1. The static hypothesis prevents the entire
figure *ABCD* from containing more than wages and
interest. There is, then, no area in it representing
entrepreneur's profit; and EBC, which equals AECD
of Fig. 1, is the product of labor solely, since the
rectangle AECD measures the least amount that can
be ascribed to labor.

As we have, throughout this study, kept constantly before our eyes the fact that, whenever one
man comes into the force, the capital changes its
forms and adapts itself to the number of men who
are to use it, so we have to keep as constantly in
mind the fact that the modes of labor itself have to
change in a parallel way. A working force may be
built up, unit by unit, so that the enlargement of the
force seems to be quantitative; but the change in
labor, abstractly regarded, is mainly qualitative.
More effort is expended, as the force enlarges; but
it shows itself, not so much in doing things that
were formerly left entirely undone, as it does in
doing nearly everything in a more perfect manner.
If the work is agricultural, the ground will be more
evenly fertilized, the seed more uniformly distributed, etc. This is one type of change that labor, as
a process, undergoes when workers become more
numerous. Another type of change is that which
is caused by the altered character of the tools and

Changes in
the charac-
ter of labor
caused by
quantitative
changes of
labor and
capital.

other appliances that a laborer has to use, as the force becomes larger, while the amount of the capital remains the same. Every change in the instruments with which men work changes the mechanical movements in which work consists. Labor, however, is capable of being measured in units, as though it were homogeneous; and there is a practical method of measuring the product of all of it.

It will be remembered that, in an early chapter, we described a zone of indifference, within which an employer can take a very few more men, at the rate of wages that he is now paying, without sustaining a loss. In a great establishment, there is often such a limited elasticity in the size of the working force. If the establishment were a great farm, an extra man might somewhere be employed without being forced to do any gleaning in which he would produce perceptibly less than other men. This man's product would, as we have said, *express* the rate of wages. Men on the zone of indifference are also an aid in adjusting wages. Our whole study requires that a **Importance of the social zone of indifference.** man on this zone in one industry shall be as productive as a man on the similar zone in another industry. It requires, in fact, that there shall be a comprehensive zone of indifference extending through the whole industrial field, and that labor on all parts of this social zone shall be uniformly productive. It is now doubly clear that labor on all parts of the industrial field has the same degree of productivity that it has on the marginal zone.

The practical usefulness of this zone lies in its influence in facilitating competition. A single unit of labor, in seeking employment, always has alternatives open to it. A young man who has not mastered a particular craft has many employments open to him, and can count on getting about what he is worth, anywhere on this social zone; and one who, after learning one trade, has to take up another may often get a new employment on some new part of this comprehensive area. An *entrepreneur* who is entering a sub-group, as a competitor of the men who are already there, can gather a force of workers for his mill by withdrawing men from this large social area of indifference — from which they may be taken without causing disturbances, either within any sub-group or in the relations between the different sub-groups. The scientific importance of this zone, however, depends on the test that it affords of the productive power of all labor. If only the adjustments which have lately been described have already taken place, and if labor and capital are now apportioned in a nicely accurate way among the different industries, the product realized from labor on this zone has become an indicator of the product that may be attributed to labor everywhere.

Antecedent adjustments in order that this zone may afford a standard of the productivity of all labor.

CHAPTER XXII

THE LAW OF ECONOMIC CAUSATION APPLIED TO THE PRODUCTS OF CONCRETE INSTRUMENTS

As capital always consists in goods, it should be possible to account for the whole earnings of it by tracing the amount that is specifically created by each productive instrument. Studies of capital proper should be confirmed at every point by parallel studies of capital-goods, and they can be. There is a simple way of showing the causal connection between all-capital and all-interest, by showing the detailed connection between each piece of capital-goods and its concrete product, or rent.

In the classical idea of rent there is something which is contrary to popular notions on the subject.

The popular conception of rent. In practical life, almost any concrete instrument of production may become a rent earner; and the thing that is most frequently spoken of as securing this kind of income is a building. One may, for example, "rent" an office, an apartment, a dwelling, a warehouse, etc. Although the hiring of any one of these involves hiring a certain quantity of land, that quantity is frequently minute and is not prominent in the minds of the parties to the transaction. In popular usage, the term rent also designates the earnings of many things to which no land is attached in the letting: one may, for example, "rent" a ship, a carriage, a horse, a tool, or any other of a hundred concrete things.

334

This use of terms in popular speech rests in reality on the distinction between capital and capital-goods. Interest is the fraction of itself that permanent capital earns; and the capital in the case, while it is certainly not thought of as a disembodied abstraction, is nevertheless regarded as permanent wealth, the concrete and changing forms of which are left entirely out of sight. Interest is not a fraction of buildings, ships, horses, etc.: it is a fraction of the permanent fund that an endless series of such shifting things embodies.

The distinction between capital and capital-goods the basis of it.

With rent, on the contrary, it is the concrete forms that come into prominence. Every instrument that helps to constitute the permanent fund of capital earns, during its active existence, a certain definite quantity of wealth, which can be measured in a lump sum. The axe may earn two dollars; the spade, four dollars; the boat, fifty dollars; the building, a hundred thousand dollars, etc. In all this there is no idea of a percentage connected with these earnings. We can, however, reduce that part of the gross product of an instrument which is really a net income to a percentage of the value of the instrument. If we do this, we shall have reduced the rent, with a certain deduction, to the form of interest. If we make a distinction between the gross earnings of the instrument and the net earnings, by deducting from the gross earnings the amount that is necessary to replace the instrument when it is worn out, the net earnings can be treated as interest on the value of the instrument. If we follow the usage of the market, we shall, then, use the term rent to include the whole gross earnings. Thus, the rent of a house is what the tenant pays for it. But, if the landlord keeps the house in repair and replaces it when it is worn out, merely from what the tenant pays, he must set aside a sinking fund for that purpose; and only what is left will become an available income.[1] If we make this calculation in the case of every instrument in use, we shall have the net earnings of all the capital-goods that exist, and we can reduce this amount to the form of interest, by comparing it with the amount of the capital that the goods embody. We can, for this purpose, get the net income of the instruments in dollars, estimate the aggregate value of the instruments in dollars, get the ratio between the two quantities and, stating the ratio in a decimal fraction, have the rate of interest — the percentage of itself that capital earns in a given time. If, on the other hand, we simply make a list of all the instruments that are in use, without reference to their value, and compute the lump sums that they can earn in a given time, we shall have the gross earnings of the instruments in the form of an aggregate rent. This rent, however, includes a sinking fund that offsets the wear which causes deterioration of the whole mass of instruments during this time. In dynamic conditions land usually increases in value, while in a static state it does not. But even in a static state most things deteriorate by use. If we deduct the sinking fund thus made necessary from the gross rent, we have what we may term net rent, or the part of the gross rent that is really income. This is what the owners of the instruments can use with impunity for personal consumption.

Net rent is, then, nothing more than interest

The mode of translating rent into interest.

---

[1] Where a building stands on land that is increasing in value, a crude kind of book-keeping treats the increased value of the land as an offset for the diminished value of the building, and therefore reserves no sinking fund from the earnings of the building for the replacement of the structure when it shall be worn out. The whole rent that the tenant pays is, in that case, not very inaccurately regarded as the rent of land and building.

regarded from another point of view: it is an aggregate of lump sums, each of which represents the net earnings of some instrument. It is identical in amount with interest, and it becomes interest the moment that we reduce it to a fraction of the value of the instruments that earn it. In a static state, the only difference between net rent and interest lies in the manner of computing them. State how many dollars all capital-goods of every kind earn, above the cost of repairing and replacing them, and you have told what is the net rent of all capital-goods. It is the same as the whole amount of interest, but you translate it into a rate of interest by comparing it with the value of the capital-goods.

Net rent and interest identical sums computed in different ways.

We shall regard the product of permanent capital as interest, the gross product of all capital-goods as gross rent, and this same amount, less the cost of replacing the goods, as net rent. Herein we are following practical usage in the choice of terms, and we are expressing a distinction that business men make between rent and rent-producers, on the one hand, and interest and interest-producers, on the other.

Science has proposed a different distinction between rent and interest. It has tried to confine the former term to the product of land,—and that, too, without taking account of changes in the value of land,—defining it as what a tenant pays to his landlord for the use of the "original and indestructible" properties of the soil. This usage probably would never have grown up, if the science of political economy had originated in America, where land has always been a commercial article, and where the man who buys a piece of it reckons whether he can get as good interest on his investment in that form as he can in any other. It is, then, obviously very important to know whether the usage that is prevalent in ordinary life is not, after all, really more accurate, and hence more scientific.

The two distinctions that are usually cited as differentiating land and other instruments are: (1) The quantity of land is absolutely fixed, while instruments may be multiplied; and (2) the earnings of land consist in differential quantities, obtained by comparing the yield of good land with that of poor. " The rent of a piece of land," says the definition, in effect, "is what it produces, minus the product of the poorest land in use that is tilled or otherwise utilized by the application of the same amount of labor and capital." The rigidly fixed amount of land, then, on the one hand, and the differential way of reckoning the product of it, on the other, are the facts on which science has based its practice of treating this agent as unlike capital and as distinct from it as an economic agent.

Let us see how much, in a static study, these distinctions amount to. That capital, in the aggregate, should be fixed in amount, is one of the conditions of the static state. This assumption, moreover, expresses what is true at any one moment in a dynamic state. The gross amount of capital in the world cannot be instantly changed, and the rate of interest at this moment is based on the gross amount existing at this moment. If dynamic changes were not to occur, the present amount would be the permanent one, and all capital could be treated, like land, as a fixed quantity. The idea that land is fixed in amount, and that capital can be increased at will and to any extent, is really based on an error which one encounters in economic discussions with wearisome frequency. It is true, indeed, that if one particular kind of instrument is highly productive, we can multiply the number of such things at will; and we shall, in fact, multiply it till we reduce the earnings of these goods. We thus bring the returns of the capital that is invested in them down to the rate that corresponds to the general earnings of social capital. The value of the instrument appears to be fixed by its cost, while the number of instruments of this kind is varied according to the earnings. A piece of land, on the other hand, earns an amount that the Ricardian formula measures; and the value of the land is the capitalization of the earnings. Land, of course, has no cost value, since it is furnished by nature. In this view, it looks as if, in the case of land, quantity were fixed, earnings fixed and value conformed to earnings. It looks as though, in the case of capital-goods, quantity were variable, value were variable and earnings were brought into a relation to the value by a change of quantity.

Let us look again and more carefully. What we are really comparing is land in general and capital in one particular form. In the terms of our table, we are noting the quantity of all land, as an all-around agent of social production, and that of the capital employed in a *particular sub-group*. In one case we are taking a social view, and in the other a local view. This is a method that has been adopted in many other connections — and never without confusion.

Confusion resulting from comparing all land with one kind of capital-goods.

Let us, then, rather compare *all* land with *all* other capital-goods: let us take all society into the field of view. In every group and sub-group there is land, and in every one there is capital in the form of artificial instruments. Neither the one agent nor the other can be increased in the aggregate at will. At any one time, the amount of artificial capital in existence is as fixed as is the amount of land.

Within any short time it is impossible to increase the general fund of artificial capital enough to make a perceptible difference in the conditions of social industry. At any one time we have to deal with a definite quantity of land, in combination with a definite amount of capital in artificial forms. Moreover, the distinction between land and other capital-goods, based on the notion that land cannot be increased and that other things can be, has obviously no validity in a static study; for the static assumption itself precludes all increase of capital.

Let us see where, if ever, the distinction holds good: let us take a limited view, confining ourselves to a particular sub-group. Is it true, even here, that land cannot be increased, and that capital in other forms can be? The distinction has as little application here as it has in the general view. We can, of course, move more land into this sub-group by taking it out of others. Land is, in the economic sense, mobile; since we can cease to use land for one kind of product and devote it to another. In exactly the same way, we can increase the amount of capital in artificial forms — we can take capital out of one industry and put it into another. In the particular sub-group on which we are concentrating attention, we can have more tools and machines, if we want them. If we are looking at the shoe manufacturing business, we can have as many stitching machines, pegging machines, etc., as we wish; but we can have them quickly only by diverting capital from other forms of investment. In a static condition of society, however, we never shall do this, for an economic influence prevents it.

Is there a limit on the amount of land that, consistently with economic laws, we can use in this industry, and no limit on the capital that we can thus consistently put there? Is there an economic consideration that virtually says: "For the best results you must have exactly so much land in this business, while the amount of capital that you may have is an uncertain and variable amount? On the contrary, the quantity of land is fixed in exactly the same way as is the quantity of capital in other shapes. Land is mobile; artificial capital is mobile; and the law of variation that we have described in an earlier chapter determines exactly how much land there shall be in each sub-group, and exactly how much capital in other forms there shall be.[1] Put in too much land, and the product of the land, estimated in goods, is reduced, the value of the goods is reduced, and these two influences act concurrently to make you take out the excess. Put in too much capital in other forms, and the same thing happens. The unit of capital then produces too few goods, and goods of too small value. Hence the excess vanishes. *Both land and artificial capital are mobile, and the quantities of them in one sub-group are fixed by a single law.*

The result of the action of this law is that there is, in every sub-group, a normal amount of land and also a normal amount of capital in other forms. If you change either amount, you change it for the worse; for, when you apportion either your land or your other capital badly, you get a smaller income. One peculiarity of land is here to be noticed, in connection with the fact that artificial capital has no special adaptation to any particular industry. It changes its outward forms freely, as it goes out of one industry and into another. There is nothing about its form that ties it permanently to one occupation. Some forms of capital, indeed, are very durable; and when capital is invested in them, it cannot easily be taken out. Not all the capital can be withdrawn from such an investment without a great deal of *Land and artificial capital are transferred from group to group in different ways.*

[1] See pp. 297–299.

delay, for it is there to stay till the instrument wears out. In general, however, there are enough kinds of capital-goods in every industry that are quickly perishable, requiring frequent renewal, to make it possible to change the form of the capital quickly and without much waste.

Land, on the other hand, has to be moved bodily, when it is moved at all. It is possible to change the form of improvements connected with it, though doing this too quickly involves a waste; but the land itself has to be transferred from group to group as it is. We cannot wait for one kind of land to perish and for a different kind of land to take its place. The process by which we can move capital without waste, if we take time enough to do it, is not available in the case of the indestructible elements in the soil. When we move land from sub-group to sub-group, we take it, with all its qualities as they are, from one to the other. Land has, moreover, its special adaptations, and it never develops its full productive power unless those adaptations are respected. Land that is good for grazing or for forestry is not equally good for wheat cultivation, land that is good for market gardening is not equally good for building sites, and land that is good for building sites for one purpose is not equally good for building sites for another purpose.

This fact makes it necessary to modify the law that apportions land among the different sub-groups.

Special adaptations of land are to be considered. That land which has a special adaptation for one use may be devoted definitely to that use, with no moral possibility of taking it out of it. If it is necessary to reduce the quantity of land thus employed, that which should be taken out of this department of business is land that is less preëminently adapted to it. There is, for example, some land so well adapted for grazing and so ill adapted for tillage that taking it out of the former use and putting it into the latter would be a pure waste. On the other hand, there is a great deal of marginal land that is adapted to either use. In making the adjustment of quantity between the two industries, we respect the peculiarities of the land that has marked adaptations and move only that which can be used indifferently for either purpose. Some land, too, is so supremely well adapted to be used in building sites for mercantile structures that we can never think of using it for anything else. There is, however, marginal land that is as well adapted for mercantile uses as it is for residence uses; and when we reduce the amount of land that is devoted to the one purpose and increase the amount devoted to another, we do it by transferring some of this indifferent land.

We shall see, when we get our ultimate measure of value, that there is such a thing as a unit of true capital in the form of land.[1] For economic purposes, land is to be measured, not by the acre or by the square foot, but by units of productive efficiency. Thus, there may be much capital concentrated in a small piece of land in the heart of New York City, while there may be very little of it in a whole township in the Rocky Mountains. But the law that apportions land among different sub-groups so locates it that every unit of it — that is, every unit of the capital that it embodies — goes where it will do the most good. Land that is supremely well adapted to one use and ill adapted to another represents many units of capital in the one use and few in the other. Suppose, now, that it were necessary to take some land out of the former of these employments and to put it into the latter. Should we think of taking

Units of capital in land;

---

[1] See Ch. XXIV.

land that, in its present employment, represents ten units of capital and put it where it will represent only one unit? That would be suicidal. We shall, in fact, transfer some of the land which represents one unit of capital where it is and will represent the same amount in the place where we are to put it. That is, we shall try to move land from sub-group to sub-group without rudely destroying the productive power that depends on its adaptations. Land that is worth more per foot or per acre where it is than it can ever be worth in any other sub-group, will stay where it is. Land that can be moved

their tendency toward a maximum total productivity and toward a uniform specific productivity. without any such waste as we have described will be moved freely, till an adjustment is reached which gives two results: (1) Land, as a whole, will be so placed as to develop its maximum productive power — which is equivalent to saying that it will embody the largest number of units of capital that it is capable of embodying. (2) All units of capital in land will, of course, be uniformly productive.

With this reservation about the kinds of land that will be chosen, to be taken out of one use and put into another, the principle that locates land among the different sub-groups is identical with the principle that locates capital in other forms among them. Capital, in all forms, is brought to a uniformity of productive power per unit: capital, as a whole, is brought to its highest efficiency. Mislocating capital of any kind is reducing the total efficiency of the fund. Locating capital of all kinds according to the law of apportionment that we have outlined gives to the whole of it the largest possible power to produce. In a static hypothesis, we assume that this adjustment is made and kept — that the quantity of land and of other capital in each sub-group is fixed.

We now have to see that the earning power of

land and that of the other forms of capital are determined in exactly the same way. Here we take issue with the second claim of the classical economist concerning land — namely, that its earnings consist only of surpluses, or differential quantities, while the earnings of capital are determined otherwise. We shall find that two things are true: (1) The earnings of every kind of capital-goods can be brought into the form of surpluses, or differential quantities; and land is not unique in this particular. (2) The returns that capital of any kind can secure for its owner are determined directly and not residually. The positive power of each bit of land to create wealth fixes the rent of it, just as the positive power of each unit of capital to create wealth fixes the interest on it. The *entrepreneur* who hires land does not make over the rent to the landlord because, after paying other claims, he has a certain remainder in his possession. That fact would never compel him to part with the remainder. He pays over this remainder, indeed; but he does it because each bit of land has a positive power to produce, and the landlord can make the tenant pay the value of the specific product of it. If this particular *entrepreneur* will not pay for a piece of land what it produces, another will. Competition forces the user of any productive agent to give to the owner of it the amount that it brings into existence. What it earns for its owner is determined directly, not residually.

There are in use lands of every grade, and there are in use artificial instruments of every grade. The lowest grade of every instrument produces nothing, and is a no-rent article. Higher grades of every instrument, land included, produce something; and, if there is any advantage in calculating the amount of that something by saying that it is a product of

The earnings of all instruments may be viewed as surpluses, but the amounts are not fixed residually.

A differential form for all static incomes.

the good instrument minus the product of the poorest one, that calculation will always yield a correct result, since the product of the poorest one is nothing.

This method of calculation reduces the rent of everything to a differential quantity; but *whether there is any significance in the fact* that it is such a differential quantity or not, depends on how the margin of utilization is located. What is it that fixes the grade of the poorest instrument in use, and determines that all poorer ones shall be neglected or abandoned? We shall see that there is a single principle which locates this margin everywhere — which determines how poor a grade of land it will pay to cultivate, how poor instruments it will pay to use and how poor a quality of laborers it will be profitable to employ. The product of any productive agent is, in fact, just what it can add to the marginal product of capital and labor. If the groups are in a normal condition, these marginal earnings are uniform in all of them and are the standards of social wages and interest. The product of any specific agent is what it can add to the product of the labor and the capital that work with it, when these products are thus computed on a marginal basis.

For measuring a unit of labor we need a standard, and we shall soon get it. Provisionally we may use, as a unit, a day's labor of a man of average quality.

Provisional units of labor and capital.

The term "average quality," it may be admitted, requires and will soon receive definition. Capital, also, has to be measured in units; and we may provisionally take, as a unit, whatever improvement can be made in the working equipment of any group by a certain number of days' labor of the standard or average kind. Additional labor put into the shops that make instruments of production will have the effect of turning out either more tools or better ones.

In one case, they make a quantitative addition to the capital-goods; in the other case, they make a qualitative addition; but in any case they make an addition, and we now need to recognize the fact that this increase of productive wealth, which is due solely to the labor of a certain number of men working for a given time, can be treated as a unit of capital.

From the studies that we have already made, we know that such units of labor and such units of capital create definite amounts of produce. The product of a marginal unit is obviously a definable thing; for if labor, in any combination in which it finds itself, produces less than the marginal amount, it will get out of the combination. Also, if a unit of capital anywhere produces less than its marginal product, it will disentangle itself from the combination that has handicapped it, and will bestow itself at a point where it will be marginal capital and will get its normal return.

Now we are ready to locate the margin of utilization, not alone of land, but of all other instruments. There is land so poor that it adds nothing to the marginal product of the labor and the capital that are combined with it. If it were one grade poorer, it would yield less than this amount, and the labor and the capital would withdraw from it and would seek to locate themselves elsewhere on the margin of employment, where they could make normal earnings. This land is the poorest that can be used, without in some degree wasting the other agents. A better grade of land, however, adds something to the marginal product of labor and capital used in connection with it; and this addition is the true product of this land — the rent of the land. It is the gross product of the land, minus the wages and the interest of the labor and the capital that work on it.

A general margin of utilization for all instruments.

It seems, then, that wages and interest, rather than the product of the poorest land in use, tilled with a certain amount of labor and capital, constitute the standard by which the product of land is to be measured. The fact is that wages and interest *locate* *the margin.* They determine how poor a grade of land it will pay to utilize. We follow the gradations of land downward till we get a piece that adds nothing to the marginal product of labor and capital, which is the same as saying that a piece produces nothing more than wages and interest. There we stop. We thus extend the margin of utilization of land just to the point at which wages and interest are afforded. The term "gross product of marginal land, tilled with a certain amount of labor and capital " is a cumbersome expression for " the wages and the interest of that amount of labor and capital." [1]

How in the case of land this margin is located.

---

[1] This is not the only objection to using the old expression. A more serious objection lies in the possible implication that, if we were to extend the margin, we should necessarily increase rent, and should do it by virtue of the extension. A forced or blundering extension of the margin, however, would not add to rent. The location of the margin is not the cause of rent. The power of land to add something to wages and interest is that cause, and wages and interest are the true subtrahend to be used in determining rent.

Let us revert to what is certainly a general and defensible formula for rent. It is a net product. It is what any instrument can add to the marginal product of labor and capital. It is what the industrial world would lose outright, if that instrument were taken away. The advance of the margin of utilization is a circumstance that *accompanies and reveals* an increase in the productive power, and in the consequent rent, of an agent of production. Nothing can make a good piece of land produce more than it now does that will not also make the poorest piece in use produce something more. Whatever does this will also have the effect of making a still poorer piece — which formerly produced a minus quantity, if it was used at all, since it handicapped the agents combined with it — produce something. This piece of land, by virtue of a change of conditions, ceases to be a drag on labor and on auxiliary capital, and is promoted to the position of no-rent land. Land that is still poorer,

The rent of anything else is, in like manner, its true product. It is what society would not have without it. If the labor and the auxiliary capital that are used on an antiquated ship, a worn-out machine or an old building can be just as well used elsewhere, by becoming marginal labor and capital, society gains nothing by using these things; and their product — that is, their rent — is *nil*. These instruments have lost their combining power, or their capacity to enter into a combination with labor and capital in a way that adds something to the independent product of these agents.

It is clear that we can always measure the rent of a good instrument of any kind, by comparing the product of it with that of an instrument that is at the point of abandonment. The rent is always the net product, minus nothing; and the poorest instrument is the one that produces nothing. There is,

and that, if used at all, would have inflicted a still greater loss on the agents that combined themselves with it, now inflicts a smaller loss on them. It is promoted from the position of land that is by two degrees below the marginal grade to land that is but one degree below it. In short, an all-around increase of rent has taken place : land of every sort has acquired an increased productive power or a smaller destructive power. Land that produced something now produces more ; land that produced nothing now produces something ; land that destroyed a small amount now neither destroys nor produces anything ; lands that would have destroyed larger quantities, if they had been used, under the new conditions destroy less. An all-around infusion of productive power into land carries with it an extension of the margin of utilization. We utilize all grades to the zero line, and that is now below the former line.

In saying that the rates of wages and of interest locate the margin of land, we do not overlook the fact that the product of labor on marginal land enters in a minute degree into the determination of wages and interest. This point has been fully discussed in an earlier chapter. In the main, wages are what a unit of labor can produce by adding itself to all the other labor and to the great mass of capital, including instruments of all kinds and land of all grades, that are already in use.

A valueless periphrase.

however, no value in this periphrase; and there is some danger in using it. It is simpler to say: *The rent of any instrument is its net product.* This, the only product that is imputable to it, is what it can add to the marginal product of the agents used in connection with it. This formula removes the danger that comes from supposing that the extension of the margin of utilization is the cause of an increase of rent. The truth is, that it is the increase of rent which extends the margin.

In pure theory one might even measure wages in the concrete way in which we are measuring the product of instruments; for he might apply the rent formula to men of different personal qualities.

The possibility of reducing all wages to rent of personal superiority.

There are to be found workers with so little power to create wealth that it does not pay to intrust any capital to their hands. Rather than give to them a bit of land, with the tools and seeds needed for cultivation, it would be expedient to add the land to the holdings of some efficient producer, who already has an adequate amount of it. There the piece would be a marginal increment of land, adding itself to the other productive agents in the *entrepreneur's* hands, and it would make a net addition to his output of produce. This net addition would be the product normally imputable to the land. It would be a larger product than the land could create in the hands of the inefficient worker. Auxiliary capital, too, cannot profitably be left in inefficient hands. It is better to withdraw it and make marginal capital of it elsewhere. This application would afford the four types of rent to which attention was called in the thirteenth chapter.[1] We applied the principle which is familiar in connection with land first to capital in its entirety and then to the social force of

[1] See note on page 192.

labor in its entirety; and we thus obtained a general law of interest and wages. We then applied this principle concretely to particular capital goods, and in a like way we may apply it to particular men. There are, in fact, few no-rent men in actual employment; and the reason for this is clear, since work involves a sacrifice, and it does not pay to incur the sacrifice unless the earnings be a positive quantity. In those times and places in which child labor has been employed, with little regard for the welfare of the victims, labor that was not at the no-rent point, but very near it, has been pressed into service. But, where the sacrifice entailed by labor is, in some way, neutralized by a benefit that work confers, labor which creates literally nothing may sometimes be employed. Lunatics or prisoners may be kept at work, in order that they may secure fresh air and exercise, even though the amount of capital that they use, if it were withdrawn from their hands and turned into marginal capital, would produce as much as it does when it is used by them. In such a case the product imputable to their labor is *nil*.

The existence of any no-rent labor enables us to make the rent formula general and to apply it to every concrete agent of production. Men, land and capital-goods of other kinds produce something that can be measured by this formula. The product of any one of them is the difference between what is created by the aid of it and what the same coöperating agents that are now combined with it could produce, if they were relegated to the position of marginal agents of their several kinds. This is one way of saying that the product of any agent is what it creates as a net income; and we can deduct the product created by the poorest agent of the kind, — which is nothing, — if we wish to do so. The product of any

The rent made formula universal.

agent is, in short, what it contributes to the total output of industry; and the reduction of such a product to a differential sum is useless, since finding what any agent adds to the marginal product of other agents combined with it is all that is necessary.

The location of the several margins of utilization is effected by one comprehensive law. *Entrepreneurs* stop using anything, when they find that it adds nothing to the marginal product of other agents. Independently of all considerations of humanity, they would, from mere self-interest, stop employing the labor of a child or of a disabled person, if his work added nothing to the interest of the capital that they would have to put into his hands. They would likewise throw any instrument out of use, when it lost its combining power — its capacity to add to the independent product imputable to laborers and to other instruments combined with it. The margins of utilization of men, of tools, of land, etc., are all fixed in the same way; and they all advance and recede according to one universal law. While this advance and this recession are subjects of study under economic dynamics, we may note now the universality of the law that locates them at any one time. All depends on the quantities of the several agents that are brought together. If capital of all kinds, including land, were very abundant, it would be possible to employ very poor grades of labor. The abundant capital would mean a high rate of wages; and this might render unnecessary the work of children, invalids, cripples and aged persons. Abundant capital would, however, lead to the employment of such able-bodied persons as might formerly have been excluded from employment, because they were below the grade of intelligence or skill that, under the former conditions, was requisite. For such workers, increasing abundance of capital would extend the margin of employment. Again, an abundance of labor would, so far as it went, insure the employment of poor lands, poor tools, poor buildings, etc. In practice, this would mean that perishable instruments would have a long lifetime. We should repair the old ship and sail it a year or two longer than we should if labor were scarcer; and we should likewise prolong the use of the worn tool, the rickety machine, etc. In a static state, there is in use a constant quantity of perishable tools of every kind. If a machine steadily deteriorates from the time it is made, and if we make one every year and use it for six years, we have six such machines in constant use. But if we use each one for seven years, we have seven in constant use. Much labor calls for a great number of instruments, and one way to get them is to use each one for a longer time. When the world is crowded with people, the margin of utilization of all capital-goods is pressed far outward — just as, in familiar theories, is the margin of cultivation of land.

How, in a static state, margins are maintained and how quantities of the several agents are kept constant.

Nothing is really labor, in the economic sense, that consists in the effort of laborers who are below the marginal grade; and nothing is really capital that consists in instruments of any kind — land, tools, buildings, etc. — that are at or beyond the point of abandonment. True labor is always productive, though there may be unproductive effort. In the same way, true capital is always productive, though there are land and tools that are too poor to create anything. In the case of laborers, therefore, the marginal line separates persons who represent true labor from persons who do not; and in the case of instruments, the marginal line separates those that embody true capital from those that do not.

CHAPTER XXIII

THE RELATION OF ALL RENTS TO VALUE AND
THUS TO GROUP DISTRIBUTION

ONE detail of great importance remains to be supplied in the outline of the theory of wages and interest. This is a unit for measuring wealth in all its forms. Both wages and interest change when the quantity of capital changes, and a unit is needed for so measuring capital as to give a result that is an absolute sum. Such a unit will soon be supplied. It is best, however, before leaving the subject of rents and beginning the quest for an ultimate unit of value, that we should make sure that no embarrassment has been created by resolving all wages and interest into surpluses that are of the nature of rents. It has, for example, been a current belief that "rent is not an element in value" and that interest is such an element. In discovering that rent and interest are, in substance, identical, though they are differently viewed and computed, it would seem that we have found either that interest is not, or that rent is, an element in
Rent universally an element in the determining of values.
determining value. The fact is, that rent is universally an element in the determining of values and prices. Moreover, as values have an influence that controls group distribution, whatever controls them governs that general division of the social income that takes place between the different specific industries, or groups.

354

We have noticed the nice apportionment of labor and capital among the different sub-groups which is necessary in order that values may be normal. There must be in each sub-group, not only the exact amount of capital that unhindered competition would put there, but also the exact amount of every kind of capital that competition would put there, or else values are in a disturbed and abnormal state. There must be the right amounts of fixed capital and of circulating capital, and there must be the right amount of land as compared with fixed capital in other forms. If you take out of one occupation a quantity of land that perfectly free competition would naturally place there and put it into another occupation, you cause to be created less of one product, and more of another, than the perfect action of natural law calls for. Exactly the same thing is true of every agent of production. When competition has its way, it puts a certain amount of each agent into each sub-group; and you cannot make the amount less or more without making the quantity of the product smaller or greater, and the price of it greater or smaller, than a perfect action of natural law requires. Wherever the quantity of a product is unnatural, the value of it is also unnatural.

It appears, then, that the amount of a productive agent that is at work in a sub-group is an element determining the value of the product. The amounts of all kinds of natural agents that are present in any sub-group are, likewise, the regular determinants of value. They are such, because of the amounts of different goods that they create; for the product of every one of the agents enters into the supply of the goods that is put on the market.

This product of an agent, concretely regarded, is the rent of it. Thus, the rent of the tool in the

Values dependent on the apportionment of labor and capital among the producing groups.

The product of an agent that is assigned to a group is the rent of that agent.

shoe factory is essentially the number of pairs of shoes the existence of which can be traced to the tool. Similarly, the rent of a square rod of land utilized by the shoe factory is essentially the number of pairs of shoes the creation of which is referable to that amount of land. Regard the land as marginal, contract the area occupied by the shoe factory just enough to take out a square rod of it, leave the other capital unchanged in amount — although changed in shape, because of the contracted area — and you find that you produce a certain number of shoes the less every year. The reduction of the output due to the withdrawal of the land, or the addition that would be due to the restoration of it, is the rent of the land. The real rent of land, as of everything else, consists in goods that the land virtually creates; and these enter into the supply of such goods and help to determine their value. Rent is primarily to be regarded as a product traceable to a concrete agent, or as a distinguishable part of supply. The rent of land, then, as the concrete product imputable to land, is emphatically an element in determining value. The rents of all the agents of production constitute, when society is in a natural static condition, the entire supply of goods; and the supply that is furnished by any one of them — or, in other words, the concrete rent of it — is, of course, one of the value-determining elements.

Land not an exception. The product of it an element in supply.

So far as values are merely relative, it is the apportionment of the producing agents among the different sub-groups that determines them. Moving any one of the agents from sub-group to sub-group changes values; and, as we have said, putting a perfectly normal amount of each agent into each sub-group makes relative values normal. There is a sense, however, in which values are not merely reciprocal;

for it is possible to get an absolute unit of value, by means of which we can add all values and get a sum total. If article A is worth a half of article B, and a third of article C, this fact enables us to state the value of any one in terms of the other two; but it does not enable us to get the sum total of the value of all three. Reciprocal comparisons yield no sums. If, however, the values of A, B and C can be measured in something that is distinct from them all, we can get the sum of the values of those three things.

Now, it is possible to get such a sum total of values; and, whenever we get it, we shall find that rent is an element in determining it. Rent is product, as we have said; and the sum of all the products of the different agents that are at work, measured in terms of an absolute unit of value, gives the total of all values produced. Every agent must create just what it does, or the sum of values created will be different from what it is. Suppress or diminish the productive action of an agent — or reduce the rent of it — and you reduce the sum of values created. Disturb the natural apportionment of the producing agents among the sub-groups, and you somewhat reduce their aggregate productivity — that is, reduce the sum of values that they create, if values be measured in absolute units.

The possibility of getting a sum of values.

Rent, then, is an element in determining, not only relative values, but the sum of values created. It is all this, because it is itself identical with supply. The rent of the land in a particular industry is the part of the supply of the product of that industry which is traceable to the land. The rent of all land used in production is that part of the supply of commodities in general that is traceable to land. Rent and imputed supply, or partial supply traced to one agent, are synonymous terms; and comparative sup-

Rent an element in constituting such a sum.

ply fixes relative values, while total supply fixes total values.

"Rent is not an element in price" — such is the classical statement on the subject. It even expresses a view that is now prevalent. The expression itself however, is vague. It seems to mean that the fact of rent plays no part in the adjustment of values, and that things would exchange for one another in exactly the ratios in which they now do, if there were no such thing as rent.

The claim that rent is not an element in adjusting values refuted by defining rent as product imputable to a concrete agent.

But, if one defines rent as product imputable to a concrete agent, the impossibility of maintaining such a claim becomes apparent. Even if one were to restrict the term rent to the product created by land, the claim that it is not an element in adjusting market values would be absurd; for it would amount to saying that a certain part of the output of every kind of goods has no effect on their market value. The "price" referred to in the formula is, of course, the market value expressed in units of currency.

What the classical economists have really tried to prove is that, so far as price is concerned, it is of no consequence who gets rent. Their argument merely establishes the fact that the destination of rent, as an income or share in distribution, is of no importance in affecting prices. The proof that is given is essentially the following· Of the supply of such an article as wheat, some part comes from no-rent

The traditional argument for proving that rent is not an element in adjusting values.

land. The demand for this cereal has brought this land into utilization, by raising the price to the point at which it can profitably be cultivated. At this price a certain definite quantity of wheat is wanted, but it cannot be had without resorting to this land of lowest quality. The price, therefore, conforms to the cost of production on this area. The crop that is here secured is conceived of as in a sense the "most expensive" part of the supply of wheat, or the part that is raised at "the greatest disadvantage." Whether, from an *entrepreneur's* point of view, a bushel of wheat procured by using labor and auxiliary capital on no-rent land is really created at a greater disadvantage and is more costly than a bushel that is raised on good land, is a problem that is worthy of further attention; and we will return to it. We shall find that to the *entrepreneur* the cost of all the different bushels is uniform, and that it is equal to the price, if static law works perfectly. What we now have to note is that the cost of wheat raised on no-rent land, as well as that of other wheat, does certainly equal and express the normal price of this cereal.

If the proprietor of superior land were to say, "I will take no rent for it," this would not make wheat cheaper. The supply would not be changed; for the same quantity would be raised, the marginal amount raised on the no-rent land would be needed and would be bought at the former price, and all other parts of the supply would command the same rate. The farmers who use the good tract of land would still be able to sell their wheat at the price that they now get for it, and they would add the remitted rent to their own gains. This condition, however, leaves rent in existence, and not reduced in the slightest degree in amount. It leaves it, indeed, in the hands of the farmers instead of in those of the landlords; but the price of wheat is not affected by this transfer. What the argument really establishes is the fact that it makes no difference, so far as price is concerned, whether landlords or farmers pocket the income called rent — the money received for that part of the wheat crop that is traceable to land.

The argument may be carried farther. The farmers

may say, "We will not keep the rent, but will pass it on to our laborers. We will divide it, in a *pro rata* way, among all who work on the farms." This, again, will not make wheat cheaper; for the marginal quantity of it will still be needed and will be paid for at a rate that makes good the cost of getting it. Therefore, whether landlords, farmers or laborers absorb rent, the rent will exist, so long as land adds its quota to the supply; and the price will be constant.

We may go still further with the argument. The laborers may decline to take the premium on wages which the farmers offer to give to them. In their beneficence, they may resolve to give it to the public. Even this will not affect the price of the wheat supply, as a whole. If the farmers sell the wheat and give the money that would represent rent to the laborers, the only way in which these men can give it to the public will be by some eccentric and arbitrary plan of distribution. The wheat will still have been sold at the regular rate. If, however, the rent is made over to the workers in kind, and if they are determined not to keep it, they will have to devise a method of giving away that part of the supply. Whatever is sold will, despite all these complications, bring the former price.

This whole argument concerns, not the existence of rent, but the disposition of it as an income. Not one of the hypotheses that have here been made, following the line of the classical argument, annihilates the element, rent: the product attributable to land still exists. There is a definite number of bushels of wheat somewhere in the granaries that has been brought into existence by the agency of good land. This wheat is, in reality, the rent of the land; and some one has the value of it as an income. The fact that one person rather than another has this income is not anything that affects values, and this is all that the traditional argument proves. It establishes the fact that the European system of landlord and tenant leaves values where they would be, if the land were the property of the cultivators or of the nation as a whole. Under either of these conditions, rent would exist; and it would constitute an element in supply that would affect value.[1]

The argument really proves that systems of landholding do not determine values.

It is a striking fact — but one hitherto much neglected — that similar conclusions apply to the product of every other agent. The principle of rent may be applied, as we have seen, to the concrete products of all artificial capital-goods, and even to those of workmen. In the same inaccurate sense in which it may be said that the rent of land is not an element in price, the rents of tools, etc., and those of men themselves, or interest and wages, are not elements in price. It makes no difference who gets these amounts. Price remains the same, whether we take one of them away from the persons who now get it and bestow it on others, or leave it where it is. We can repeat, word for word, the argument concerning the rent of land, making it apply to the

The traditional argument repeated and applied to capital-goods and to laborers.

---

[1] The hypothesis that comes nearest to annihilating rent is one that makes all land free, and allows laborers and capitalists to resort to all parts of it at their pleasure. Thus, if ten men wished to cultivate an acre of very productive land, they might do it ; and if an eleventh man chose to add himself to their number, he would be admitted. Such an arrangement would be practically impossible; and, in mere theory, the effect of it would be to reduce rent, by causing an unnatural crowding of good land, and to scatter what rent remained in a *pro rata* fashion among laborers and capitalists. It would, incidentally, cause the relative amounts of goods produced to vary from the present relative amounts ; and so it would affect comparative prices. It would also reduce the absolute quantity of value produced. For a discussion of this subject, see an article on Marshall's *Principles of Economics,* in the *Political Science Quarterly* for March, 1891.

rent of men or to that of artificial instruments, and it will be as true in the one case as in the other. The differential product of artificial instruments of superior quality still constitutes the interest on the capital that they embody, and the differential product of men of superior quality constitutes wages.

Artificial instruments of production are virtually loaned for hire, when the capitalist loans "money" with which to buy them or have them made. What goes to the capitalist is really the earnings of the instruments; but it goes in the form of an annual fraction of the money that he has advanced; and it is thought of in this form, and termed interest rather than rent. If the capitalist says, "I will take none of this interest," the earnings of the instruments simply remain in the hands of the *entrepreneur*. The price of the products is unaffected. Some of these products, as we have seen, are created by the use of no-rent instruments; and the price is sufficient to justify the use of these instruments. At that price the public demands a certain quantity; and this cannot be secured without using the no-rent instruments, except in ways that are even more costly. The quantity will be secured and the no-rent instruments will be used. With that quantity of product in the market, the price will justify the using of these instruments. The *entrepreneur* will now keep the rent that the capitalist makes over to him, but the value of the goods produced will not be changed.

The *entrepreneur* may refuse to keep the gain and may pass it on to his workmen; but it exists still, as the rent of concrete instruments of production or — what is the same thing — as the interest on the capital that is in them. This second transfer produces no more effect on price than did the first. The value of the goods is still enough to justify using the marginal instruments. If the workmen in certain factories were to refuse to receive this rent, it might be passed on to the purchasers of the particular goods that were made in these establishments, in the shape of a discount from the market value of these goods; but the price of similar goods would remain the same as before. The rent of the good tools, etc., used in these factories, — or the interest on the capital in them, — would still be in existence; but the purchasers of the particular goods made by this capital would have it. It makes no difference whether capitalists, *entrepreneurs*, laborers or favored customers get this interest: prices are not affected by transfers of it from one class to another. In reality, the existence of the interest, or the rent of the capital-goods, is of importance. It is a part of the supply of the goods; and, like every other part of the supply, it is a regular determinant of price.

Exactly the same principles apply to labor and wages. There are a few no-rent laborers at work, though they are not numerous; and what they create is really an infinitesimal part of the supply of goods. If they were more numerous than they are, it would be possible to point to a considerable part of the supply of any one kind of goods and say that this part had been created entirely by capital in the hands of no-rent men — capital working at the " greatest disadvantage." The public needs this part of the supply and is willing to buy it at the rate at which it pays to produce it by entrusting capital to these marginal workers. In such hands, the capital creates less than it creates elsewhere, and the *entrepreneur* has to pay for the capital; so that, in terms of interest, this part of the supply of the product is the " costliest " part, since the *entrepreneur* must use more capital in order to bring a given number of goods into existence by the aid of poor labor than he would use with good labor. Five thousand dollars entrusted to a no-rent man may create no more than would five hundred entrusted to an average worker. The cost of all parts of the supply is, however, uniform. The cost of what is produced by hiring capital, paying interest on it and entrusting it to no-rent men, resolves itself wholly into interest, while that of most parts of the supply consists partly of wages ; but the amount of the cost of the several parts is the same, and the value of all parts is equal.

The consideration of such conditions, artificial though they be, under which owners of capital-goods of any kind should refuse to accept the incomes from them, reveals the generic fact that the ownership of an income is not, but that the existence of it is, a determinant of price. Exactly this can, however, be shown to be true of wages. In the same sense in which the interest on artificial capital and the rent of land are not elements in price, wages have no effect on price. If good workers were to relinquish their claims against their employers and work for nothing, the price of the goods would still conform to their marginal utility. It would, incidentally,

Wages not a price-deter-mining ele-ment, if rent is not so.

equal the cost of creating them by means of the labor of no-rent workers, even if the *entrepreneurs* should pocket the relinquished wages, or should pass them on to capitalists, as a premium on interest, or to favored customers, as a discount on the market value of goods. But wages would exist in any of these cases, even if the wage-earners did not get them ; and prices would be the same as though distribution had not been tampered with.

This hypothesis has an unnatural sound, for there are very few no-rent laborers in the field.   Men who produce nothing, get nothing; and the cases are rare in which such persons work at all. They work only where the sacrifice that labor entails is, in some way, offset by a personal benefit; and this is the same as saying that they work only where labor entails no real sacrifice. Yet the proposition, that what has been claimed concerning rent is equally true of wages, is perfectly sound. If there is any sense in which land is not an element in price, then *in the same sense* wages are not an element. The important kernel of truth in both of these statements is the insistence upon the fact that *the identity of the persons* who receive these incomes is immaterial as affecting prices. It is not true, however, that the *existence* of these rewards is thus unimportant. On the contrary, rent of land, rent of concrete instruments and rent of men are all components of the supply of goods — that is, are price determiners.

If wages are not an element in price, then rent is not so; and this is an absurdity. Wages, as a whole, are the rent of social labor as a whole; and the wages of laborers in a group are the rent of the labor in that group. We may here cease to treat as rent producers laborers in the concrete or men of different grades of producing ability. We may now bring into view a permanent force of labor, as such, measured in units. The no-rent laborer embodies not a single unit of labor; and though he can put forth effort, he cannot himself produce anything. But the man of the highest grade, the very high-rent laborer, represents many units of labor in the abstract, for he has the power to create a large product. Measuring the working force in units, we may get from the formula that expresses the law of interest a surplus, or differential amount, which is the rent of pure labor, as such.

The argu-
ment ap-
plied to all
labor and
capital as
permanent
agents of
production.

Let us assume that the number of units of labor
is fixed, that capital increases unit by unit, that the
amount of capital is measured along the line AD,
and that the prod-
uctivity of suc-
cessive units of it
declines along the
curve BC. AECD
is, then, interest
and EBC is the
surplus, or the
rent of labor.

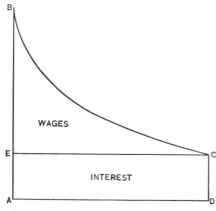

In this view,
the last unit of
the supply of the
product is the one
that is created by the final unit of capital, unaided
by labor.   In our former study, we noticed the
virtual isolation of this final unit and of its product.
Add a unit of capital and you get a certain net
addition to the output of goods, and that without
any change in the laboring force.   Take away
a unit of capital and you make a net deduction
from the product, and that, too, without any change
in the laboring force.   The addition that you make
in the one case and the deduction that you make in
the other are the products of the units of capital that
you respectively add and subtract.   If you neither
add nor subtract any capital, but leave the amount as
it is, there is in the output of the industry a certain
final or marginal amount that is entirely due to the
presence of the final unit of capital — an amount in
the production of which labor does not coöperate.

Now, if the traditional reasoning about land and
its products has validity, the same kind of reasoning
is valid here.   The price of the goods must be suffi-

ciently high to enable the *entrepreneur* to create a certain marginal portion of them by the use of this final unit of capital, unaided by labor. The fact that the earlier units of capital — aided, as they are, by labor — produce " at better advantage " does not affect the price, since that equals the cost of the marginal unit of the supply, which is traceable to the marginal unit of capital. If we can conceive such a thing as an entire working force refusing to accept wages, while continuing to work, then we must accept the conclusion that the *entrepreneurs* will pocket the gain. They will, obviously, be under no necessity for passing it over to the public; since, by the action of the law of value, they can always get from the public a price that equals the cost of that marginal unit of the product into which labor does not enter. If the *entrepreneurs* choose to dispose of this gain by making it over to capitalists, the effect on price will be *nil;* and nothing short of presenting it to the public as a gratuity, by arbitrarily and unnecessarily throwing off something from the price of the whole supply, will cause the price to change. In short, total wages, or the rent of the whole force of social labor, bears the same relation to price as does the rent of land.

Real wages are the goods that labor itself, apart from capital, produces. These goods, like those which land produces, are a component in the supply of the goods and an element in price, although the question who gets them has no bearing on price. If real wages, or the distinct product of labor, were to grow smaller, the absolute value created in a year would become less, and the relative values of different commodities would be affected. A reduction of the contribution that labor makes to the output of different kinds of goods would, however, affect the supplies of the several kinds of goods unequally;

since labor creates a certain part of the supply of (say) woollen cloth and a different part of the supply of steel. A horizontal shrinkage of wages, or of the product of labor, would cause the output of woollen cloth and of steel to contract unequally and would thus affect their relative values.

The argument becomes a reductio ad absurdum

Rent is always product — that is, the part of the total product that can be traced to a distinguishable agent of production. The statement that product is not an element in value is, then, obviously an absurdity; just as the assertion that any component element in product is not an element in value is an absurdity. We have just seen that a general shrinkage of the product of labor would reduce the product of different kinds of goods unevenly; for, since labor enters into the different industries in unequal proportions, this would

The result of a general shrinkage in the product of one agent.

change relative values. For a similar reason, a shrinkage in the product of artificial capital would also have this effect. This capital enters in unlike proportions into the production of different kinds of goods; and if the whole product of it were to become less, the comparative quantities of different commodities in the market would be changed. Even the gross amount of every rent is an element in relative value; and the rent that is realized from any agent of production in a particular sub-group — or, in other words, the contribution that this agent makes to the product of the sub-group — is obviously an element in adjusting relative values. In this respect the rents of land, of artificial capital and of laborers are all alike. It would be absurd to assert, broadly and vaguely, that wages are not an element in price; and it is equally fallacious to say, in the same vague and sweeping way, that the rent of land is not such an element. These propositions are all specific applications of one principle. Rent is product; product controls values;

the existence of any part of any product is important, as fixing the price of the product. But the question who gets this product is not thus important; and the destination of rent as an income is not, in this direct way, a factor in value.

The idea that different parts of a product can be created by an *entrepreneur* at greater or less advantage to himself, or at greater or less cost, is fallacious. It is *entrepreneur's* cost that figures in connection with the permanent or " natural " adjustment of values : in a static state all things tend, in the long run, to sell for what they cost the *entrepreneur*.[1] To him it makes no difference whether he hires one agent or another, or the two together; since he gets the same results for the same outlay in all cases. When he uses good land and gets a given amount of produce with very little labor, he is employing much of the first agent and relatively little of the second ; but he is virtually buying the product of the land at its market value, and he is buying the product of labor also at its value. Hiring an agent is buying the product of the agent, and the values of all parts of the same product are uniform. When the *entrepreneur* uses the poorest land and pays nothing for it, he is employing one rent-paying agent instead of two; but he gets the produce at the same price per unit, neither more nor less. In a perfectly static state, in the case of any one commodity, cost is as uniform as is price.

The rent of any agent comes into existence in the hands of the *entrepreneur*, and it consists in the goods that the agent produces. The selling of the goods

All parts of a product are created by an entrepreneur at equal advantage to himself.

---

[1] Final utility is, of course, the determinant of value ; but, by changes in the comparative amounts of different articles, those which have equal costs, in the sense here defined, come to have equal final utilities and market values.

puts the rent into the form of money, but it is still in the *entrepreneur's* possession.   When he pays this rent to the owner of the productive agent, rent becomes to the *entrepreneur* a cost.   In a static state, all the *entrepreneur's* costs consist in such rent claims made on him by laborers and capitalists.   As rents created in the shop are products, and as rents received by owners of productive agents are incomes, so rents paid by *entrepreneurs* are costs.   All rents are, at the proper stage of their existence, thus paid by *entrepreneurs ;* and at this stage rents and costs are synonymous.   Costs are then determinants of value.   The broader statement is that rents are products, originally and fundamentally ; that the quantities of products fix values ; and that values, as thus fixed, influence the income that each specific industry, taken as a whole, can get.[1]

The way in which rents are identical with *entrepreneurs' costs.*

NOTE. — For the earliest statement of the theory advanced in this chapter the reader is referred to an extended supplementary note in a monograph on *The Possibility of a Scientific Law of Wages*, published by the American Economic Association, in March, 1889.   At the same date there appeared, in Professor Wieser's work on *Natural Value* (Chapter XII), an argument maintaining that the part of rent that is not differential, but general, is an element in price making ; while even the differential portion may be such an element, provided the land that earns this income is devoted to " secondary or derivative " uses.   In Professor Marshall's *Principles of Economics* (Book V, Chapter VIII), it is shown that, by reason of the competition of different agricultural uses of land with each other, the amount of land devoted to a particular crop may be limited, the supply of that kind of produce may be reduced and

[1] Total rent is total supply and is one determinant of value. Value is the determinant of group distribution ; but, as we have seen, group distribution tends to adjust itself so as to annihilate profits and insure uniformity in wages and interest.   The tendency of labor and capital to uniformity of productive power is the most fundamental of these facts.

the price may be influenced by this limitation of the supply.
The reader will see that in the argument presented in the
present work the contention is made that all rents, even
though they may be reduced to differential quantities, are
essentially contributions to the supply of goods and elements
in the determining of values, and also that all the rents that
have been enumerated are, in this respect, on a parity.

In a work on *The Theory of Wages*, by Mr. Herbert M.
Thompson, published in 1892, the view is maintained that rents
"*in the aggregate*" are elements that enter into the expenses of
production, as do wages, profits, and interest considered as
aggregates, and that "the analogy which subsists between land
and other agents of production is a very close one." This
theory has a near kinship with the one here advanced.

In Part III, Chapter IV, of his work on *Principles of Social
Economics*, Mr. George Gunton criticises on quite different
grounds the traditional view of the relation of rent to prices.

In connection with all early discussions of rent, and particularly with that of Ricardo, it is to be recalled that at the time
when they appeared the distinction between the statics and the
dynamics of the subject was not consciously drawn by any one.
The impulse to study rent came from a dynamic fact — namely,
the increasing density of population and the increasing cost of
food products that is traceable to the action of the law of diminishing returns in agriculture. It was to be expected that
a writer of that period, in presenting the standard to which
under the conditions of a single year rent tends to conform —
which is a static subject — would be led to make incursions
into dynamic territory. These are wholly admissible, when
they are made for the purpose of showing how a static adjustment is brought about. We explain the forces that keep the
surface of a pool of water level by showing what movements
would bring the surface to the level, if the waters were injected
into the pool in irregular fashion and in a way to make the
surface originally uneven. References like this to dynamic
economic forces are needed in explaining the adjustments of
the industrial groups and of values, wages and interest; and
they are equally in order in explaining ground rent, when that
is singled out as a special and unique product. It is to be recalled, however, that the mode of treatment that merges statics
and dynamics, without making a conscious distinction between
them, must result in giving a formula for measuring rent that,

if it were applied without amendment in dynamic conditions, would give a result either larger or smaller than the actual returns that accrue from the use of land. When society is in the midst of the disturbances that inventions, migrations and a comprehensive reorganization of the business world create, what is actually gained by the use of a piece of land often contains theoretical static rent, with an element of *entrepreneur's* profit added or a loss deducted. It is prospective profit that lures *entrepreneurs* to the occupation of wholly new areas of ground, and a rigorous application of an economic test is necessary in order to determine how much of the composite gain is true rent. Moreover, the conditions afforded by such a dynamic state make the Ricardian formula, which gives a correct measure of rent in a static state, inadequate for making such a separation of the composite income and isolating rent from all admixtures. For the scientific isolating and measuring of rent in a dynamic society, we need, first, a formula that is akin to the one used by Ricardo and, secondly, a further formula that will account for the difference between the theoretical rent that the Ricardian formula directly affords and a different rent, strictly static, toward which actual rent is tending. The discussion of the dynamics of rent must, however, be reserved for a later volume.

CHAPTER XXIV

THE UNIT FOR MEASURING INDUSTRIAL AGENTS AND THEIR PRODUCTS

WE are ready for the supplying of the last detail that is necessary, in order to make the statement of the law of wages and interest intelligible. There is before us the picture of social labor coöperating with social capital. Both are governed by the law of diminishing returns, and their earnings are fixed by the productivity of their final units. The labor in the case is a permanent force, and the capital is a permanent fund. Each exists in an endless succession of concrete forms, which change whenever the quantity of either agent changes. Particular increments of capital consist in distinguishable elements in concrete instruments, rather than in particular instruments in their entirety. Both capital and labor have to be apportioned, by a nice adjustment, among all the groups and sub-groups of society, if either value, wages or interest is to be normal. Every separate increment of labor and capital has to be apportioned in the same way and by the same play of forces. Wages, then, conform to the product of the final increment of social labor and interest to the product of the final increment of social capital. Both of these incomes may be translated into the form of rents of concrete producers; and these, like all products, are elements in determining values.

Summary of conclusions thus far attained.

373

This statement will be complete enough to reveal all the general and essential facts of distribution, when we know how we may measure labor, capital and their products. But we need, evidently, a universally usable measure of values.

In the statement of the law of diminishing returns, as applied to capital, it was said that the successive units of capital produce less and less. Provisionally, the "doses" of capital are measured in terms of money;[1] but it is necessary to know exactly what the money ultimately represents. When, in our illustration, it is assumed that the capital of a society increases from ten thousand dollars to a million, does this mean, at bottom, that the capital comes to represent a hundred times as much labor as it did before or a hundred times as much personal sacrifice? If it means either of these things, it is still necessary to find some way in which to express a measurement of labor or of sacrifice.

An ultimate measure of capital and of products is needed;

Moreover, when what we are measuring is social capital and the social product, it is clear that we must have some unit that will give us absolute sums. In a way, the capital of a group might be measured by comparing it with the capital of another group; but this process would never give us the total capital of the whole industrial system. So, also, might the product of one group be compared with the product of another; but that would yield no sum total of products. Interest is a ratio between the sum of the

and this must yield absolute sums.

[1] It is clear that the product of capital cannot, in such connections as these, be the basis of the measurement of capital. If we say that whatever produces a unit of consumers' wealth is a unit of capital, we assert nothing by adding that, at any one time, all units of capital are equally productive. On the other hand, when we say that a series of units of capital show diminishing returns, while still measuring the units by their products, we assert what is a self-contradiction.

products of all the separate capitals and the sum of the capitals themselves. For these purposes, — and for more than it is now necessary to enumerate, — a universal unit for measuring economic values is necessary, if the law of final productivity is to have scientific exactness.

The entire study of wealth is, indeed, meaningless unless there be a unit for measuring it; for the questions to be answered are quantitative. How great is the wealth of a nation? Such inquiries demand that the thing which is studied shall be measured in units of some kind and that the result shall be stated as an absolute amount. Mere reciprocal comparisons give no sums. The commodity A may be regularly exchanged in the market for B, and the two together for C; but that fact gives us no intimation as to the total value of the three. Ratios of exchange alone afford no answer to the economist's chief inquiries.

Reciprocal comparisons inadequate for measuring values.

The actual wealth of a community consists in heterogeneous things. If they are ever added together, it must be because there is some one element present in all of them and this element is absolutely measured. Thus, unlike things can be weighed and their total weight can be stated in a sum, because they all gravitate toward the earth and exert a force on whatever resists their movement. A unit of weight may, therefore, be applied successively to many such apparently unlike things, in order to measure one element common to all of them. In like manner, there is one element that is common to all the diverse things that appear in the inventory of social wealth. In every commodity there is a power of a certain kind which can be measured.

Difficulty caused by the heterogeneity of the things to be measured. Need of finding a common element in them.

Amounts of wealth are usually stated in money : thus, we say a man is " worth a million dollars." This, however, does not mean merely that he could sell all he has for a million of our bulky silver coins. The thought in the minds of the men who use money as a standard of value runs forward to the power that resides in the coins. They will buy goods or they will set men working. There resides in each one of them a certain amount of influence on human well-being. The rich man in the illustration wields a power of this kind, and it is a million times as great as that which resides in one of the coins. The intuitions that are at the basis of this popular mode of speech are nearer to absolute truth than much of economic analysis. They discern a power of things over men, lay hold of an available unit of that power, apply it to the diverse goods and state the measurement in a sum.[1]

Effective utility is the name by which this potency of goods will here be designated. It is the power that a particular unit of a commodity has to change the status of its possessor and to promote him in the scale of well-being. Give to a man a barrel of flour and you make him by so much better off. You do not save him from starvation, though he may live for a time on the food that you furnish. If you had not given him the flour, he would have got it by some sacrifice; and what you have done is, in effect, to save him from the sacrifice. This effect measures the value

Real signifi-cance of the monetary unit of measure-ment of values.

Effective utility the basis of values.

[1] The substance of this chapter was published in the *Yale Review* for November, 1892, and, as thus published, was a continuation of an article that was printed in the *New Englander* in 1881. In that earlier study the power residing in all economic goods was termed "effective utility." The entity thus defined is closely identified with the " final " or " marginal " utility of Professor Jevons and the Austrian economists whose researches were then unknown to me. The manner of approaching the law of value differed from that adopted by the European economists, and led to a certain distinctive view of the nature of that law. According to this view value is always subjective and social. It gauges the power of things over society in its entirety.

of the flour. Take away a barrel of flour that the man now has, estimate the real detriment that he suffers, and you measure the effective utility in another way. He must have food and will get it by a sacrifice of some kind. He may not fully replace the loss of the flour; for he may live on maize, and in that case the utility of the barrel of flour is gauged by the cost of the maize and the unsatisfied want of a better quality of food.

It will appear that this power of substituting one thing for another, in repairing the injury caused by the loss of that other thing, plays a very comprehensive part in determining values. In the case of many articles the substitute resorted to is quite different in kind from the thing that it replaces. Having parted with one means of well-being, the man proceeds, as best he can, to make himself as well off generally as he was before. If he is to gauge the real importance to himself of a particular saddle horse, he may, perhaps, do it by ascertaining how many hours he must work in order to get enough in the way of boats, guns or a tennis outfit, etc., to afford as much pleasure as he can get from the horse. The mental process in the case is, first, a balancing of one pleasure as against another and, secondly, a measuring of the substituted pleasure by its cost. By the two operations the owner of the horse determines how much it is effectively worth to him. The final measure in the case is one of pain; for the ultimate injury that is done to a man by depriving him of any one means of pleasure, resolves itself into putting him under the necessity of enduring a certain amount of personal sacrifice in the effort to secure something that will effectually replace it.

It is this process, in which men are continually engaged, of determining how important it is to have

How sacrifice may measure effective utilities.

one thing by ascertaining how much it will cost to get a very different thing, that reveals one special significance of a study of effective utility. Men pursue happiness in the generic, and the form in which it may come is secondary. The measurement of well-being, thus regarded in the abstract, is an occult but dominant fact in exchanges. A man may have a monopoly of one means of promoting happiness, yet he cannot set his own price for his wares. That is fixed by the cost entailed on the community by the effort to secure, by any means whatever, an equal quantity of happiness. With many possible ladders to Elysium, the toll for the use of one is limited. Effective utility, whatever be its form, is measured in the market in a purely quantitative way.

Society the measurer.   It is measured by society, as a whole; and in this lies the significance of the phrase, " measure of effective *social* utility," which, in earlier studies by the present writer, has been used as a synonym of value. It was on the word " social " that emphasis was laid. The price of a thing gauges its importance, not to one man, but to all men, as organically related to each other. The efficient serving power of an article varies in the case of different individual users, but to society as a whole it is constant. A civilized man is a specialist. He produces unit after unit of one kind of product and hands them over to society. Into the mysteries of distinctly social psychology, therefore, the measuring process that gauges value must be traced. Essentially simple in nature is the operation — simpler even than the act of the man who decides how important a horse is to himself by seeing how long he must work to get a boat and a tennis outfit.

In this connection it is now necessary to give definiteness of meaning to the word " social." There is such a thing as a unit of social improvement or detriment. It happens, however, that the detriment is more available for measuring purposes than is the improvement; and so the final unit of value is the sacrifice entailed by a quantity of distinctly social labor. Society, in short, sets value upon a thing by ascertaining how much work is necessary to replace it or to get an equivalent for it.

A unit of social disutility available for measuring values.

In its simplest form, division of labor means that one kind of commodity is carried to completion by one man. He is a specialist, to the extent of being a maker of entire shoes, or clocks, or tables. Working on raw material taken from nature, he hands it over to the community in condition for final use. But the differentiating of labor has, of course, gone far beyond the point where any man begins the making of a thing and completes it. Most work is now done by highly complex groups, and the individual's function is limited to a minute but distinguishable part of the operation. The principle that we are studying is, however, not affected by this fact; and we may gain clearness by first examining a society of a more primitive type, in which it may be assumed that whole articles are made by individual workers. As such goods leave the maker's hands day after day, in a continuous supply, they seek purchasers. No one man will take many, but society will take them all. We may even assume, without vitiating the principle to be studied, that every man in the community takes at least one. That each class of goods is *made in great numbers by one man* and *consumed singly by many men*, is the essential thing to be noted.

A simple illustrative society.

It is the users of an article who can best gauge the well-being that it gives them, and they make the estimate continually. Shall I buy this article? Will the paying for it trench on my income and make me go without something that is of greater importance? Is this article or some other of equal cost the more desirable? Such comparisons of services rendered by different articles are going on in the minds of the many consumers who constitute the purchasing public. These comparisons alone give us only rude ratios, not sums; and the ratios are different in the case of all the different members of the communty. If each man could measure the usefulness of an article by the effort that it costs him to get it, and if he could attain a fixed unit of effort, he could state the utility of a number of different articles in a sum total. Similarly, if all society acts in reality as one man, it makes such measurements of all commodities, and the trouble arising from the fact that there are many measurers disappears. A market secures this result, for society acts as a unit — like an individual buyer.

In measuring well-being human sensibility is under a limitation which is akin to that under which the eye finds itself in measuring light. It is possible to pronounce two lights equal; but it is not possible to tell, by the mere effect on the eye, how much brighter one light is than another. It is possible to say that two pleasures are equal, but not to say that one is just twice as great as the other. It is, however, practicable to determine when a pain and a pleasure offset each other; and if we can compare many kinds of pleasure with one kind of pain, we can, as a result, both compare pleasures with each other and obtain a sum total of many different ones. If a man knows that he would walk a mile for one gratification, and that he would do this twice over for another, he has the means of knowing that the good afforded by the second is twice as great as that afforded by the first, and that the gain insured by the two together is an offset for three walks of a mile each. Some-

Users of goods measure their comparative utilities, but get no sums by this means.

Units of cost that would measure utilities in sums.

Psychological difficulty encountered in comparing utilities.

Ratios of equality attainable as between pleasure and pleasure, and also between pleasure and pain.

How pain may afford a common measure of dissimilar pleasures.

thing like this society does, but it does not do it thus crudely.

At the beginning of an attempt to measure wealth by labor, whatever be the method adopted, there presents itself the difficulty that wealth is created by work aided by instruments. There is capital in the case, and this is the fruit of a sacrifice termed abstinence. None of our material comforts are brought into existence merely by the unaided efforts of laborers. This difficulty may be surmounted by taking marginal labor as the test of cost. Let the capital of an establishment remain exactly as large as it is, but introduce a small supply of extra labor, and whatever of product is created by the addition is virtually due to labor only. A part of the supply of every article that is put upon the market may be said to be traceable to the presence of a final increment of work. Take a man or two out of each of the shops that produce this article, leaving the capital unchanged, and this increment of the product will cease to be created. Restore the men, but make no other change, and this marginal part of the product will reappear. This virtually unaided labor is the only kind that can measure values. Attempts to use labor standards have come short of success, because of their failure to isolate from capital the labor to which products are due. As earlier chapters of this book have shown, the product of marginal work is the virtual product of all work; and this fact enables us to disentangle all labor from the capital it uses, and to find what part of the entire product of the industry is distinctly traceable to it.

Work, moreover, consists of concrete acts of men; and these are as unlike in themselves as are the miscellaneous articles that are to be measured by them. Can we make one sum of the labor involved in cut-

Abstinence one sacrifice involved in producing goods,

but not in producing that part of the supply which is specifically traceable to labor.

Virtually unaided labor the measurer of values.

Kinds of work unlike and therefore incapable of being added.

ting wood, in playing violins, in setting type, etc ? Adding the unlike acts that constitute social labor is, it appears, as difficult as adding the products that constitute social wealth. There is need of a pervasive element in the actions, and one that can be measured. Such an element can be found; for, as

Sacrifice a common element.

utility is common to all commodities, so personal sacrifice is common to all varieties of labor. There is service rendered to man, on the one hand, and there is burden imposed upon him, on the other. Social self-service — the act of mankind ministering to its own needs — constitutes the whole economic process.

A point to be found at which social costs of production offset and measure social gains.

Man works on nature to make it useful, and experiences a painful reaction in his own person during the process. Improved nature then works on man, the consumer, and has a counterbalancing and favorable action upon him. If we can find the point at which the unfavorable reaction exactly counterbalances and measures the favorable one, we can then estimate pleasure in terms of pain.

Work becomes more costly to the man who performs it, as the hours of the day succeed each other. The burden of it is at first light, but becomes heavy. Burdensome to a nearly insupportable degree it becomes in the afternoon or evening hours of the really struggling members of the " submerged tenth " of society, while it is lighter at the end of the day's

The increasing costliness of the labor of the later hours of the working day.

work of higher grade. In all cases, however, it is the later hours that burden the laborer and test his willingness to continue in the shop. He may work for two hours with pleasure, for four with cheerfulness, for eight with submission, and for ten with incipient rebellion.

The actual number of hours spent in labor in a highly organized society is, of course, not left wholly to the choice of the individual. When working in companies, there is an advantage in beginning and ending together. The principle that determines the length of the normal working day operates, however, in spite of this fact; and it may be revealed by a study of simpler conditions. We will, then, for the moment forget that gangs of men are tied to the steam whistle.

An isolated worker is the user of his own products, and he naturally works each day till it does not pay to work longer. Additional product might be gained by prolonging the toil, but the advantage of having it could not compensate for the sacrifice of making it. The man is already tired, and he feels the confinement of his occupation. He wants both rest and freedom. Nature is luring him from the shop, and the comforts of his home are calling to him. His normal work-day ends when these calls have their way, and this occurs at the moment when the gains and the losses of production are equal. *The normal work-day of a man who consumes his own products.*

The gains that are due to the successive hours of labor diminish from the first onward, and the last product the man secures is the least useful of all. If he can work but one hour, he will create that of which the type is food, the life-sustaining things for daily use. If he adds a second hour, it will be spent in getting what still rates as a necessity. With more time available, he will add comforts to his list; and he may end with a positive luxury. In any case, it is the least of his gains for which he works last and hardest. Left to himself and nature, he must work during a part of the day to sustain life and he must refrain from working during a part of it for the same reason. Between the point of no-work, at which he would starve, and that of nothing-but-work, at which he would die from exhaustion, there is the point of *The diminishing utility of successive units of income gained by prolonging the work of a day.* *The point of equilibrium of inducements to work and to cease working.*

balanced gain and loss. If he stops just there, the net gain from labor is at its greatest.

In determining whether it will pay to prolong work for an eleventh hour during each day of the year, the man goes through that balancing of one pleasure against another and that balancing of each pleasure against fatiguing work to which attention has been called. For the final hours of all days in a year the man will get a miscellaneous list of pleasures, and will decide whether the sum total of them offsets the sacrifice of almost three hundred final hours of labor. This is a difficult decision, but the man will make it; and in doing so, he will get a unit of final utility in terms of equivalent pain. We pursue no farther the analysis of the method by which, in the individual mind, it is decided whether it will pay to work eleven hours a day. We are safe in assuming that the man arrives at a judgment on this point. What we now wish to know is how society arrives at this judgment. Individual psychology is not a subject of our investigations; but the manner in which a psychological process in the individual gives a social result is distinctly included in our field of study.

If the duration of a working-day is measured on a horizontal line, and the gains and the sacrifices entailed by it are measured by vertical distances from that line, we may make a simple figure that represents the facts concerning a free and isolated laborer.

AB is the length of the day, while AC is the pain of the earliest labor, and BD that of the last. AE represents the gain secured by the first product, and BD that of the last. BD is, in fact, two coinciding lines, of which one measures the burden of the final labor, and the other the gain of the final consumption. The area ACDB measures the total sacrifice involved in the day's labor; AEDB, the total gain; and CED, a surplus gain, representing the net benefit of a day of industry. All gains below the line CD are exactly offset by costs.

The man that we are studying is a society by himself: he makes things and he alone uses them. The line BD is his unit of value, which measures the effective utility of everything that he makes. Though AE may measure the absolute bene-

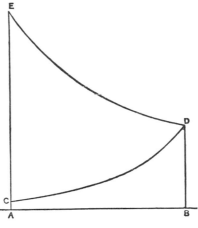

fit conferred by the loaf that satisfies hunger, the real importance of having that loaf is far less. If this necessary article were taken away, the man would devote a final hour to bread-making, and would go without the article otherwise secured by that final increment of work. Destroy his day's supply of food, and what he goes without will be luxuries naturally secured by the terminal period of labor. BD measures the utility of those luxuries, and it measures therefore the *effective* service rendered by the supply of necessaries that are produced in an equal period of work. Any article on the line between E and D will have a true importance measured by BD; since, if it were lost, there would be diverted to the replacing of it some work that would otherwise secure an article having an importance measured by that line. As it is of no more real consequence to the man to keep one of these articles than it is to ·keep any other, BD measures the subjective value of each of them.

The effective utilities of goods produced by like amounts of labor equal.

This state-
ment appli-
cable to
products of
society in its
entirety.

Of a society regarded as a unit the same is true.
It produces for itself, and the burden of its final labor
measures the utility of its final products, which is
the same as the effective utility of any of its products
created by the same expenditure of working time.
Take away the articles that the society gains by the
labor of a morning hour, — the necessary food, clothing and shelter that it absolutely must have, — and
to make good the loss it will divert the work performed at the approach of evening, which would
otherwise have produced the final luxuries on its
list of goods. To society the net importance of the
different grades of commodities is equal: take away
one variety entire, and terminal labor will be made to
replace it. The things otherwise produced by that
final labor will be the ones really lost, and their
utility is measured by the burden entailed in the
creating of them.

If we arrange, as on the opposite page, a series of
descending curves to represent the lessening absolute
utility of the things consumed by a society, we shall
get a representation of a social unit of value — a
quantity that measures wealth in all its forms.
We now have a descending curve for each member
of society. The goods indicated by the upper section
of the several curves, between EE^v and the dotted
line designated by the figure 1, are the most essential
things used by society. They are to be treated as
the product of the first period of the social working
day, and the absolute service that they render to
society is measured approximately by lines falling
from EE^v, etc., to the line AA^v. These goods will
differ in the case of different consumers; but, taken
collectively, they may be treated as a social complement of goods of the highest importance. We will
term them complement number one, including the

society's necessaries of life. Complements numbers two, three, four and five also are designated in the figure. The variety of the goods represented increases as the complements succeed each other ; and that of

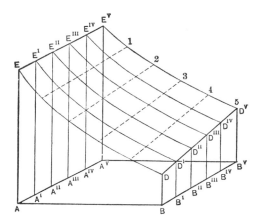

number five, containing the luxuries, is very diverse. What is true of the isolated man is likewise true here. The effective utility of the different complements is uniform and is measured by the lines from DD^v to the line BB^v. Destroy any one of them, except the last, and society will replace it and go without the last. The burden entailed is, in short, always that of the final period of labor.

If we make the lines BD, B'D', etc., numerous and contiguous, so that they fill the area BD D^vB^v this area becomes the measure of the absolute utility of the last social complement of goods consumed. It is the measure also of the effective utility of each one of the earlier complements and, still further, of the disutility of the labor that produces the final complement. It thus represents a social aggregate of sacrifice, and this is the unit that is most available for measuring all values. Everything that is produced

and also the nature of the unit that measures all values.

by one hour of social labor, whether that labor be performed early in the day or late, possesses an effective social utility that equals the absolute utility of the final complement of goods consumed ; and this, again, is counterpoised and measured by the sacrifice which all society undergoes in the labor of its final hour.

Difficulty arising from the fact that individuals make particular things and society uses them.

Single things are, however, in our illustration, produced by individuals and consumed by society in its entirety. The relations of man and society must, then, be studied. As applied to social complements of goods, the law is simple enough ; since it is society as a whole that makes and uses them. A complement of the kind referred to comes from all men and goes to all men. The social organism gets each complement by labor, and measures the importance of it by the labor of creating the final complement. Collective labor secures and measures collective gain.

We noticed that the different complements of goods are of unequal absolute utility, since they minister to wants of varied degrees of intensity. Bread and the other necessaries of life are absolutely more important than jewelry and other luxuries ; but in effective utility the complements are all on a par, since, if any one of them were destroyed, the result would be to make the community go without the last. In like manner, the periods of labor are of unequal degrees of absolute burdensomeness, since the last hour is the most wearying and irksome ; yet they are all on a par in

Periods of labor are equal in *effective* disutility,

effective burdensomeness, as will appear from a similar test. As we gauged the virtual importance of a thing to its owner by supposing that it were taken away and seeing how much worse off the man would thus become, so we may now estimate the virtual sacrifice involved in the labor of a particular hour by making it unnecessary and seeing how much better off the man would then be. If you supply by a gift the product that an isolated man usually makes in the first and easiest working hour of the day, you thereby save him the necessity of working through the last and hardest hour. You shorten the day by one hour, in supplying the product of any equal period; and the deduction is, of course, made at the latter end, where sacrifice is at its greatest. Similarly, if we could make nature supply gratuitously any one of the successive complements of goods that enter into the consumption of society, the effect would be to shorten the social working day by the omission of the most wearing and irksome period. The effective disutility of all labor is, it thus appears, gauged by the absolute disutility of the concluding work of the day.

It follows that, in the case of an isolated man, we may measure the subjective value of goods by the mere duration of the work that creates them. All goods made in an hour are equal in effective utility and all hours of labor are of equal effective disutility. Destroy the product of an hour's work, and you injure the man by a fixed amount; make any hour's work unnecessary, by making nature freely supply what is produced in that period, and you benefit the man by a fixed amount. Unit of product and unit of labor are alike represented by the line BD of the diagram. The product of two hours' work will always be of just twice as much subjective value as is the product of one. *and this makes it possible to use the labor of any period of a given length as a unit for measuring values.*

In the case of society as a whole, the values of different complements of social goods are, in like manner, measured by the mere duration of the collective labor that creates them. The effective sacrifice entailed by labor varies directly as its duration, and the effective utility of products created in different parts of the day varies in the same way. The unit *In the case of society the measurement is in terms of the duration of collective labor.*

of utility and of disutility is the area BDD'B'. In the subjective valuations of society, as an organic whole, the product of two hours' labor is always worth just twice as much as is the product of one. Mere labor time is an accurate gauge of the values of different complements of goods.

Is it also an adequate gauge of the values of different articles that enter into the complement? Here we introduce a complication. Neither the pain nor the duration of labor will now serve our purpose. The essential feature of the valuation of a complement, in its entirety, is the fact that the same collective personage creates and uses the whole of it. But when a man creates an article and makes it over to society, the condition changes; for he experiences the burden of the production and society gets the benefit. The final disutility of his labor then stands in no connection with the final utility of society's goods. Though the social organism, as a whole, will work till what it gets offsets what it suffers, will a man also work till what society gets from him offsets what he suffers? Obviously, when the enjoying falls to one party and the suffering to another, there is no offsetting in the case. There is, therefore, no equivalent established between the disutility of such work and the utility of its product.

Yet there is an equivalent between the man's sacrifices and his own enjoyments. The pain that he undergoes in making his own product is a payment for other men's products, for it is the personal cost of what he gets. In like manner, the pain that all other men suffer in making products for him represents the cost to them of what they get from him. Between cost and gain there is still an equivalent, and it will furnish us a unit for appraising specific commodities.

If A makes the article W, B makes X, C makes

Such measurements simple when applied to social complements of consumers' goods, but more difficult when applied to single articles;

since the disutility incurred by a producer is not in a measurable quantitative ratio to the utility secured by consumers.

Y and D makes Z, and if each gets and uses some part of each product, we have a miniature society in which the relations are clear. A sells to B, C and D; and the effective social utility of W is measured by the pain undergone by B, C and D in creating, in the final period of the day, articles in exchange for it. If money is used in the transactions, and if the price of W and that of X are equal, it is because the last unit of the supply of each commodity, as it is made over to the miniature society for consumption, imparts to the society as a whole a uniform addition to its enjoyments. That addition is in each case measured by the pain of working through the final period of the day in order to get it. Price is, then, an indication of the *social cost of acquisition* of different commodities.

Back of the figure ABCDE, which represents the sacrifice, the gain and the surplus of benefit realized

A man's effective sacrifice in making one thing is measurable in terms of the effective benefit that he gets from using other things.

Price an indication of social cost of acquisition.

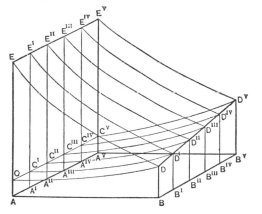

Figure illustrating the manner in which marginal social gain and marginal social sacrifice quantitatively coincide;

by one laborer in a working day, let us place a series of similar figures, setting forth the same facts for each member of our miniature society.

The curves ascending from C, C', C'', C''', C^{iv} and C^v represent the increased cost entailed by the labor of successive hours in the case of all the men. The curves descending from E, E', etc., show the lessening gains afforded by different increments of things consumed. D, D', D'', etc., are points of equilibrium of gain and loss; and the lines descending from D, D', D'', etc., to B, B', B'', etc., measure sacrifice entailed on all society by its final period of labor.

If the figures were multiplied in number and were so drawn that the lines of one should be contiguous to the similar lines of the other, then the course of the ascending curved surface that follows the lines CD, C'D', etc., would indicate the increased costliness of the work of all society, as the hours of labor in a day succeed each other; and that of the descending surface ED, E'D', etc., would represent the diminishing utility of all things consumed. The volume between these curved surfaces and the vertical plane CC^vEE^v would measure the total surplus realized by society as a whole in consequence of its work. The area of the vertical plane BDD^vB^v expresses the pain suffered by society as a whole in the final period of daily labor, *and this is the ultimate unit of*

and in so doing furnish an ultimate unit of value.

value. So far as the selling price of a thing corresponds with labor of any kind, it corresponds with the terminal labor that society, the consumer, puts forth in order to get it. If it is as anxious to have more of one product as it is to have more of another, it will be as willing to add a minute to the length of its day in order to obtain the one as it will in order to get the other. By laws that are now wholly familiar, the two things will sell for the same price; and this price is the gauge of the uniform cost, in the labor at the end of successive days, that the acquisition of the two things entails on society.

The value of a thing, then, is the measure of the effective service that it renders to society as a whole.

This service is estimated subjectively. The standard for measuring it is the sacrifice, in final periods of labor, entailed on society in acquiring it. By establishing an equality between the gratification conferred on itself by articles different in kind and the element pain, which is here homogeneous, society is able to compare the quantities of gratification in the different cases with each other. The price of things corresponds to the pain of acquisition, of which the unit is the sacrifice entailed on society by the work of the final period in each of a series of days; and the sacrifice involved in the collective labor of one such final period is like that which is imposed by another. *The value of one article the measure of the effective service that it renders to society as a whole.*

The burden of labor entailed on a man in the making of an article has no fixed relation to its market value. The product of one hour's work of an eminent lawyer, an artist or a business manager may sell for as much as that of a month's work of an engine stoker, a seamstress or a stone-breaker. Here and there are " prisoners of poverty," putting life itself into products of which a wagon-load can literally be bought for a prima donna's song. Wherever there is exceptional personal power or position, giving to any producer the advantage of a monopoly, there is a divergence between cost and value, if by these terms we mean the cost to the producer and the value in the market. Compare, for example, the labor involved in maintaining telephones with the rates demanded for the use of them. Yet of monopolized products, as of others, our rule holds good : they sell according to the disutility of the terminal social labor expended in order to acquire them. Differences in wealth between different producers cause the costs of different units of the supply of a given commodity to vary, so that not all correspond to the market value. The rich worker stops producing early, while the sacrifice *The measure of the value of a particular article not the sacrifice incurred by the men who produce it, but the sacrifice incurred by society in acquiring it*

entailed is still small; but his product sells as well as if it cost much more sacrifice.[1]

If we say that the prices of goods correspond with the amount and the *efficiency* of the labor that creates them, we say what is equivalent to the above proposition. The efficiency that figures in the case is power and willingness to produce a given effect, and the willingness is as essential as the power. The man of great capacity who is too rich to put forth much effort is not an efficient laborer. Moreover, the effect that gauges the efficiency of the worker is the amount of wealth that he creates, and this must be measured by the units that we have just attained. Efficiency in a worker is, in reality, power to draw out labor on the part of society. It is capacity to offer that for which society will work in return. Hence goods must sell at rates that are in accordance with the quantity and the efficiency of the work which creates them.

There is, then, a way in which we can measure the efficiency of every worker; and by comparing the measurements we can see how much one laborer excels another. A, the weaver, and B, the carpenter, are working on such unlike products that, even though we may know how much the one contributes toward the making of a piece of cloth and how much the other contributes toward the building of a house, we still have trouble in comparing directly the quantities of these dissimilar products and thus gauging the comparative efficiency of the two workers.

Running through the unlike products is the one common element, power to give social gratification; and the amount of this gratification is measured by the

---

[1] In the figure, this fact is rudely expressed by the fact that the line BD is shorter than the line B'D'. The lines representing costs between these two would not, however, actually lengthen at a perfectly uniform rate and thus make the line DD straight.

amount of social labor that it induces. Every worker's personal power registers itself in the quantity of this composite labor that he is able to draw out. If A, by working for a year, can induce society to work two minutes, and if B, in the same way, can induce it to work three minutes, the former is only two-thirds as efficient as the latter. The labor of each one of a thousand men working in as many different trades may thus be measured, and the amounts given by the different measurements may be added, compared and averaged. If we regard the thousand workers as constituting a complete industrial society, an average worker is one who can induce the whole body, in return for all of his own labor, to work for him for a thousandth part of every day.

Three things can be measured in terms of this ulti- as well as capital and mate standard of value — namely, consumers' wealth, consumers' capital and labor. Goods for consumption induce wealth. social labor and are valuable in proportion to the amount of it that they severally draw out. Capital creates consumers' wealth and thus indirectly induces social labor. The capital itself can be measured by means of this social labor which, through its product, it induces. The work of an individual creates consumers' wealth, draws out social labor and records the degree of its own efficiency by the amount of such labor it gets control of. Though our study has taken us into a region of abstractions, it has not taken us out of the world of reality; for every artisan who is plying his trade actually possesses the power over society that has here been analyzed, and so do the tools in the artisans' hands and the finished products on the merchants' shelves. Induced social labor gauges the power of all of them.[1]

[1] On page 343 it has been stated that there is "a unit for measuring true capital in the form of land." This measurement is made

by gauging the productive efficiency of each piece of land in terms of the social labor that, as a producing agent, it calls out.

There are questions of some subtlety to be answered before the theory of the ultimate unit of value can be made complete. One of them has reference to the indirect way in which the labor of an individual producer makes itself felt as a power throughout society. He may be making something that is consumed by a limited part of society ; and yet he is able to induce, in return for his special product, labor that is literally social, since it enlists every member of society in a certain *pro rata* proportion. He can cause every one to work for the nth part of his working day. It would be a simplification that would amount to inaccuracy to say that he can make them all work for any fixed period of time, such as a minute; for each person who contributes to the social labor that gauges values of all kinds must contribute an accurately adjusted share of his own labor, and a minute would be a larger fraction of one man's day than of another's. It is accurate enough for our purpose, however, to say that the social labor is made up of a fixed fraction of a day's labor of every individual. In ways direct and indirect one producer can draw out the composite labor that is thus defined.

If, for a simple illustration, we assume that twenty men constitute an isolated society, and if we cause the first of them to make something which is directly consumed by only five of the others, there are fourteen whose labor he can draw out only through a series of intermediate exchanges; and the principle that governs these exchanges is of great importance. A, the first producer, can directly induce labor on the part of B, C, D, E and F. In order that he may cause G to labor, he must offer to him some product created by one of the men for whom he works directly. By performing additional labor for B, getting a second share of B's product and presenting it to G, A may insure work on G's part ; and in similar ways he may cause all the others to labor. There may be men in the society who do not consume any of the products made by B, C, D, E and F, the men for whom A produces directly ; and A's connection with them may be still more indirect. It may be necessary that A should work still further for B, giving a bit of B's special product to G and some of G's product to H, in order to induce the last-named member of the little society to work. By a chain of connection that is mainly indirect, one worker is always able to exercise over all workers that power which we have described.

The important point in this connection is the nature of the influences that act on the individuals who furnish this chain of connection. These influences are psychological. A motive is presented to B by something that A does for him, and it is the character of this motive that needs carefully to be noted. Something in A's product is a final utility to B. In the goods produced by A there is an element that enters into the final and least important increment of the wealth that B consumes ; and yet this final consumption on B's part is important enough for him to cause him to work in the final period of his day, when the service is most burdensome. As has been shown, it is the consumption which is least important which offsets the work that entails the most sacrifice. When B's product is given to A and passed on to G, there is in it an element that is a final utility to G and causes him to do work which offsets and measures the benefit that he gets. By a chain of connection, every link in which is made by a subjective experience of an individual, the first worker in the society reaches and influences all the others. A offers a marginal gratification to B and gets from him a marginal sacrifice; and when, in turn, A gives some of B's product to G, there is the same balancing of inducements and the same result.

Importance attaches to these facts, because they enable us to avoid a difficulty that has been fatal to a certain labor measure of value. If we say that the value of an article corresponds to the amount of labor " of average quality " that has been expended in producing it, we must find a way to average different kinds of labor ; and we can do this only by means of the values of the products that different kinds of labor create. These values, in turn, we are obliged to measure by average labor, and we thus find ourselves reasoning in a circle. A commodity is, however, actually measured for value on the basis' of the social service that it renders. By means of the chain of purely subjective connections that have here been described, it can diffuse benefits throughout society. At every point in the connection an individual receives a marginal pleasure and subjects himself to a marginal sacrifice. All society, in the end, incurs a marginal sacrifice that measures the value of this kind of goods. *The individual labor which made the commodity is the economic equivalent of the social labor that is induced by it and that measures its value, and in this way individual labor performed in making an article corresponds with and expresses the value of it ;* but the value of a commodity is not derived from the labor that is back of it in the making. It is derived from the social service that is before us in the using. The value of the labor of making the article is derivative. It comes through the product of the labor, from the social effect that the product will produce.

The definitions of the static state that have been given in the earlier chapters of this book have not in any way depended on the definition of a unit of labor that has just been offered. Society is static, if labor and capital are able to move from group to group, even though they do not do so because the inducement is lacking.

This implies merely that men do not change their occupations and that the young workers who enter any group merely fill the places of the old workers who withdraw from it. It is not necessary that individual laborers should be tested in a way that would measure in any kind of scientific units the work that they perform. A young man who is about to choose an occupation may embody many units of labor or only a few ; but the essence of the static state is that, within the range of employments for which his capacities fit him, he should be as strongly impelled in one direction as in another. If, in connection with this description of the static state, we speak provisionally of units of labor, the idea that the expression is intended to convey is that of a certain power to produce merely physical results. When a man is digging in a trench, he may be thought of, in a rude way, as embodying a unit of labor, if he throws out in a day an average amount of earth. When the man is in a textile mill, he may similarly be thought of as embodying a unit of labor, if his presence causes the production of so much of the fabric there made as to mark him as an average worker. Values and units of values do not enter into such a measurement.

It is now possible, however, to use the true unit of labor in defining the static state ; but this affords a new definition of it. The amount of labor that is potentially in a man is measured by the social labor that he can induce when all workers, as well as all capital, are apportioned among the groups in a normal or static way. If there is a misadjustment of the agents of production, these agents produce different amounts and nearly always smaller amounts than they would in a static state. The actual work that a man then does counts as fewer units of labor than there are potentially in him. The static state can, then, be identified as the one in which every man's actual work represents his potential working power, as measured in scientific units.

Some part of the output of every kind of goods is traceable to capital, and thus to the sacrifice termed abstinence; and the personal sacrifice entailed by abstinence may be measured in terms of that which is entailed by labor. On this point the study of Professor F. H. Giddings, in the *Quarterly Journal of Economics* for January, 1890, is valuable. Since, however, the creating of a bit of capital secures an endless income, the social labor that the act of abstinence really draws out is also endless. By saving a thousand dollars now, I secure a power to serve society in a minute degree and to draw a return service from society forever. But there is not a calculable connection between the present cost of the abstaining, as measured by its equivalent in social labor, and the value of the earnings of the capital (say) fifty years hence, as measured in terms of social labor of that date. A full study of this point would detain us too long.

CHAPTER XXV

STATIC STANDARDS IN A DYNAMIC SOCIETY

IF this study were to be absolutely restricted to The limits
the field of social economic statics, as sharply defined, of a static
it should stop at this point; for in going farther it reached.
enters on the field of economic dynamics. We have
seen that the second natural division of political
economy which is devoted to social economic statics,
includes phenomena that are due to exchanges —
to the fact that society acts as an organism in producing wealth. That division, however, includes nothing
that is due to continuing evolution in the organism.
When we state those facts concerning distribution
which are due merely to the organized method of
creating wealth, we have told all that we can, while
keeping strictly within the limits of this part of the
science; for we have presented in their entirety
the static laws of distribution, as they would act in
the absence of organic change and of the friction
and the disturbance that it causes.[1]

We now have before us a picture of a static industrial world — not a dead world, but one filled with
living and acting men. It produces and consumes
wealth; but the kinds of wealth that it creates and
uses, and the quantities that it creates of all the
various kinds, remain unchanged. Its methods and

[1] If present plans are realized, the dynamic laws of distribution
will be stated in a later work; and, if that were now ready for
publication, the present one would end here.

its tools are unvarying, and there is no change in the amount or in the character of the labor and the capital that do the producing work. This society acts and lives, but does so in a changeless manner. It is divided, for productive purposes, into groups and sub-groups, and there is no change in the size of any of them. This absence of any flow of labor or of capital from one group to another is the sure outward sign of the static condition.

Values are here "natural" in the Ricardian sense, for everything sells at its "cost of production" and no *entrepreneur* makes a profit. The cost of producing a given thing is uniform in all the different establishments that make it. Wages and interest also are natural, in the same sense; for workmen everywhere get what their work alone produces and capitalists get what capital alone produces. Moreover, the product of labor per unit is uniform throughout the whole system of groups and sub-groups, so that a man can gain nothing by passing from one group to another. The productive power of capital is also everywhere the same. Isolate the static forces — shield society absolutely from the influence of change and disturbance — and it takes this shape.

The sense in which, in a static society, values, wages and interest are "natural."

This picture is, of course, completely imaginary. A static society is an impossible one; for the forces that bring men together in the social state have in themselves the power to make society change its form and its mode of action. In reality, the social structure grows and improves daily, and will do so to the end of time; and it is this growth that makes the social condition tolerable and opens before it inspiring possibilities.

Five general changes are, as we said at the outset, continually going on : population is increasing, capital is increasing, industrial methods are changing, the modes of organizing labor and capital for productive purposes are changing, human wants are multiplying and refining. Every one of these changes, moreover, results from a perfectly normal cause, and it is wholly in accordance with nature that they should all go on together. A changeless society would, in this view, be unnatural; for it would bear little resemblance to the society that nature really calls for. Changes that are actually in progress

Values also are forever altering, and the alterations are in accordance with normal tendencies. Similarly, the rate of wages is rising and the rate of interest is falling, and these changes are natural. Profits in a particular sub-group, or in a particular establishment within a sub-group, are continually appearing and then slowly vanishing; and this appearance and disappearance of profits is entirely in accordance with forces of nature. Everything that is keeping society out of that condition which we have described as static is natural, in a broad sense, since it is in harmony with sociological laws and results from influences that are inherent in men and in their environment. Yet we have called static standards of value, wages and interest, in a certain narrower sense, natural standards; and we have been right in so doing. and are natural, though they disturb static adjustments.

The description of the purely static state, in fact, deals with realities. It is imaginary only by its omissions; for it presents an essential part of the forces that act in the real, dynamic world. The influences that bring about the group adjustment that we have just described, and all that it involves, are not imaginary: they are as real as anything on earth. They are always acting in the midst of the most violent disturbances that dynamic forces produce. As an illustration we have used the sea. A static ocean is imaginary, for there never was such a thing; but The essential realism of a static theory.

there has never been a moment in the history of the stormiest seas, when the dominant forces that controlled them were not those which, if left entirely alone, would reduce their waters to a static condition. Gravity, fluidity, pressure, and nothing else, would have the effect of making the sea level and motionless. With all the movements that winds and tides produce, these influences are still the dominant ones. The ocean does not leave its bed, and the depth of it does not greatly change. The surface, considering its size, shows only trifling irregularities. If we take only a bird's eye view of the ocean, we are tempted to say that a static philosophy of it is sufficient and that we may treat waves and currents as minor aberrations due to "disturbing influences."

Such a physical science would, however, never serve its purpose. Changes must be accounted for, even though a body may keep a form that approximates the static one. A social science that should not deal with evolution would likewise be entirely unsatisfying, since change and movement are in the highest degree important. The forces of change, however, can never be understood without first having a knowledge of the forces of rest. Without a knowledge of the action of fluidity and pressure, one could never comprehend the effect of wind upon the ocean; and without a knowledge of the shape to which competition alone would reduce society one could never understand the action of the changes that we have termed dynamic.

A dynamic society tends, at each instant, toward a certain static adjustment. The static state which has here been pictured is the one toward which society is at every instant tending, under the influence of competition. The static system of groups and sub-groups should, then, be thought of as an ideal arrangement, projecting itself through the disturbed and changing group system of actual society just as the imaginary level surface of the sea projects itself through the waves. We need, above all things, to see the static society as it is. It is not a monstrosity unconnected with the real world: it is a shape and a mode of action that the real world carries within it. That we may grasp the essential reality of it, we must describe, at least in outline, the movements that are going on and show how static forces are related to them; for, unless it be seen that these forces are really working, we shall encounter the accusation that our whole science is a sublimation of theory. What we have to see is how static laws operate in a dynamic state. How do the standards of value, wages and interest — which, in the Ricardian sense, are natural — make themselves effective, in the midst of such violent movements as are going on? This we must know, if we are to understand the importance of static theory.

Every one of the five dynamic changes above specified disturbs the static adjustment of society: after any one of them, static law sets itself at work to produce a new adjustment. In actual life it cannot complete this rearranging work before a new disturbance occurs; and so the actual state of society is always somewhat different from the state to which static forces alone are tending to bring it. An endless series of changes of a single kind would cause value, wages and interest forever to differ from static values, wages and interest. What the world actually experiences, however, is a perpetual series of each one of the five typical changes, going on together: population is continually increasing, capital is growing, methods of production are perpetually improving, a great centralization of industry is going on, and wants are forever increasing in number and variety.

Forces of movement capable of being understood only after a study of forces of rest.

Dynamic movements to be examined, first singly, and then in concurrent action.

By the aid of static theory, we can begin to make dynamic studies; and the first step is to examine each one of these changes separately, in order to see, first, how it causes actual values, wages and interest to differ from static standards and, secondly, how it causes the standards themselves to change. It remains for dynamic theory to show what happens when all these changes go on together. To this end we must ascertain what is the grand resultant of five different types of social change, all of which are continually in progress. Obviously, from all these changes two general results must follow : first, values, wages and interest will differ from the static standards ; secondly, the static standards themselves will always be changing. The ultimate fruit of a dynamic theory is an ability to account for the direction and the rate of these changes.

Our study, therefore, should reveal — in no detail, indeed, but in the most general way — what is the effect of each of the five changes that have been called dynamic. It should show how each of them, separately considered, takes society out of the static condition, and what kind of changes it produces ; and it should also show, in the same brief way, how these five changes affect society, when they are all in progress together.

How dynamic movements neutralize each other.

In fact, they largely neutralize one another, so far as group arrangements are concerned, and cause the actual form of society to hover much nearer to the theoretical static form than would be possible if these influences worked separately. Values, wages, interest and profits are much nearer to what they would be under the influence of competition alone than it would be possible to have them if there were fewer disturbing forces working.

Variations from the static standards are not the only things to be accounted for. They are a part of what economic dynamics has to investigate but they are a relatively small part. The whole science of economic friction, which accounts for the variations of actual values, wages and interest from certain natural standards, is a smaller science than that which accounts for changes in the standards themselves. Every one of the great dynamic changes alters those static values and changes those static rates of wages and interest toward which actual rates are tending. The kind of dynamic change that is most useful for the illustration of this point is brought about by an improvement in the methods of production. Thus, an invention makes it possible to produce something more cheaply. It first gives a profit to *entrepreneurs* and then, in the way that we have described, adds something to wages and interest. This is equivalent to a creation of new wealth. It has made a definite addition to the income of society, and from the moment when the improved method has been put into operation the static standard of wages has been higher. The rate toward which the pay of labor is now tending is not what it was before the invention was applied, but it is a new and higher rate. Wages now tend to equal what labor can now produce, and this is more than it could formerly produce. When the full fruits of this invention shall have diffused themselves throughout society, the earnings of labor will equal the new standard rate.

Let another invention be made that also effects an economy in production. It also creates a profit; and this profit, like the first, is an elusive sum, which *entrepreneurs* grasp but cannot hold. This sum, like the former one, slips in time through their fingers and bestows itself on all members of society. At the moment when the second invention is applied, then, there is a new and still higher standard established

Variations from static standards and changes in those standards to be considered.

How invention, for example, affects the static stand ard of wages.

for actual wages; and they will pursue that standard till they reach it, though before they do so a still remoter and higher standard will be before them.

How intermittent inventions would affect standards of wages and variations from the standards.

If improvements in production occurred only at intervals long enough to allow a complete diffusion of the fruits of one improvement before another one should be made, the results would be simple. At a given time, one static standard for wages would be established; and, by the influence of competition, the actual pay of labor would be made to conform to it. Then another, and a higher, static standard would be established; and during the following interval wages would slowly be brought up to that level. Then a still higher standard would result from some further invention, and actual wages would pursue and overtake that one. There would, in short, be a succession of static standards for wages, each of which would be somewhat higher than the former one; and the actual rate would move upward, overtaking first one of the standards, then another, and then another. At distant intervals, but only temporarily, would the actual and the static rate coincide.

How a continuous improvement in method would affect them.

If, instead of occurring at intervals considerably separated, the improvements in industrial methods were continually taking place, — if one followed another so closely that, when the second occurred, the fruits of the first were only beginning to make their impression on the earnings of labor, — then, as a result, we should have the standard of wages moving continuously upward and actual wages steadily pursuing the standard rate in its upward movement, but always remaining by a certain interval behind it.

This process represents the actual condition of industry. Improvements are, in fact, occurring so rapidly as to tread upon one another's heels. They take place in all the different groups and sub-groups of which society is composed, and every one of them does its minute part toward pushing upward the standard of pay for all labor.   Obediently to the laws of competition, the actual rate of pay responds to the influence of the improvement and moves in pursuit of the rising standard.   But it never reaches that standard: at no one instant of time is the pay of labor what it will be, when the full effects of improvements that have recently been made shall have taken their final shape, as an addition to the earnings of laborers and capitalists.   In every single instant there is a static standard — and this is the point that is now of importance for us — which is defined by the principles that we have described.   Select that society which is fullest of life and of economic disturbances, the most enterprising of societies, and you will find that it is subjected to the most revolutionary changes.   On any particular day we can say that static law governs that society, establishing for workers a rate of pay that is higher than the actual rate; though, after an interval that dynamic principles can account for, the actual rate will reach it.   The society is thus dominated by static law; for the standard of pay for labor at this moment is what the actual pay would be, if we were to stop all dynamic changes and let the fruits of the changes that have thus far been made convert themselves into additions to wages and interest.   Dynamic science studies the variation of the present actual rates from the static standards and the interval that it will take to make them coincide with those present normal rates.   It studies the velocity of the upward moving standard of wages and that of the pursuing rate of actual wages, as well as the rapidity of the downward moving normal rate of interest and that of the pursuing actual rate.

Velocities of movement and amounts of variation from standards are dynamic subjects.

We have frequently used the sea as an illustration of the static and the dynamic aspects of industrial life, and it will again serve our purpose here. There is, then, an ideal surface of the ocean, perfectly level, which projects itself through the actual waves. Stop the winds, letting the waves subside and the troughs between them become filled, and the sea will take an actual surface that will conform to this imaginary one. This is like what would happen, if the dynamic movements of society were to stop and allow competition to do its work, in diffusing profits and making earnings normal. If, however, there were at work some force that continually raised the static surface of the water, so that a calm occurring to-morrow would bring the water to a level that would be higher than that which would result from a calm to-day, the case would resemble that of the world of industry.

Improve-
ments in
method
afford new
sums for
distribution.

The improvements that are going on make additions to the whole income of the world. They disturb existing static adjustments, indeed, and in this respect they act like winds that toss up waves; but they do more than this, for they raise the entire height of the future sea, waves and all. For this also we can present a marine illustration. Pile somewhere on the surface of the sea a mountain of water and then let it subside, sending its great waves in rings that widen till they reach the outermost parts of the ocean. This makes disturbances, of course, for it takes the surface of the water out of that level and motionless state in which static law may be supposed to have left it; but it adds new water to the ocean and, when the surface shall again be quiet, it will be somewhat higher than it was before. Such a single mountain of water, piled somewhere upon the smooth sea, illustrates what happens, whenever a single improvement in production is so made that static law is left alone to dispose of the fruits of it. The addition to the wealth of society is like the addition to the waters of the sea, for the improvement has made the real earnings of men vary from the theoretical rate and has raised that theoretical rate itself. Such waves, piled upon the ocean at such intervals that each one would subside before its successor appeared, would act like those improvements which come at considerable intervals. Each wave would disturb the existing surface of the sea and make the new surface higher than was the former one.

Now, let the mountains of new water come in such quick succession that, just as one is beginning to subside, another makes its appearance. Let them be scattered all over the ocean, so that the ring-like waves, as they move outward, intersect one another in every direction. At every instant the waters are trying to conform to some static level, but at no two successive moments are they trying to conform to the same level; for they are pursuing an ideal and level surface that is continuously rising. Now we have the figure of what is occurring in society — the figure that describes the movement of wages, which move ever upward, hovering always about a static standard but never for two successive moments about the same standard.

These changes themselves and their effects are all subjects for economic dynamics. Static science recognizes one natural standard of wages for one time; but static laws, pure and simple, as they work in an actual and dynamic society, never give the same rate at different dates, but rather an endless succession of static rates. Dynamic forces create conditions in which there must be one static rate of pay to-day, a higher one to-morrow, and a third and still higher one the day

Illustration

The new elements of gain change static standards of income.

folłowing. This is the fundamental fact about the action of static law in the world as it is.

Dynamic science deals with profits in their original state, as normally created by improvements in industry, in the proceeds of which the *entrepreneurs* have a share; while static science deals with them in their later and permanent state, as they are transmuted into increments of wages and interest. How some employer is now getting rich, dynamic science can tell us; but how it is that wage-earners are getting benefits from improvements of an earlier day, static science tells us. Profits, it is important to note, are larger when they become additions to wages and interest than they were when they existed in their initial shape, as *entrepreneurs'* gains. When they slip out of the employer's hands, they grow. In the diffusing they become greater in the aggregate. The competitive law that gives them over in the end to laborers and capitalists thus gives more to these classes than it takes away from *entrepreneurs.* The whole output of industry is at its maximum when the agents, labor and capital, are apportioned among the groups in a perfectly normal way; and that is when they have moved to the groups where profits have existed, till these gains have vanished and wages and interest have absorbed the whole social income.

The interval between actual wages and the static standard is the result of friction; for, if competition worked without let or hindrance, pure business profit would be annihilated as fast as it could be created — *entrepreneurs,* as such, could never get and keep any income. The annihilation would consist in converting profit into another type of income and making it larger in the operation of conversion. Dynamic theory has to account for the whole of that friction on which *entrepreneurs'* shares depend; while static

Profits a subject for Economic Dynamics; the ultimate disposal of them a subject for Economic Statics.

Friction a dynamic element.

law determines what wages will be, when the friction shall have been completely overcome, and what they would be at this instant, if friction were immediately to vanish.

Dynamic theory reveals a causal connection between the interval of which we have been speaking and the rate at which wages are increasing. Were it not for that interval, *entrepreneurs*, as such, would get nothing, however much they might add to the world's productive power. They would have no incentive in self-interest to make any improvements, and it is clear that additions which are difficult and costly would be in danger of not being made. Profit is the lure that insures improvement, and improvement is the source of permanent additions to wages. To secure progress, this lure must be sufficient to make men overcome obstructions and take risks. The difference between the actual pay of labor and the rate toward which, at a particular date, it tends, measures the incentive that is offered to the men who make progress possible. Because to-day laborers are not getting the fruit of the improvement that was made yesterday, employers can make something; and because they can make something transiently for themselves, they make permanent additions to wages.

Dynamic theory has to show how great is the interval that insures the maximum rate of progress — how much *entrepreneurs* need, in the way of profit, in order to make them do all that they can do to keep wages moving upward. This subject is intricate, as are all subjects in dynamics; but very simple is that static theory which shows that, however great may be the profits, wage-earners will in the end get the lion's share. The vast sums that to-day are accruing to the rich, who do the marshalling of the industrial line, are bound, under static law, to add

A causal connection between variations that depend on friction and the rate of increase of the social income.

themselves with an increase to wages and interest.
They add themselves, moreover, chiefly to wages.
By the time that they have done this, indeed, gains
from new sources will be accruing to the captains of
industry, so that there will always be profits. But
this gain will not long be obtained from any one
source; for, if we can identify the profits of to-day,
we shall have something that static law will claim as
its own and will by to-morrow, as it were, make over
mainly to laborers and to the owners of the tools of
work. Dynamic forces, then, account to-day for the
existence of an income that static forces will begin to
dispose of to-morrow.

The velocity with which all standards move is a
subject for the latter part of the theory of distribution. Velocities, directions of movement, obstructions, intervals — with these dynamics must deal, and
with none of them has static theory, as such, anything to do. It does deal, however, with near goals.
It tells what the rate of wages would shortly be, if
evolution were to cease. Static forces, then, are of
vital importance in the midst of all manner of social
changes. For study here we have singled out one
alone of the typical dynamic changes — that, namely,
which takes place in methods of production; and we
have examined the effect of it on one of the shares
in distribution, namely, wages. But each one of
the other four dynamic changes similarly transforms
society and changes values, wages and interest.

It is clear that static law is entirely operative
under dynamic conditions. Not one jot nor one
tittle is taken from its full efficiency by inventions,
by new organizations, by growth of population, etc.
Let there be, for example, an increase of population.
It is impossible that this increase shall occur in
such a way that every group and every sub-group

Profits
largely un-
transformed
increments
of wages.

An illustra-
tion of the
action of
static law in
dynamic
conditions.

will naturally and without any further adjustment have its normal share of new laborers. The increase of the working population is likely to be in some degree localized. One geographical locality will have more of it than another has; and in the geographical locality where the population is densest it is impossible that all the different sub-groups in the industrial system shall be equally well represented. If the newcomers drift to a section where (say) textile manufacturing is a specialty, these industries will get more than their share of the new labor.

Under these circumstances, a diffusion of the local excess of population will take place. As all industry uses land, such a local excess of inhabitants may be treated as an overcrowding of land, even though the occupations that flourish in the more densely populated region are not mainly agricultural. One of the permanent static laws which we have presented in the foregoing chapters now calls for what we have treated as a re-apportionment of land among the sub-groups. Literally, it results in a certain dispersion of labor and capital over the large area that is at their disposal. Rent is at its maximum, as we have seen, only when land is in a certain combination with labor and with capital; and each section of the land must have a certain normal share of each of the other productive agents combined with it. But this condition is impossible, where an undue proportion of the population originally locates itself in some one place. Static law must, then, make a local diffusion of the excess.   An influence that will cause the overplus of population to move is the tendency that it has to diffuse itself among different groups and sub-groups; for in the crowded neighborhood these are unevenly represented, and to reach them in natural proportions the labor must migrate.   There is a definite number of men who are, as it were, due to the shoe-making trade, and a certain other number who are due to iron smelting, etc. Every occupation, under static law, has its claim on a certain definite proportion of the new laborers who are coming on the scene, and it will get them by such a diffusion. The mere crowding of land itself is a further influence that acts in the same way.

If the influx of population occurred all at once and then stopped, there would be a time when values, wages and interest would all be unnatural, in the sense of deviating from static standards. Then they would slowly approach those standards and would ultimately reach them. So long as an undue proportion of population is in any one sub-group, values cannot be natural in the static sense. Moreover, while the groups are out of balance, the whole amount of wealth produced is somewhat less than it normally should be, and neither wages nor interest is at the static maximum. The influence, then, that apportions the new working force among the different sub-groups readjusts values by raising some and lowering others. In the second place, it steadily raises both wages and interest, by causing both labor and capital to produce in the aggregate more than they did before.

A second increase of population, also more or less localized, would cause another disturbance and another re-adjustment like that we have just described ; and a long series of such enlargements of population would, so far as this one influence goes, cause values, wages and interest first to deviate from the static standards, then slowly to conform to them and then to deviate from them again.

When the growth of population is not intermittent, but continuous, the effect is to cause a perpetual de-

viation from the normal standards.   Some groups The con-
and sub-groups are, so to say, the receiving ground tinuous
growth of
for the new laborers and pass them on to the other population
and static
sub-groups in which they are to stay permanently. law.
The receiving ground is necessarily overcrowded ,
and, though there may come a time when it parts
with laborers as rapidly as it gets them, something of
the effect of the original overcrowding continues
forever.   This single dynamic influence, increase of
population, causes the values of things produced by
the groups and sub-groups to which the labor comes
earliest to be unduly low — meaning by "unduly"
that they are lower than the rates at which a static
adjustment would fix them.   It also causes the values
of other things to be, in the same special sense, unduly
high.

What we have said about the increase of labor is Increase of
equally true of the increase of capital.   We could, capital and
static law.
indeed, substitute the term "capital " for "labor " in
the entire foregoing statement and so make it describe
what occurs by reason of the fact that the fund of
productive wealth is enlarging.   The influx of capital must, in the same way, be at first somewhat localized.   It is not possible that it should originally
appear in each of the different sub-groups or in each
of the localities in exactly the proportion in which
static law will finally place it, and for this reason
capital must move.   There must be the recombina-
tion of land and of auxiliary capital that the law of
rent requires ; and until static law has in these ways
asserted itself values will not be natural.   In the
interim, the sub-groups that are the receiving grounds
for the new capital will turn out an excess of products, receiving lower prices for them.

An intermittent growth of capital might cause
values to be abnormal, then normal and then abnor-

mal again; but a continuous growth of capital will keep values in some small degree perpetually abnormal, in the special and narrow sense of the term, for it will cause them always to differ from the static standards. In the finer and truer sense, it is natural that they should thus differ from these standards; since it is entirely in accordance with nature that capital should steadily increase and that the increase of it should be in a measure localized. The values which in a dynamic society are in accordance with nature — and thus, in the higher sense of the term, natural — are the values that deviate from the static standard by a natural interval. The localized increase of capital, like that of labor, keeps general wages and interest by a real, though slight, interval below the static standards. The lower actual rates are in a true sense natural, if the distance between them and the standard rates is a normal one.

Variations that are natural, when a dynamic change is steady and continuous.

Let us now apply these principles to the third dynamic change which we have noticed — that resulting from inventions or improvements in method. The effect of this change on value is much less steady than is that of an increase of population or of capital. Inventions appear now here, now there and now elsewhere. They lower the price first of one thing and then of another; and, from the moment when the labor-saving machine begins to work in producing a particular article, there is a new static standard of value for that article and for all others. When the machine shall have produced its full effects, more of the goods produced by it will be constantly offered for sale and the price of them will be lower. From the outset this lower price is the static or, in the narrow sense, the natural price. At first the actual price is higher than this, but it tends gradually to conform to it.

If inventions were confined to one group and if they occurred intermittently, the standard value of the product of that group would first go down with a sudden drop, then it would remain stationary awhile and then, as the result of the next improvement, it would drop again. If the standard continued stationary long enough, actual value might fall to the static level and remain there for a while. Static value dropping and coming to a halt, actual value gradually falling but at intervals overtaking the descending standard—such is the condition of an industry in which inventions are made, as it were, by fits and starts.

If improvements go on continuously in one industry and in no others, the actual value of the goods there produced is always pursuing a standard of value that is steadily descending. Both values are falling, but there is an interval between them; and, if the interval is a normal one, the actual value may be said to be natural in the true sense of being in conformity with nature. The dynamic standard of value is a moving one; and actual value is as natural law would have it, when it moves in the same direction and remains at the proper interval behind this standard value. Whenever the value of only one thing thus descends, that of every other thing rises. The products of the groups in which there are no labor-saving inventions are, so far as this influence goes, always rising in value ; and, moreover, they are always pursuing a rising standard that keeps ahead of them. If the improvements are altogether localized in A''' of our tabular group system, then the values of B''', C''' and D''' are not at any one moment as high as they will be when the output of A''' shall become larger. Static law requires that the output of A''' shall thus become larger. An uninterrupted succession of labor-saving inventions in the sub-group A'''

Continuous improvement of method and natural variations from static standards.

How actual values may pursue changing static values.

causes the actual value of A''' to pursue a descending standard, but never to overtake it, and it causes the values of B''', C''' and D''' to pursue ascending standards, but never to overtake them.

The creation of a new want also has a very disturbing effect in the group systems, if it requires an absolutely new product to gratify it. It then calls for the creation of a new producing group and the attraction of labor and capital from old groups. As a rule, however, the changes in the wants of the consuming public call for qualitative changes in products that are already made, rather than for wholly new products. Every such change, too, has its own effect on value, wages and interest. A new want calls for a new static adjustment of all values, and with that there is required a new adjustment of wages and of interest. A continuous series of new wants brings about a continuous change in the standards of value, wages and interest; and the actual market is in perpetual agitation, due to its perpetual effort to conform to the shifting demands. As a rule, the new want somewhat lowers the values of products that satisfy old wants.

New wants and static adjustments.

Dynamic influences that are mutually neutralizing, so far as movements of labor and capital in the group system are concerned.

Dynamic influences largely neutralize each other, so far as apportionment of labor and capital in different parts of the group system is concerned; and a fundamental fact about them is that, coming together as they do, they actually keep values, wages and interest comparatively near to their static standards. They cause a perpetual shifting of value, a continuous rise of wages and a continuous fall in the rate of interest; and they cause the actual pay for labor and for capital to differ from theoretical static rates far less than they would if the dynamic influences were less active and numerous. We are confronted, therefore, by the striking fact that, for the accuracy of its working in a world of reality, static law is dependent on dynamic influences. If a fluid, for example, is viscous, the surface of it does not readily subside to a perfectly level plane, but it does so far more readily if it is agitated at many points at once. Again, a measure of wheat may have an irregular surface while the measure rests on the floor, but it will take a level surface if you shake it. Similarly, static law has to encounter friction, which makes actual values, wages and interest slow in conforming to theoretical standards; but agitation helps to overcome the friction. The standards themselves change the less, because different dynamic movements neutralize each other.

The efficiency of static forces in proportion to the activity and diversity of dynamic ones.

If the increase of labor were localized and if it were confined to a place in which only the group A in our table were represented, it would have very disturbing effects and would keep values, wages and interest far removed from static standards. But this increase in the working population takes place, in fact, in B, C, D, etc., and in all the sub-groups within each of them. Comparatively little relocating of labor is therefore required: it is relatively easy for the new men to put themselves where pure static law would place them. If population were increasing in this general and diffused way and if capital were not increasing, there would be a steady fall of general wages and a steady rise of interest; but, in fact, capital also is growing in amount. It is even growing more rapidly in quantity than is population, and the growth of it neutralizes the depressing influence on wages that increase of population by itself would have. There is, indeed, an actual disturbance of wages and interest caused by the excess of the new capital in amount, as compared with the new labor; for it is only by reason of the fact that one of these economic agents increases faster than the other that distribution is affected. The disturbance

The concurrent growth of capital and of population.

that is due to the difference between the two rates of growth is far less than would be the disturbance occasioned by an increase in the amount of one of the agents alone.

, If improvements in production were confined to a single group or sub-group, they would have very disruptive effects; but they occur in all the sub-groups of the system, and with some approach to continuity.

If the constant multiplying of the output of A''' stood alone, it would call for a perpetual fall of the relative value of it, as well as for constant readjustments of wages and interest. But, as improvements occur also in the B, C, and D groups, the adjustments of value that have to be made are relatively small. While the rate of wages rises more rapidly when improvements are numerous, the pay of laborers conforms much more closely to the static standard where improvements are numerous and well diffused than it would if the improvements were localized. Clearly, where the output of A''', B''', C''' and H''' were all growing larger together, there would be less necessity that men and capital should go from one group to another than there would be if the output of one were increasing, while that of the others remained fixed. Widely diffused improvements, then, help to keep society near to the shape that static law calls for.

The same generalization is true of the changes that take place in consumption. If new wants are numerous and of many kinds, they shift labor far less violently from group to group, and disturb values far less, than would the appearance of a single new want. If society should begin to produce and to use only one entirely new commodity, the fact would call for a quick moving of capital and labor from point to point; but, since there is, in fact, a constant refining of wants and a corresponding constant improvement in the quality of products, the shifting that is called for is far less violent. Labor and capital can remain in the mills that now employ them, but they must produce higher and higher grades of goods.

It is the growth of new wants that in this way neutralizes the effect of all the product-multiplying influences that go on. A glut of consumers' goods would come forthwith, if expanding desires did not make a new market for the output of the mills. The want of commodities which are unlike any that have Simulta-formerly been produced does at times make its neous ap-pearance of appearance; but the demand for improvements and new wants and of new refinements in the qualities of goods that are already productive methods. consumed is the constant fact, and this opens a very general market. Nearly everything that a man uses can be improved in quality; and, as a rule, the improved articles can be made by the same men who now produce them. It follows, therefore, that, with more and more refined wants developing, productive energy sets itself at work throughout the great system and enlarges the output of every group, by making goods finer rather than more numerous. This causes no disastrous transfers of labor and capital from one part of the system to another and it produces no general glut.

The multiplying and the refining of wants — or, in other words, the dynamics of consumption — furnish the elastic market that is needed. If this movement merely keeps pace with the dynamics of production, grave evils are averted and, in the main, the economic world goes on peacefully in the way of larger and larger production. As the dynamic movements are not entirely steady, symmetrical and mutually compensatory, there are some irregular transfers of labor and capital from group to group;

Steady
currents of
labor and
capital.

These the
resultants
of opposing
forces, and
reduced in
violence.

yet, on the other hand, there are noticeable some comparatively steady currents of labor and capital. These agents are regularly flowing in certain directions. Thus, increase of population, in itself, would cause labor and capital to flow steadily downward in the sub-group system. Under its influence alone, man and equipment would have to increase in a disproportionate way in the agricultural sub-groups and in the mining sub-groups, both of which produce what we have defined as elementary utilities. The increase of population would call for more food and more raw material, and the effort to get these things out of the earth would reveal the action of the law of diminishing returns. It would take a larger and larger fraction of the population to feed the whole of it. Wages, as we know, would have to fall ; and this means that laborers would be forced to take their pay in the shape of cheaper and coarser goods. Form utilities would have to be less amply represented in the general product of industry, and elementary utilities would predominate in the consumption of the world. Moreover, as it is the lowest sub-groups that create these elementary utilities, labor and capital would move thither.

The increase of the amount of social capital, however, neutralizes this effect. Though it reduces the *rate* of interest, it enlarges the *gross amount* of it and thus increases the incomes of the members of that class whose consumption has already reached the level of comfort and luxury. This, of itself, calls for more form utility ; for it induces a refining and improving of products to a greater extent than it causes the multiplying of them. Moreover, the increase of capital raises the rate of wages, and this means qualitative improvements in the goods that workmen consume. As the upper sub-groups create

form utilities, the growth of capital, considered apart
from other influences, moves labor and capital from
the sub-groups that are at the bottom of the series
to those which are higher. Improvement in method, or the gaining of new
productive power by the industrial world, if it acted
merely as a labor-saving influence, would cause labor
and capital to move downward in the series of sub-
groups, from A''' toward A, from B''' toward B, etc.
This, however, is because the field for such improvements is rather in the upper sub-groups than in the
lower ones. Agricultural machinery was, for a time,
invented and applied very rapidly ; but, unless chem-
istry shall come in some striking way to the aid of
agriculture, it will probably be other parts of the field
that will, in the long run, show the greatest improvements. If no other effect is to be expected from a
machine than that less labor will be used in the industry
that adopts it, then the progress of invention will, of
course, cause labor to mass itself in those industries
in which labor saving takes place the more slowly
and on the smaller scale.

The full effect of such an influence as that of mechanical improvements may be described as follows:
We may first assume that there is no new product
created and no multiplying of former products.
The output of A''', B''', C''', etc., are to remain
as they are, however rapidly invention proceeds.
Improvements in machines and methods now occur,
but they mass themselves in the upper sub-groups
of the different series. If all the labor that was
formerly in A''', A'', B''', B'', etc., remains there, it
can be employed for only a short period in each day.
In that case its earnings will be small. But the
earnings of laborers in A will be much larger, and
competition will transfer a portion of the labor from

A''' and A'' to A. This will bring the productive power of labor in the upper sub-groups and that of labor in the lower sub-groups to an equality, and the ultimate effect of all this will be that the working day will be shortened in every industry.

Now let the improvement in method act, not as a labor saver, but as a product multiplier, and the effect is the reverse of this. The labor in A''' and A'' may, for the most part, remain there and give rein to its new productive power. Enlarged production, however, means raising the qualitative grades of goods more than it multiplies them in number. Less productive energy is required at A, where raw materials are created, and more at A', A'' and A''', where the fashioning of the materials is done. There is, in short, a relatively smaller amount of elementary utility represented in the consumption of the world, and there is a comparatively larger amount of form utility.

Unlike effects of labor saving and of product multiplying.

A certain amount of improvement in method does, in fact, take place in the lowest sub-groups, where the crudest materials are produced; and it has the effect of moving labor upward in the series to the sub-groups that produce finer utilities. This happens because of the comparatively rigid and inelastic character of the demand for these crude products and the highly elastic character of the demand for form utilities. Our more luxurious living shows itself in the care with which we fashion things, and not in the mere multiplying of the number of them, with the result that our consumption of raw materials does not increase as rapidly as our consumption of wealth in its finer forms. On the whole, therefore, the flow of labor and capital is continually upward in the sub-group series; for it can find outlets for its new power only in this way.

Effects of quickened production in the lower sub-groups compared with the same thing in the upper ones.

Organization has in these respects the same effect as improvement in method. As a practical fact, it takes place in the upper sub-groups, rather than in the lowest ones. It is not in farming that the great consolidations are going on. If organization acted merely as a labor saver, and not as a product multiplier, it would cause labor and capital to mass themselves in mining and agriculture; for men who were thrown out of employment in mills would be forced to betake themselves largely to farming and kindred occupations. Acting as it does, however, and multiplying products, it compels the making of finer grades of them and moves the productive agents forever upward in the series.

In discussing the effect of the two great product-multiplying influences, industrial method and organization, we have tacitly introduced the fifth and last of the dynamic influences that we are considering — namely, the multiplying of wants. It is because the want of form utilities is indefinitely expansive, while that of elementary utilities is relatively inexpansive, that we have, as the resultant of all changes, the steady upward movement of labor and of capital in the sub-group series. Moreover, some general groups create products which, with all the qualitative refinements that can be imparted to them, satisfy less elastic demands than do some other products. With the steady upward flow of labor and of capital in the sub-group series, there is also a flow from those groups which cater to less elastic demands toward those which cater to more elastic ones.

Effects of the unequal expansiveness of wants catered to by different sub-groups and by different general groups.

These steady and stream-like movements would not, of themselves, have disturbing and disruptive effects; and they would not impose any hardship on labor or cause any waste of capital. It is the irregular movements that do this. The labor saving that is effected at some single point in the system changes the location of labor. Inventions are not made and applied simultaneously in A''', B''', C''', etc.; but, unless they are, there must be movements of labor from one of the sub-groups to others and back again. On the whole, an efficient machine is to some extent

Two regular movements of labor and capital, due to all the foregoing causes, contrasted with irregular movements due to one cause.

a labor expeller. If it is introduced at A''', it will cause an enlarged output of the product, A'''; but the amount of this increased output that the market will take will not be enough to keep all of the original laborers at work there. It will, however, create a new demand for them elsewhere; so that machinery can never be rightly treated as a labor expeller, if the whole field of industry is kept in view. The invention that is made and applied at A''' does not displace labor from the entire upper range of sub-groups. In A''', B''' and C''', taken together, there is probably as much labor as ever; but the machine at A''' creates a need of comparatively more men at B''' and C''' and of comparatively fewer at A'''. When, in turn, an invention is made at B''', the movement will be away from that point to A''' and C'''. In irregular ways, therefore, must labor move to and fro within the range of sub-groups that are on the same horizontal level. While the general and slow current of labor is upward within the whole group system, there are irregular and sudden movements to the right and the left of each range of coördinate sub-groups; and it is these that cause hardship for laborers.

It is only in the most hasty and the most general way that we can now speak of these dynamic movements. They form a part of the subject of the concluding division of economic theory. There are, indeed, in progress some movements of capital that we cannot even notice. We must, however, give attention to two essential facts: (1) There is a steady upward movement of labor and capital in the group series; and (2) there are irregular and disturbing movements taking place within each range of coördinate sub-groups.

It would appear, if we were to go one step farther into the dynamic part of our study, that, so far as improvements are well diffused within a range of sub-groups, they neutralize each other's disturbing effects. Whenever inventions at A''', B''' and C''' come nearly together, they remove the necessity for transferring much labor to new positions. It would also appear that the steady upward flow of labor reduces the violence of the horizontal movements that have to take place. As new labor is always entering the uppermost range of sub-groups, it may be that no men will have to leave A''' and go to B''', even though a new machine is introduced at A'''. The enlarging of the force at B''' may be effected by turning to that point some of the labor that is flowing upward from the lower sub-groups.

Still further, it would appear, if we were to continue this study, that movements of capital take much of the violence away from the movements of labor that are entailed by inventions. Not toward greater and greater hardships for the working class, but toward smaller hardships and larger gains is the world tending, as the result of economic dynamics.

All this would become clear, if it were possible to pursue the study into the dynamic region. We have now before us, however, the problem of defining static standards of value, wages and interest, in a state in which all five of the grand dynamic movements are going on together. At each instant there is a certain definite adjustment of labor and of capital in the sub-group system that static forces, of themselves, would

The two important movements of labor: — (1) the steady upward flow in the sub-group systems, and (2) the movements to and fro among sub-groups in the same horizontal range.

Mutually neutralizing effects of improvements diffused among sub-groups of the same range.

Effect of movements of capital in reducing the violence of movements of labor.

THE DISTRIBUTION OF WEALTH

An exact adjustment of labor and capital in the group system called for, at each instant, by static law.

make. Static law calls for a certain exact amount of labor and a certain amount of capital at A', B'', C'', etc., respectively. This static adjustment, if it could be made in a moment, would insure at once the amount of output of each kind of goods that is "natural" under the conditions that exist at this moment; and it would thus make the values of all products natural. Likewise, it would insure natural wages, or the rates of pay that would everywhere conform to the product of labor. It would adjust interest on the same plan, making it everywhere coincide with the product of capital. It would reduce pure profits everywhere to zero. These things would ensue if, at any one moment, dynamic changes and all friction were to cease.

This is, of course, a recapitulation. We have already had the picture of the perfect static adjustment before us; but we have not had before us the fact that some static adjustments require much time, while others require only a little, and that there are

Different amounts of time required for different parts of this general adjustment.

a number of different standards which figure in the natural adjustment of wages and of interest. Within a single year the pay of labor may gravitate rapidly toward a certain standard, while that standard may for a decade, or even a century, slowly gravitate toward a remoter standard.

The moving of labor and capital to the sub-groups in which static forces would put them involves some local migration of workingmen and even of capitalists. A certain number of them may have to change their residences, and this is something that encounters

The assimilation of a new method a more rapid process than the local transfer of labor.

friction and requires time. The assimilation of methods may, however, go on more rapidly. It may be that, when one *entrepreneur* has hit upon a new and successful way of producing something, his competitors can get possession of it within a few years; although, by reason of patents, they may not do this for a longer period.   In general, however, transfers of labor from place to place go on comparatively slowly and those of capital go on more rapidly; while the abandoning of poor methods of production and the placing of all competitors in one business on a plane of high efficiency is sometimes a quick process and sometimes a slow one.

One way of defining the static standard toward which, at each moment, a dynamic society is tending, is to suppose that all dynamic influences should cease at once, while static laws continue to operate for an indefinite time.   On this plan, we should have to wait, before realizing the static condition, long enough to allow the slowest adjustments that are in progress to be carried through quite to completion.   If it takes fifty years to locate labor geographically in the way that static law calls for, even though it requires only five years to unify the methods of production that are in vogue, we must wait fifty years for the complete realization of the static state.   We should thus bring the development of new methods of production to a standstill now, instead of forty-five years hence.   If we stopped all dynamic changes in the year 1900 and waited until 1950 for population to locate itself in a natural way, the methods of production in the subgroup that we took for illustration would be brought to uniformity in 1905 and these processes would then continue in use without further modification for forty-five years longer.

This is one scientific way of defining the state toward which at this moment society is tending under the influence of static forces and of no others.   It would be reached, if we were to paralyze the dynamic forces all at once and wait long enough for the slowest static adjustments to be made.[1]   The state toward

One mode of creating, for purposes of study, a complete static state.

---

[1] It would have been possible to allow mechanical inventions and

which society is now tending, at the outset of the long period, is one that cannot be completely reached until the slowest adjustment that static law calls for has had time to complete itself. In our illustration, that adjustment is the movement of population; and, as this movement requires fifty years, natural values, natural wages and natural interest are not realized within less than that long period. They will come when population is rightly distributed, and not earlier.

Under the influence of static forces, and of these only, society is actually tending toward this remote adjustment; and, if all friction could be removed, it would at once attain it. Friction, however, has this effect: it allows quick-acting dynamic movements to occur over and over again, within the long period that is required for a slow acting static adjustment. In the fifty years that may be needed to move a mass of population from the densely peopled East to the sparsely settled West, hundreds of machines may be invented and values may in each case be adjusted at the level that each machine at once requires. We must, therefore, recognize standards of value, etc., that differ from the ultimate standards.

other improvements to go on until 1945; since, if they were to cease at that date, the five remaining years would suffice to bring industrial methods to uniformity. In the year 1950 the geographical movements of population called for by the conditions existing in 1900 would have been completed and society would have been reduced to a static condition, but for the fact that some minor geographical changes of residence would have been called for by the progress in method occurring in the latter part of the period ; and, as these would require further time, a completely static adjustment would not be realized in 1950. Moreover, if we could disregard these induced and minor changes of residence, it would still be true that the static adjustment realized in this way in 1950 would not be the result of the action of *static forces only* on society, as it was in 1900. It would be, in part, the result of certain dynamic forces acting for forty-five years.

CHAPTER XXVI

PROXIMATE STATIC STANDARDS

IF, under the influence of competition, labor can go exactly to the points where it is wanted in a period of fifty years, if capital can do the same in twenty-five years and if the best method of producing some article can come into general use in ten years, it will be necessary to stop all dynamic changes and to wait through the full fifty years' period, in order that either value, wages or interest shall be reduced absolutely to the rate at which static law alone would fix it. It may be, however, that the fifty years' period that labor occupies in adjusting itself within the group system is made necessary by the obstacles that are in the way of migrating from one geographical locality to another. It may, for instance, be easy for the son of a miner to become a machinist, instead of following in his father's footsteps; and if many young men do this, there is an exodus of labor from the mining subgroup and an influx of labor into the machinist's trade. Where, however, the change carries men from one country to another, it is a slow and costly process. Within the limits of a single small country, labor may be able to dispose itself in the way that static law requires within ten years and capital may do so within a shorter time. Even these local adjustments, with others that can always be made quickly, suffice to bring value, wages and interest within the

Obstacles in the way of certain parts of a general static adjustment.

431

Quasi-static adjustments.

small country to certain quasi-static levels. They approximate the levels that would be reached, if we were rigorously to repress dynamic changes within the one small territory and were to let static forces there continue to work.

When population surges in a wave of migration from Ireland, Germany and Italy to the United States, the movement is a part of the generic operation of giving to the population of the world, as a whole, a natural geographical distribution. In a study that has the world in its purview, this migration is to be considered in the study of economic statics. It is as though there were too much water in the Indian Ocean and the surplus were bringing the sea, as a whole, to an equilibrium by rushing into the Atlantic. In the Atlantic, however, the movement is highly dynamic. The whole surface is rising and the whole body of the water is

What is a part of a static adjustment for the entire world may be, in effect, a dynamic influence in a part of it.

full of violent currents. An influx of men from Asia into America would be one of the movements that would tend to bring the distribution of population in the entire world to an equilibrium; but in America, separately considered, it would constitute a great and typical dynamic change.

The same thing is true of many other movements. When Asia shall copy the mills and the machines of America, the act will be a part of the operation of unifying the industrial processes of the world. This process tends to bring about an equilibrium in the industry of the world; and it is, in this view, a

A static unification of method in America and Asia the cause of grand dynamics in Asia.

static process. In Asia itself, nevertheless, it is an eminently dynamic process; for it is much as though inventions were there rapidly going on in every mechanical field. The reaction that America would experience, in turn, would be highly dynamic in America. Something of this kind is, without doubt, before the people of these two contrasted regions. That which is a static adjustment within the world as a whole may create a dynamic movement within a limited part of the world.

We are, however, immediately concerned with natural standards of wages and interest within limited parts of the world: we wish to know what now fixes the rate about which wages fluctuate in the United States, in England or in Italy. This problem it is possible to solve. There is a rate of wages that would be realized within the limits of the United States, if dynamic changes within that area were at once to cease and if competition were there to work without any obstructions. This rate would differ from the one that would be realized, if the whole world were brought into a static equilibrium. Not till labor and capital are distributed over the world in such a way that there is nowhere any reason for migrating — not till methods of production are, in a way, unified on a world-wide scale, and not till consumers' wants are normal, can the rate of pay for laboring humanity as a whole be natural. After reducing one country only to a static condition, this universal adjustment still remains to be made. The rate of wages that is realized in the one country differs by a certain interval from the ultimate standard, even though it is fixed at a certain proximate static level.

The possibility of limiting, in a local way, the scope of an economic study.

It is possible to study the activities of a limited part of the world by themselves, without being unscientific. Throughout our study we have, indeed, spoken of society without assigning to it any territorial limits. We have tacitly assumed that competition extends through it and that such an influence as a mechanical invention originating in any part of this organism will produce effects in every other part.

Does this organism include all humanity? In a sense, it does; for, unless there is a country that, with all its people, could sink beneath the sea without producing economic changes in other countries, there is none that is outside of the world organism with which the economist must ultimately deal. It would be more than heroic theorizing, however, — for it would be unnatural theorizing, — that should assume that the whole world is bound in so close an organization that there is, even in theory, only one rate of wages, one rate of interest and one standard of value for each commodity throughout the whole of it.

The relation that different parts of the earth sustain to each other furnishes the most difficult and the most fruitful study within the theory of economic dynamics. In view of what Europe and America are doing and are about to do in Asia, this study is as important to the practical man as it is fascinating to the theorist. Already does economic society include the whole world; for trade already unites its parts, so that a change in one part is felt in some degree in every other. Yet there are demarcations to be recognized within this great area. One general boundary is drawn about the civilized nations that constitute the economic centre of the world. Within the area included by this line, economic influences are active — each part is sensitive to influences that originate in other parts. Here there is a strong tendency toward uniform values and toward uniform rates of wages and interest. Across the general boundary, on the other hand, such influences act in a comparatively feeble way. In the inner and the outer areas there are great differences in values and in the rates of wages and of interest.

It is possible to study the economy of this civilized centre of the world, as a unit, and still to proceed on a

The sense in which society includes all mankind.

Demarcations to be recognized within the universal society.

An economic central area in the world.

scientific plan. Europe, America and whatever other continents and islands are in close connection with them constitute this centre, which may be treated as a complete society, with an environing world acting on it. This central society trades with the outer zone, and it sends labor and capital thither. Whether it will or not, it gradually instructs the people of the outlying zone in industrial method. For business purposes it is, in this way, assimilating belt after belt of the outer zone to itself—that is, the civilized economic society is absorbing parts of the uncivilized and loosely bound area. Ultimately all will have been absorbed; and, if we can now establish economic principles that work within the centre, our theory will in the end apply to the world as a whole.

Relations between the centre and outer zone.

Let us, then, limit our studies to this economic centre. Under these conditions, the importation of goods into it is to be regarded as equivalent to producing them in an indirect way; and this process is naturally resorted to, when it costs less than the production of them in a direct way. All that the people of the centre get, in the way of consumers' goods, we may, then, consider that they directly or indirectly produce.

Importation from the outer area an indirect mode of production.

Laborers come into the area; but this is to be regarded as an influence that quickens the increase of population which would, in any case, take place. When laborers go out of this area, the movement retards the increase of population. The moving of capital out of the region or into it is to be regarded as merely changing the natural rate of increase of capital. If a new method of production is ever borrowed from people in the outer zone, the effect in the centre is the same as if it were there invented.

How an influx or an efflux of labor or of capital is to be regarded.

In attaining now a static standard of wages and interest for the centre itself, we assume, first, that

labor and capital there remain fixed in amount.
This cuts off immigration and emigration, as well as
the natural increase in the population. We assume
that methods of production remain unchanged, and
this cuts off any copying of foreign arts. We assume,
too, that other economic elements remain unchanged,
that competition goes on with no hindrances and that,
within the area that we have in view, static rates
of wages and interest are realized. In addition to
repressing wholly new dynamic influences, we have
stopped impulses that are communicated by the outer
region to the central zone. We saw that, in fact,
certain unifying movements in the world, as a whole,
are bringing it all toward a static equilibrium; and
we also saw that such movements, in their effect on
a limited region, are equivalent to dynamic changes.
These we have cut off, as we have cut off new dynamic
changes; and the effect is to produce a local static
state, which gives the standard of wages and interest
toward which local rates are practically tending.

The wages that are thus made generally to rule in
the civilized heart of the business world contain an
element that we may designate as quasi-profit. In this
there is something akin to profits, *entrepreneurs'* gains,
which we identified as an income that will soon slip
from *entrepreneurs* and assume the form of an addition to wages and interest. This income, thus transferred to laborers, will early raise wages in the central
area; but the barrier that separates this region from
the outer zone will long retard the effect that in the
end it will produce on wages there. Perfect and
world-wide competition would give to laborers in
China benefits from the invention of shoe-making
machinery that now accrue to those in America; but,
since such perfect and general competition does not
exist, the gain that is on its way to the labor of

The mode of creating, within the centre, a completely static state.

Quasi-profits an element in wages at the economic centre.

the world pauses long in the hands of the laborers of the civilized part of it. This premium which appears in the pay of laborers of Europe and America, as compared with that of men of Asia and Africa, is quasi-profit: it is a gain from a dynamic source only partially diffused. Friction prevents the men of the outer world from sharing it now, although in the remote future static forces, acting throughout the world, will give it to them.

Mere advantage in point of time thus gives an advantage in point of wages and interest. It is the leaders in the adoption of fruitful methods of creating goods who get profits; while imitators, who straggle into line long after an invention has been made, may barely save their wages and interest. Men who labor in a region that leads in inventions may enjoy forever the quasi-profits that inventions give; for some fruit of each improvement may escape from the hands of the *entrepreneurs* who adopt it early and, becoming wages for the men who there labor, may continue long in this shape. The Golconda of the future, the region of limitless wealth, is to be the region where the greatest dynamic influences originate. A lead in the race that all humanity is running is to determine the comparative wealth of countries and of continents. Wealth is to abide with the swifter runners.

Tidal waves cause large areas of the sea to rise higher than the general static level of it, and they cause other large areas to fall below that level.

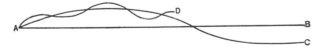

Thus, the line AB represents the static level of the entire ocean. The double curve AC represents the surface as it is elevated here and depressed there by a tidal wave. The wavy line AD represents the upper surface of the tidal swell, as it is thrown into local waves by the wind. At any one instant the actual surface is here above and there below the normal surface of the tidal wave itself. Now, giving to this figure an economic meaning, let AB represent the ultimate static level of wages in the entire world. Let all dynamic influences definitely cease, leaving a world-wide competition in free play, and AB will represent the general rate of pay for labor. But, in fact, increased power of production, with that friction which prevents the fruits of it from being shared equally by all mankind, has caused the pay of civilized laborers to conform, in a general way, to the rate described by the upper part of the curve AC and that of the uncivilized laborers to take the level indicated by the lower part of it. And local influences within the civilized area have caused wages here and there to vary from the standard indicated by the upper part of AC, so that the pay of men in different parts of Europe and America conforms to the varying levels described by the line AD. At one point the rate is above the general standard that prevails in the economic centre of the world and at another point it is below that level.

Three typical standards of wages.

There is, then, an ultimate static standard of wages for the whole world, a quasi-static standard for the civilized part of the world, and a local and quasi-static level of wages for every part of that civilized section. The pay of a man in any particular part of Europe or America tends, under the influence of competition, to conform to this local and quasi-static rate. Also, very slowly and through long periods this standard rate itself tends toward the ultimate static standard for the world as a whole.

It will never, however, reach that ultimate stand- *These are never to be brought to equality.* ard. Here the hydraulic illustration, in its present shape, fails. The tidal wave is made by withdrawing water from one part of the sea and carrying it to another part ; and, if the attracting influence were removed, the level of the whole would become uniform. The greater productivity of labor in the civilized part of the world is not, on the other hand, secured by any deduction from the productivity of labor elsewhere : it is the result of new increments of product that are conjured out of non-existence by civilization itself. As we said in an earlier chapter, the wave that represents the superior productivity of the advanced region must be made by pouring new water on a part of the surface of the ocean and by checking the flow of that water to other parts.

Imagine dams extending from Labrador to Green- *Illustration.* land, from Greenland to Norway and from Africa to the nearest point of South America. They would enclose a vast area of the northern Atlantic Ocean ; and, if water were to gather within this reservoir, the surface of it could be held at a higher level than that of the outlying seas. This illustration shows the true relation of wages in the civilized states to those in the uncivilized ones, for the superior level may be permanent. Even if the dam were imperfect, so that the water slowly flowed into the outer sea and tended to raise the level of it till it coincided with the falling level within the barrier, new water might enter so much more rapidly as to maintain or increase the superiority of the level there. So dynamic influences, calling new produce into existence in the advanced countries of the world, may preserve or may even increase the superiority in productive power that labor there enjoys, as compared with other labor.

The effect of endlessly recurring dynamic gains.

Dynamic gains, endlessly recurring, sustain the quasi-static rate of wages in favored parts of the world. It is primarily with this superior standard, and with the numerous local standards that compose it, that for practical reasons theory should deal. The men of America need to know what fixes the rate of pay for labor in America, as those of Massachusetts need to know what fixes the local rate there. This dominant influence is in every place the product that is there traceable to labor only. It is the rate which would there be realized, if in that locality dynamic influences were to cease and static forces were to operate alone. The specific product of labor in that locality is disentangled from the distinct product of capital in the way that has been fully described in the foregoing chapters of this book.

Economics concerned primarily with locally static rates of gain and with influences that are locally dynamic.

The relation of proximate standards of wages to ultimate standards.

The relation between the world, as a whole, and its various parts presents no real difficulty in a theory of distribution. There are proximate standards of wages and there are ultimate ones ; and the local pay of labor may tend quickly toward the proximate standard and always remain near it, while this standard itself tends slowly toward the ultimate one. What is true of wages is equally true of interest and other elements. One difficulty in the way of the theory is, however, more serious. To many persons any theory based on competition may seem to have somewhat of the character of theoretical romance. Will not competition itself soon be a thing of the past ? There are forming on every side trusts and other consolidations of capital that threaten to extinguish competition and to introduce a regime of monopoly within much of the business field. Have we, then, completed the theory of competitive distribution, only to find that the fact on which the whole of it is predicated has ceased to be ? If, when competition was at its best, theories of natural values, natural wages and natural interest seemed to have a character of unreality, what is to be said of them when competition appears to be a vanishing element? It remains for economic dynamics to show that competition is an inextinguishable force. The consolidations of the present period change the mode of its action, but they do not destroy it; and therefore they in no wise invalidate a theory that assumes the existence of it. At no point have we minimized the obstacles that static forces encounter. Everywhere in life are there variations from results that static theory alone calls for. Dynamic theory, if it were quite complete, would give results from which, in actual life, there would be no variation; for it is a part of the function of this division of the science to account for every element of friction, as well as for every change and movement that actual life shows. Among the lesser tasks that it will set for itself is that of reducing to clear formulas the principles which govern trusts, labor unions and other consolidations. It will deal with protective tariffs, which modify values; immigration laws, which affect wages; and currency laws, which influence movements of capital and rates of interest. It will undertake a larger work, when it tries to reduce to law the growth of population and of capital, and a still larger one, when it shall try to determine the conditions that govern the rapidity with which methods of production change and become more fruitful.

Movement is the general subject of dynamic economics. The direction and the velocity of changes in the economic world are always what it seeks to account for. In studying wages it will deal with an actual rise in the rate; in studying interest, with a fall in the rate and an increase in the gross amount; in

Competition inextinguishable.

Elements of friction and variation that a dynamic theory must deal with.

Changes to be anticipated in connection with wages, interest and profits.

studying profits, with the alternate appearing and vanishing of this element of gain.   Conditions of local and of world-wide prosperity are other subjects for it; and among the conditioning causes of prosperity are political policies, national and international. There is, indeed, in mundane affairs little of importance for humanity that does not fall within the scope of this division of the theory of political economy.

The extent, the difficulty and the fruitfulness of the dynamic field.

But the task of developing this branch of science is so large that the execution of it will occupy generations of workers.   As limitless as any other scientific field is the domain of economic dynamics; and, though early results may be modest, the value of any of them will be great enough to reward the hardest labor, while the unreached areas that will open before the explorer's eye, at every step in advance, will lure him to work that for difficulty and for fruitfulness will surpass any which has thus far been undertaken.   Yet, whatever movements the dynamic division of economic science may discover and explain, static laws will never cease to be dominant.   All real knowledge of the laws of movement depends upon an adequate knowledge of the laws of rest.

INDEX

443